CW01669686

Berlitz

Turkey

Front cover: Nemrut Dağı

Right: evil eye amulet

TOP 10 ATTRACTIONS

Aspendos. The site of an amazingly well-preserved Roman theatre. See page 107.

Blue Mosque. Its interior is aglow with thousands of decorated tiles. See page 31.

Gaziantep Archaeological Museum. Hundreds of square metres of vivid Roman mosaics, the best in the Midd East, form the heart of this astonishi collection. See page 122.

Hagia Sophia. Completed in AD537, it ranks among the wonders of the world. See page 28.

Pamukkale. Mineral-rich springs formed its irresistible travertine terraces. See page 79.

Ephesus. Its Roman ruins are the most extensive in the Mediterranean. See page 74.

Patara. Turkey's longest continuous beach, its dunes romantically encroaching on the ruins of an ancient city. See page 97.

Ölüdeniz. Pine-clad hills and white-sand beaches back the turquoise waters of this beautiful stretch of coastline. See page 93.

Topkapı Palace. Centuries of Ottoman pomp and power are on display. See page 34.

Nemrut Dağı. Huge stone heads stare from a mountaintop in the Mesopotamian basin. See page 124.

A PERFECT TOUR

Days 1–2 İstanbul

Enter Topkapı Palace early, then see Aya Sofya and the Blue Mosque. Have lunch nearby before strolling west via the Grand Bazaar to the Sülemaniye mosque, later descending to the colourful Spice Bazaar. The next day, take a ferry up the Bosphorus, visiting various museums or waterside villas. Return in the evening to sample Beyoğlu's nightlife.

Days 3–4 Bursa to Assos

Hire a car and take the ferry to Mudanya or Yalova, ports for Bursa. Tour Bursa then set off west for Çanakkale, perhaps making it to Troy before sunset. The following day, cross to Eceabat for the battlefields of Gallipoli. Return to the mainland and head for Assos, watching the sunset over Lésvos from the acropolis before dinner.

Days 5–6 Ayvalık to Pamukkale

After a morning swim, head down the Aegean coast to Ayvalık, in time for lunch. Explore nearby Pergamon before continuing south to Selçuk. Spend the next morning at Ephesus, then stop at Priene, Miletus or Didyma after lunch. Next head inland to Pamukkale in time for sunset.

Days 7–8 On to Patara

After viewing the terraces and ancient Hierapolis, loop round via Aphrodisias, lunching at adjacent Geyre village, before continuing to Highway 400 en route to Dalyan. Get up early for a river cruise to Kaunos. Then drive east, pausing for lunch at Kaya Köyü, before visiting two sites from among Tlos, Pınara, Xanthos or the Letoön. Arrive at Gelemiş, gateway to Patara beach and ruins.

OF TURKEY

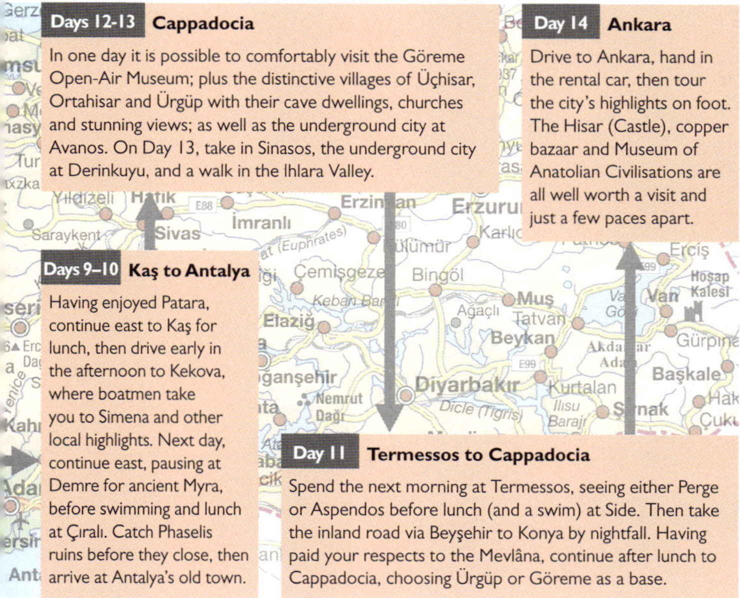

Days 9–10 **Kaş to Antalya**

Having enjoyed Patara, continue east to Kaş for lunch, then drive early in the afternoon to Kekova, where boatmen take you to Simena and other local highlights. Next day, continue east, pausing at Demre for ancient Myra, before swimming and lunch at Çıralı. Catch Phaselis ruins before they close, then arrive at Antalya's old town.

Day 11 **Termessos to Cappadocia**

Spend the next morning at Termessos, seeing either Perge or Aspendos before lunch (and a swim) at Side. Then take the inland road via Beyşehir to Konya by nightfall. Having paid your respects to the Mevlâna, continue after lunch to Cappadocia, choosing Ürgüp or Göreme as a base.

Days 12-13 **Cappadocia**

In one day it is possible to comfortably visit the Göreme Open-Air Museum; plus the distinctive villages of Üçhisar, Ortahisar and Ürgüp with their cave dwellings, churches and stunning views; as well as the underground city at Avanos. On Day 13, take in Sinasos, the underground city at Derinkuyu, and a walk in the Ihlara Valley.

Day 14 **Ankara**

Drive to Ankara, hand in the rental car, then tour the city's highlights on foot. The Hisar (Castle), copper bazaar and Museum of Anatolian Civilisations are all well worth a visit and just a few paces apart.

CONTENTS

Features

INTRODUCTION

Today, Turkey is one of the world's favourite holiday playgrounds, and this land that bridges Europe and Asia has accommodated a stampede of travellers for millennia (although many of the earlier visitors came dressed in armour and had conquest and plunder on their minds). To experience the richness of this nation you need only follow paths well beaten since ancient times. Since the earliest prehistoric cultures of Anatolia this has been the crossroads of civilisations: the Hittites, Greeks, Persians, Romans, Byzantines, Seljuks, Crusaders, Mongols, Ottomans, French, British and Italians have all passed through and left their imprint on this most complex and beautiful of societies.

In İstanbul, climb the staircase outside the waterfront entrance to the Egyptian Bazaar and you will find yourself in the Rüstem Paşa Camii, a gem of a mosque designed by the great Ottoman architect Sinan and awash with magnificent İznik tiles. At Termessos, on the Mediterranean coast, scramble up a steep mountain path and before you lies an ancient Greek theatre perched spectacularly on the edge of a precipice. In the Ihlara Valley in Cappadocia, insignificant holes in the cliff open out into jewel-like cave-churches rich in glorious Byzantine frescoes. In Antakya, another cave-church is, astoundingly, where saints Peter, Paul and Barnabas gathered in secret to create and name their new religion – Christianity.

Of the many fabulous experiences that await you in Turkey, one well worth seeking out is the pleasure of swimming from beaches at Patara, Olympos, Side or Phaselis, raising your head from the warm Mediterranean waters, and looking back

Serving Turkish tea

towards a shore littered with the remains of ancient, once-thriving cities: a ruined temple here, a granary there, a bath complex rising from the scrub. Or there's the unsettling sensation of looking over the side of a boat gliding over the waters of the Kekova Sound to see Roman mosaics and columns glistening beneath the surface.

Size and Landscape

Geographically, Turkey is huge, with 7,200km (4,500 miles) of coast, and land frontiers with Armenia, Azerbaijan, Bulgaria, Georgia, Greece, Iran, Iraq and Syria. The border between Europe and Asia runs through the middle of İstanbul, along the Bosphorus, one of the most strategically important waterways in the world.

The country's landscape is as varied as it is huge. Sculpted cliffs, punctuated by golden beaches and lapped by indigo and turquoise seas, line the Aegean and Mediterranean coasts, their valleys a sea of greenhouses producing, among many other things, some of the most delicious tomatoes in the world. A little way inland, valleys give way to rocky mountains clad in pine forests, their lower slopes filled with orchards that flutter with pink and white blossoms in spring. Behind the mountains stretch the vast rolling grasslands of the Anatolian plateau with its fiercely hot summers and bitterly cold winters.

In the southeast, ancient Mesopotamia (the Near East), so famed for its fertility that some claim it to be the original Garden of Eden, lies between the Euphrates and Tigris rivers. The government has created a vast network of dams based on the two rivers, to generate hydroelectricity and irrigate the semi-desert to the southeast – great for Turkey, not so good for the desert countries to the south, for whom the rivers are, quite literally, a lifeline, or for the Kurds, some of whom claim the region as an independent state.

Mount Ararat

In the border territories of the far east, the mountains again soar skywards, culminating in the massive bulk of Mount Ararat, Turkey's highest peak at 5,137 metres (16,853ft). This, according to legend, is the last resting place of Noah's Ark. Beyond this region lie the steppes of Central Asia, from where several waves of invaders have arrived to shape Turkey's people and culture.

Atatürk's Legacy

There is a famous Turkish saying, coined like so much in Turkey by Kemal Atatürk, '*Ne mutlu Türküm diyene!*' (Happy is he who calls himself a Turk.) There are few countries as patriotic, but astonishingly, Turkey as it exists today has been a country for less than 100 years, carved by Atatürk from the wreckage of the Ottoman Empire at the end of World War I. He was building a nation and needed to create an identity that would bring people together. The Ottomans were discredited,

> **Facts and figures**
>
> There are over 81,5 million people in Turkey, of whom nearly half are under 25 and 18 percent are Kurds. 99.8 percent are Muslim (about 20 percent of these Alevi, a branch of Shia Islam). 97.9 percent of men and 90.3 percent of women are literate.

seen as cruel and decadent rulers, so he looked further back into history and settled on the Turks, who began arriving in the Anatolian peninsula during the 11th century AD. Yet relatively few people in Turkey today are ethnically Turkish; people are far more likely to admit to Circassian, Bosnian, Bulgarian, Greek or Albanian ancestry, a consequence of the Ottoman Empire's rapid collapse from the early 19th century onwards.

Atatürk also endowed the country with one of the world's most progressive constitutions – a democratic, strictly secular, republican form of government – and one of the world's largest standing armies. For decades, the two reinforced each other. The army, which idolises Atatürk even more than the general populace, sees itself as the guardian of his legacy. It has stepped in three times in bloodless coups to remove ostensibly unsuitable governments, whether incompetent or overtly sectarian. A religious party that won an election and took power in 1997 was banned and its government toppled. While a religious party again holds office, it does so under the implicit understanding that it would not attempt to introduce religious law.

People and Religion

The vast bulk of the population is Muslim, either Sunni or Alevi. Islam in Turkey is generally an open, welcoming brand of the religion. The visitor is made to feel at home and the secular, emancipated society created by Atatürk is still clearly visible in contemporary culture and both men's and women's fashions. The muezzin's call to prayer competes with honking horns and pop music blaring from hundreds of sound systems; the object of the age-old ritual of bargaining is as likely to be a mobile phone or cheap watch as it is a bag of spices or a kilim. Even those young İstanbul women who have adopted the headscarf may well have chosen a colourful designer version that highlights rather than conceals what is beneath.

Turkey nurtures many subcultures within its borders. İstanbul, İzmir and Ankara have a sophisticated international lifestyle; a casual, beachfront charm typifies the coastal resorts. Yet go only a few kilometres inland and you see an entirely different country, peopled by chickens and goats, squat women in headscarves, cardigans and baggy trousers, and men with voluptuous moustaches and flat caps. This is a country where women work the fields, a flock of small children tugging at their clothes, while the men hang out in tea shops playing backgammon and righting the ills of the world.

Young faces of Turkey

A staging-point for armies and empires throughout its history, Turkey still walks the delicate tightrope between East and West, looking for friends and influence in both directions, and acting as a moderate buffer zone in the current tense political atmosphere. So far, it has succeeded admirably.

A BRIEF HISTORY

At ancient Troy, myth and historical evidence suggest that three millennia ago the Greek Odysseus rolled a large wooden horse through the city gates as a gift. The rest of the story is told in the *Iliad*: soldiers crept out of the horse under cover of darkness, overpowered Troy's defenders and freed Helen, whose face, it is said, launched a thousand ships. Nearby, at Gallipoli, more than 250,000 troops on both sides were killed or wounded during fighting in 1915. At Pergamon and Ephesus, farther south along the Aegean coast, great libraries attracted the ancient world's scholars. And in Constantinople/İstanbul, at Konya and at Edirne, the Byzantines, Seljuks and Ottomans established their respective empires.

With so many events having unfolded across its coasts, plains and mountains, Turkey is rich in tales of conquest and glory, and the landscape is strewn with the remains of the places where these events transpired. For much of its long history Turkey has been at or near the centre of the world.

Conquerors and the Conquered

In around 9000 BC, Palaeolithic peoples were painting caves at Belbaşı and Beldibi near Antalya. By 6250 BC, flourishing towns existed. Çatalhöyük, south of Konya, is considered the second-oldest known town (after Jericho). It had a population of around 5,000, and is the first place in the world to have used irrigation and domesticated sheep and pigs. Other, as yet unexcavated and possibly older settlements are known to exist nearby.

By the 2nd millennium BC, written history was in the making. In the west, Troy was already 1,000 years old. The Hittites crossed the Caucasus to establish a stronghold in central Anatolia, leaving behind them sites such as Boğazköy (Hattuşa), Yazılıkaya, Alacahöyük and Karatepe, south of Ankara. After

Hattuşa, the ancient Hittite capital in Anatolia

the collapse of the Hittite civilisation in the 13th century BC, successive waves of colonists arrived from the Balkan peninsula until about 800 BC. The Phrygians moved down from Thrace, taking over most of central and western Turkey. Little now remains of their empire, other than the ruined city at Gordion, home to King Midas of the golden touch. The Lydians settled in Sardis, near the Aegean coast, their fortunes reaching a pinnacle under the fabulously rich King Croesus, who invented coins and dice. The wild coast of the southwest Mediterranean was the territory of the Lycians, described by the Hittites as a proudly independent, matriarchal society. The people of Xanthos twice took this desire for independence to extremes, preferring mass suicide to surrender to Persians and Romans in turn. As Greek city-states took root around the coast from Pergamon to Aspendos, theatres, temples, colonnaded agoras and bathhouses appeared. Wealth was spurred by growing international trade, both east to Asia and west to Europe.

Pergamon

This affluent society tempted envious outsiders, and in 546 BC the Persians, led by Cyrus II, swept west from Persepolis, conquering much of Anatolia. Their hegemony was only broken in 334 BC by the next great imperialist, Alexander the Great, who conquered territory as far as India. Over the next two centuries, the original cultures and languages of ancient Anatolia were gradually engulfed by Hellenistic civilisation.

In 133 BC, King Attalos III of Pergamon left his kingdom to the Romans. From this toehold, the Romans expanded rapidly, unifying the many city-states and kingdoms of Anatolia as the province of Asia Minor. With the Romans came the relative calm and prosperity of the *pax romana*, although the 3rd century AD saw violent invasions by the Goths and Persians.

Early Christians

Southeastern Turkey had long been integral to Biblical history; Abraham lived at Harran and Noah's Ark is said to have grounded on Mount Ararat. From the 1st century AD, Christianity began taking hold across the Roman Empire. In Antakya (Antioch), saints Peter, Paul and Barnabas first founded and named the Christian religion. St Paul, brought up in Tarsus as Saul the tax collector before his blinding revelation on the road to Damascus, followed an itinerary that may well be the envy of a modern traveller, preaching at Alexandria Troas, Assos, Ephesus, Patara, Myra and elsewhere in Asia Minor. St John the Evangelist settled in Ephesus, allegedly in the company of the Virgin Mary. The early Christian inhabitants of Cappadocia found that the cave-riddled landscape was ideally suited to hermetic monasticism and to the construction of simple underground churches, of which more than 600 continue to impart a sense of spirituality.

From AD 312 onwards, Emperor Constantine strongly favoured Christianity, although he himself only converted on his deathbed. Constantine dispatched his mother, Helena (later made a saint), to the Holy Land where she conveniently identified Christ's place of execution and tomb, and returned home with large numbers of relics, including enough of the True Cross to build a boat. By 325, Christianity had splintered into so many heretical factions that Constantine was forced to call a conference in Nicaea (modern İznik), which laid down the basic tenets of the faith, the Nicene Creed.

Meanwhile, the western part of the empire was under increasing pressure from invading barbarians. Between 322 and 330, Constantine moved from Rome to his new capital, Constantinople, built around an old Greek fishing port, Byzantium. The empire split into independently ruled eastern and western halves a few decades after Constantine's death in 337. The western portion, still ruled from Rome, but starved of resources, limped on until its demise in AD 476.

Immortal words

It was in 47 BC, after the Battle of Zela, in Asia Minor, that Julius Caesar uttered his immortal words 'Veni. Vidi. Vici.' (I came. I saw. I conquered.)

Byzantines and Seljuks

The eastern (Byzantine) empire by contrast flourished. Constantinople grew ever more splendid, with vast palaces and great churches, of which the finest was Hagia Sophia, built by Emperor Justinian, and still standing today. However the imperial frontiers were repeatedly tested, by the Slavs in the west, the Avars from Central Asia and the Sassanid Persians in the southeast. In 647, Islamic religion entered Anatolia in the form of Arab warriors who reached the gates of Constantinople in 673 before being repulsed – after a four-year siege. A second attack in 717–18 took most of the empire's eastern provinces. Islam brought a new civilisation, religion, language and script. Christians were tolerated, but held inferior civil status and paid more tax – good incentives to convert. Some Christians espoused iconoclasm, replacing the faces on many frescoes and mosaics with geometric motifs. Under the Macedonian dynasty, inaugurated in 867, icon-worship was restored and the fightback began, but it was 1018 before the Byzantines recovered all their possessions.

Within decades, there was a new threat in the form of the Seljuks, who traced their origins to the Asian steppes. In 1071, at the Battle of Manzikert, they routed the Byzantine Army, capturing the emperor. From their capital in Konya, the Seljuks expanded their Sultanate of Rum at the expense of the Byzantine Empire. Ruins of the *kervansarays* (inns), bridges and roads they built across their holdings to accommodate increased trade along the Silk Route attest to their immense but short-lived power. They were toppled by the 13th-century Mongol invasions of Genghis Khan.

Hagia Sophia mosaic

In both northeast Anatolia and southerly Cilicia, the Armenians took advantage of Byzantine weakness to carve out semi-independent states after the late 11th century. From the west, Christian Europe marched east on a holy crusade against the Muslim infidel. Byzantine land was decimated by the passing armies, while the western invaders also set up Latin principalities in Antioch, Edessa and Jerusalem. In 1204, the Fourth Crusade did not bother to attack the Muslims of the Holy Land, but instead ransacked Constantinople and set up a new Latin Empire. The Byzantine emperors, who fled to Nicaea, only recovered their city in 1261.

Crusaders sack Constantinople

Enter the Ottomans

The Ottomans first appeared as a local clan who helped the Seljuks defeat a Mongol detachment in the 1220s and were given land near Eskişehir in central Anatolia in gratitude. But they gradually took over the Seljuk Empire and, over the next 200 years or so, one sultan after another planted the Ottoman standard on new territories. In 1402, the Mongols reappeared under Timur, and temporarily checked the Ottoman advance by defeating Sultan Beyazit I. But in 1453, Mehmet II finally conquered Constantinople, renaming it İstanbul and breaking ground for an opulent new palace, the Topkapı.

By 1520, Selim I had brought Palestine, Egypt and Syria under Ottoman control, and imposed Sunni orthodoxy as the

Süleyman the Magnificent

state religion, with the caliphate relocated to İstanbul. Between 1520 and 1566, the Ottoman Empire reached its zenith under Süleyman the Magnificent, who doubled the size of the empire, adding lands from northern Africa and Iraq to the Balkans and Hungary. He was also an able administrator and, with the help of his architect Sinan, built some of the empire's greatest monuments. Unfortunately, he was not as wise in his choice of a favourite wife. Roxelana was an ambitious former concubine who convinced the sultan to murder his son Mustafa; her own son Beyazit; and Ibrahim Paşa, his son-in-law, grand vizier (prime minister) and closest advisor – all to promote the succession of her useless first-born son, Selim.

Decline and Fall

Selim II, known to history as 'the Sot', drowned drunk in his bath, but not before the Ottomans suffered their first significant naval defeat at Lepanto in 1571 – though they conquered Cyprus earlier the same year, and retook North Africa in 1578. But under further unenlightened and often debauched sultans, the empire began to crumble. By 1792, the Ottomans had lost most of their European holdings, and by the early 19th century the empire was powerless to prevent Serbia, Greece, Egypt and other territories from declaring independence. The Janissaries, originally a praetorian guard of Christian slave-recruits fanatically dedicated to the sultan, became far too powerful; in 1826, Sultan Mahmut II used loyal forces to massacre them.

At the same time, Europe exerted increasing pressure on the 'sick man of Europe', occasioning numerous, often ineffectual reforms by later sultans. In 1853–6, the Ottomans were saved from Russian domination by siding with the French and British during the Crimean War. Despite increased commercial development and the adoption of some western models in education, the military and the civil service, decline continued through the 19th century. The first effective challenge to Sultan Abdülhamid's autocratic power came from the Committee for Union and Progress (CUP), whose 1908 revolution led to the re-opening of parliament and restoration of the liberal 1876 constitution.

These reforms failed to stop further Ottoman losses during the Balkan Wars of 1912–13 and World War I, in which Turkey sided with the Central powers, and the Anatolian peninsula became one of the main charnel-houses of the conflict. Out of a population of about 21 million, civilian Ottoman victims of disease, slaughter and starvation included approximately 1 million Armenians, 500,000 Greek Orthodox, 500,000 Syriac Christians and 2 million Muslim Turks; the Ottoman armies suffered nearly 800,000 fatalities.

Birth of a Nation

During 1919, the victorious British, French, Greeks and Italians moved in to carve up what was left of the Ottoman Empire; the Greek landing at Smyrna/İzmir in particular goaded hitherto passive Turks into action. Mustafa Kemal, a popular Ottoman general, rallied a resistance movement which ratified the so-called National Pact, declaring the minimum acceptable borders of an independent Turkey; in April 1920 the so-called Nationalists convened the first Grand National Assembly. Over the three-year course of a bloody, see-saw war, the Nationalists under Kemal

Atatürk

halted or co-opted the French and Italians and finally in late summer 1922 crushed the Greek expeditionary armies, who retreated in disorder.

In November 1922 the Grand National Assembly abolished the sultanate. On 24 July 1923, the Treaty of Lausanne was ratified, recognising the frontiers won by the Nationalist armies, and completely nullifying the Allied-imposed Treaty of Sèvres from 1920, which had provided for an independent Armenia and Kurdistan. Another Lausanne clause stipulated population exchanges: nearly 1.5 million Anatolian Greek Orthodox, and 400,000 Muslims resident in Greece, switched homelands.

Kemal, now president of the new Turkish Republic, oversaw successive secularist reforms. Polygamy was banned, education for women made mandatory, the fez and turban prohibited, the caliphate abolished, dervish orders outlawed, the Muslim lunar calendar replaced with the Georgian calendar, and Arabic script replaced with a modified Latin alphabet. Surnames, once informal, were made obligatory; Kemal took as his Atatürk (Father Turk).

Into the Present

After strict economic autarky, political stagnation and self-imposed isolation during the 1930s and World War II, Turkey found – in 1946, when Russian threats were renewed – a sponsor in the USA. Massive American aid poured into the country, which joined NATO in 1952, and the first multiparty elections were won by Adnan Menderes' opposition Democrat Party. Menderes oversaw improvements to rural living conditions while encouraging private enterprise and more religious freedom, but at the cost of economic instability and the antagonism of the urban secularist elite – plus the armed forces. He was overthrown in 1960 by the first of several military coups; the army has always viewed itself as the guarantor of Atatürk's secular legacy, guarding it against economic and social disorder. After 1960, unstable civilian regimes presided over a chaotic society, punctuated by Turkey's invasion of Cyprus in 1974 and a harsh coup in 1980.

Since the definitive return to civilian rule in 1983 under technocrat Turgut Özal, Turkey has made astonishing progress, although industrialisation, vastly improved infrastructure and a place at the G20 top table have come in tandem with periodic high unemployment, corruption, continued para-state violence against dissidents, a chequered human rights record, hyperinflation and urban terrorist attacks by al-Qaeda affiliates or Kurdish separatists. From 1984 onwards the army confronted a full-bore insurrection in the east by the Kurdish PKK organisation, which is still active along the eastern borders, prompting recent

Father of the Nation

Born in the now-Greek northern Aegean port of Salonica in 1881, Mustafa Kemal Atatürk had a glittering military career, in spite of early revolutionary tendencies, but really made his reputation during World War I when he took over the defence of Gallipoli, beating off the Allied attack. He then led the revolution that led the country to victory in the War of Independence, established a republic in place of the sultanate and became its first president, secularising the state, liberating women and westernising the nation. He died from cirrhosis of the liver, on 10 November 1938, at the age of only 57, at the Dolmahbaçe Palace, İstanbul.

A Turkish flag flies in the Blue Mosque.

incursions by the army into northern Iraq.

The secularist edifice began to crumble – quite literally – with a catastrophic August 1999 earthquake in northwestern Turkey, in which nearly 40,000 died. The army was upbraided for poor handling of the emergency and Greek rescue teams were the first foreigners on the scene, leading to a sustained rapprochement between the two nations. A severe 2001 economic crash preceded landmark 2002 elections, won decisively by an Islamist party, AK, who formed the first non-coalition government in decades – repeating this feat twice, in 2007 and 2011.

Turkey has been a European Union membership candidate since 1999, but only under AK has it adopted necessary significant reforms. Accession talks began in 2005, but continued Turkish occupation of northern Cyprus (plus opposition from many European countries) remain major stumbling blocks. Enthusiasm for EU membership has waned as doubters tout the advantages of being instead a regional power with orientation eastwards. In 2013, the government's plan to develop Istanbul's Gezi Park provoked a sit-in protest which was brutally broken up by the police, leading to violent clashes. More than 5,000 demonstrations were held across the country in the following months as over 3,5 million people stood up in defence of freedom of expression and of the press, and right to assembly. A series of corruption scandals in recent years has undermined public confidence in the ruling AK Party.

Historical Landmarks

6500 BC Neolithic peoples settle near Konya.
1100 BC First Greek colonies on Aegean coast.
800 BC Phrygian, Lydian and Lycian cultures begin to flourish.
546 BC Persians, under Cyrus II (the Great), invade.
334 BC Alexander the Great defeats the Persians.
130 BC Romans create province of Asia Minor.
AD 40 St Paul begins preaching Christianity.
325 Constantine convenes first ecumenical council at Nicaea.
330 Constantinople becomes capital of eastern Roman Empire.
1071 Seljuks enter Anatolia.
1204 Crusaders sack Constantinople.
1453 Mehmet II conquers Constantinople, ending Byzantine Empire.
1520–66 Reign of Süleyman the Magnificent.
1683–1792 Ottomans lose much of their European territory.
1912–13 Ottomans lose remaining European territories in Balkan Wars.
1914–18 Turks fight in World War I as one of the Central Powers.
1919–1922 War of Independence against Greece, Italy, France.
1923 Turkish Republic is established, with Atatürk as president.
1924–38 Atatürk imposes secularisation and modernisation.
1950 First free elections, won by Adnan Menderes.
1960 Menderes deposed by first military coup.
1974 Turkey invades northern Cyprus.
1983 Return to civilian rule under Turgut Özal.
1984 PKK launches guerilla insurrection in southeast.
1999 Earthquake kills tens of thousands in northwestern Turkey.
2002 Islamist AK Party forms majority government.
2005 Negotiations begin on Turkey joining the EU.
2007 Second AK electoral victory.
2011 AK wins general election for the third time, but with an insufficient majority for drafting a new constitution.
2014 AK leader Recep Tayyip Erdoğan elected President of Turkey.

CHP

WHERE TO GO

Mosques, minarets, bazaars stacked high with spices, ancient ruins lapped by turquoise waters, churches aglow with frescoes – the mere mention of Turkey launches a seemingly endless stream of exotic images, few living up to the splendour of reality. Nowhere does the cultural wealth of this nation that straddles Europe and Asia come to light more vividly than in İstanbul, the city that bestrides both continents.

İSTANBUL

Its name, according to some, comes from the Greek *eis tin polin*, 'at the city.' There were many centuries when people throughout the world would refer to 'the city'; everyone knew they were talking about this fascinating metropolis that has been known successively as Byzantium, Constantinople and finally **İstanbul** ❶. The city has witnessed the passing of Greeks and Romans, flowered in the 6th century under the Emperor Justinian, and rose from ruin and neglect during the 15th century, when Ottoman Sultan Mehmet II set about building mosques, monuments and the magnificent Topkapı Palace. Now as vast real-estate development and modernization have changed the city into a giant construction site, rapid gentrification and an appetite for public green spaces has provoked many social protests, most notably those in Gezi Park in 2013.

The city's stunning setting on the hilly terrain of two continents, bisected by boat-choked waterways, is bound to disorient the newcomer, while the monuments, scents and the omnipresence of the exotic can be overwhelming. İstanbul is a city to savour at leisure, whether it be pausing to catch a

Busy İstiklâl Caddesi in Taksim

glimpse of the minaret-pierced skyline or sitting down with a carpet-dealer for your umpteenth glass of ultra-sweet black tea.

Begin in the old city, where a staggering wealth of sights are within walking distance, then venture across the Golden Horn on the Galata Bridge into modern Beyoğlu and other sections of this city that sprawls along both sides of the Bosphorus.

Sultanahmet

Set on a small peninsula overlooking the Bosphorus and the Golden Horn, this is the historical centre of the city and was, for over 1,500 years, the heart of the Byzantine and Ottoman empires. Here, you can view some of the city's finest museums, step into some of the world's most hallowed religious structures, wander through royal palaces, view ancient ruins, barter at İstanbul's acclaimed bazaars, dine in a Byzantine cistern and sleep in a finely restored Ottoman house. You can do all this quite comfortably on foot.

Hagia Sophia (Aya Sofya)

From the time of its completion under the Emperor Justinian in 537, **Hagia Sophia** Ⓐ (Aya Sofya) or the Church of Holy Wisdom (www.ayasofyamuzesi.gov.tr; Tue–Sun 9am–5pm, until 7pm in summer) was the largest and most important church in the Christian world. This astonishing building quickly assumed similar stature in the Islamic world when the Ottoman sultans appropriated it as a mosque some nine centuries later, adding the four minarets. In 1936, Atatürk converted the structure to

Weeping Column

Hagia Sophia's most popular attraction is the Weeping Column in the north aisle. According to legend, Justinian cured a hangover by resting his forehead on it. Since then, the moisture that gathers on its brass- and marble-clad surface is said to cure many ailments.

The awe-inspiring interior of the Hagia Sophia

a museum, although Christians and Muslims alike still lay claim to it.

Contributing in no small part to the overpowering presence of Hagia Sophia is its dome, which was not eclipsed in size until St Peter's rose in Rome 1,000 years later. In designing the dome, Byzantine architects seemingly accomplished the impossible – the massive structure seems to float over the interior of the church, an illusion created by using hollow bricks made of light, porous clay.

Inside, pride of place undoubtedly belongs to the **mosaics**, many commissioned by Justinian to ensure that his church would be the most splendid in Christendom. In the 16th century, Süleyman the Magnificent, in accordance with Islamic law forbidding representation of man or animal, ordered the mosaics to be covered. Fortunately, the protective plaster inadvertently saved the mosaics for posterity. Ongoing restorations continue to reveal the sheer splendour of these works, many in gold, portraying saints and angels. Two of the most important show the Madonna and Child, and Christ flanked by the Virgin Mary and John the Baptist. For a look at more secular images, walk to the far end of the south gallery, where the 11th-century Empress Zoë improvised a convenient way to portray a succession of husbands – when one would pass on, she would simply have the image of his face replaced with that of his successor. On view for the ages is Zoë's last husband, Constantine IX Monomachos. The beautiful İmaret building (soup kitchen) of Hagia Sophia, built in 1743, now houses the Carpet and Kilim Museum. It has a fine collection of historic carpets, some dating from the 14th and 15th centuries.

Across from the entrance of Hagia Sophia, **Haseki Hürrem Sultan Hamamı** (www.ayasofyahamami.com; daily 8am–10pm), is a sumptuous bathhouse built by Mimar Sinan in 1556 for

Visiting Mosques

Mosques are free to enter and typically open to visitors from about 9am until dusk, except at prayer times. You must remove your shoes; leave them by the door or take a bag large enough to carry them with you. Bare arms are forbidden and women must cover their heads. You may borrow a scarf at larger mosques, but it's best to carry your own. Do not disturb or take pictures of people who are praying. On exit, give a small tip to the shoe guard, if there is one, and a donation to the mosque.

Mosques have four crucial architectural elements: a courtyard with a *şadırvan* (ablutions fountain) for ritual washing before prayer; a mihrab, the niche that points towards Mecca to mark the direction to face when praying; a mimber, the pulpit for sermons; and a minaret, the tower from which the muezzin calls time for prayer (usually taped these days). Women have a separate section, and there may also be an attached medrese (religious school), and an imaret (soup-kitchen/hostel for travellers and dervishes).

Roxelana, the favourite wife of Süleyman the Magnificent.

The Blue Mosque and Surroundings

The Blue Mosque, designed to rival Hagia Sophia

In the 16th century Sultan Ahmet I commissioned a mosque within the shadow of Hagia Sophia, designed to rival it. The **Sultan Ahmet Camii** **B**, better known as the **Blue Mosque** (best to visit early in the morning) had six minarets, equal to the number adorning the Great Mosque in Mecca. To quell the resulting outrage, Sultan Ahmet was forced to donate a seventh minaret to Mecca. Entering from Sultanahmet Square, pass through the forecourt and side doors (only the faithful can walk through the massive main portal), and you will find yourself standing beneath a canopy of airy domes. The space is bathed in the light of 260 stained-glass windows and aglow with 20,000 blue İznik tiles (from the ceramics-manufacturing city to the south of İstanbul; see page 57).

Several buildings surrounding the mosque once housed shops, alms houses and other establishments that serviced the needs of the faithful. These now include the **Arasta Bazaar** (www.arastabazaar.com), a good shopping area for crafts, which leads to the Büyük Saray Mozaikleri **Müzesi** (Museum of Great Palace Mosaics; www.ayasofyamuzesi.com.tr; Tue–Sun 9am–5pm, until 6pm in summer). This shelters a magnificent stretch of mosaic pavement, once the great hall of Justinian's Byzantine imperial palace. Not uncovered until the mid-20th century, the mosaics are in splendid condition and colourfully depict flora, fauna, scenes from mythology and, with some degree of pomp, the occasional emperor.

The Egyptian obelisk

Just opposite the Blue Mosque is the **Hippodrome**, site of the 100,000-seat stadium that for much of İstanbul's history hosted chariot races, circuses and other entertainments, as well as mass assemblies and an occasional outburst of public violence. It was here, in 1826, that Sultan Mahmut II oversaw the slaughter of the Janissaries, the dangerously powerful and frequently mutinous royal guard. Little remains of the actual structure, but three monuments continue to grace a large greensward at the centre of what was once the chariot track: the **Yılanlı Sütun** (Serpentine Column), taken from the Temple of Apollo at Delphi; the **Ormetaş** (Knitted Column) of Constantine VII Porphyogenitus, and the **Dikilitaş** (obelisk of Pharaoh Thutmose) that Byzantine Emperor Theodosius I brought from Alexandria in AD 390.

Under the Byzantine and Ottoman empires, Hagia Sophia and the Blue Mosque were surrounded by the palaces of the powerful elite. On the western edge of the Hippodrome, the 16th-century stone Ibrahim Paşa Sarayı (Ibrahim Paşa Palace) is now home to the furniture, carpets and other holdings of the **Turk ve Islam Eserlei Müzesi** (Turkish and Islamic Arts Museum; closed for renovation), providing an insight into Ottoman lifestyles. The tenant for whom the palace is named was a one-time confidant of Süleyman the Magnificent who, like so many, fell out of favour and was strangled.

A little further along the road, the **Yerebatan Sarnıcı** **C** (Underground Palace or Basilica Cistern; www.yerebatan sarnici.com; daily 9am–5.30pm) is one of the many vast water tanks the Byzantines built to ensure that the city would be supplied with fresh water during sieges, often reusing older Greek masonry. Among the latter are two famous blocks with carved Medusa heads, one upside down and one on its side, used as column bases; the columns and elaborate arches reflected in the rippling waters produce an eerily fascinating atmosphere. The space is used for concerts during cultural festivals. The **Binbirdirek Sarnıçı**on nearby Klodfarer Caddesi (the Cistern of 1,001 Columns; www.binbirdirek.com; daily 8am–midnight for sightseeing) is an even older 4th-century cistern, with 224 columns – in spite of its name.

Archaeological Museum

Near the Topkapı gate, the **Arkeoloji Müzesi** (Archaeological Museum; www.istanbularkeoloji.com.tr; all sections Tue–Sun 9am–5pm, last admission 4pm) will help you put things in perspective. An exhibit on İstanbul history nicely explains the city's Greek, Roman, Byzantine and Ottoman past, and gathered here are prize examples of statuary and other artefacts from Troy, Ephesus, Aphrodisias and the many other important archaeological sites throughout Turkey. The star exhibit is the magnificent Alexander Sarcophagus from Sidon.

The complex also includes the **Eski Şark Eserleri Müzesi** (Museum of the Ancient Orient), which houses some

Stolen horses

The four bronze horses that once graced the Hippodrome were pillaged by Crusaders on their way home from the Holy Land. They are now inside St Mark's Cathedral in Venice (with replicas on the facade).

astonishing artefacts, including the world's first surviving peace treaty and the gateway of Babylon. The nearby **Cinili Köşk** (Tiled Pavilion) was built in 1472 as an imperial sports pavilion. It is covered inside in colourful İznik tiles, with other Ottoman ceramics on display.

Topkapı Palace

The very stones of the **Topkapı Palace** **D** (Topkapı Sarayı) ooze wealth, pleasure and intrigue. This vast residence and administrative centre of the sultans has seen plenty of all three. It consists of an alluring maze of ornate, jewel-filled state rooms, fountain-cooled gardens, and the famous harem, and is set on a lovely hilltop overlooking the confluence of the Sea of Marmara and the Bosphorus.

The various palace pavilions and living quarters are clustered around four courtyards. Cross the first one, the **Court of the Janissaries**, to reach the ticket office. This large open space was the precinct of an elite corps of guards serving the sultan. They were Christian by birth, recruited as young boys from the Balkans, and trained to be soldiers. Janissaries, however, were far more than a professional army – well educated in Islam and civic affairs, they filled some of the highest posts in the palace, ensuring that the sultan was surrounded by loyal retainers. The Ottoman mint (now a civic museum) is in this courtyard, as is the ancient Byzantine church, Aya Irini Kilisesi (Church of Saint Irene), now used as a concert hall and exhibition space.

After you pass Bâb-i-Selam (Gate of Salvation), you will find yourself in the Second Court. The palace kitchens line one side. A couple of rooms have been reconstructed to give some idea of what it was like as a staff of hundreds prepared meals for the palace's 4,000 residents. The various sculleries and oven rooms now display porcelain and glassware. You will notice a disproportionately large collection of Chinese celadon dinnerware, a court favourite because it allegedly changed colour on contact with poisoned food.

The **Divan-i-Humayun** (Imperial Council Chamber), known as *kubbealti* (literally, beneath the cupola) because of its distinctive cupola-like tower, was where the grand vizier met with the Council of State, more familiarly called the 'divan' because members reclined on the couches that line the walls. These proceedings were sometimes observed by the sultan from behind a screen known as the Eye of the Sultan. The many-domed **Inner Treasury**, one of several halls housing the famed Topkapı treasures, displays an extensive collection of arms and armour.

Entrance to the Harem

The **Harem** is an intriguing warren of apartments and courtyards, incorporating about 400 rooms in all (of which you can visit about 40 on the mandatory guided tour). Life here was neither licentious nor, for most of the inhabitants, particularly enjoyable. However, true to the meaning of the word harem, or forbidden, what transpired here was shrouded in mystery, and residents of the complex had little or no contact with the outside world. Aside from the sultan's mother (the valide sultan) and his official wives, who lived in luxury, the Harem also housed, in conditions akin to slavery, hordes of eunuchs, concubines and ladies-in-waiting.

The Kafes, or Veliaht Dairesi (Golden Cage, Apartment of the Heir-Apparent) was a prison. In it lived brothers and other close male relatives of the sultan who might be in line for the throne. Confined here, they could cause little trouble and, circumspect as their lives were, they were unlikely to have access to any treasonous plots. The practice was an improvement upon the wholesale fratricide in which new sultans once engaged to ensure their place on the throne, but it did not breed good rulers. Much of the Harem, especially the apartments occupied by the valide sultan and the sultan himself, are sumptuously domed and tiled, culminating in the Hünkar Sofrasi (Imperial Hall), where the sultan entertained his preferred visitors.

While the Harem was where intimacies of day-to-day life at the Ottoman court transpired, the Third Court was the sultan's official domain. Here, beyond the Bâb-i-Saadet (Gate of Felicity), he received state visitors in the ornate **Arz Odası** (Audience Chamber) – conversing with them only through the grand vizier, as a sultan did not deign to speak directly to anyone but a high-ranking member of court. The Third Court also houses the **Treasury**, where you can view the palace's lustrous collection of 3.5kg (8lb) emeralds, the 84-carat 'Spoonmaker' diamond (so called because a peasant allegedly traded the gem for three spoons), and room after room of other jewels and gaudy jewel-encrusted swords, books and garments. The **Pavilion of the Holy Mantle** houses sacred relics of the Prophet Mohammed (including hairs

Ticket info

The Topkapı (www.topkapisarayi.gov.tr) is open Wed–Mon 9am–4.45pm, until 6.45pm in summer; separate tickets for the Hagia Irene and Harem. Tickets can be purchased at the main ticket office in the First Court. Alternatively, consider buying the Istanbul Museum Pass (http://museumpassistanbuldistributor.com).

from his beard) and is therefore a place of great religious importance for Muslims.

The **Fourth Court** is the most pleasant and relaxed precinct of the palace, laced with gardens, summer houses and pools. The **Sünnet Odasi** is a richly tiled pavilion in which young princes were circumcised. The Revan Köskü and Bagdat Köskü are two unusually elaborate kiosks to which sultans would retreat to catch a breeze and look out over the city and waterways below. You can do the same from one of the terraces or in the pleasant restaurant.

Tower of Justice, Topkapı Palace

The Bazaars to Süleymaniye Camii

Below the palace the workaday waterside neighbourhood of Eminönü bustles with crowds coming and going from the Bosphorus ferries, the Sirkeci railway station and the Galata Bridge. The **Mısır Çarşısı** (Egyptian or Spice Bazaar; www.misircarsisi.org; daily 8am–7.30pm; free) is just a few steps from the ferry docks. Stacked high with bags of spices, nuts and dried fruits, this market opened for business in the 17th century to generate revenue for the **Yeni Camii** (New Mosque) next door. The little **Rüstem Paşa Camii** **E** up a flight of steps in front of the waterside entrance to the bazaar, may well be the most beautiful mosque in İstanbul. The facade and interior are covered entirely in İznik tiles arrayed in a distinctive circular pattern.

Tiled ceiling detail

The Grand Bazaar

The Egyptian Bazaar is only a fraction of the size of the **Kapalı Carşı** F (Grand Bazaar; http://kapalicarsi.com.tr; Mon–Sat 9.30am–7pm; free), where up to 4,000 shops, selling everything from mops to mint-condition antiques, line a covered warren of 65 streets. The streets between the two covered markets are clogged with vendors' stalls, handcarts transporting sacks of spices, and all manner of exotic hubbub.

Two recent fires, one in 1954 and another in 1974, came close to destroying the bazaar, but restorations have retained the tiles, ironwork and other elements of the original Ottoman style, including its 18 distinctive fountains. The bazaar grew from a small warehouse built under Mehmet the Conqueror in the mid-15th century to support a neighbourhood devoted to commerce, supplied by Turkey's position at the western end of the fabled Silk Road. Merchants decided to connect their establishments with arcades, and eventually the huge complex was gated. It's easy to lose your bearings in the maze of little lanes and hard to escape without buying something. At the centre of the complex dealers specialise in antiques and fine jewellery, while the Old Book Bazaar is outside the main market and just to the west.

Beyazit District and Süleymaniye Camii

Just to the west of the main entrance is Beyazit Square. The forum of the Byzantine Emperor Theodosius, built in AD 393, once stood here, as did a wooden palace occupied by Mehmet the Conqueror before he moved his court to Topkapı Palace. Mehmet later used the old palace as a retirement home for elderly ladies of his harem. On the south side are the somewhat austere buildings of **İstanbul University** (www.istanbul.edu.tr), formerly the Ottoman War Ministry.

The **Süleymaniye Camii** **G** (daily, 9am–5.30pm), just north of the university, is the largest mosque in İstanbul, situated high on a hill overlooking the Golden Horn. Considered to be the highest achievement of Mimar Sinan, Süleyman the Magnificent's master architect, it is austerely beautiful, with a vast dome supported by four columns and elegant proportions that lend a spiritual air to the space. Süleyman, his wife Roxelana and Sinan are all buried in the grounds.

The streets to the west of Süleymaniye Camii lie in the shadow of the **Aqueduct of Valens**, begun in the 4th century

Inside the Egyptian Bazaar

Friday prayers in Süleymaniye Camii

as part of the extensive system of reservoirs, cisterns and waterways that supplied the city. A little further west is the enclave of Fatih (meaning 'the Conqueror'). The Fatih monument commemorates the conquest of İstanbul by Mehmet II in 1453. He is buried next to the **Fatih Camii** (Victory Mosque), the first mosque to rise above Ottoman İstanbul. The original structure and its attendant schools and alms houses were levelled in a 1776 earthquake and, while the mosque that stands in its place has never been completed, it is the centre of a large and devout religious community.

The Golden Horn

This fabled waterway is a fjord-like inlet separating the old and new cities. At the far end (easily reached by ferry from the Galata Bridge) is one of the most hallowed sights in Islam. Only Mecca, Medina and Jerusalem are more visited by pilgrims than the **Eyüp Camii** (tomb Tue–Sun 9.30am– 4.30pm except at prayer times; donations), burial place of Eyüp Al-Ansari, the standard bearer of the Prophet Mohammed, who was killed carrying the Islamic banner during the 7th-century Arab siege of Constantinople. His tomb was already a revered monument when Mehmet the Conqueror built the mosque in the 15th century. Rebuilt in 1800 after an earthquake, the mosque and tile-covered tomb are reached by a series of peaceful, shaded courtyards. For centuries Ottoman sultans were crowned here and the tombs of many Ottoman notables surround the complex. For a fabulous city view, a cable car leads from here up the hill to the **Pierre Loti Café**.

Nearby, the **Sveti Stefan Bulgar Kilisesi** (Church of Saint Stefan of the Bulgars; admission only by caretaker), once at the centre of the thriving local Bulgarian community, is also one of the most unusual structures in the city. Constructed entirely of cast iron, the church was actually built in Vienna in 1870 and shipped in pieces to İstanbul on more than 100 barges.

Directly west are two remarkable remnants of the Byzantine era. The city's western boundaries are entirely walled in, from the Golden Horn to the Sea of Marmara,

Mimar Sinan, Master Architect

Mimar Sinan (1489–1588) was the greatest of all Ottoman architects. Born into an Armenian Christian family in a village near Kayseri, he was selected for Janissary training and worked his way through the ranks to become a military engineer before being appointed architect to the Darüs-Saadet (Abode of Felicity) by Süleyman the Magnificent in 1536. Over the next 50 years, he was involved in the design and construction of 34 palaces, 79 mosques, 33 hamams, 19 tombs, 55 schools, 12 kervansarays, 16 külliyeler (charitable institutions) and 7 medreses. He regarded the Selimiye Camii in Edirne as his masterpiece; others suggest that the Süleymaniye Camii in İstanbul was greater.

Frescoes of saints in the Kariye Müzesi

with the **fortifications** started by Theodosius II in 413. When the walls were destroyed by an earthquake in 447, a workforce of more than 65,000 civilians rebuilt them in just two months, barely completing the job before the legions of Attila the Hun reached the city and were successfully repelled.

The former Monastery of St Saviour in Chora, now known as the **Kariye Müzesi** **H** (www.ayasofyamuzesi.gov.tr; Thu–Tue 9am–5pm, until 6pm in summer), is practically within sight of the walls. Its magnificent mosaics and frescoes were created by Grand Logethete Theodore Metochites in 1316–21. Considered to be among the world's finest surviving examples of Byzantine art, they present a detailed, highly emotional account of the life of Christ. Due to restoration work, some parts of the museum may be closed.

The **Rahmi M Koç Museum** (Hasköy Caddesi; www.rmk-museum.com.tr; Tue–Fri 10am–5pm, Sat–Sun 10am–6pm, until 8pm in summer) housed in an old iron foundry on the south side of the Golden Horn is a fascinating private collection of anything involving science, technology and transport, from an 1898 steam car to a 1940s American submarine.

New İstanbul

Across the Golden Horn from 'Old Stamboul' is the 'new' city, often referred to as Beyoğlu, which is actually the name of one of several neighbourhoods that climb the hill from the shores of the Golden Horn and the Bosphorus. There were settlements here long before Christ, and this part of İstanbul is new only in the sense that this was the foreigners' enclave from the arrival of the Genoese in the 14th century. Many of the buildings are in early 20th century Art Nouveau style. Modern high-rise İstanbul is further northeast, in the newer business districts of Maçka and Maslak.

Cross the Golden Horn on the **Galata Bridge**, pausing midway to take in the view. Looking back, Topkapı Palace rises to the left, while the domes and minarets of Hagia Sophia and the Blue Mosque fill the middle horizon, and the massive dome on Süleymaniye Camii is to the right. Climbing the hillside ahead of you are the buildings of the new town, with the conical roof of the cylindrical 14th-century Galata Tower rising above them.

Karaköy

Before heading uphill, explore the waterfront district of Karaköy. Once the province of European traders, it is still a port district, with

Tram on İstiklâl Caddesi

shipping offices, chandlers, and docks that serve Bosphorus ferries and ocean-going cruise-liners.

Overlooking the Bosphorus near the mouth of the Golden Horn, **İstanbul Modern** I (www.istanbulmodern.org; Tue–Sun 10am–6pm, Thu until 8pm) on Meclis-i-Mebusan Caddesi was originally a customs warehouse on the pier of Karaköy. It now houses a permanent collection of modern Turkish paintings, sculpture, photography, video and sound installations, as well as touring exhibitions, an arthouse cinema and chic first floor café-bar with fabulous views.

Galata Tower to Pera

Back beside the Galata Bridge, board the **Tünel**, a short, steep underground train built by the French in 1875 to link their waterfront offices and hillside residences. At the top, **Tünel Meydani** (Tünel Square) is surrounded by shops and cafés. It is also the southern end of the antique tram line that runs along **İstiklâl Caddesi** to Taksim Square.

At the high point of the hill, **Galata Kulesi** J (Galata Tower; observation deck daily 9am–5pm, until 7pm in summer; restaurant offering dinner and belly dancing shows at 8pm, book in advance) is part of a 14th-century fortifications network built by the Genoese. In the shadow of the tower are modern art research centre SALT Galata (www.saltonline.org), a hangout of the local art crowd as well as several synagogues, some established more than 500 years ago by Sephardic refugees from Spain, invited to the Ottoman Empire by Sultan Beyazit II.

Dracula's head

Just inland from the Galata Bridge, Voyvoda Caddesi is named after the 15th-century prince (*voyvoda*) Vlad III of Wallachia, more familiarly known as Count Dracula. He was a fierce enemy of the Ottoman regime, and after his 1476 death in battle, his severed head was brought to the city from Romania and put on public display.

The largest one, Neve Shalom Synagogue, (www.nevesalom.org) has been attacked twice by Islamist terrorists in recent years – in 1986 and again in 2003, with 47 fatalities in total.

Galipdede Caddesi continues up the hillside through an intriguing neighbourhood of narrow alleyways and stepped streets. The **Galata Mevlevîhanesi** Ⓚ (Galata Mevlevî Hall; www.galatamevlevihanesimuzesi.gov.tr; daily 9am–5pm, until 7pm in summer) is a former *tekke* (monastery) of the Mevlevî dervish order (see page 118) and now (officially) a museum of calligraphy and dervish memorabilia. Regular public performances of the order's distinctive whirling, trance-inducing dance, are held Sun at 5pm. Nearby are many music shops

Galata Tower

Until the early 20th century, İstiklâl Caddesi (Independence Street) was known as the Grande Rue de Pera, and in its smart shops and cafés European residents of the surrounding **Pera** neighbourhood could outfit themselves in Parisian finery, enjoy French pastries and comport themselves as they would at home. Many of the Belle Époque buildings house foreign consulates, originally built as full embassies before the capital was moved to Ankara. Rising above this architectural hodgepodge and adding to the sense of bygone cosmopolitanism are the steeples of Anglican, Dutch Reformed, Franciscan and Greek Orthodox churches.

Built in 1892 to billet passengers travelling on the Orient Express, the **Pera Palace Hotel** has a guest list that includes Mata Hari, numerous royals and statesmen, and Agatha Christie, who wrote *Murder on the Orient Express* here. Her room and the one once occupied by Atatürk have been cordoned off for public viewing. Almost opposite, the equally old Hotel Bristol has come back to life as the **Pera Museum/Pera Müzesi** Ⓛ (www.peramuzesi.org.tr; Tue–Sat 10am–7pm, Sun noon–6pm; free Fri 6–10pm), with a fine collection of paintings and Ottoman ceramics, hosting special events as well. Nearby, at İstiklâl Caddesi 136, an elegant 19th-century townhouse has been transformed into a three storey ultra-modern exhibition space called **SALT** (www.saltonline.org; Tue–Sat noon–8pm, Sun noon–6pm) with a good English language bookstore and a panoramic restaurant.

To Taksim

About halfway up İstiklâl Caddesi, a more Turkish atmosphere asserts itself on the alleys and arcades that branch off **Galatasaray Meydanı** (Galatasaray Square). The square is another bastion of European İstanbul, named after a former lycée where Ottoman children were schooled in the French language and Western manners. The **Çiçek Pasajı** (Flower Passage; www.tarihicicekpasaji.com), just off the square, is now surrounded by smart restaurants. At the adjoining **Balık Pazarı** (Fish Market), the fishmongers standing behind voluminous displays of the daily catch, are no small part of the market's appeal and the market is lined with restaurants. In the evening itinerant musicians entertain diners, but you'll get a better, cheaper fish meal along Nevizade Sokak, which separates the two. Further to the south, in the Çukurcuma district, modern design shops can be found alongside antiques and bric-a-brac. The **Mazumiyet Müzesi**

M (Museum of Innocence; www.mazumiyetmuzesi.org; Tue–Sun 10am–6pm, Thu until 9pm) in a dark red townhouse, was created by Orhan Pamuk and based on his novel *Museum of Innocence* (the ticket printed at the back of the book permits free entry). Housed in a dark red townhouse, the museum explores life in Istanbul in the second half of 20th century.

The main function of vast **Taksim Meydanı** (Taksim Square), at the northern end of İstiklâl Caddesi, appears to be to accommodate a constant flow of traffic that streams around the Italian-designed **Cumhuriyet Anıtı** (Republic Monument), erected in 1928 to celebrate Atatürk's establishment of a Turkish democracy. A governmental proposal to build a shopping centre on the site of Gezi Park, the only green space in this area, triggered social protests and the rise of the Occupy Gezi movement. The **Atatürk Kültür Merkezi** (Atatürk Cultural Centre) used to be the city's largest concert hall, but is now closed.

At the Fish Market

Beşiktaş

Eventually, the royal inhabitants of Topkapı Palace followed the wave of Westernisation and moved across the river to build lavish palaces along the European shore of the Bosphorus. Their mirrored and gilded interiors

Stopped clocks

Atatürk died in a simple room in the harem complex of the Dolmabahçe, at 9.05am, on 10 November 1938. All the palace clocks have been stopped to mark that exact time.

reflect not prosperity but the 19th-century decline of the Ottoman Empire.

Sultan Abdülmecid sited the **Dolmabahçe Sarayı** Ⓝ (Dolmabahçe Palace; www.millisaraylar.gov.tr; Tue–Wed and Fri–Sun 9am–4pm or until the daily quota of 3,000 tickets is exhausted; guided tours only) in the 17th-century imperial gardens (Dolmabahçe means 'filled-in garden'). The sultan intended the move to symbolize the Ottoman Empire's unveiling the mysteries shrouding Topkapı Palace; Dolmabahçe, however, proved to be a white elephant from the day the soon-bankrupt sultan moved his court here in 1854. Gilded in silver and clad in marble, as per the specifications of the Armenian architects who designed it, the palace is an ornate extravaganza that has long outlasted the crumbling empire it was meant to reinforce. Ironically, the staunch republican Atatürk lived here in the last days of his presidency.

Abdülmecid's brother and successor, Abdülaziz, had far fewer funds to draw upon when, in 1863, he built his own palace on the opposite side of the Bosphorus, the smaller and relatively modest **Beylerbeyi Sarayı** (www.millisaraylar.gov.tr; Tue–Wed and Fri–Sun 9.30am–7pm) and lavished attention on a royal garden, now **Yıldız Park**, a leafy hillside refuge where his harem was allowed to roam the paths and enjoy the kiosks and pleasure pavilions in relative freedom.

In the 1880s the park became less secluded when Sultan Abdülhamid II commissioned the 62-room **Yıldız Sarayı** (www.millisaraylar.gov.tr; Tue–Wed and Fri–Sun 9.30am–7pm) to accommodate visiting foreign dignitaries. The sultan eventually moved in as well. You can still see furnishings he made himself and the tools he used to craft them.

Along the Bosphorus just beyond the Dolmabahçe palace is the **Deniz Müzesi** (Maritime Museum; www.denizmuzeleri.tsk.tr; Tue–Sun 9am–5pm, also Sat–Sun 10am–6pm in summer). Dry-docked here is an extraordinary fleet that includes imperial caiques and Ottoman war galleys. Other memorabilia ranges from cannons to mementos from Atatürk's yacht.

On the hill above, the **Askeri Müzesi** (Military Museum; www.tsk.tr; Tue–Wed and Fri–Sun 9am–5pm) tells the story of more than 600 years of Ottoman campaigns and defences. The museum's displays include many *sayebanalari*, elaborately woven tents that sheltered sultans and other royalty on the battlefield, and what is alleged to be fragments of the chain that the last Byzantines stretched across the Golden Horn in a vain attempt to thwart an Ottoman sea attack during the siege of Constantinople in 1453.

Inside the Yildiz Pavillion

Maiden's Tower

Along the Bosphorus

The **Bosphorus** cuts a broad swath through İstanbul, providing a direct artery between the Black Sea and the Sea of Marmara and marking the boundary between Europe and Asia. Millions of ferry-borne commuters criss-cross it each day, dodging under the bows of the supertankers sailing from Russian and Ukrainian ports. It has been a vitally important shipping lane since antiquity and is rich in the city's earliest mythological associations. Jason and his Argonauts allegedly sailed its course en route to and from Colchis. The strait's name comes from Bous (cow) and Poros (crossing place), a reference to an incident in Greek legend in which Zeus turns his lover, Io, into a cow, at which his wife, Hera, spitefully conjures up a gadfly to sting the beast and force her into the stream. Aside from their legendary and historical importance, the straits are also lovely, and a boat trip upstream from the Eminönü docks provides rewarding views of waterside mosques and fortresses, colourful villages, and the distinctive wooden villas known as *yalis*, all backed by forested hills.

Directly opposite Karaköy, Üsküdar and Kadiköy are the main residential suburbs of Asian İstanbul, fairly conservative and traditional in character, with a fine collection of mosques. Offshore, Leander's or the **Maiden's Tower (Kız Kalesi)** is an 18th-century addition to a 12th-century island fortress, used variously as a quarantine centre, lighthouse, maritime tollgate and now, a combination museum-restaurant. Legend has it that a princess was walled up here to protect her from a prophecy that she would die of a snakebite. Perhaps inevitably, the snake wriggled into a basket of fruit and she met her appointed end.

Also in Üsküdar are the **Haydarpaşa Station**, terminus of the Asian railway, closed following a fire in 2010, and the **Selimiye Barracks**, home of Florence Nightingale's original hospital. From there, it is only a short walk to the moving **British War Cemetery**, final resting place for casualties of the Crimean War and World War I.

Back on the European side of the river, at the western foot of the **Bosphorus Bridge**, is the former fishing village of **Ortaköy (Mesahoro)**, now an enclave of brightly painted wooden houses, a trendy market stalls on the waterfront square and sophisticated cafés or restaurants for well-dressed urbanites. A far less secular sight is elegant **Ortaköy Camii**, these days overshadowed by the lower Bosphorus Bridge, which also shelters the Beylerbey Sarayı (see page 48).

Arnavutköy, the former Greek settlement of Mega Revma, is just upriver. This is a far quieter town, and its

Martial music

At the Askeri Müzesi, there is a performance of *mehter*, Ottoman martial music, by a Janissary band in full regalia, daily at 3pm and 4pm. This stirring sound was one of the great influences behind Souza's military marches.

atmospheric waterfront is lined with beautifully preserved wooden houses and trendy cafés.

Neighbouring **Bebek** is one of the city's wealthiest enclaves, but the presence of the Bosphorus University and an attendant intellectual community lends the town a Bohemian air. The most impressive of the many lavish waterside villas here is the Art Nouveau-style **Hıdıv Sarayı** (Khedive's Palace), which belongs to the Egyptian consulate. The town's famous landmark is the far more imposing fortress of **Rumeli Hisarı** (Thu–Tue 9.30am–4.30pm), massive fortifications assembled by Mehmet II in 1452. Across the channel, completing the pair of sentinels overlooking this narrow stretch of water, rises another early Ottoman castle, **Anadolu Hisarı** (closed to the public).

The next two villages, **Emirgan** on the European side and **Kanlıca** on the Asian side, mirror each other from opposite riverbanks. Each is famous for its local speciality – Emirgan for tulips, which bloom in a hillside park, and Kanlica for sugared yogurt, served in several waterfront cafés. At Emirgan, the **Sakip Sabancı Museum** (İstinye Caddesi; www.sakipsabanciimuzesi,org; Tue–Sun 10am–6pm, until 10pm

Who Rules the Waves?

In 1936, the Montreux Convention declared the Bosphorus to be an international waterway because of its strategic importance. The only such waterway bounded by a single country, it is governed by international maritime law, and commercial vessels of any nation enjoy unfettered passage (though there are severe tonnage restrictions on military shipping). In 1936, some 150 ships a year passed through the straits; today it is well over 45,000, thanks in part to the burgeoning Central Asian oilfields. The Turks are nervously expecting a major disaster involving one of the supertankers, and accordingly have strenuously encouraged the construction of overland pipelines to ship Central Asian petroleum.

Wed and Fri) is a private art museum. Several rooms have been kept as they were when the Sabancı family lived here, and the collection also includes decorative arts, Ottoman calligraphy and paintings by leading Turkish artists from the 19th century to the present day. The café has live music during Sunday brunch.

Boats on the Bosphorus

At the **Sadberk Hanım Müzesi** in Büyükdere (www.sadberkhanimmuzesi.org.tr; Thu–Tue 10am–5pm), two waterfront houses contain a magnificent collection of Turkish carpets, tiles and archaeological artefacts amassed by one of Turkey's wealthiest businessmen, the late Vehbi Koç.

AROUND İSTANBUL

The Princes' Islands

Only 20km (12 miles) offshore in the Sea of Marmara, the Princes' Islands have been providing a place of escape for centuries, though some notable residents – political dissidents, an exiled Leon Trotsky among them – have not sought their restful beaches and forests by choice. Since the mid-19th century, the four small inhabited islands have lured well-to-do city dwellers. Today, visitors sail over from the Bostancı or Kabataş docks to explore the islands' rugged beauty and considerable charm on foot, bicycle or horse-drawn carriage – there are no cars except for a few official ones on Büyükada.

Phaeton on the carless Büyükada

Büyükada (Pringipo) is the largest and most visited of the islands, with many wooden mansions surrounded by lush gardens. Trotsky lived on Çankaya Caddesi in the main town. The most notable structure, topping one of the island's two hills, is the Byzantine monastery of St George. Its three chapels and alleged healing fountain are still pilgrimage sites of great importance to Orthodox Christians.

Heybeli (Halki), the other large island, is less developed, but its terraces of wooden houses are often in better condition than those of Büyükada. The island's Greek Orthodox School of Theology has a famous collection of Byzantine manuscripts, but is not open to the public. Of greatest interest to most visitors are the island's forest paths and lovely, unspoilt beaches. **Burgazada (Antigoni)** has an excellent museum devoted to Turkey's premier short-story writer, Sait Faik (www.saitfailmuzesi.org; Wed–Sun 10am–6.30pm, free). **Kınalıdada (Proti)** is barren and almost completely covered by summer residences (many Armenian-owned), but is said to have the cleanest swimming water of the four islands.

Edirne

In its graceful bridges and other roadside monuments, the Via Egnatia from İstanbul to **Edirne** ❷ (today the D100 road) still shows traces of the imperial legions, Byzantines, Ottomans and invading armies who have travelled its length since Roman times. Edirne, 235km (146 miles) northwest of İstanbul on the parallel E80 motorway, lies near the modern Greek border at the heart of the ancient, war-prone region of Thrace. Despite these ancient roots, the city owes most of its outstanding monuments, especially its remarkable mosques, to the Ottomans.

Formerly known as Hadrianopolis after the emperor who made the outpost the capital of Roman Thrace, Edirne fell to the Ottomans in 1361, and served as capital of the growing Ottoman Empire from 1413 to 1458. It was from here that Mehmet II marched on Constantinople. Long after Edirne lost its role as capital, sultans continued to retreat here to hunt and relax in royal splendour.

The **Selimiye Camii** dominates the city from atop a knoll. This beautiful mosque, completed in 1574, is one of the finest in Turkey, and in building it the great Ottoman architect, Mimar Sinan, set out to surpass Hagia Sophia in majesty. The dome, supported on eight columns set unobtrusively into the walls, creates a stunning celestial effect and, at almost 32 metres (104ft) in diameter and almost 45 metres (146ft) high, it is indeed larger than that of Hagia Sophia, if only by a hair's breadth. Inside, exquisite tilework, 999 windows and lacey stonework imbue the massive space with light and serenity. Outside, four identical minarets surround the dome, lifting the entire structure heavenward. The mosque's collection of calligraphy, as well as ceramics and furnishings from

Selimiye Camii in Edirne

throughout Thrace, are kept in the adjoining **Türk-Islâm Eserleri Müzesi** (Museum of Turkish and Islamic Art; www.edirnemuzesi.gov.tr; daily 8am–5pm, 9am–5pm in summer), originally a medrese (religious school).

You will also see displays devoted to the more earthbound art of *yağlı güreş* (oil wrestling), a popular local sport originally used as part of the soldiers' training. A statue of two wrestlers looms over Hürriyet Meydanı, Edirne's main square. Championship matches are held each summer at Kırkpınar, just outside the city.

The aptly named **Eski Cami** (Old Mosque) predates its more impressive neighbour by almost two centuries and, though its beauty derives mainly from the simplicity of the square plan, its walls are covered in elaborate calligraphy. Surrounding it is evocative evidence of Edirne's importance as a trading centre: the domed, 15th-century *bedesten* (lockable market), the larger Semiz **Ali Paşa Bazaar**, and the **Rüstem Paşa Kervansaray**, which as a hotel conversion continues to house travellers as it has for more than four centuries. A third historic mosque, the 15th-century **Üç Şerefeli Cami** (Mosque of the Three Balconies), just north of the markets, is named for the balconies circling its graceful minarets. Next door the Sokullu Paşa Hamamı, built by Sinan, still functions.

The İkinci **Beyazit Külliyesi** (Beyazit II Complex; http://saglikmuzesi-en.trakya.edu.tr) lies just north of the city, on an island in the willow-lined River Tunca, reached via the gracefully arched, two-stage **Beyazit Bridge**. Seen from midstream the 15th-century complex, the largest of many such charitable institutions built throughout the Ottoman Empire, is especially remarkable, as hospitals, schools, storehouses and the mosque are clustered beneath a sea of domes. The most evocative of the buildings here may well be the Timarhane, or madhouse, quite enlightened for its time, in which peaceful gardens and splashing fountains were intended to soothe the inmates. It now houses a bizarre little museum of health (daily 9am–6pm).

İznik

It takes a little imagination to evoke the days when the lakeside farming town of **İznik** ❸, equidistant from Yalova port and Bursa, was an important political centre. In AD 325, what was then Nicaea (Nikaia) hosted the First Ecumenical Council of the early Christian church that proclaimed the Nicene Creed, establishing the basic tenets of Christian faith still followed today. In 787, the town hosted another council to resolve the Iconoclast controversy, decreeing that icons could be worshipped, not as idols, but as conduits to holy personages.

The city briefly became capital of the Byzantine Empire in the 13th century when the brutal arrival of the Fourth Crusade forced the

Oil wrestling

The organised sport of *yağli güreş* (oil wrestling) dates from 1360, when Süleyman Paşa invited 40 champions to wrestle for Allah and the sultan. By dawn next day, the last two were dead of exhaustion, but where each hero had fallen, a spring gushed from the ground. An oil-wrestling festival is held outside Edirne every July; 1,000 wrestlers take part.

The busy city of Bursa

Lascarid emperors to flee Constantinople. In 1331, it was captured by the Ottoman Orhan Gazi and renamed İznik. During the next century its craftsmen, many imported from Persia, began shipping their famous tiles throughout the Ottoman Empire. Unfortunately, the tiles are not much in evidence in İznik itself. A few originals are on display in the **İznik Müzesi** (İznik Museum; daily 8am–5pm), alongside ancient coins, Byzantine jewellery and a bronze statuette of a dancing Pan. The museum occupies a former *imaret* (hostel) built in 1388 to shelter dervishes and members of the Ahi trade guild.

Across the street, one-room **Yeşil Cami** (Green Mosque) dates from the same period as the museum and is typical of the Seljuk style. The multicoloured tiles that cover the minaret are modern replacements from Kütahya. Also evocative is the **Aya Sofya Müzesi** (Holy Wisdom Museum; Tue–Sun 9am–5pm) in the eponymous church, which retains damaged floor mosaics and a faint fresco of Christ, John the Baptist and the Virgin. Of the four original town gates, at the points of the compass, the most impressive are the easterly **Lefke Kapısı** and the northerly **İstanbul Kapısı**, both triple-layered affairs built by (or to honour) Emperor Hadrian around the time of his AD 123 visit.

Bursa

To see some of Turkey's finest examples of İznik tiles, you need only drive an hour or so west to **Bursa ❹**. This busy, park-spangled city, famous for silk production, peaches, mosques and tombs, sits at the base of 2,543-metre (8,342ft) **Mount Uludağ**, its slopes reached by cable car.

The hillside neighbourhood of **Yeşil**, just above the city centre, is home to two of the city's most famous monuments. The early 15th-century **Yeşil Cami** (Green Mosque) is considered to be one of the great Ottoman masterpieces, and no small part of its beauty derives from the blue and green tiles that adorn its walls to a height of 5 metres (16ft). Especially beautiful tiles decorate the sultan's loge, just above the foyer, and white marble etched with feathery designs covers the elegant entranceway.

Living in the Shadows

Each November, Bursa holds a festival celebrating the shadowpuppet theatre that originated here in the 14th century. Local lore has it that Karagöz, a stonemason, and Hacivat, his foreman, broke the tedium of their labours on Orhan Gazi Camii by entertaining their co-workers with humorous, often ribald skits. The pair became such a popular distraction that Sultan Orhan had them beheaded. Regretting his cruelty and missing the pranksters, the sultan arranged to have them immortalised as shadow puppets – Karagöz as a black-eyed, turbaned knave and Hacivat as his hapless cohort.

The nearby **Yeşil Türbe** (Green Mausoleum; daily 9am–6pm; free) houses the sarcophagus of Sultan Mehmet I Celebi and his various offspring. The 19th-century exterior tiles, mediocre post-earthquake replacements of the originals, are in turn being supplanted by new, high-quality İznik work. The interior, however, is awash in a sea of brilliant tilework laid by Tabriz craftsmen during the 1420s.

The Old Centre

The presence of so many Ottoman works in Bursa is a reflection of the city's role in the nascent Ottoman Empire. In about 1312 Osman Gazi laid siege to Byzantine Bursa, which finally fell to his son Orhan in 1326. Orhan proclaimed himself sultan, and the unified empire that began to flourish under his capable stewardship became known as Ottoman, from Osmanli, the clan of Osman. To celebrate his victory, Orhan erected an elegant mosque, the **Orhan Gazi Camii** (much rebuilt since its 1336 foundation).

Among the city's other mosques are two that seem to belong to the realm of the dead. **Emir Sultan Camii**, just east of Yeşil Cami, rises from the midst of graveyards popular with the devout, and the early 15th-century **Muradiye Külliyesi**, comprising a mosque, hamam and, is surrounded by the ten, often ornate tombs of Sultan Murat II and later members of the Ottoman dynasty, many of whom were victims of fratricide, murdered to keep them from interfering with a smooth succession. Nearby, the 19th-century **Hüsnu Züber Evi** (Tue–Sun 10am–5pm) is a restored Ottoman house with a small collection of carved wooden implements made by former owner Hüsnu Züber.

The 20 domes of Bursa's largest mosque, **Ulu Cami**, are allegedly a bargain that Sultan Beyazit I struck when he couldn't fulfil his vow to build 20 mosques if he was victorious at the 1396 Battle of Nikopolis. The fountain beneath the central dome is yet another compromise, made necessary when a local homeowner refused to sell her property to make room for the mosque. The presence of the fountain precludes any possibility of praying on land not donated willingly.

The Ulu Cami is at the edge of Bursa's old commercial district, where the 14th-century covered market *comprises* a confusing warren of little streets where cabinetmakers, cloth merchants and goldsmiths ply their ages-old trades. At the centre of the marketplace is the 1490-vintage **Koza Hanı** (Silk Cocoon Hall), occupied by silk dealers, whose trade – despite decline since the 18th century – is still a vital part of the local economy. In late June and early July, silk breeders fill the courtyard with their little white cocoons, to be auctioned. At other times, the surrounding shops are filled with fabulously sensual silks, from scarves and ties to shirts and richly coloured bolts of cloth.

Headstones in the cemetery at the Muradiye Külliyesi

The elegant suburb of **Çekirge**, 4km (2.5 miles) west of the centre, is the best place to stay, with many hotels built on bubbling thermal springs. The Eski Kaplıca and Yeni Kaplıca are both wonderful historic public baths. The heart of the district is the hilltop Birinci Murat Camii, which looks more like a Byzantine church with its brickwork – tradition asserts the builders were all Christian.

THE AEGEAN COAST

Turkey's Aegean coast has been a cultural crossroads for more than 3,000 years. Greeks migrated here early in the 1st millennium BC and founded its marvellous cities. In succeeding centuries, the Persians appeared from the east; Alexander the Great's army marched down from the northwest; the Romans added the area to their empire; Arabs attacked from the south; the Crusaders established military outposts; the Ottoman Empire expanded; and climactic World War I battles were waged. The Aegean coast thus offers the traveller an unparalleled picture of the past – with a backdrop of lovely beaches and old towns, imposing ruins and moving battlefield sites.

Çanakkale

The narrow strait separating Europe from Asia, known in Classical times as the Hellespont and now called the Dardanelles, has proved strategically irresistible to centuries of armies – the Persian Xerxes crossed the strait via a bridge of boats in 480 BC, on his unsuccessful campaign to conquer Greece, and Alexander crossed it going the other way 146 years later, on his (successful) march into Asia. In World War I, one of the bloodiest campaigns of this bloodiest of wars was waged just across the strait at Gallipoli.

Sea of love

The narrow, dangerously surging waters of the Dardanelles have proved irresistible to romantic swimmers – in ancient times, Leander swam across them by night to visit his lover, Hero, until drowning. The English poet Lord Byron repeated the feat (and surviving) in 1810.

Çanakkale, a lively navy and university town with a pleasant seafront promenade, makes a good base. The compact old quarter shows traces

Port at Canakkale

of a multicultural past in its synagogue, Armenian church, and well-restored bazaar. The **Archaeology Museum** (1.5km/1 mile south of the town centre on the Troy road; daily 8am–5.30pm) has as highlights of its collection two ornately carved sarcophagi.

Gallipoli

Çanakkale is also a convenient departure point for a visit to the **World War I battlefields** of **Gallipoli ❺**. Here, in late April 1915, Allied forces launched a massive campaign against Turkish troops to gain control of the Dardanelles and, ultimately, İstanbul. The German commander handed over to his deputy, a young Turkish officer called Mustafa Kemal (later known as Atatürk), who waged a brilliantly ruthless defence of the peninsula. In the months of fighting that followed, more than 46,000 Allied troops and 86,000 Turkish troops were killed and over 140,000 were wounded, out of half of million men on both sides. By January 1916, the Allied troops had retreated in defeat.

A replica of the wooden horse of Troy, Çanakkale

Tours to Gallipoli leave from Çanakkale; you can also take the car ferry to Eceabat or Kilitbahir and explore the region on your own. Well-tended cemeteries and other monuments to the dead mark the former battlefields on the peninsula. There's an excellent museum at the Kabatepe Information Centre, 9km (6 miles) northwest of Eceabat (daily 9am–6pm), with archival photos, maps, military hardware and touching letters home. Tours tend to visit only the ANZAC and Turkish memorials just north of Kabatepe; if you want to see the English and French sites on the far south cape, you'll need your own transport. The peninsula, incidentally, is ideal for mountain-biking.

Troy

The road to **Troy 6**, Highway E87, runs 30km (19 miles) south from Çanakkale. The modest ruins of this legendary city lie just west, looking towards the sea (daily 9am–7pm in summer; 8am–5pm in winter).

Homer's famous tale was long believed to be myth, but in 1871 a German businessman named Heinrich Schliemann began excavations at the site and uncovered nine layers of a prosperous city that had stood on the site for at least 4,000 years, including evidence that a battle had taken place at about the time of *The Iliad*. Parts of the massive east wall and gate still stand, a paved chariot ramp leading into the city is intact, and trenches and foundations mark the streets and houses of the ancient town. Stand on the ramparts and look over the Troad plain to the sea, where the thousand ships of King Agamemnon laid siege to Troy.

Gold, bronze and silver artefacts, plus jewellery, that Schliemann assembled in 1873 as 'Priam's Treasure' had nothing to do with the Trojan king, as he claimed, but are in fact some 1,200 years earlier in date. They were first spirited away to a museum in Berlin by Schliemann himself, from where they were stolen by the Red Army at the end of World War II. The cache, now the subject of litigation, resurfaced during 1993 in Russia; other objects recovered later are in İstanbul and Ankara. You will need a guide or an archaeological guidebook (available in the site shop) to make sense of the ruins, but it is well worth the effort.

The Iliad

Homer's story, told in *The Iliad*, is familiar: Paris, son of King Priam of Troy, abducted Helen, wife of Menelaos of Sparta, and took her back to Troy where she was received as his wife. Menelaos immediately appealed to his brother, the great Argive king Agamemnon, and together they amassed an army to get Helen back. For 10 years, the Greeks, including Achilles and Odysseus, tried to conquer the city. Finally, Odysseus hatched a scheme – the Greeks would present the Trojans with a gift of a great wooden horse and pretend to retreat. But the horse was hollow and filled with Greek soldiers; that night, as the Trojans celebrated their victory, the soldiers crept out and opened the gates to the invading Greek army.

Assos acropolis, looking up from the surrounding poppies

Behramkale (Assos)

Called Assos in ancient times, **Behramkale** is a divided town: most of its inhabitants live around the imposing ruins, set on a hill, the remainder in the small port below.

Assos ❼ (daily 9.30am–7.30, 8am–5pm in winter) may have been a Hittite settlement of the 13th century BC, but its true rise began around 950 BC when settlers from the Greek island of Lesbos just opposite took root here. They constructed a terraced city, much of which remains, on an impregnable site above Aegean shipping routes. In the 4th century BC, Hermias, a former student of Plato, rose to power, instituted a regime based on the Platonic notion of the philosopher-king and founded a school of philosophy, attracting Aristotle, who eventually married the eunuch-king's niece. After Hermias's execution by the Persians, the city passed from one ruling power to the next; the medieval Ottomans dismantled much of the ancient town for building stone.

The view from the ancient **acropolis** is wonderful – down the coast, and over to Lesbos. During the 1980s, inappropriate concrete was used to reconstruct the columns of the 6th-century BC **Temple of Athena**; remedial work is now sourcing stone from the original quarries. Around lie sparse remains of the ancient agora, gymnasium and theatre and the intact, simply proportioned 14th-century **Murad Hüdavendigar Camii**. The necropolis is well preserved, strewn with pieces of the limestone sarcophagi for which ancient Assos was famous, and about 3km (2 miles) of the old city walls still stand.

The little harbour at the bottom of a steeply twisting road, once used to ship out the acorns from which the region formerly made a living, has a compact collection of restaurants and hotels popular with the İstanbul trendy set. There's no real beach – the closest proper one is at Kadırga, a 45-minute walk (or 4km/2.5-miles drive) east.

Ayvalık

Follow the coast road around the Gulf of Edremit to charming **Ayvalık** ❽, 131km (81 miles) south of Behramkale. Founded by Ottoman Greeks in the 16th century, it was a prosperous, ethnically Greek town left all but empty after its inhabitants were ejected from Turkey in 1923. It's been resettled by Muslims from Crete and Mytilini, but its square stone houses and narrow, winding streets overhung with balconies and lined with lovely carved doorways still feel Greek. Stop at the busy central **bazaar** where cobblers and metalsmiths ply their

Ayvalık's new harbour

trades. Tall minarets mark the city's mosques, all former Greek Orthodox churches; note especially the **Saatlı Cami** (formerly Agios Ioannis), named after its clocktower.

The best beaches are several kilometres south of the city at **Sarımsaklı**, heavily developed with lines of holiday hotels, bars and restaurants. Boat excursions leave from Ayvalık's main waterfront every morning. The trip lasts for most of the day and includes the nearby islands such as **Alibey Adası (Cunda)**, with its miniature, Greek-built version of Ayvalık town, and makes frequent stops for a swim.

Pergamon

Pergamon ❾, 54km (33 miles) south of Ayvalık on Highway E87/550, was once the royal capital of the Attalids, and the most magnificent Hellenistic city in Asia Minor. Give yourself plenty of time here, for this was one of the greatest and most beautiful of all Greek cities, and its ruins speak eloquently of its past.

The city became famous in the 3rd century BC when Lysimakhos, a general in Alexander's army, deposited his considerable treasure behind its walls for safe-keeping before dying in battle in 281 BC. His eunuch-steward, Philetaeros, inherited the lot and set about founding a dynasty, adopting a nephew, Eumenes, to succeed him. Under Eumenes I and his descendants (variously named Attalos and Eumenes), the Attalid rulers of Pergamon defeated the Gauls, allied themselves with Rome, and steadily increased their wealth through war and exploitation of the surrounding silver mines and pasturelands. By the time Attalos III bequeathed the city to the Romans in 133 BC, the population was over 100,000 strong, immense by the standards of the day.

The ruins

The ruins are scattered across a large area. Start your visit at the Acropolis, on a rocky hill 6km (4 miles) above modern

Ancient ruins at Pergamon

Bergama, and then explore the Asklepion near the town. Both the Asklepion and Acropolis are open daily 8am–5pm in winter, until 7pm in summer (Asklepion from 8.30am); separate entrance fees. Limited parking is available outside both archaeological zones, with site maps on sale.

Near the summit of the Acropolis, the Corinthian columns of the 2nd-century AD **Temple of Trajan** have been partially restored. The north stoa once housed Pergamon's famous library, founded by Attalos II. It contained 200,000 volumes, partly written on papyrus and partly on bound parchment, a material the scribes invented when Egypt, fearing that the Pergamon library would outshine the one at Alexandria, banned the export of papyrus. The library was a magnet for scholars and historians until the 4th century AD.

Below is what's left of the Temple of Athena and the Altar of Zeus, the latter excavated by the German Karl Humann during the 1880s. Its magnificent frieze, depicting the battle between gods and titans, now has pride of place in Berlin's Pergamon Museum, along with a collection of other choice portable art from the site.

A staircase leads down to the **theatre**, which spectacularly backs onto a vast panoramic valley. Beautifully preserved, its 80 rows of seats could accommodate 10,000 people. Performances took place on a removable wooden stage (you can still see holes for the supporting posts). As in most ancient arenas, the acoustics are superb: a conversationally pitched voice can be heard clearly from the highest seats. Just offstage is the Temple of Dionysos.

Ancient medicine

Classical procedures were systematic, but had striking differences from modern medical practices. The patient would sleep in the temple, after which the physician interpreted the resulting dream and prescribed treatment, be it fasting, sacrifice to the gods or exercise, accordingly. Relaxation and private contemplation were also considered crucial, something we are finally learning again today.

The Asklepion is situated well below the Acropolis. Built in the 2nd century AD under the Romans, it was a centre of ancient medicine. Galen (129–202 AD), perhaps the world's first anatomist and physiologist, trained here before he joined the court of Marcus Aurelius in Rome. Besides a stoa and a theatre, the most impressive remains here are circular temples of Asklepios and Telesphoros.

The town

In the town itself, stop at the **Kızıl Avvlu** (Red Basilica; daily 8am–5pm, 9am–7pm in summer). Founded in the 2nd century AD as a temple to three Egyptian deities, it was later converted to a basilica and became one of the Seven Churches of Asia Minor, as referred to in the biblical Books of Revelations. The **Pergamon Arkeoloji Müsezi** (Archaeological Museum; daily 8am–5pm; 9am–7pm in summer) has those finds from the site not in Berlin.

İzmir and Çeşme

Turkey's second city, **İzmir** ⑩, 80km (48 miles) south of Bergama on the coast road, is the gritty industrial centre of the region. The city claims to be the birthplace of Homer, but its known history starts with Alexander the Great, who had a dream that inspired his generals to build a fortified settlement here shortly after Alexander's demise. As Smyrna, it prospered under the Romans, suffered under Arab invasions, and enjoyed a long period of prosperity as part of the Byzantine Empire, most notably as a key stop on the Silk Route from Asia. The early 20th century brought disaster. İzmir always had a large Greek, Armenian and Levantine population and, after the defeat of the Ottoman Empire during World War I, the city was occupied by the Greek army in 1919. The large force pressed inland, inciting resistance from the Nationalist Turks under Mustafa Kemal. On 9 September 1922, the victorious Turks entered İzmir after a disorderly Greek retreat; thousands of Armenian and Greek civilians died, and a fire – almost certainly the result of arson – destroyed 70 percent of the city.

İzmir clock tower

The current incarnation of İzmir, with its wide, tree-lined boulevards and characterless buildings, is built on those ruins; only the northerly district of Alsancak, with its ornate Belle Époque mansions, escaped the blaze. Another survival is the Roman agora (daily 8am–5pm; in summer 9am–7pm), just east and inland from the modern **bazaar** (leather is a great buy here). The harbour is best appreciated from the seafront promenade, **Birinci Kordon**, or **Konak Meydanı**, the city's main square with an ornate mosque (1748) and late 19th-century clock tower. Several streets south, in Turgutreis Parkı, stand the city's very good **archaeological and ethnographic museums** (both daily 8am–5pm, 9am–7pm in summer).

Just 75km (46 miles) west of İzmir by fast motorway, **Çeşme** ⓫ is one of the most charming Aegean resorts, crowned by a Genoese castle and flanked by a massive marina. The best local beaches are 9km (6 miles) south at **Altınkum** – scarcely developed white-sand coves. **Dalyan**, 4km (2.5 miles north, is the place to go for quality seafood tavernas. **Ilıca**, east of Dalyan, is a spa-resort with natural hot springs; **Alaçatı**, some 10km (6 miles) east of Çeşme, is a fine old Greek-built town that is the weekend retreat of choice for İzmir trendies, with boutique hotels installed in many of the old mansions.

Sardis (Sart)

Ancient **Sardis** ⓬ (90km/55 miles east of İzmir on Highway E96/300; daily 8am–5pm, 9am–7pm in summer), lies near the junction of the roads from Ephesus, Smyrna, Pergamon and inner Anatolia – a strategic position that made it, for centuries, the chief city of Asia Minor. Cyrus II (the Great), leader of the Persians, took note of this rich prize, and Croesus, last of the Lydian kings, unsure if he should attack first or wait to be attacked, consulted the oracle at Delphi. The ever-ambiguous oracle replied that if Croesus attacked he would destroy a great empire. Croesus did so, but the empire destroyed was his own. Cyrus used Sardis as the base for his conquest of Asia Minor and his assaults on Greece. Sardis then passed from ruler to ruler over the next centuries until, in AD 17, it was destroyed by an earthquake; what remains are ruins of the Roman rebuilding of this fabled city, like Pergamon one of the Seven Churches of Revelations.

The ruins are spread over a large area. The huge **Temple of Artemis**, originally founded by Croesus but rebuilt by Alexander the Great, was never finished; eventually, its stones were looted for use in other buildings. It now consists of a huge foundation with 15 massive Ionic columns, while its setting – amid forested hills and angular rock pinnacles – is very beautiful. About 1,300 metres/yds to the northeast, the **Marble Court** of the 3rd-century AD gymnasium has been restored. A nearby **synagogue**, also restored, was probably given to the local Jewish community by a Roman emperor in the 2nd century AD; original floor mosaics remain. Entry to this zone is via a marble-paved Roman avenue.

Library of Celsus at Ephesus

Ephesus

The gleaming marble monuments of **Ephesus** ⓭, 79km (49 miles) south of İzmir on the E87, comprise one of the best-preserved ancient cities on the Mediterranean. The site is open daily from 8am, closing at 5pm in winter, 8.30am–7pm in summer. Plan your visit carefully. In high season, arrive early or late to avoid the heat and the tour buses; invest in a site map; and take water. From the car park at the bottom gate, there are taxis or a free shuttle to the top gate, leaving you an easier walk downhill. Allow time also to visit the adjacent village of Selçuk – the Selçuk museum will illuminate your visit to the ancient city, while Selçuk itself is the site of the great Temple of Artemis, one of the seven wonders of the ancient world.

Set on a sheltered harbour at the mouth of a river, Ephesus was originally built by immigrant Athenians in about 1000 BC and dedicated to Artemis. It was conquered by King Croesus, and then held, in relatively peaceful succession, by the Persians, Alexander and the Romans, eventually declining due to its harbour silting up during the Byzantine era. Both St Paul and St John the Evangelist preached here , and the city was the site of two church councils. Paul wrote one of his most famous epistles to the Ephesians.

Begin your tour at the uppermost **Magnesian Gate**, from where caravans bound for the east departed in the past. The **Street of Kuretes** heads downhill past the East Gymnasium, Upper Agora and **Odeon**, an intimate theatre for poetry readings and music. The small **Temple of Hadrian** lies farther down the street on your right. Dedicated in the 2nd century AD,

Rich as Croesus

The mountains that surround Sardis are rich in gold ore, and coins were first minted here by the city's last Lydian ruler, King Croesus (560–546 BC), who literally coined the phrase 'rich as Croesus', flaunting his fortune by giving away 10 tons of gold.

The theatre in Ephesus

this gracious structure, fronted by Corinthian columns, has been restored; the friezes you see are plaster and the originals are in the museum in Selçuk. Behind it are the **Baths of Scholastica**, with their very public communal toilets and beautifully draped, headless statue of the bath's benefactor. Opposite is a large mosaic that presumably fronted a row of shops. Beyond this, steps lead up to the **terrace houses** (daily 8/8.30am–5pm). These were home to citizens of Ephesus in the Roman imperial and early Byzantine period, and give an idea of what life was like for the well-to-do.

On the corner with the so-called Marble Avenue is the city's **brothel**, marked by a footprint in the stone and some graphic decoration. Rooms surround a central atrium and, in the main reception room, a mosaic depicting the four seasons covers the floor – winter and autumn are the best preserved.

As you turn onto Marble Avenue, the **Library of Celsus**, on your left, is another structure that has been extensively restored

Ephesus mosaic

by the Austrian excavators. It was erected in the 2nd century AD by the Roman Consul Gaius Julius Aquila, who was subsequently buried in an ornate sarcophagus under the building's western wall. The library housed 12,000 scrolls that were stored in niches separated from the outer walls, to protect them from heat and humidity. Goths destroyed the library in AD 262. Beside this, the Lower Agora leads to the incomplete Temple of Serapis.

Back on Marble Avenue, continue to the **theatre**. Started by the Greeks, the structure that stands today is almost entirely Roman – and heavily, if not to say tastelessly, restored. A huge semi-circle backed by Mount Pion, the theatre could seat 24,000. Notice that the pitch increases as you climb up the rows of seats, allowing a clear view of the stage for spectators in the upper reaches. As well as watching plays, viewers over the centuries heard the preaching of St Paul; today, the theatre hosts music and folk-dance performances during the May Ephesus Festival.

The theatre stands at one end of the **Arcadian Way**, the colonnaded main street that runs to the middle harbour gate. Built in the 5th century AD, it was the model of an urban thoroughfare, its shopfronts protected by covered walkways illuminated at night with lamps (only Rome and Antioch shared this distinction). Towards the far end are the massive 2nd-century **Harbour Baths and Gymnasium**. To their right, the **Church of the Virgin Mary** was the first church in history so dedicated.

Back on Marble Avenue, turn left to pass the 70,000-seat **stadium** – a venue for everything from chariot races to gladiatorial contests – and the 2nd-century **Gymnasium of Vedius**. A well-preserved monumental gate on the west side was the city's main entrance. The car park lies beyond.

Selçuk

Selçuk town began its rise to prominence in the 5th century AD, when the harbour at Ephesus silted up. St John the Evangelist died here in about AD 100, and was buried on **Ayasoluk Hill**, which is a good spot to begin your tour. Several hundred years after John's death, the Emperor Justinian constructed an ornate basilica which, until its destruction in the 15th century by the Mongols, was one of the largest in the world. A castle sits atop Ayasoluk Hill; its ramparts provide a fine view. Below it, the **İsa Bey Camii** is an elegant 14th-century mosque.

A quick scramble down the hill brings you to the **archaeological museum**. Its wonderful collection of artefacts from Ephesus and other nearby sights includes a bronze statuette of Eros riding a dolphin, a fine wall-painting of Socrates from a reconstructed terrace-house salon, a collection of early crucifixes and various representations of the Virgin and the saints, some fine sarcophagi, and several statues of the many-breasted Artemis, mistress of beasts.

The popular resort of Kuşadası

Just out of town, it's hard to imagine how a former wonder of the ancient world could be a less impressive sight than the **Temple of Artemis**, but centuries of neglect and looting have taken their toll. Let your creativity reign, however, and you may be able to re-erect the 127 marble columns, recreate the magnificent friezes and imagine the goddess of the hunt at home and at rest. Another outlying place of interest is **Meryemana**, the House of the Virgin Mary, on the road from Ephesus to Bülbüldağı. Legend has it that St John and the Virgin lived in this simple dwelling after the death of Christ. Although the story is unsubstantiated, the house has been recognised by the Vatican and is usually thronged with pilgrims.

Kuşadası

Kuşadası, 20km (12 miles) southwest of Selçuk on Route 515, is one of the most popular resorts on the Aegean coast, a port for cruise ships and tour boats and, as such, has become a jumping-off point for group tours to Ephesus. It's a busy place, with some good restaurants and hotels, and the small old centre is atmospheric. To the south of town lies the mountainous **Dilek Yarımadası Milli Park** (Dilek Peninsula National Park), with several good pebble beaches along its north shore. Some 15km (9 miles) north stretches sandy Pamucak beach which, if the wind isn't too strong, also has good swimming.

Pamukkale and Hierapolis

From Kuşadası, Route E87 turns east into Turkey's interior, and the striking scenery and ruins at **Pamukkale** and **Hierapolis ⓮**, 170km/105 miles inland (daily 8am–5pm, 9am–7pm in summer).

You will see Pamukkale in the distance as a tall, chalky outcrop rising high above the surrounding plain. Come closer and the rocks will resolve into fantastic shapes resembling flowers, birds, waterfalls. The source of this strange beauty is a spring that, for the past 14,000 years, has burbled up from the top of the plateau, putting out a stream of warm, calcium-rich water that, as it dribbles over the side and cools, precipitates into the hard white chalk called travertine.

The Antique Pool at Pamukkale

The ancient city of Hierapolis may have been founded by Eumenes II of Pergamon. Favoured by the Romans, it became prosperous from trade in wool and an unusual marble coloured by the seepage of minerals. It was also a spa whose waters were said to cure rheumatism. A large Jewish community laid the foundations for the growth of Christianity, and there were once hundreds of churches here (some of which still stand). The city suffered under Arab attacks, and was virtually abandoned by the 12th century when it passed into Seljuk hands.

While you can hike up from **Pamukkale Köyü**, a village at the base of the plateau, the main entrance is via a road which winds up the back of the site and through the ruins of Hierapolis. From the top, it is almost irresistible to climb down onto the **travertine terraces**. Pools of milky water are everywhere, but with algae and erosion problems, most areas are closed off with only one walking trail open at any one time. Remove your shoes before stepping in. For a proper bath in the curative waters, visit the once-sacred Antique Pool.

Once cured, step out into the largely Roman ruins. A narrow road leads past the 4th-century AD nymphaeum,

Pamukkale's travertine terraces

or fountainhouse, to the Temple of Apollo. Started in the Hellenistic period and probably completed in the 3rd century AD, it is set on a shelf of natural rock. Not much remains of it. While excavating the temple foundation, Italian archaeologists were troubled by noxious gas seeping from the rock in the Plutonium next door. This sanctuary, dedicated to Pluto, is set over a stream that runs through a deep, natural cutting in the rock. The gas, which includes sulphurous compounds, rises from the water. It is deadly; only eunuchs, according to ancient writers, were immune to its toxicity. Farther along is a restored Roman theatre. Many of the stage buildings have been preserved and, in June, this is the venue for an international song festival. Farther east, past the city walls, is the 5th-century Martyrion of St Philip.

Continue through the triple-arched northerly city gate. The arcades on the right were originally Roman baths, which were later converted to a church. Just past them is the ancient city's **necropolis**, dating back to the Hellenistic period, probably the largest cemetery in Asia Minor. For sanitary reasons, burial was not permitted inside the city proper. The tombs, some elaborately designed and inscribed, were surrounded by gardens, and tended by special guilds.

The nearby village of **Karakhayıt** has other travertine formations, rainbow-streaked by minerals, as well as a number of hot springs. This is the main tourist centre, with plenty of large spa hotels and a good bazaar. There are two natural mud pools at nearby Karakbaşı and Gölemezli.

Aphrodisias

On the way back to the coast, take Route 585 south through fertile countryside to **Aphrodisias ⓯**, 80km/50 miles from Pamukkale (daily 8am–5pm, until 7pm in summer). Named for the Greek goddess of love, the city was a cultural centre, known for its school of sculpture and devotion to Aphrodite.

Aphrodisias Gateway

The carefully excavated ruins, built mainly from the local blue-veined marble, give the city an other-worldly air.

Set on a 600-metre (1,900ft) -high plateau, and ringed with craggy, marble-veined mountains, Aphrodisias is a strikingly beautiful place. The ruins, most of which date to the 1st and 2nd centuries AD, were obscured by the village of Geyre until 1956, when an earthquake struck. The villagers were relocated a short distance to the west, and excavations have revealed an entire ancient city on a par with Ephesus.

A path loops around the site. The 1st-century **theatre** is beautifully preserved; behind the stage is a large square, or tetrastoön, where Roman and Byzantine citizens might have congregated after a performance. Follow the path anticlockwise from the theatre; below is the **Sebasteion**. This 1st-century complex, consisting of twin porticos and a central paved area, was probably first constructed as a shrine to Aphrodite, and later became a place to honour the Roman emperors. Making an emperor divine and equal to the ancient gods was a way to legitimise Roman hegemony in the east. A double agora lies just west, its blue-grey marble columns almost indistinguishable from the surrounding poplar trees. Beyond it are the well-preserved **Baths of Hadrian**.

North of the agora, the so-called Bishop's Palace probably began life as the Roman governor's residence. Next are the remains of the **Temple of Aphrodite**. Begun in the 1st century BC, by the 5th century AD the temple had been converted into a Christian basilica and the great statue of the goddess of love that stood here was largely destroyed, her battered torso incorporated into a Byzantine wall. Just north is the school of philosophy, while to the east stands the fully restored Tetrapylon, which marked the intersection of two ancient roads.

Perhaps the finest structure in Aphrodisias is the **stadium**, the best preserved in Anatolia. It was built in the 1st century AD and designed to seat 30,000 spectators. The competitions staged here emulated Delphi's Pythian Games – foot racing, boxing and wrestling; music, oratory and drama. Prizes were modest, and contestants entered simply for the privilege of competition. The **museum** houses all statuary from the site that hasn't been transferred to major Turkish museums.

Priene

Back on the coast, some 37km (23 miles) from Kuşadası, **Priene** ⓰ (daily 8am–5pm, until 7pm in summer) is an ancient Ionian city superbly set on pine-clad terraces high on Samsun Dağı. It was probably first settled by Greeks in the 11th century BC. The city whose ruins remain today was laid out in the 4th century BC on a grid system. As the harbour silted up, the wealth of Priene declined, invaders or renovators lost interest, and so it remains an almost purely Hellenistic city.

Temple of Athena Polias, Priene

The ruins are a gentle climb up through the southeast gate from the car park. Main streets run east–west and are intersected by smaller lanes, creating 'insula,' which contain either four private houses or the city's public and religious buildings. Note the drainage gutters on the sides of the streets, and the grooves in the centre, which were worn by chariot wheels. Just south of the main street is the 2nd-century BC ***bouleuterion***, or council house. Rows of seats on three sides enclose a small stage; a speaker's recess, where speakers stood to address the council, is on the fourth. Across the street are the scanty remains of the sacred stoa, the agora and the Temple of Zeus, which formed the heart of the city. Farther along the main street is a largely residential section of thick-walled houses, their rooms opening off a central courtyard.

On a terrace above the main street stands the **Temple of Athena Polias**. Built in part with contributions from Alexander the Great, it is one of the most harmoniously designed temples on the Aegean coast and served as a model for students of architecture for centuries; five of the original 30 Ionic columns have been re-erected. At the 4th-century BC **theatre**, front-row VIP seating and stage building are largely intact. Finally, if it's not too hot and you are feeling exceptionally energetic, climb to the top of the Acropolis. It will take you more than an hour, but the view is magnificent.

Miletus and Didyma

Some 14km (9 miles) west, then south of Priene, **Miletus** ⓱ (Milet; daily 8am–5pm, 9am–7pm in summer) is actually the oldest of the ancient Ionian cities. The highlight here is the 2nd-century AD theatre, with seats for 15,000 and fine reliefs on the stage building. Another site standout is the exquisite İlyas Bey Camii, dating from 1404, with a banded dome and finely carved mihrab. Nearby, there is a small museum of local finds.

Just 36km (22 miles) south of Priene, **Didyma** ⓲ (Didim; daily 8.30am–5.30pm, 8am–7pm in summer) was home to a magnificent **Temple of Apollo** and an oracle, and from its

The head of Medusa at Didyma

Bronze Age origins was always a sacred precinct, never a town. An early shrine was destroyed by the Persians, and a new temple was planned when Alexander the Great retook the region. Its grand scale almost ensured that it would never be completed and, although work went on for some five centuries, it never was.

Try to visit towards sunset, when the temple's columns glow in the fading light. The temple was designed to be bounded by 108 columns in double rows (some of which have been re-erected), all set on an imposingly high *crepidoma*, or stepped platform. Just below the ticket booth, notice two reliefs of Medusa heads. In a well below the heads, pilgrims would purify themselves, then make their way to the temple shrine, where they would receive the oracle's answers. Further inside the temple is the foundation of the naiskos, the great hall that contained the cult statue and sacred spring.

Bodrum

Set on two curved bays, **Bodrum** ⓳, 125km (78 miles) from Didyma, is one of Turkey's premier resorts, a rich town that's full of posh yachts, boutiques, restaurants and lively nightlife. The Aegean is never long out of sight, but as the town itself has no beach, many tourist hotels are strung out along the sands of the nearby peninsula.

Known in ancient times as Halikarnassos, the place was colonised by Greeks in the 11th century BC, nurtured Herodotus in the 5th century BC, enjoyed semi-autonomy under the Hecatomnid kings during the Persian era, and declined slowly after Alexander passed through. In the 15th century, the Knights of St John built a castle here; in later centuries the peninsula was home to a largely Greek Orthodox

Opening times

The castle is open daily 8am–5pm, until 7pm in summer. Check locally before visiting.

A view of Bodrum's castle from the harbour

population and, although the Greeks were expelled in 1922, the area retains a vaguely Greek feel.

The modern town of Bodrum is dominated by the **Castle of St Peter** on its peninsula, for years the only Christian outpost in Anatolia. Many of the stones in the castle were salvaged from the Mausoleum of Halikarnassos, final resting place of the 4th-century BC Hecatomnid ruler Mausoleus, and one of the seven wonders of the ancient world. St Peter's surrendered to the Ottomans in 1523 and today the castle is a multi-level maze of courtyards, rooms, moats and cisterns. Much of it is given over to the **Museum of Underwater Archaeology**. Don't miss the Glass Wreck Hall, where a Byzantine ship and its cargo, *c.*1025, are housed; the Uluburun Wreck Hall, containing one of the world's oldest ships, which sank in the 14th century BC; and the Hall of the Carian Princess, with the lavish contents of a tomb dating to about 360 BC. The **towers** offer splendid views across the town and harbour. In the **English Tower** the banqueting hall has been restored, and you can read the graffiti carved in the window niches by homesick knights. Bodrum's bazaar lies just north of the castle. The site of the ancient mausoleum (daily 8am–5pm, until 7pm in summer) is two blocks above the harbour; little is left of the mausoleum itself.

A peninsula extends west of Bodrum, with towns and beaches served by both boat and bus. On the south shore, **Kargı** has a fine sand beach and camels to ride, **Karaincir** is another good beach with public access, while **Akyarlar** boasts some good restaurants. In the far west, **Gümüşlük** is a relatively 'alternative' resort with another long beach and the ruins of ancient Myndos. On the north shore, **Türkbükü** fancies itself the St Tropez of Turkey and gets a well-heeled Turkish clientele.

MEDITERRANEAN COAST

The southern ('Turquoise') coast of Turkey is one of the most beautiful on the Mediterranean, with long sandy beaches, crystal-clear waters and pleasant resorts. This craggy landscape also cradles the evocative ruins of past civilisations, centuries-old cities and spectacular mountain scenery.

Marmaris and the Datça Peninsula

Marmaris is a brash, boisterous resort town and yacht port whose saving grace is a fleet of boats ensuring an easy getaway to more idyllic places. Aside from a seemingly endless line of harbourside drinking establishments, the allure of Marmaris consists of its beautiful setting on a bay framed on both sides by pine-forested slopes and cliffs, and the small, whitewashed old town. An exploration of the narrow lanes begins at the souvenir-filled bazaar and ends at the **castle** (daily 8.30am–noon and 1–5.30pm), built shortly after a huge Ottoman fleet sailed successfully against nearby Rhodes in 1522. Most of the resort hotels are stretched along İçmeler beach, round the bay to the west, and the closest decent beach.

Datça, 69km (43 miles) west along the eponymous peninsula, proves a workaday market and real-estate town, its town beaches too ordinary to draw may foreign tourists. There's more appeal in **Eski Datça**, 3km (2 miles) inland, a stone-built village that has been restored by Turkish alternative types. From here to the end of the peninsula, the scenery – some of the least spoiled along Turkey's Mediterranean coast – becomes ever more dramatic, with defiles, forested crags, almond orchards. There are the side turnings down to the excellent beaches of **Ova Bükü** and **Palamut Bükü**, both with plenty of accommodation and eating opportunities.

A pretty cove on the Lycian Coast

The theatre at Knidos

Palamut Bükü is the last attraction before **Knidos** ⓴ (daily 8.30am–7pm), a 7th-century BC Dorian Greek settlement draped over a windswept headland commanding the juncture of the Aegean and the Mediterranean seas. This position on major shipping lanes earned Knidos a prominent role in the ancient world. Aside from the rough-hewn beauty of the city's ruined temples, agora, theatre and Byzantine church, as well as some curiosities such as the sundial used by the astronomer Eudoxos, Knidos is more famous for what's no longer here. The city's famed lion tomb is now in the British Museum, as is a statue of the goddess Demeter, both unearthed by archaeologists in the 1850s. Most famous in antiquity was the long-lost, 4th-century BC statue of Aphrodite by Praxiteles. Pliny praised the sculpted nude as the finest statue in the world, and travellers sailed here from all over the ancient world to see it. The road in from Datça is now mostly paved, but you too may sail in on a boat trip from Datça harbour.

Dalyan

The relaxed resort of **Dalyan** ㉑ is 75km (46 miles) east of Marmaris, although much closer to the Dalaman airport. The former agricultural town is lapped by a slow-moving, reed-lined river, the Dalyan Cayı, beneath a cliff perforated with 4th-century BC Carian rock tombs. Pleasant as these environs are, a visitor will not be here too long before boarding a boat and embarking on some extraordinary excursions. A short way upstream the river opens into **Lake Köyceğiz**, a former gulf long isolated from the sea, whose reed-beds shelter a rich bird life. Boatmen usually ferry their passengers upstream first to the **Ilıca mud baths** (40°C) on the riverbank, and then may continue to the **Sultaniye thermal springs** (also 40°) on the lake's south shore; the facilities are a bit basic, but a soak in the warm, mineral-rich waters is quite soothing.

About 1km (0.5 miles) downstream from Dalyan, boats pull dock below the ruins of the city of **Kaunos** (daily 8.30–5pm, until 7pm in summer), famous in antiquity for figs and malaria. Settled in the 9th century BC by the Carians, the city much later passed through Greek and Roman hands and was closely allied with the Lycian civilisation farther east along the coast. This mixed heritage accounts for the presence of Roman baths, a Greek-style theatre, a Byzantine basilica and Lyciantype rock tombs, with elaborate facades suggesting temples. Impressive remnants of the extensive 4th-century BC walls loom just north.

Beyond Kaunos, the river emerges at **İstuzu Beach**. Aside from some makeshift

Loggerhead turtle

Between June and September each year, huge female loggerhead turtles weighing up to 180kg (350lb) drag themselves up onto 17 beaches around Turkey. Each lays around 100 leathery eggs, which take two months to hatch, the babies scurrying in the moonlight down to the relative safety of the surf.

Magnificently situated Ölüdeniz

snack bars either end, this flat, sandy beach, 3.5km (2 miles) long, is blessedly devoid of manmade incursions, to protect its status as a breeding ground of the loggerhead turtle *(Caretta caretta)*. You are likely to see the creatures' tracks, but not the turtles themselves, as the beach is off-limits at night during the breeding season.

Fethiye

This busy commercial town, 90km (55 miles) east of Dalyan along Highway 400, is more concerned with the here and now than with the ancient past. Founded in the 5th century BC as Telmessos, it changed hands – and name – several times, to Anastasiopolis and Makri under the Byzantines and finally to Fethiye in the 1930s, in honour of a pioneering Ottoman military pilot.

Earthquakes, the most severe in 1857 and 1957, destroyed the medieval settlement, and most of the ancient one. Just a few temple- or free-standing tombs stand in the streets or are cut into the cliffs bounding Fethiye to the south; the ancient theatre has been excavated; a Crusader castle tops the hill behind; and the local museum is replete with local archaeological finds. More compelling, perhaps, are the lively bazaar, and general air of an ordinary Turkish town. Excursion boats depart from here on day-trips to the islands of the Gulf of Fethiye, or multi-day cruises taking in **Gemiler Adası** with its Byzantine ruins, Kalkan and Kekova.

Ölüdeniz and Kaya Köyü

Turkey's most famous beach, **Ölüdeniz** ㉒, 12km (7 miles) south of Fethiye, is much touted on travel posters, the turquoise waters of the lagoon backed by white beaches and forested hillsides. The immediate area is a national park; the drawback is that the whole of the valley flanking the approach road is a solid mass of holiday accommodation, and the area is heaving all season, with most arrivals on cheap mass-market package tours that cater to families and young singles. Unspoilt it isn't. To enjoy this lovely coast in quieter surroundings, seek out the beach at **Kıdrak**, 3km (2 miles) east, or take the short boat excursion to '**Butterfly Valley'** and its beach, inaccessible by road.

Kaya Köyü (the medieval Levissi), in a secluded uplands between Fethiye and Ölüdeniz, is a strange ghost town. Its 600 houses and three churches have been abandoned since their Greek Orthodox inhabitants were ousted during the population exchange in 1923. The whole place is now a protected monument (daily 8.30am–5pm).

The Ruins of the Lycian Heartland

The tall coastal mountains and fertile valleys east and south of Fethiye and Ölüdeniz cradled the Lycian civilisation.

Establishing themselves here even before the Hittite era, the Lycians formed a democratic federation of 23 towns that continued to function even when ultimate control was ceded to successive conquerors, including the Persians, Greeks, Alexander, the Rhodians and eventually imperial Rome. The Lycians left behind bountiful traces of their presence, from their coinage to their rock tombs, and a collection of ruined cities that can be reached easily from turn-offs along Highway 400.

Tlos and Pınara

The ruins of Tlos and Pınara crown hilltops on opposite sides of the valley of the Xanthos river, now known as the Eşen Cayı. At **Tlos** (35km/22 miles from Fethiye; daily 8am–5pm, until 7pm in summer), the most extensive ruins from the city's lengthy past are its 7th-century BC rock tombs, a Roman theatre juxtaposed against the peaks of the Akdağ range and the Yedi Kapı baths. Relief carvings are unusually rich; one tomb bears depictions of the mythical Bellerophon riding the winged horse Pegasus, while the theatre stage has a block decorated with an eagle and a garlanded youth.

Tlos carpet craftswoman

Beyond Tlos, a narrow but paved road leads to the mouth of the **Saklıkent**

gorge (dawn to dusk). Some 300 metres (1,000ft) high and 18km (11 miles) long, this is the longest and deepest gorge in Turkey. Its first 2km (1 mile) is accessible only by a catwalk, then path that follows the base of the towering rock face through icy water pouring out of the limestone mountains of the Gombe Akdaği.

Saklıkent Gorge, the longest and deepest gorge in Turkey

Pınara (across the valley and 20km/12 miles south of Tlos; daily 8am–5pm, until 7pm in summer) is less accessible than its neighbour, with final dirt-road approach from the village of Minare. You may well find yourself alone among the ruins scattered among olive trees at the base of a massive cliff honeycombed with tombs. Intricately carved tombs are also among the best-preserved structures in the town below; the so-called Royal Tomb is decorated with depictions of cityscapes and scenes of what appears to be a religious festival. Across the cultivated plain, the theatre is exquisite – small and perfectly formed, and never modified by the Romans.

The Letoön and Xanthos

The **Letoön** (16km/10 miles south of Pınara; daily 8am–5pm, until 7pm in summer), was a religious sanctuary, a shrine to the goddess Leto and an assembly ground at which Lycians celebrated festivals. The first of the **three temples**, dating to the 3rd century BC, is dedicated to Leto, and French archaeologists have recently re-erected three of its columns, plus most of the walls. The other two temples honour her twin offspring, Artemis and Apollo. A mosaic on the floor of one temple symbolises both twins, with a bow and quiver for Artemis and a lyre for Apollo. The partly waterlogged nymphaeum is well tenanted by noisy frogs; there is also a well-preserved theatre.

Xanthos (directly across the valley from the Letoön; daily 8am–5pm, until 7pm in summer) was the most important of the Lycian cities and its ruins are extensive. The city was noted for its fierce pride and stubborn independence; the residents of Xanthos twice set their city and themselves ablaze in a mass suicide, rather than surrender to the Persian general Harpagos in 540 BC or the Roman general Brutus in 42 BC.

Like the other Lycian cities, Xanthos is littered with **rock tombs**, including a 5th-century BC pillar tomb with 250 lines describing the exploits of a champion local wrestler;

Ruins at the Letoön

this is the most extensive known script in the Lycian language. The so-called Harpy Tomb is richly carved with figures that are half-woman and half-bird and appear to be ushering the dead into the afterlife. These reliefs are not the originals – they and many other artefacts were carried away from Xanthos in 1842 by archaeologist Charles Fellows. Most, including the Ionic temple known as the Nereid Monument, are now in the British Museum. Among immovable monuments in Xanthos, the city gate and theatre are Roman, the monastery and mosaic-decorated basilica are Byzantine.

Fragments in Patara

Patara

The principal port of Lycia, **Patara** ㉓ is 18km (11 miles) south of Xanthos (daily 8am–5pm, until 7pm in summer). An oracle of Apollo resided here, in a still-unlocated temple; Hannibal and St Paul were among the city's many noted visitors. St Nicholas (who later became identified with Santa Claus) was born in Patara in AD 270, the son of a wealthy trader. Today, the ruined ancient city is steadily being excavated, and kept free of the nearby, drifting sand dunes.

The Patara area's other great attraction is a magnificent 15km (9-mile) long blonde-sand **beach**. All development has been kept blessedly far inland at cheerful **Gelemiş** resort, thanks to the ruins and the presence of loggerhead turtles.

Kalkan and Kaş

Relatively free of important ruins, Kalkan and its near neighbour Kaş, both former Greek fishing villages, offer the ruin-weary traveller bougainvillea-shaded café terraces, breezy seaside promenades and plenty of retail therapy. Both are charming resorts and excellent bases from which to explore the coast. **Kalkan**, 13km (8 miles) east of the Patara turn-off on Highway 400, is marginally the smaller of the two towns. The old quarter of stone-built, tile-roofed houses, some occupied by shops, restaurants and *pansiyons*, clings to a steep hillside descending to a small harbour. This is, however, completely enveloped by a burgeoning quarter, most of it second-home developments aimed at foreign purchasers. Kalkan does not a sandy beach, merely a small pebble cove in town and diving platforms on the flanks of the deep bay. Those in need of a real beach make the 6km (4-mile) trip east along the coast to **Kaputaş**, a popular, much photographed beauty spot reached from narrow steps off the roadside and the outflow of an eponymous gorge.

Kaş ❷❹, a once-sleepy port, 27km (16 miles) east of Kalkan along Highway 400, is now quite lively – especially after dark in high season. However, it retains an easygoing air and a more varied clientele than Kalkan, and the setting, along a curving bay beneath limestone cliffs and olive groves, is lovely.

Lycian culture

Leto was a nymph who had the misfortune of attracting Zeus, thus invoking the wrath of his jealous wife, Hera. Pregnant and in flight from Hera, Leto was befriended by wolves who led her to the Xanthos River to refresh herself. The incident allegedly gave the Lycian culture its name, which derives from the Greek *lykos*, wolf. Leto was not without a vengeful side of her own – she turned some local shepherds who refused her water into frogs.

The narrow central streets are lined with small houses and the occasional rock tomb, while a small Greek-style theatre looks out to sea a short walk west from the mosque in the town centre. Kaş is an obligatory port of call for *gulet* trips along the Turquoise Coast, and also the crossing-point to the Greek islet of Kastellórizo just opposite, the remotest of the Dodecanese islands. A modern marina lies at the western end of the town. Both Kaş and Kastellórizo are now official ports of entry/exit for their respective countries, and in season there's at least one daily scheduled ferry in each direction, allowing day-trips.

Old houses in Kaş

Kekova

Kekova Island ㉕ gives its name to a beautiful and fascinating marine landscape just east of Kaş. You can also drive into the region, following a 20km (12-mile) road off Highway 400 towards the village of **Üçağız** from a turn-off about 18km (11 miles) east of Kaş. Little coastal villages overlook placid inlets, and the seabed beneath the warm waters is divided by the foundations of Roman houses or harbour-works, with Lycian tombs occasionally, and romantically, jutting out of the water.

Üçağız is the larger of the two settlements here, both protected from concrete expansion by existing within

Picturesque Kale

archaeological zones, though arrived touristically in a small way. Local fishermen are willing to forsake their lines and nets to ferry passengers to various points of interest. At **Tersane**, the remains of a ruined Byzantine basilica form a picturesque backdrop to a popular spot for swimming from a pebble beach. The north shore of the island is home to the underwater ruins known as **Batık Şehir** (Sunken City), though snorkelling above them is banned to preclude antiquity theft.

The village of **Kale**, reachable by 45-minute walk or another boat ride, huddles beneath a castle built by the crusading Knights of St John atop the acropolis of ancient Simena. The scramble up the narrow path to the ramparts rewards the visitor with sweeping views and an ancient theatre carved into the living rock inside the castle. Down below, the little harbour is studded with half-submerged Lycian tombs. The incongruous presence of a helicopter landing-pad can be attributed to wealthy Turkish businessman Rahmi Koç, who retreats to a simple house in the village and has endowed several local institutions.

Demre and Myra

Demre, about 35km (21 miles) east of Kaş, is home to the ancient city of Myra and the Byzantine **Church of St**

Nicholas (daily 8.30am–5.30pm, 9am–7pm in summer), built in the 4th century AD during, or just after, St Nicholas's tenure as the local bishop.

The saint's remains were stolen by religious pirates in 1087 and taken to Bari, Italy, but the little basilica still commemorates the saint, whose reputation for generosity seems to have originated from his practice of giving coins to poor households by anonymously dropping them down the chimney. Aside from the *synthronon* (bishops' seating) in the central apse, remains of the original church are difficult to locate among the reconstruction of 1043, and the 1862 renovations that added a belfry and vaulted ceiling over the nave, sponsored by Tsar Nicholas I; Nicholas is the patron saint of Russia, and Russian pilgrims come here in force. Best of the faded Byzantine frescoes are the Communion of the Apostles in the north apse.

A short walk or drive north of town brings you to **Myra** (daily 8am–5pm, 9am–7pm in summer). This riverside city was an important centre of Lycian commerce, as evidenced by its impressive monuments – particularly a well-preserved theatre with 35 rows of seats and fine comedy and tragedy masks on the stage masonry. The main group of tombs, some in imitation of wood-beamed Lycian domestic dwellings, are in the palisade west of the theatre; there are more at the so-called River Necropolis, 1500m upstream.

From Demre, Highway 400 follows the indented coastline east for 30km (18 miles) to Finike, from where a 34km (21-mile) steep detour north

Busy saint

As a saint, Nicholas is one of the busiest. Not only is he Santa Claus, but he is also patron saint of Russia, Greece, prisoners, sailors, travellers, unmarried girls, pawnbrokers, merchants and children. The image of the jolly red man with a white beard was a 20th-century invention by the Coca-Cola company.

Comedy and tragedy masks in Myra

along Highway 635 brings you to the ruins of **Arykanda** (daily 8am–5pm, 9am–7pm in summer). These cling precipitously to a south-facing hillside to either side of a ravine. Tombs, the agora, a basilica with surviving floor mosaics, a small theatre and a stadium have been excavated. Most impressive are the main baths, with walls, windows and a plunge-pool still intact.

Olympos and Phaselis

Continuing about 35km (22 miles) east, then north, from Finike, a side road leads to **Olympos** ㉖, a long-abandoned port city straddling a tree-shaded stream that disappears into a broad beach just beyond a natural defile guarded by two Byzantine-Genoese forts. The ruins here (daily 8am–5pm, 9am–7pm in summer) are a bit scanty and overgrown, but the setting and opportunity for swimming from the pine-backed beach is memorable. Just before the site entrance is a long series of backpacker-orientated 'treehouse'-style lodges of varying comfort.

Olympos is also the ancient name of the local mountain (one of many summits so called in the ancient world), today called **Tahtalı Dağ** (2366 metres/7690ft). It's easily visible from **Çıralı**, an alternative base for visiting ancient Olympos, with numerous, more comfortable *pansiyons* and a separate access road just beyond the first one. Çıralı has two major attractions: a long, scenic beach strictly protected from over-development, with the ruins at one end, and the **Chimaera** (*Yanartaş* in Turkish), a short way inland from the north end of the beach. Several natural-gas vents here issue eerie flames from the bare rock, as they were doing millennia ago when sailors on Roman trading ships recorded a natural beacon along this part of the coast; they are best viewed at night. It was here that the mythical Bellerophon supposedly defeated the dragon-like fire-breathing Chimaera. There is also an adjacent small shrine to the blacksmith-god Hephaestos, revered wherever fire or lava issued from the earth.

Phaselis (25km/15 miles east of Olympos; daily 8.30am–5pm, 9am–7pm in summer) is a former colony of Rhodes and a strategically placed commercial post that traded widely across the Mediterranean, from Egypt to Rome. Phaselitans acquired quite a reputation in antiquity for being both obsequious and venal. The 7th-century BC founders of the city are said to have purchased the territory for some dried fish; their descendants helped both Mausolus of Halikarnassos

Flame of the Chimaera

and Alexander without any prompting, and raised money by selling citizenship for the meagre sum of 100 drachmas. The baths, theatre, aqueduct and wide central street nestle in pine groves around three natural harbours – excursion boats still arrive at the southerly one, and all lend themselves to a swim and a long picnic.

Antalya

Busy **Antalya** ㉗, 50km (30 miles) north of Phaselis, was one of the major cities of ancient Pamphylia, founded as a Pergamene colony during the 2nd century BC by Attalos II. While the rest of the coast survives on tomatoes, citrus fruit and tourism, Antalya is Turkey's fastest-growing city, spreading round a broad bay beneath the Beydağları range. The mega-resort hotels are mainly east of town at Lara; however, it's **Kaleici**, the old town surrounding the harbour, that will interest most visitors.

Antalya's most famous landmarks crown the bluffs that surround the harbour. The Seljuk **Saat Kulesi** (clocktower) is built into a fragment of the Roman and Ottoman walls, near the so-called Castle Gate and the entrance to the bazaar. **Mehmet Paşa Camii**, a mosque in front of the clocktower, was built in the 16th century, while a much earlier mosque nearby is most famous for its distinctive **Yivli Minare** (Fluted Minaret); the mosque itself is now a municipal art gallery and the courtyards of its adjoining medrese (theological school) have been glassed over to accommodate shops. Southeast along Atatürk Caddesi, **Hadrian's Gate**, a rather pompous, three-arched monument, honours the emperor's visit to the city in AD 130. **Hıdırlık Kulesi**, a contemporaneous stone tower down on the shore, may have served as a lighthouse.

Narrow cobblestone lanes wind down towards the harbour. Many of the Ottoman houses, built in the 19th century, now accommodate shops, *pansiyons* and restaurants. Among them is the **Kesık Minare** (Broken Minaret), an eclectic structure that has served as a Roman temple, a Byzantine church and an Ottoman mosque. The downhill walk ends at the old port, a favourite location for an evening promenade.

West of the old town, **Konyaaltı** is the main city beach, its promenade lined by restaurants, cafés, sports facilities and the occasional upmarket hotel. The **Antalya Müzesi** (daily 8am–5pm, 9am–7pm in summer), at the western edge of the town centre, houses a world-class archaeology collection. Many of the exhibits are from Perge and range from a game board to a pantheon of statuary. Other highlights include mosaics from Xanthos, a silver reliquary that once held the bones of St Nicholas, and Bronze Age burial goods and votive figurines from Elmalı, in the local mountains.

Hadrians Gate in Antalya

Ruins of the Antalyan Coast

Some of the most extraordinary ancient sites in Turkey make an easy day-trip from Antalya. The neighbouring Pamphylian cities of Perge, Aspendos and Side long predate Antalya, passing through the hands of the Persians and Alexander the Great before becoming a Roman imperial backwater.

Termessos

In a mountainous national park 30km (19 miles) northwest of Antalya, **Termessos** ㉘ (daily 8am–5pm, 9am–7pm in summer) is one of the most dramatically situated, which allowed it quasi-independence even under the Romans. The city's impregnable position stopped even Alexander the Great, who was deterred by the shower of boulders the citizenry launched from the ramparts above. The climb up to the evocative ruins

The great theatre at Aspendos

is still arduous. The theatre's setting – one side abutting a deep gorge and another built into a cliff – is as dramatic as any performance on its stage. A large gymnasium adjoins extensive baths with an elaborate water-collection system, and beyond the odeon and temple complex a hillside is eerily littered with more than 100 tombs.

Temple of Athena and Apollo, Side

Perge and Aspendos

East of Antalya, the coast is backed by a broad plain. **Perge**, 15km/8 miles from town along Highway 400 (daily 8.30am–5.30pm, 9am–7pm in summer) is not as spectacularly situated as Termessos, but it is unusually well-preserved. Remains of the mundane, including agora shops which still retain their mosaic flooring, and streets rutted by chariot wheels, make it easy to get a sense of everyday life. Monumental Perge is still standing, too, from the red Hellenistic Gate to the huge theatre, baths and stadium, one of the most complete in the ancient world. Continuing east, past the purpose-built golf and beach resort of **Belek**, you come to **Aspendos** ㉙ (25km/16 miles east of Perge; daily 8am–5pm, 9am–7pm in summer). The 15,000-seat **theatre** here, built in the 2nd century AD, is probably the best-preserved Roman theatre in the world. The stage, stage building, seats and portico under which spectators gathered in the event of rain are still here, looking much as they did thousands of years ago. The theatre was still in such good repair centuries after

Timber tryst

It was not the romance of Side's seaside setting that brought Antony and Cleopatra here; rather, the Egyptian queen was trying to strike a deal with Antony for the timber that still carpets the mountainsides to the north of the city.

its construction that the Seljuks used it as a kervansaray when they occupied the city leaving distinctive zigzag plasterwork over the stage. The theatre continues to host performances during the annual summer Aspendos Opera and Ballet Festival. High above the theatre, on the acropolis, stand a nymphaeum and a basilica; in the distance you can see what remains of an aqueduct.

Side

Side ㉚, 22km/14 miles east of Aspendos, is two places: the ruined port evocatively set on a stony headland and a beach resort given over to the worst excesses of package tourism. They are inextricably intertwined – ruins are interspersed with modern souvenir shops, bars and sand dunes, and thus probably more true to Side's past than many other ancient sites. Walking through the monumental gates or looking up the theatre's tiers of 20,000 seats, it is possible to imagine Side ('pomegranate' in ancient Anatolian) as the trysting place of Antony and Cleopatra. It was also the centre of a thriving slave trade. The ruins of the **Temples of Athena and Apollo** (daily 8am–5pm, 9am–7pm in summer) are particularly spectacular, poised to catch the sunset at the tip of the peninsula. The **archaeological museum** (daily 8am–5pm, 9am–7pm in summer) stands opposite the theatre.

Alanya

Most of the seaside city of **Alanya** ㉛, 110km (70 miles) east of Antalya, is relatively new. Though a settlement was already well established here in 44 BC, when Antony presented Alanya to Cleopatra, its heyday came later, when Seljuk Sultan Alâeddin Keykubad built his summer residence here in 1221.

The older city crowns a peninsula where Ottoman houses cluster beneath the 7km (4 miles) of walls and 150 towers that surround the castle. Within the enclosure, the inner fortress (daily 8.30am–5pm, 9am–7.30pm in summer) shelters a ruined Byzantine church with 6th-century frescoes. More popular, though, are the ramparts that afford magnificent sea views – and from which executioners once hurled the condemned to their deaths. Far below, the harbourside **Kızılkule** (Red Tower) now houses the ethnographic museum (daily 8am–5pm, 9am–7pm in summer).

Either side of the castle promontory stretch long beaches and the boisterous modern city. The **Alanya Müzesi** (Alanya

Byzantine church in Alanya

Museum; Tue–Sun 8am–5pm, 9am–7.30pm in summer) houses some artefacts from nearby ruins, including a tablet inscribed in Phoenician, kilims and Ottoman furnishings. The nearby **Damlataş Mağarasi** (Cave of Dripping Stones; daily 10am–7am) has elegant stalagmites and is said to be beneficial to asthma-sufferers.

CENTRAL ANATOLIA

A vast, river-slashed plateau, circled by mountains, the Anatolian heartland is relatively little visited but has some of Turkey's most fascinating attractions. These include Çatalhöyük, the world's second-oldest town; Hattuşa, capital of the Hittite Empire; the glorious Byzantine rock churches of Cappadocia; and Ankara, the country's flourishing capital city.

Ankara

Start your exploration in **Ankara** ㉜, chosen in 1923 as the new capital of Turkey both for its geographic location at the centre of the country and for its lack of associations with the hated Ottomans. It already had a considerable history as a major centre for the Hittites, Galatians and Gauls – better known as the Galatians of Paul's epistle. Over the past 90 years, Ankara has grown from a dusty market town of 20,000 people to a vibrant city of over four million.

Between AD 622, when it was taken by the Sassanid Persians, and AD 838, when it was sacked by the Arabs, Ankara lived under constant threat from invaders. Its defenders numbered only a fraction of the population of the earlier city and, rather than quarry new stone, they reused material from older buildings to build up the city's defences. The ramparts of **Ankara Kalesi**, mainly dating to the 9th century, are at their most spectacular to the west where a line of triangular towers jut out from the wall. Step through the main gate, and a winding path through little streets – where houses have hardly changed over the past century – takes you left to the innermost point of the castle. Unfortunately, the Ottoman tower is kept locked, but from its base, there is still a fine view. Various old mansions within the walls are now home to restaurants or souvenir shops.

Hittite relief, Museum of Anatolian Civilisations

Down the slope to the southwest is the **Anadolu Medeniyetleri Müzesi** (Museum of Anatolian Civilisations; Kadife Sokak; Mon–Sat 8.30am–5.30pm, until 7pm in summer; some halls closed for renovation). Housed in a former *han* (market with workshops) built by Grand Vizier Mahmut Paşa, this is a truly world-class museum. It showcases the pre-Classical civilisations of Anatolia, from the Palaeolithic, via Neolithic Çatalhöyük, the Assyrian traders of Küllepe and pre-Hittite Alacahöyük, to the Phrygians and Urartians. There are also collections from the Hittite and Late Hittite eras. The contents of the Great Tumulus at Gordion include some very fine Phrygian woodcarvings in astonishingly good condition after 2,700 years. Other things to look out for include Neolithic frescoes from Çatalhöyük, vast Hittite stone sculptures and the exquisite Bronze Age stags found in Alacahöyük.

The Anıtkabir, the imposing mausoleum of Kemal Atatürk

Across the rail lines in Tandoğan district looms the **Anıtkabir**, the massively imposing Mausoleum of Kemal Atatürk (Anıt Caddesi; daily 9am–noon and 1–5pm, until 4pm in winter; evening sound and light show). The vast tomb hall was built between 1944 and 1953 in a mixture of styles, with stone donated by every province of Turkey. The great man's body, however, is buried in a chamber far below.

Hattuşa, nearly three hours' drive east of Ankara (mostly on the E88) beside the modern village of Boğazkale, was the capital of the Hittite empire from about 1400 BC onwards. The site (Tue–Sun 8am–5pm) is distinguished by nearly 6km (4 miles) of perimeter walls, pierced by four surviving gates (including the famous Aslanlıkapı, named after a pair of flanking relief lions). Inside the walls are smaller citadels, and the Büyük Mabet (Great Temple) dedicated to the two main Hittite deities. There was another temple 3km (2 miles) east at **Yazılıkaya** (same hours); the temple is mostly gone but two ravines flanking its foundations contain fine reliefs of the Hittite pantheon.

Cappadocia

Southeast of Ankara, nature and human ingenuity have together shaped magical **Cappadocia** ❸❸. Allow yourself plenty of time – aside from the region's distinctive caves and geological formations, its orchards, fields and forested stream valleys invite unhurried walks, horse rides, or even a hot-air balloon trip. In winter, snow adds a fairy-tale dimension to the already startling landscape.

About 30 million years ago, three nearby volcanoes covered this region in deep layers of ash and mud that solidified into tuff. This soft rock, shaped by the elements into whimsically conical spires called 'fairy chimneys', proved heaven-sent when the inhabitants embraced Christianity – and found that their faith put them at odds with Romans, Arabs and even other Christians. Digging into the pliant tuff, they built secret churches, dwellings, and underground cities that protected up to 20,000 souls from marauders. Even in times of peace, cave dwellings lent themselves ideally to the monastic lifestyle espoused by St Basil (AD 330–379), born in nearby Caesarea (Kayseri). Over the years, the ease of digging into the soft tuff has made troglodytes of many Cappadocians. Every village in the region is, at least in part, hacked out of weirdly shaped outcrops.

Cappadocia sentinels

Üçhisar

Ürgüp and Nearby Villages

Transport hub Nevşehir is the largest town in Cappadocia, though **Ürgüp**, tucked into a canyon 23km (14 miles) east, is far more appealing, with its cliffside cave dwellings, cobbled streets lined with handsome Greek-built houses and lively centre. Ürgüp is within reach of some remarkable villages. **Mustafapaşa (Sinasos)** is not only near the Göreme Valley and its cave churches, but itself presents an appealing mix of Greek and Seljuk architecture. **Ortahisar** huddles beneath a fantastic, 85-metre (240ft) -high rock formation riddled with cave dwellings. At one time this comprised the entire village, and for a small fee you can explore the former dwellings, long since abandoned. **Üçhisar** has also outgrown the tunnelled rock, topped with a fortress (daily summer 7am–8pm), that rises from the village centre, with stunning views over much of Cappadocia.

Göreme

This small town, 7km (4 miles) northwest of Ürgüp, has one big attraction: the **Göreme Açık Hava Müzesi** (Göreme Open-Air Museum; daily 8am–7pm, until 5pm in winter). The former monastic community, dug into cliffs above a verdant valley, was endowed with more than 30 churches from the 9th to the 12th centuries; many of them are decorated with strikingly beautiful, primitive frescoes.

The best-preserved cave-church in Cappadocia, the **Karanlık Kilise** (Dark Church), is here with its brilliantly restored frescoes. Most of the other shrines take their names from an object or image contained in their cramped interiors. The Çarıklı Kilise (Sandal Church) is named for the footprints embedded in the floor, said to be those of Christ. The Yılanlı Kilise (Dragon Church) contains a fresco of St George slaying the dragon. Another fresco in this church depicts a full-breasted but hirsute St Onouphrios, a hermit saint of the Egyptian desert. The breasts may reflect an obscure legend in which he was originally a woman, Onouphria, who prayed to god to be made a hermaphrodite in order to not lose her virginity to a persistent suitor.

The Underground Cities

Kaymaklı and **Derinkuyu**, respectively 21 and 29km (13 and 18 miles) south of Nevşehir (both daily 8am–7pm, until 5pm in winter), are vast underground cities that descend many levels into the earth. They were elaborately equipped with dormitories, sanitation systems, kitchens, wine-pressing facilities, cemeteries and other amenities, all designed to house thousands of refugees for years on end. Comforting as these must have been for those in need of a safe haven, be warned that the narrow passages can induce claustrophobia. Another underground city,

Karanlık Kilise, Göreme Open-Air Museum

Ihlara Valley

Özkonak (same hours as above) was discovered in 1972 near **Avanos**; excavations are still underway and visitors can enter only the top four of 10 floors. Avanos, an appealing town on the Kızılırmak ('Red River'), Turkey's longest, has long been renowned for its pottery industry.

The Ihlara Valley

For centuries, this gorge, 100km (60 miles) southwest of Ürgüp, was a lost world. More than 100 metres (330ft) deep and well off the beaten path, it provided a perfect hideout for early Christians. Over the years, inhabitants dug over 100 churches and monasteries into the cliffs. Reached by steep staircases or paths from the villages of Ihlara, Selime and Belisırma (daily 8am–7pm, until 5pm in winter), the Ihlara provides excellent hikes along its 16km (10 mile) length and the opportunity to explore the dozen frescoed churches that are open to the public.

Konya

Konya ㉞, amidst endless grain fields due south of Ankara, was a Hittite settlement, an important Roman outpost, a focus of early Christianity and a Seljuk capital. It would then have settled into relative obscurity were it not for the Sufi mystic Celaleddin Rumi – the Mevlâna – who founded the sect known as the Mevlevî, or the Whirling Dervishes. The **Mevlâna Tekkesi** (daily 9am–6.30pm, until 4.40pm in winter) is among the most important pilgrimage destinations in the Islamic world, visited by thousands paying homage to this great teacher.

Rumi was born in Central Asia in 1207 and fled to Konya when he was 20. Here he met his mentor, a wandering dervish named Sems-i-Tabriz. Rumi devoted himself to study with Sems and was inconsolable when his master disappeared (possibly murdered by jealous colleagues). Turning himself to Sufi teachings, he was inspired to write several volumes of spiritual poetry, the *Mathnawi*. Rumi taught his growing band of disciples to shun ostentation, embrace love and charity, and elevate the position of women.

Beneath a distinctive blue dome spreads the 15th-century monastery of the dervishes and the earlier mausoleum of the Mevlâna. The deceptively humble entranceway lies beyond the dervishes' tiny monastic cells and the gardens that once sustained the community. Inside, beyond a library where the dervishes would study, the tomb of Mevlâna rests on a pedestal, surrounded by the coffins of his eldest son and his father. The adjoining circular hall is the ***semahane***, where the *sema* ceremony was originally performed. Reed flutes and other instruments that accompany the dance are on display, as are some rare Seljuk carpets presented to the Melvâna as gifts.

Mevlâna Tekkesi

Some 800 metres/yds west, the **Karatay Medrese** (daily 9am–noon and

1–5pm) is an extensively tiled Seljuk theological school whose dome is decorated with a dramatic representation of the firmaments, once used for astronomical study. A collection of rare tiles and other ceramics are on display in adjoining galleries, grouped around a fountain-cooled courtyard. This medrese and the neighbouring **İnce Minare Medrese** (Seminary of the Slender Minaret; Tue–Sun 9am–6.40pm, until 4.40pm in winter) are graced with elegant Seljuk portals ornately tiled in geometric patterns and – a reminder that these were among the first structures built by the nomadic Seljuks – resemble the entrances to tents. The minaret of the İnce Minare Medrese is beautifully tiled but was severely truncated by lightning in 1901;

Whirling Dervishes

The brotherhood that Rumi founded is best known to outsiders for its distinctive *sema*, a ceremony in which dancers whirl to symbolically free themselves of earthly ties. The position of the arms, with the right arm extending to heaven and the left to the floor, conveys the notion that the dancers are conduits through which the grace of God is flowing to humanity. The dancers' garments also have symbolic significance. The hat represents a tombstone, the cloak is the tomb (and is shed during the dance to represent escape from earthly bonds) and the white skirt is the funeral shroud.

Though the Mevlevî order has been forbidden to practise openly since all religious brotherhoods were banned in 1925, the government has continued to promote the *sema* for its folkloric merit; today, an increasing number of dancers also openly follow the teachings of the Mevlâna, without official interference. Folkloric dervishes perform in Konya during an annual December festival, though you can see more genuine observances at other times in İstanbul (see page 45).

Whirling Dervishes

inside is a collection of stone- and woodwork, much of it salvaged from a nearby Seljuk palace. On the knoll between the two medreses, the 13th-century **Alâeddin Camii** has a forest of 42 interior Roman columns, and a finely carved ebony *mimber*.

Çatalhöyük

Çatalhöyük ㉟ just off the road some 40km (25 miles) southeast of Konya (www.catalhoyuk.com; daily 8am–5pm; free); is still more of a working archaeological dig than conventional tourist attraction (the best finds are in Ankara), but it has been designated a World Heritage Site by Unesco and is fascinating for students of prehistory. Between about 6250 and 5400 BC, Çatalhöyük was a prosperous town of some 5,000 people. Rich and poor lived crowded into houses which ran directly onto one another with no streets between them. The only way to gain entry was by climbing

Early traders

Çatalhöyük contains the earliest evidence in the world of the irrigation of crops and domestication of animals. The people wove textiles, had simple carpets and traded in luxury goods such as black, glass-like obsidian, a rock widely prized for making axes, daggers and mirrors.

through holes in the roofs. Most striking are some wall murals showing hunting scenes and what may be a nearby volcano in eruption.

THE EAST

Eastern Turkey is a hard but immensely rewarding place to travel. The terrain can be challenging and the roads lonely, with long distances between anything; journeys require careful planning. The easiest approach is along the Mediterranean beyond Alanya, with the coast highway passing the enormous Armenian castle (and beach) at **Anamur** ㊱, the Hellenistic/Roman town at Uzuncaburç, and a Byzantine double castle at **Kızkalesi** ㊲ (with another good beach). At Mersin a motorway commences, bypassing dusty Tarsus – hometown to St Paul, and where Cleopatra first met Antony – and Adana en route to the Hatay.

The Hatay and Antakya (Antioch)

A narrow finger of land pointing south towards Syria, the **Hatay** feels more Arabic than Turkish – until 1938 it was indeed part of Syria. This final stretch of the Turkish Mediterranean coast is traditionally Muslim, having little contact with foreign tourists or even sophisticated city-Turks: a fascinating, ancient realm where Hittite and Biblical cultures meet. The regional capital, **Antakya** ㊳ began life as Antioch in about 300 BC, its population soon swelling to nearly half a million. Remains of former glory are few, yet an intense atmosphere seeps through the narrow alleys of the bazaar, making it one of the most charming cities in southeastern Turkey. The

Archaeological Museum (Gündüz Caddesi 1; daily summer 9am–6.30pm, winter 8.30am–4.30pm) is home to a world-class collection of some 50 Roman mosaics. Most of them, carefully removed from Roman villas in nearby Harbiye (the ancient Daphne), date from the 2nd and 3rd centuries AD, and seem to leap off the walls.

During Roman rule, Antioch had a large Jewish community and was crucial in the history of early Christianity. St Peter allegedly lived here from AD 47 to 54, frequently joined by the much-travelled Paul of Tarsus and St Barnabas. As a result, Antioch was later the seat of the powerful Patriarchate of Asia, a rival Christian centre to Constantinople – chiefly notorious for its heretical scholars. The tiny cave church of **Sen Piyer Kilisesi** (St Peter's Cave), 2km (1 mile) off Kurtuluş Caddesi, northeast of the city centre, is generally regarded as the first Christian church (daily 9am–7pm,

Roman mosaic in Antakya

8am–5pm in winter). It was here that the saints first termed their new religion Christianity (Acts 11:26). The fancy facade was built by the Crusaders.

The early church attracted many extremists, including various ascetic monks and other spiritual acrobats like St Simeon Stylites the Younger (AD 521–597), who was inspired aged 7 to climb a column on a windy promontory later named **Samandağ** (Simeon's Mountain). He spent the rest of his life on top, fasting and praying, only descending to change to a new column on occasion. The **Aya Simeon Manastırı** (St Simeon's Monastery) grew around his final pillar until an earthquake brought the entire complex into its present state of ruins.

Northern Mesopotamia

Turkey's share of Mesopotamia is of course dominated by the upper reaches of the Euphrates and Tigris rivers, along which the Turks have built a series of giant hydroelectric dams and irrigation canals to turn the neglected barren flatlands into an agricultural powerhouse. A number of remarkable Roman cities and mosaics have been discovered – and drowned – in the process.

The most notable of these is Hellenistic/Roman **Zeugma**, now mostly under the waters of the Birecik dam; fortunately vast extents of mosaic flooring were rescued in time and now form the centrepiece of the **Archeological Museum** (daily 9am–7pm, 8am–5pm in winter) in the booming, one-million-strong city of **Gaziantep** ❸❾, 35km (22 miles) west. Itself just 100km (62 miles) from Aleppo in Syria, the Arab influence in lifestyle and cuisine – especially in its famous pistachio-based sweets using nuts from the local orchards – is unmistakable. A progressive mayor has seen to the restoration of Gaziantep's remaining old quarters, which once had substantial Christian and Jewish populations.

About 75km (47 miles) south of the **Atatürk Barajı**, now the fourth-largest dam in the world, lies the old town of **Şanlıurfa** ❹, purportedly the birthplace of Abraham, the father of Judaism. According to local Muslim legend, the cruel Assyrian King Nimrod had Abraham launched from a catapult in the city's citadel, to fall into a pile of burning wood. Happily, God (or Allah) intervened and turned the fire to water and the faggots to fish. Today, visitors pray at the **Hızır İbrahim Halilullah complex**, which includes a cave said to be the birthplace of the prophet, and visit a large reservoir full of holy carp.

Gaziantep copper craftsman

Some 45km/28 miles south lies **Harran**, with its strange beehive-style mud-built dwellings (now only used as barns), Kurd- and Arab-populated like Şanlıurfa. From here Abraham decided to move into the land of Canaan; under Assyrian rule there was a Temple of Sin, god of the moon, famous for its star readers and savants. Later, Byzantine Emperor Julian the Apostate supposedly worshipped here in AD 363 en route to his fatal encounter with Shapur II of Persia farther east. And Harran was a stronghold of the Sabians, planet-worshippers who also used the Sin temple and whose rites only vanished completely long after the arrival of Islam.

The next notable place beyond Şanlıurfa is **Mardin** ⓿41, spectacularly sited on a castellated crag overlooking the Mesopotamian plain. This small city has an extraordinarily mixed population of Kurds, Arabs, Turks and Syriac Christians, with secular and sacred architecture to match; it has of late become trendy with big-city Turks, for whom a number of high-end hotels and restaurants have opened.

The crowning glory of this region, however, is **Nemrut Dağı** ⓿42, the only physical legacy of the Commagene kingdom, a tiny state on the upper Euphrates that flourished briefly during the first century BC, managing to stay out of Roman (and Parthian) hands for some time. Built by King Antiochus I Theos (ruled 70–38 BC) for his own glory, this fabulous pile of stones and statuary rivals the greatest efforts of the self-deifying, pyramid-building Egyptian pharaohs.

Nemrut Dağı, sacred site of the Commagene dynasty

There is now a road up to the 2,150-metre (7,053ft) summit, and excursions are offered from many of the region's cities (though under your own power it's far more pleasant to stay in the village of Karadut at the base of the mountain). You will be told that you *must* make a visit at sunrise, but this is cold and involves getting up in the small hours; sunset is just as dramatic, and warmer, while mid-day is blissfully uncrowded.

Artificial terraces below Antiochus's presumed burial tumulus are studded with vast statue-heads of Apollo, Tyche, Zeus and Hercules, along with the megalomaniac Antiochus, who included himself in the roll-call of divinities. There are more colossal heads (including two eagles) detached from their bodies on the west terrace, in better condition.

The Far East

Beyond the Mesopotamian plain, the landscape becomes ever more rugged, a high plateau striated by mountain chains under snow eight months of the year, but as before the rewards are commensurate with the trials. From the overwhelmingly Kurdish city of **Diyarbakır**, easily reached from Mardin, it's a straightforward trip to emerald-green **Lake Van**, Turkey's largest at an altitude of 1,650 metres (5,500ft), with the nicely restored Armenian church of **Akdamar** ❸ on the eponymous islet. Around Van town itself are more ancient Armenian churches, and the Kurdish-built **Hoşap Kalesi** with a striped bridge below.

North from Van, **Mount Ararat** (Ağrı Dağı; supposedly the last resting place of Noah's Ark), overlooks the engaging pastiche of **İshak Paşa Sarayı** outside the functional town of Doğubeyazit. Next stop for most travellers will be Kars, which bears many marks of its long occupation by Russians and Armenians, and is the natural gateway to **Ani** ❹ (daily 8am–5pm, 9am–7pm in summer), the medieval capital of the Bagratid Armenians, right on the Armenian border.

WHAT TO DO

Exploring classical remains and enjoying the Ottoman Empire's splendours, with some time to relax on a beach, could keep you happily occupied in Turkey. Sooner or later, you will also find yourself immersed in a wealth of other activities.

SHOPPING

Most larger Turkish cities have one at least partially covered bazaar at their centre, and this warren of stalls is still a major shopping precinct despite inroads from modern malls. Any number of small shops usually spill out onto the pavements of the streets surrounding the bazaar. A street market also usually springs up somewhere in town once or twice a week, selling fresh fish, meat and produce alongside ordinary household items.

The most essential tool a visitor can bring to these venues is at least a modicum of skill at bargaining. This age-old art is both an intrinsic part of shopping (except for foodstuffs, which are fixed-price) and a social custom; in fact, it's fair to say that not to engage in at least some negotiating is rude.

Bazaars

In these mainstays of Turkish commerce, a walk down crowded lanes past stalls selling everything from spices to mops is tinged with no small amount of exotic flavour.

In İstanbul

The **Mısır Çarşisi** (Egyptian or Spice Bazaar), near Galata Bridge, houses an especially appealing selection of nuts, spices,

Copperware in İstanbul's Grand Bazaar

dried fruits and sweets – as well as nargiles (hubble-bubbles) and every manner of spare parts and compressed tobacco for them – beneath its atmospheric, 17th-century vaulted ceilings. The **Kapalı Carşi** (Covered Bazaar) is perhaps best approached for its colourful atmosphere rather than as a bargain-filled paradise, since tourist-orientated goods tend to be a bit tacky and many of the more solid goods offered are ordinary items geared to locals. Some exceptions include the gold jewellery, antiques and carpets sold in shops near the centre of the bazaar, where you can find dealers of international renown who trade regularly with New York and London; some silver goods, especially those made and sold in the northeastern corner in what is known as the Kalcılar Han; and the old books and prints in the Old Book Bazaar, near the western gate. The Arasta Bazaar behind the Blue Mosque has some interesting, relatively upmarket souvenir shops.

The Art of Bargaining

While there are no hard-and-fast rules on how to strike a deal with a wily merchant, remember two basics: however clever you think you are, the seller has the advantage of years of experience and will inevitably gain the upper hand (that is, a profit will be made no matter how hard you bargain). It is okay to be casual in the early stages of the negotiation in order to get some idea of price, but the one sure way to infuriate any seller is to engage in hard bargaining when you have no intention of buying. The whole process of buying and selling is charming and entertaining, inevitably accompanied by a glass of *çay* (tea) and, if you are female, lavish compliments.

It may seem absurd, but whatever price is suggested, come back with an option of roughly a quarter. This gives you both room to wriggle, plead and negotiate until you arrive at a final price that is half or 60 percent of what the seller originally proposed.

Elsewhere

Bursa has one of Turkey's most atmospheric bazaars, founded in the 14th century but now housed in a beautifully restored 19th-century structure. This is the place for textiles, with thick cotton towels a local speciality, along with silk goods at knock-down prices. Allow time and you can have clothes tailored for you while you visit the local spa. On the resort circuit, both Bodrum and **Marmaris** have large, well-stocked bazaars catering to the many visitors who sail over from the Greek islands of Kos and Rhodes opposite, though the quality of goods in the marketplaces of Fethiye and Kaş is generally superior.

İstanbul's Old Book Bazaar

Inland, the *bedesten* (lockable valuables hall) of Kayseri near Cappadocia is now a carpet market, while there's also a covered bazaar devoted to woollens and more carpets. Ankara has a famous copper bazaar, the Samanpazarı, along Salman Sokağı.

What to Buy

Carpets and Kilims. It would be a shame to leave Turkey without at least one rug, so look forward to the experience, which can be a highlight of your holiday. The crucial point is to do your homework so that you have some idea of prices and quality – and that means being tough enough not to succumb to the first temptation. Walk into any carpet shop

Rugs will be laid at your feet

and abandon yourself to the dealer. You will be offered a seat and a cup of tea, and the show will begin. Rug after rug will be laid at your feet with a flourish; a savvy dealer will soon detect the size, materials, colours and patterns that seem to be most appealing to you, and eventually bring out only items that match those criteria. Many connoisseurs say the best rugs have long since been brought to İstanbul, but you can still find treasures in smaller towns and villages where the carpets are made, or even in highly trafficked resorts such as Bodrum and Antalya.

If you wish to get a feel for quality and price before you start buying, you can ease into carpet-buying by visiting some of the fixed-price, state-run shops or the vast tourist emporia on the coast which have carpet-making on the premises and will show you how they are made and how to check the fabrics, dyes and quality of production, as well as offering potted summaries of the symbolism of the patterns and regional design.

Copper. Ewers, pilaf vessels, teapots, trays, sieves, and samovars handsomely handcrafted from copper were once the mainstay of a bride's dowry, and these items have found their way to many an antiques shop. Besides Ankara, Bergama, Şanlıurfa and Gaziantep are well stocked with authentic copper pieces. Likewise, copper items of modern manufacture – machine-made with a thin sheath of copper over a less expensive alloy – are among the more appealing displays of many bazaars. Some rules of thumb: if it's authentically old, it will be thick and heavy-gauge, with intricate hand-embossed designs, and expensive; if it's new, it will be quite inexpensive, with any designs likely to be pressed in by machine. Whether old or new, make sure any copper vessel you intend to use is lined with tin.

Carpet Caveats

A kilim is flat-woven (with no pile) and its pattern is clearly visible on the reverse side. If a kilim is then embroidered, it is called a cicim or sumak. Be wary of claims that dyes are natural. Synthetic dyes have been used for well over a century, and a rug made with natural dyes is likely to be quite rare and expensive. If a dealer insists that a rug is an antique, ask for proof – on the other hand, claims that a rug has been made from old saddlebags or pieces of old kilims may well be true and the result can be uniquely beautiful. If a true antique, you need an export licence.

To ensure colours will not run, rub a wet white cloth over the fabric – if it picks up colour, you know that inexpensive, non-durable dyes have been used. If the material is pure wool, a strand will crumble when lighted; pure silk will turn immediately to fine ash. Smell a rug to see if you can detect the scent of vinegar – sometimes it is applied to fade colours and 'age' a new rug to add antique value. A reputable dealer will encourage you to perform these tests.

If a rug is hand-woven, the pattern and knots that show on the reverse side will be slightly irregular and the fringe is likely to be uneven as well. The more knots to the inch, the better the quality and the clearer the pattern on the back. Price is according to the amount of work, not the size of the carpet.

A reputable shop will provide a detailed receipt and be willing to ship the rug for you; however, carrying it yourself can reduce the price considerably and also allow you to claim duty-free payments and duty-free allowances. If having it sent, use a reputable international service and ask for a shipping receipt with a tracking number.

Ceramics and tiles. The factories of İznik stopped manufacturing the town's famous tiles on a large scale centuries ago, but since 1993 there's been a modest revival of the craft, and there are now a dozen outlets for practical bathroom or kitchen tiles, trivets, house-number plaques scattered across the little town. Kütahya, southeast of İznik. is currently Turkey's largest producer of ceramic tiles, and you can find Kütahya tiles, of good quality and in attractive patterns, in shops throughout the country.

The same earth that thrust up the formations of Cappadocia also yields a bounty of onyx that shows up in bowls, boxes and every other conceivable creation; Avanos (see page 116) is chock-full of shops selling onyx and pottery made of red clay from the banks of the aptly named Red River, which runs through town.

Clothing. Turkey is one of the world's top manufacturers of fabrics and clothing. You will have no trouble finding imitations of top Western designers – and the genuine article without its label all over Turkey. For a look at fashionable Turkish couture, step into the shops along and around İstiklâl Caddesi in Istanbul (nearby Rumeli Caddesi and Halâskârgazi Caddesi are popular shopping streets); the Galleria in Ataköy on the Asian side is one of several suburban-style malls that outfit the well-to-do with local and foreign fashions. Bodrum and Kaş have some fine boutiques, while Bursa is famous for silk and cotton manufacture (see page 59).

Leather goods. Turkey produces fine leather, though there are also plenty of poor designer knock-offs and cheap tat. You will encounter tailors offering 'made-to-measure' leatherware in many resorts. Side (see page 108) and to a lesser extent Alanya on the Mediterranean coast, seem to have sold their souls to such enterprises, and almost every other shop there now promises to hand-stitch the leather item of your choice within a few hours. Although the workmanship and quality

Textiles at the Grand Bazaar in İstanbul, Turkey

of the leather is often questionable, if you stick to a simple design you will probably walk away with a durable and affordable garment.

Spices. A popular item in every bazaar, spices often come in handy assortment packets. Beware, however, of seemingly good deals on saffron – the least expensive comes from Turkey, but saffron from Iran is of far superior quality. Pine nuts (especially in Ayvalık or Bursa) can be half the cost of overseas prices.

And keep an eye out for... Blue beads *(nazar)* often worn as pendants to ward off the evil eye; curly-tipped slippers; *nargiles* (hookahs – the best have glass bowls and wood or brass hardware); meerschaum pipes carved from porous stone; inlaid chess sets and backgammon boards, from Syria; fez-style caps fashioned from old kilims; thick cotton bath towels and robes – all of these are easily portable and evocative mementos and are readily available in many bazaars and tourist shops throughout the country. Rather than buy *lokum* (Turkish delight) with its artificial preservatives and colours, keep an eye out for the healthier *cezeriye* (a carrot- and coconut-based sweet).

BATHTIME

Most towns of any size have at least one *hamam* (Turkish bath), as do many larger hotels. Very few offer mixed bathing, with either separate sections or hours for men and women. Prices are generally affordable and some of the finest baths in major cities are historic monuments. Even if they are not, this Turkish experience should not be missed.

Upon entering, you undress and wrap yourself in a large, thin cloth (a *peştamal*), which you should wear throughout the ritual (you will be handed a dry towel at the end of the

Array of spices in İstanbul's Egyptian Spice Bazaar

bath). You then enter the sauna-like main chamber, the *hararet*, which is usually domed and tiled. After cleansing yourself in basins at the sides of the room, you will be laid upon the central heated stone platform *(göbek taşı)* and soaped and massaged with a kese, a sort of large, exfoliating mitt. Before the final rinse, your masseur will skilfully blow a soapy cloth into a balloon-like ball and give you a refreshing lather. Then relax over a glass of tea or top off the bath with a deep-tissue oil massage (extra cost).

Traditional sports

As well as football, which is a national passion, traditional spectator sports include oil wrestling near Edirne (see page 55); winter camel wrestling in the Selçuk area; and *cirit*, a wild and ruthless form of polo.

OUTDOOR ACTIVITIES

Ballooning

It's worth getting up at the crack of dawn to see Cappadocia's twisted landscape from the serenity of a hot-air balloon. A memorable, expensive experience is provided by Kapadokya Balloons in Göreme (tel: 384-271 2442, www.kapadokya balloons.com). Worth every penny.

Birdwatching

As a stop on migratory routes between Europe, Asia and Africa, and with a wide range of terrain, Turkey is rich in birdlife. Among the best places to birdwatch are Kuşcenneti National Park near Bursa; the Çiğli-Sasallı bird sanctuary northwest of İzmir; and the salt lakes and freshwater marshes of Sultan Sazlığı, southeast of Cappadocia, all home (if transiently) to some 250 species.

Golf

You'll find a few links around major cities and resorts. The resort of Belek, east of Antalya, has 11 18-hole courses – some are part of luxury beach hotel complexes. Three courses near İstanbul are Klassis Golf and Country Club (tel: 0212-710 1313, www.klassisgolf.com.tr), Kemer Golf and Country Club (tel: 0212-239 7010, www.kg-cc.com) and the Istanbul Golf Club (tel: 0216-343 1660, www.igk.org.tr).

Hiking

There are many fine hiking areas in Turkey, but few well-marked and plotted trails. In the south, there are two – the Lycian Way, which dips and climbs through the mountains along the Mediterranean coast from Ölüdeniz to Antalya; and the St Paul's Trail from Perge to Yalvaç, northeast of Lake Egirdir, with a second branch starting at Aspendos, 40km (25 miles) east of Antalya and joining the first route at the Roman site of Adada. Each takes about a month to complete in total (though many people only do the best bits). English-language guidebooks are available in most Mediterranean resorts. A series of excellent trekking guides written by Kate Clow and members of the Culture Routes Society cover the Lycian Way, The St Paul Trail and the Kaçkar Mountains of northeastern Turkey. All three areas are also covered on the website www.trekkinginturkey.com.

Skiing

Turkey has plenty of downhill ski areas, until now mostly appealing to a local audience. Indisputably the best is Panandöken near Erzerum in the northeast; more convenient, if slightly less snowy, are Erciyes Dağı near Cappadocia, and Kartalkaya partway between Ankara and İstanbul. The ski centre on Uludağ near Bursa is the most established, with the most hotels, but is frankly overrated. For more information about resorts, accommodation and organised tours visit www.skiingturkey.com.

Horseriding

Cappadocia is especially well suited to riding, and several local companies hire horses and lead excursions. One of the best is based in Avanos: Akhal Teke (tel 0384-511 5171, www.akhal-tekehorsecenter.com).

A horseriding enthusiast

Sailing and Yachting

Many say the only way to explore the Aegean and Mediterranean coasts, with their many coves and inlets, is by boat. Major marinas exist in Çeşme, Kuşadası, Bodrum, Marmaris, Fethiye, Finike and Antalya; tourist offices can give information on facilities and fees. Currents and winds along the coasts can be strong; for conditions, tune into shortband waves VHF 67 for broadcasts in English at 7am and 7pm or check the website of the Turkish State Meteorological Service (www.dmi.gov.tr).

Many companies offer 'blue cruises' along the coast between Bodrum and Finike in a traditional Turkish craft, a *gulet*. Arrange such cruises either through local operators in most resorts (especially in Bodrum, Fethiye or Marmaris) or through specialists like Cavurali (tel Turkey: 0242-419 2441, www.cavurali.com), Day Dreams (tel UK: 01884-849200, www.turkishcruises.co.uk), or SCIC (tel UK: 07583 001766, www.scicsailing.eu).

Scuba Diving

The abundance of underwater antiquities makes it illegal to dive in certain Turkish waters. There are many authorised areas, however, notably near Bodrum, Ayavalık, Kalkan and Kaş. Dive shops and schools include: Körfez in Ayvalık (tel: 0266-312 4996, www.korfezdiving.com), BT Diving in Kaş (tel: 0242-836 3737, www.bougainville-turkey.com) and Kalkan Diving (tel: 0242-844 2361, www.kalkandiving.com). See also www.scubaturkiye.com and the website of the Turkish Underwater Sports Federation (www.tssf.gov.tr of).

Swimming

The most enjoyable swimming is from Mediterranean coast beaches; some of the best are at İstuzu, Patara and Ölüdeniz, of which only Ölüdeniz is likely to become crowded, while at Olympos and Phaselis you can swim from beaches backed by ancient ruins. On the Aegean coast, especially nice beaches and clear waters are near Ayvalık and Çeşme.

Windsurfing and Kite-Surfing

Bitez cove near Bodrum, Fener beach near Akyarlar and the island of Gökçeada (İmroz) are recognised as the three premier windsurfing venues on the Aegean, while at Alaçatı near Çeşme or Gökova near Marmaris you can indulge in kite-surfing. You will find schools and equipment rental available at all these locales.

ENTERTAINMENT

The State Symphony Orchestra, State Opera and State Ballet perform in İstanbul, often at Atatürk Kültür Merkezi on Taksim Square in İstanbul (tel: 0212-251 5200). The city enjoys a cultural flowering from April through July, with the successive International Film Festival, Theatre Festival (even-numbered years), and most famously the International Classical Music Festival, with name overseas acts in historic venues, followed by the Jazz Festival in July; there are other, more traditional jazz events sponsored by Akbank in September–October. For more details, contact İstanbul Foundation for Culture and Arts, Sadi Konuralp Caddesi 5, Şişhane 34433 (tel: 0212-334 0700, www.iksv.org). For other music and arts festivals around the country, see page 141.

Many establishments provide evenings of traditional music and belly-dancing for visitors. In İstanbul, one of the most authentic places to hear Gypsy musicians, with patrons providing their own dancing, is Badehane, at General Yazgan Sok 5, Tünel, Beyoğlu (tel: 0212-249 0550), with live music Wednesday and Thursday. You will find other establishments, often open only in the summer, on your travels up and down the coast and into Cappadocia; tourist offices can lead you to shows in a particular region.

In the resorts on the Aegean and Mediterranean coasts, numerous dance clubs throb late into the night. In central İstanbul the club scene is centred on İstiklâl Caddesi in Beyoğlu, where clubs currently include Babylon at

The İstanbul State Symphony Orchestra in concert at the Haghia Irene, İstanbul

Şehbender Sokağı 3, Asmalımescit (Oct–May; tel: 0212-292 7368, www.babylon.com.tr), Propaganda at Suriye Pasajı 166/10 (tel: 0212-252 7181, www.propagandaist.com), Fosil at Kemankeş Caddesi, 34C (third floor; www.fosil.com.tr) and The Hall at Küçük Bayram Sokak 7 set in a former church (tel: 0212-244 8737, www.thehallistanbul.com). In the Bosphorus suburb of Ortaköy, established clubs like Reina (www.reina.com.tr), Anjelique (www.anjelique.com.tr) and Sortie (www.sortie.com.tr) pulsate or less mainstream, but very popular Lucca (www.luccastyle.com).

CHILDREN'S TURKEY

The Turks are extremely child-friendly and the country has plenty of places to engage the young traveller. Much of the history is sufficiently lurid to grab children's attention if presented properly and even if they have had a surfeit of history, ruins are still great places to run and climb. Beaches and boats are superb for family holidays, with plenty of other possible outdoor excursions. Many larger resort hotels have kids' clubs and sports facilities which will take the little darlings off your hands for days on end. Teenagers may well be tempted by the club and bar scene in the resorts, but most clubs are not suitable for the underaged.

Certain foods (kebabs, *pide*, *lahmacun*, salad) suit children well and are healthy. There are occasional problems with food hygiene (especially in summer) and stomach upsets; generally, popular places with high turnover and cooking-to-order are safe. There is plenty of bottled water, but the stuff out of designated town-centre or roadside springs is quite potable (do not drink tap water). It is probably best to avoid the south coast in mid-summer with small children as it can get excruciatingly hot and tender skins can burn easily.

Festivals and Seasonal Events

January Selçuk: Camel Wrestling Festival, 3rd Sunday; also at Denizli, Aydın and İzmir.
February !f Istanbul International Independent Film Festival.
March İzmir: European Jazz Festival.
April İstanbul: International Film Festival. Tulip Festival in Emirgan. Ankara: International Music Festival.
May Gypsy festival at Edirne, usually 5–6 May; Marmaris: International Yachting Week; İstanbul: International Theatre Festival; Mersin International Music Festival.
June–July Aspendos Opera and Ballet Festival; İzmir (Ephesus and Çeşme too): International Music Festival; Artvin: Kafkasör Festival with bull-fighting, music and bazaars; Edirne: Traditional Kırkpinar Wrestling Tournament; İstanbul: İstanbul Classical Music Festival, and Jazz Festival; Çeşme: International Song Contest.
August Ankara: Bilkent International Anatolian Music Festival; Hacıbektaş: Hacı Bektaş Veli commemoration, with Bektaşi and Alevî music and dance.
September Bodrum: Ballet & Opera Festival around the castle; Ürgüp: Grape Harvest/Wine Festival; Avanos: Tourism and Handicrafts Festival; Antalya: International Akdeniz Song Contest.
October Antalya: Altın Portakal (Golen Orange) Film Festival; Bodrum: International Bodrum Cup yacht race; İstanbul: Akbank Jazz Festival and the International İstanbul Biennial (held odd-numbered years).
November Marmaris: International Race Week – Turkey's last sailing competition of the season; nationwide, 10 November: anniversary of the death of Atatürk.
December Bursa: International Karagöz (Puppet and Shadow Theatre) Festival; Demre: Special Mass on 6 December honouring Saint Nicholas of Myra, aka Santa Claus (Noel Baba); Konya: Mevlâna Festival, 10–17 December – 'folkloric' performances by Whirling Dervishes.

EATING OUT

The pleasures of Turkish cuisine are considerable, and travellers will find it fresh, delicious and varied. Fish caught that day, fresh vegetables and herbs, simply grilled chicken and lamb, and creamy starter-dips are the mainstays of Turkish menus. In fact, a good meal awaits you most anywhere in the country, with the spiciest (some say the best) cooking in the far southeast.

While street food and snacks are available throughout the day in most cities and resorts, you will find a full lunch from noon to 3pm and dinner from 7 to 10pm. Except in the more formal restaurants in large cities, dress is casual.

Even in İstanbul and other large towns, there are fewer full-on restaurants than there are in comparable

Döner: the classic Turkish snack

European cities. Better restaurants, accordingly, tend to be crowded, so you may want to reserve a table in advance; your hotel may do this and arrange for transport as well. Except perhaps in peak season, you shouldn't have a problem finding a seat. During the summer, many resort restaurants stay open well into the wee hours. Many close completely between October and May.

Cafe Ara on a side street off İstiklal in Taksim

Where to Eat

Especially in İstanbul and other large cities, a wide variety of establishments sell the Turkish version of 'fast food', often at stand-up counters. A *kebapcı* serves the ubiquitous staple of Turkish cuisine, the kebab; lamb is continually being roasted on a revolving spit, ready to be sliced and skewered together with roast vegetables. *Dönercis* offer roast *döner*, an initially conical mass of fatty lamb or chicken which, as the day goes on, is whittled down into thin slices served atop bread or rice. A *pideci offers pide*, the boat-shaped Turkish pizza, a delicious concoction topped with meats, vegetables, eggs or cheese.

When Turks eat a full meal out, it is usually at a *lokanta*, a simple restaurant that caters to workers at lunch and, often, to neighbourhood families in the evening. The six to eight steam-tray dishes offered at any one time are displayed in a glass case, served on request; most of these establishments offer one or two meat or fish dishes, often prepared as stews, with vegetable and rice or potato accompaniments.

A full-blown *restoran*, or restaurant, is often only marginally fancier than a *lokanta*, but can also be quite elegant. In resorts, restaurant tables spill out onto terraces. Visitors will also find a number of Europeanstyle cafés serving lighter snack meals throughout the day.

What to Eat

Turkish breakfast, available in even the most modest pansiyons, is simple and satisfying. It typically includes sliced cucumber, olives, tomato, a hard-boiled egg, yogurt, seasonal fruit and bread slices to be topped with jam or honey. Only tea or instant coffee is likely to be offered. In multistar hotels, buffet breakfast can be elaborate, with omelettes live-cooked and various charcuterie laid out. Out in town, you can patronise a counter or cart from which *börek*, a fluffy cheese pastry, is served. Later on, the most

Grilling fish with lemon

ubiquitous snack in rural areas is *gözleme*, a crepe-like delicacy stuffed with a variety of fillings.

A full meal at lunch or dinner inevitably begins with *meze*, a wide assortment of delicious hot or cold appetisers. Several *meze* platters can in fact be so satisfying that you may not feel the need for a main course.

Tasty little bites of baklava

Main courses rely on various forms of lamb or chicken; pork is not served in this Muslim country, and when beef makes an appearance it is usually ground. Just about any restaurant, no matter how simple or elaborate, will serve several variations of lamb or chicken kebabs, as well as such staples as *mantı*, a meat-filled ravioli, and *köfte*, meatballs. Fresh fish, often various kinds of bream, is the mainstay of menus along the Aegean and Mediterranean coasts, where restaurants usually display the catch on ice and serve it simply grilled with oil and lemon. In the countryside you are likely to encounter restaurants that raise trout in a pond or stream and serve it at outdoor, tree-shaded tables.

Typical vegetable accompaniments are simply prepared beans, okra or cauliflower, and salad made of tomatoes, onions, peppers, cucumbers, olives and perhaps some white cheese – greens like rocket or lettuce are relatively rare. Popular desserts include *baklava*, phyllo pastry with honey and nuts; *helva*, combinations of flour, butter, sugar and flavourings; or various milk-based puddings.

Beverages

In this predominantly Muslim country, many restaurants and cafés do not serve alcohol. It's easier to find establishments serving alcoholic beverages – often just beer and wine – in resorts than it is in some of the inland towns less visited by non-Turks.

Turkish wines, mostly made in Cappadocia or along the Aegean coast, are widespread, and many restaurants serve nothing but domestic varieties; the two largest vintners, Doluca and Kavaklıdere, dominate the market, but it's worth asking for local microwinery products. The most popular domestic beers, bottled or draught, are Efes Pilsen, Carlsberg and Tuborg, all at about 5 percent; Efes also makes 'Dark' (6.1 percent alcohol) and 'Xtra' (7.5 percent). By contrast, domestically made spirits like gin and vodka are worth avoiding in favour of imported labels. The alcoholic beverage of local choice, however, is *rakı*, similar to Greek ouzo and enjoyed before, during and after a meal, mixed with water and ice. The best brands are Efe and Burgaz, though you're likely to be offered only the mediocre Yeni.

Turkish wine

Poor-quality instant coffee, irrespective of brand, is almost always referred to as Nescafé; if you want something more satisfying, request Turkish coffee, usually served *orta şekerli* (medium sweet) or *çok şekerli* (very sweet). In major resorts, at least one café will be doing proper, European-style espressos and cappuccinos – at European prices. Tea, *çay*, is far more common, and even shopkeepers dispense it freely to their customers; it is served in small glasses, to which you can add water and sugar, but never milk, as desired.

TO HELP YOU ORDER...

Do you speak English? **İnglizce biliyormusunz?**
Waiter! **Lütfen bakarmısınız**!
What would you recommend? **Ne tavsiye edersiniz?**

TO HELP YOU READ THE MENU...

Meze (Starters)

antep ezmesi hot chili purée
cacık yogurt, cucumber and herb dip
çoban salatası a salad of tomato, cucumber, peppers, onions and parsley
haydarı thick garlic dip
imam bayıldı cold baked aubergines with tomato and onion
mücver courgette frittata
semizotu purslane leaves, usually mixed with yogurt
sigara böreği cheese-filled pastry 'cigarettes'
yaprak dolması stuffed vine leaves

Et (Meat)

döner kebab sliced roasted lamb
iskender kebab döner drenched in yogurt

karısık ızgara mixed grill
piliç roast chicken
pirzola lamb chops
şiş köfte grilled lamb meatballs

Balık (Fish), Deniz Ürünleri (Seafood)

ahtapod octopus
alabalık trout
barbunya red mullet
hamsi anchovies
kalamar squid
karides prawns
kiliç swordfish
midye mussels
palamut bonito
sardalya sardines

Sebze (Vegetables)

bakla broad beans
bamya okra
domates tomatoes
ıspanak spinach
kuru fasulye white haricots
nohut chickpeas
patates potatoes
patlıcan aubergine

Tatlı (Dessert)

dondurma Central Asian ice cream
kadayıf 'shredded wheat' filaments in syrup
keşkül vanilla almond custard
lokum Turkish delight
aşure Pulse, wheat, fruit and nut pudding
sütlaç rice pudding
tavukgöğsü boiled chicken-breast pudding

Beverages

bira beer
çay tea
kahve coffee
maden suyu mineral water
arap wine
ayran yoghurt drink

PLACES TO EAT

Meal for one, excluding alcohol:

$$$$ over £30 ($50)	**$$** £10–20 ($16–32)
$$$ £20–30 ($32–50)	**$** below £10 ($16)

İSTANBUL

Albura Kathisma $$$ *Yeni Akbıyık Cad. 26, Sultanahmet, tel: 0212-518 9710*, www.alburakathisma.com. Everywhere in this district is touristy and pricy, but at least here you get what you pay for and more – excellent service, a pleasant Ottoman architectural environment on several levels, vegetarian options amongst the typical mains, and an unusually full wine list.

Balıkçı Sabahattin $$$ *Seyit Hasan Koyu Sok. 1, Cankurturan, downhill from Sultanahmet, tel: 0212-458 1824*, www.balikcisabahattin.com. Fish specialist working out of a 1927-vintage wooden house in winter, with shaded tables out in the lane during summer; it's not bargain-basement – as the proper table nappery tells you – but the quality is high, with more Turks in attendance than tourists. Fishaphobics should know that there are no meat or strictly vegetarian items on the menu.

Banyan $$$ *Salhane Sok. 3, off Muallim Naci Caddesi, Ortaköy dock, tel: 0212-259 9060*, www.banyanrestaurant.com. A mix of Asian cuisines, from Indian to Thai, at this stylish third-floor eatery with sweeping views of the southerly Bosphorus bridge and the Ortaköy mosque. There's a cheaper fixed menu at lunch, but otherwise expect to pay dearly.

Giritli $$–$$$ Keresteci Hakki Sok., Cankurtaran/Ahirkapi, *tel: 0212-458 2270*, www.giritlirestoran.com. Nice restaurant with a beautiful garden and a good selection of *meze* and fish dishes. The tender grilled octopus is highly recommended. The fixed menu offers a good introduction to Turkish and Mediterranean cooking. Open noon–midnight daily.

Nar Lokanta $$$$ Armaggan, 5th Floor, Nuruosmaniye Cad. 65, Nuruosmaniye, *tel: 0212-522 2800*, www.narlokantasi.com. Well situated in the heart of Sultanahmet, near the entrance to the Grand Bazaar, this elegant restaurant serves traditional Anatolian and Ottoman cuisine with a menu of 50 dishes which changes weekly. It's also a showcase for local and organic Turkish products offered by Nar Gourmet, an organization that promotes Turkish food abroad. Closed Sun.

Hacı Abdullah $$ Ağa Camii Atıf Yılmaz Cad.. *9A, Beyoğlu, tel: 0212-293 8561,* www.haciabdullah.com.tr. Long-established, high-ceiling restaurant serving authentic traditional Turkish dishes. The menu changes regularly, but specialities to look out for include *hünkar beğendi kebap* (beef chunks on aubergine/cheese purée), *kuzu tandır* (roast lamb) and *ayva tatlısı* (stewed quince with clotted cream). No alcohol served.

MARMARA REGION AND AEGEAN COAST

AYVALIK

Deniz Kestanesi $$$ *Karantina Sok. 5A, tel: 0266-312-3262,* www.denizkestanesi.com. The most elegant (and expensive) seafood restaurant in the port district, with a designer interior to match. And yes sea urchin (*deniz kestanesi*) – esteemed like Viagra by Turks – features on the menu, along with local specialities like fried *papalina* (a kind of sprat) and fish roe.

BODRUM

Gambilya $$–$$$ Eski Hukumet Sk. 62, *tel: 0252-313 3362*. Cosy restaurant tucked away in the back streets of Bodrum with a pleasant semi-covered garden and tasty food prepared and served by the friendly owners, one of whom also works as a tour guide. A good place for vegetarians. The desserts and home-made lemonade are divine.

Nazik Ana $ *Eski Hükümet Sok 7, tel: 0252-313 1891*. Something of a miracle in often glitzy Bodrum: self-serve specials comprising a choice of home-style dishes, plus salad. Sweets and beer also available. The stonewalled, canopied courtyard with its wood-bench seating is a cool refuge on a summer day. Good value for money. Cash only.

BURSA

Kebapçı İskender $ *Ünlü Cad. 7A, Heykel district, tel: 0224-221 4615,* www.iskender.com. One of the chain of restaurants which claim to have invented Bursa's most famous dish, an artery-clogging pile of *döner* on *pide* slices, slathered in yogurt. That's all they serve. Cash only.

Safran Restaurant $$ *Ortapazar Caddesi, Arka Sok. 4, Hisar district, tel: 0224-224 7216,* www.safranotel.com. Chic, small restaurant attached to the eponymous hotel, with a wide-ranging menu (including meat-mushroom stews and excellent desserts).

ÇANAKKALE

Yalova $$$ Kemal Pasa Mah. Gumruk Sok. 7, *tel: 0286-217 1045.* Unusual *mezes* and what's claimed to be the town's widest range of seafood. Dardanelles-view tables upstairs, or in the ground-level conservatory of this historic building, operating as a restaurant under the third generation of management.

ÇEŞME

Medcezir Cafe $ 3057 Sok. *7/1v, tel: 0232-712 7286.* This modest restaurant near the sea offers good quality food at unbeatable prices. The staff are extremely helpful. The Greek salad, grilled fish and steaks are delicious, but the tomato and lentil soup is also a treat.

İZMİR

Deniz $$$ *Atatürk Cad. 188/B (inside İzmir Palas Hotel), tel: 0232-464 4499,* www.denizrestaurant.com.tr. Highly regarded by locals, who return here regularly for speciality seafood dishes like whole fish baked in salt, served in tastefully minimalist surroundings. Good-value set menus; booking advisable. Open all year.

SELÇUK

Ejder $$ *Cengiz Topel Cad 9, tel: 0232-892 3296*. A prime location in the pedestrian zone opposite a stork-nested aqueduct, plus a well-balanced menu of meat with an east-Anatolian flair, vegetarian platters and fresh *mezes* combine to make a winner. Cash only.

YAYLAKÖY

Yılmaz'ınYeri $$. *Top of the pass, 9km (5 miles) south of Kuşadası on the road to Söke and Priene, tel: 0256-668 1023*. The best of a cluster of meat-strong restaurants here, always crowded with locals enjoying traditional *meze* in decent portions, an infinity of kebabs, and a very reasonable wine list.

MEDITERRANEAN COAST

ANTALYA

Hasanağa $$ *Mescit Sok 15, Kaleiçi, tel: 0242-242 8105*. Popular, durable old-town restaurant, with a characterful indoor dining area, plus a delightful walled courtyard studded with citrus trees. A serve-yourself buffet *meze* table precedes fish or meat mains (less than $10). Live Turkish music most evenings. Open all year.

Vanilla $$$ *Hesapçı Sok. 33, tel: 0242-247 6013*, www.vanilla antalya.com. Chic, cozy Turkish-English-run bistro purveying mainly continental fare (steaks, fish, carpaccio, seafood risotto), with Italian/Asian dishes thrown in. First-class service from the owners. Booking advised in season.

DALYAN

Saki $–$$ *Riverbank, by Kral Bahçesi and rowboat ferry to Kaunos, tel: 0252-284 5212*. The only genuine *meyhane* (drinker's tavern) in town, yet family-run, with abundant vegetarian *meze* platters as well as meat mains and (unusually for such an establishment) desserts. Open April–Oct; cash only.

DATÇA

Culinarium $$$ Liman Mevkii, *tel: 0252-712 9770*, www.culinarium-datca.com. This stylish restaurant run by Turkish-German couple is beautifully situated on the shore with an outdoor terrace overlooking the sea. The menu is very diverse comprising seafood and meat dishes made with local produce. Home-made ice-creams and desserts are a must. Open Mar–Nov.

KALKAN

Guru's Place $$ *3.5km (2 miles) east of Kalkan*, Kalkan Kas road, *tel:* 9053-6331 1016, www.kalkanguru.com. This roadside restaurant in a family-run hotel is located on the cliffs above Kalkan. The *meze* and lamb dishes are fabulous. It offers wine and cheese tastings, as well as cooking classes (http://cookingholidayturkey.com).

KAŞ

Bahçe $$ *Top of Uzun Çarşı, behind Lion Tomb*, Ilkokul Sok. 31 *tel: 0242-836 2370*. The best cold or hot *mezes* in town, served in the garden (*bahçe*). Their seafood annexe just opposite (tel: 0242-836-2779; $$$) is also excellent, with unusual *meze* platters like marinated sea-bass fillet. Both open May to early November.

Sultan Garden $$–$$$ *Hükümet Caddesi, opposite coast guard station, tel: 0242-836 3762*, www.sultangardenrestaurant.com. The place for a romantic tête-a-tête, or a birthday dinner, featuring less common *meze* platters like *paçanga böreği* (turnovers with *pastırma*, tomato and cheese), plus good lamb-based mains. Excellent, genuinely friendly service, and good value for the location. The desserts are unforgettable. Outdoor terrace open May–Oct.

KAYAKÖYU

Cin Bal $$ *Signposted in a field, on easterly approach to village, tel: 0252-618 0066*, www.cinbal.com. A locals' favourite, this is a *kendin pişin kendin ye* place, where you buy superb lamb by the kilo and then cook it yourself at a tableside brazier (there's also *tandır kebap* for the lazy). Open all year. Cash only.

PATARA

Golden $–$$ *Central T-junction, Gelemiş resort area, tel: 0242-843 5162,* www.pataragoldenpension.com. The original (founded 1982) village restaurant here and still one of the best, specialising in trout and grills; almost uniquely in Gelemiş, open all year.

CAPPADOCIA AND CENTRAL ANATOLIA

ANKARA

Boyacızâde Konağı $$ *Berrak Sok. 9, Hisar, tel: 0312-310 2525.* Old-house restaurant next to the Museum of Anatolian Civilisations serving on several floors; fairly traditional Turkish cuisine, and splendid views from the outdoor seating.

KONYA

Somatci $$ Akçeşme Mah.Mengüç Cad. 36, *tel: 0332-351 6696,* www.somatci.com. This rustic restaurant with wooden beams and white-washed walls decorated with folk paintings serves tasty roasted pepper and walnut soup among a wide variety of other dishes. The desserts such as almond *halva* or roasted figs in honey are delicious, but extremely sweet.

MUSTAFAPAŞA (SİNASOS)

Old Greek House (Asmalı Konak) $ *Mustafapaşa (Sinasos), tel: 0384-353 5306,* www.oldgreekhouse.com. The restaurant and attached hotel occupy what was the home of the Greek Orthodox mayor before 1923, and the frescoes and original panelling are cared for as lovingly as the home-cooked fare is prepared. The menu has a varied selection of tasty dishes, with lots for vegetarians.

ÜRGÜP

Şömine $$ *Cumhuriyet Meydanı 9, tel: 0384-341 8442*, www.somineresturant.com. Local families often join travellers at the long tables on the terrace looking over the town. The hearty food, some of the best in the region, includes stews and house speciality *testi kebap* (spicy lamb with tomatoes, onions and peppers baked in a break-open clay pot).

EASTERN TURKEY

ANTAKYA

Sveyka Restaurant $ Kurtuluş Cad. *58, Hatay, tel: 0326-213 3947*, www.sveyka.com. The restaurant is truly beautiful, situated in an old mansion with a picturesque patio and wrought iron chairs and tables. The indoor decor is more elegant. The menu offers a mixture of Turkish and Middle East cooking. The meatballs in cherry sauce and Aleppan version of kebab are worth a try, as is the local dessert known as *künefe* (cheese pastry).

GAZİANTEP

İmam Çağdaş $$ *Uzun Çarşı 49, tel: 0342-231 2678*, www.imamcagdas.com. Going since 1887, this is the best restaurant in a city known for its food. The kebabs and *lahmacun* are done to perfection, as is the baklava for which the restaurant is famous. Unlicensed. Cash only.

MARDİN

Cercis Murat Konağı $$$ *Birinci Cad. 517, tel: 0482-213 6841*, www.cercismurat.com. Run exclusively by women, this creative restaurant occupies an old Syrian Christian mansion. Regional specialties, often strongly spiced with ginger, cinnamon, coriander, allspice or sumac, include *incasiye* (lamb flavoured with grape molasses, plums and chilis), *kitel raha* (Syrian-style meatballs) and *hımmısiye* (sour chickpea stew). Reservations strongly advised.

A–Z TRAVEL TIPS

A Summary of Practical Information

A

ACCOMMODATION

In general, lodgings fall into two categories: hotels *(oteller)*, found in larger towns and cities, and extending to massive resort complexes along the Aegean or Mediterranean coasts; or guest houses *(pansiyonlar)* which can mean simple, rock-bottom accommodation or, increasingly in the historic quarters of cities and towns, character-filled and comfortable bed-and-breakfast-type lodgings. There is an increasing number of delightfully restored Ottoman mansions opening as small boutique hotels in historic cities at surprisingly affordable rates. All places are officially rated on a scale effectively corresponding to a one-to-five-star system. Technically, the rating reflects the type of amenities offered (pool, restaurant, lifts, etc.) but does not reflect charm or ambience, so a highly desirable establishment can be given a lower rating than a mediocre establishment next door.

Prices are generally considerably less than for similar accommodation in Western Europe and North America, although luxury hotels in İstanbul, İzmir and Ankara charge at international levels. Breakfast – 'traditional' Turkish in simpler places, buffet-style with 'western' options in multi-starred establishments – is usually included. Many establishments have single beds only; if you want a double bed, request a *fransiz yatak* ('French' bed). Advance reservations are highly advisable at peak season.

I have a reservation. **Reservasyonim var.**
I'd like a single/double room. **Tek/çift yataklı bir oda istiyorum.**
With shower **Duşlu**
What is the price per night? **Bir gecelik oda ücreti ne kadar?**
Can I see the room? **Bakabilimiyini?**

AIRPORTS *(havalimani; see also Getting There)*

Most travellers to Istanbul arrive at **Atatürk Airport** (www.ataturk airport.com) 20km (15 miles) southwest of İstanbul. There are excellent transport links, with metro, shuttle buses and taxis to downtown İstanbul (45mins–1hr). The low-cost carrier currently flying into İstanbul, Pegasus Air (www.flypgs.com) and regional airlines (Bora and Anadolu Jet), use **Sabiha Gökçen Airport** (www.sg airport.com) at Pendik, about 46km (25 miles) from the centre of İstanbul on the Asian shore. Transport from here is slow, with buses to the city centre (6am–10pm, 1–2hr depending on traffic); the green E10 bus to Kadiköy connecting directly with ferries across the Bosphorus to Eminönü and EM22 to the Kartal metro station; or taxis which can be very expensive.

There are also a few year-round scheduled services to İzmir and Antalya, plus no-frills flights to these two airports as well as to Bodrum and Dalaman on the Aegean and Mediterranean coasts respectively. Flying into Ankara (www.esenbogaairport.com) frequently involves a change at İstanbul.

B

BUDGETING FOR YOUR TRIP

Turkey is often inexpensive compared to the euro zone, but prices have risen recently as the currency stabilises and the economy booms. Think of İstanbul, İzmir, Ankara and major resorts as separate entities to the rest of Turkey. In İstanbul or Bodrum, for example, you can get a good double room for US$100–150/£60–93; elsewhere, you can usually find one for half that amount.

Meals along the coast, and in İstanbul, tend to cost what they do in most of the European Mediterranean; inland prices drop sharply. Generally, two people can eat extremely well for about $50/£30 and have a pleasant, simple meal for about $35/£22 (with beer, not wine) and a light snack for under $20/£13. Seafood is considerably more expensive than meat, beer is on the cheap side, but wine and *rakı* are relatively dear. Coffee is more expensive than tea, especially if it's cappuccino or espresso. Petrol is about the most expensive in the world, yet local transport remains affordable; on-line specials for domestic air tickets can often nearly match bus fares.

C

CAMPING *(kamping)*

Camping is quite easy in Turkey, the campsites are mostly along the Aegean and Mediterranean coasts) and along long distance trails such as the Lycian Way or St Paul Trail. Some sites are open also in winter. The most pleasant sites, especially if you have a caravan or camper van, are the 20 or so run by the Ministry of Forestry – look for yellow lettering on brown wooden signs. Wild camping is also permitted.

CAR HIRE

To hire a car, you must be over 21 and have had a licence for a year. You will also need a credit card for the damages deposit. The major companies all have outlets in Turkey and there are also many local hire-car agencies. Antalya, Bodrum, Dalaman airport and (sometimes) İzmir airport are the least expensive places to pick up a car; İstanbul, Marmaris, Kuşadası, Çeşme and anywhere in the east are the most expensive. Booking on-line will often be much cheaper, especially for longer periods. If you have an accident when driving a hire car in Turkey, notify the police immediately; insurance claims are invalid unless accompanied by an official accident report *(kaza raporu)*.

CLIMATE

Turkey is given to great extremes of climate. Expect high summer temperatures everywhere, cold, damp winters in İstanbul and Cappadocia (where, as elsewhere in Central Anatolia, it can be bitterly cold and snowy), and mild winters on the Mediterranean and Aegean coasts. Especially pleasant times to visit Turkey are spring and autumn, when temperatures are moderate and crowds are thin.

CLOTHING

Although Turks have become inured to the sight of tourists clad in shorts and T-shirts tramping through their cities, they do not like the practice. This is an Islamic country and while they do not expect you to wear the veil, keeping your shoulders and knees covered away from the beach is only polite. It's a necessity if you are planning to visit any mosques. The general summer dress is lightweight trousers and short-sleeved button-down or polo shirts for men, and trousers and blouses, skirts, or dresses for women. Bathing suits, vests, brief shorts and other skimpy attire are not to be worn anywhere other than the beach. A hat and sunglasses are necessities in summer and sensible at most times.

From October through to April you will need a pullover or two in the south; in the centre and north, including İstanbul, you may need full-blown winter gear as temperatures fall, rain is common and it will usually snow at some point.

Only the most expensive restaurants in İstanbul require jacket-and-tie formality, but you will want to dress well for dinner in better restaurants anywhere in the country.

CRIME AND SAFETY

Turkey is relatively safe, and even in İstanbul crime is rarely more serious than pick-pocketing or purse-snatching; be especially careful in crowded markets and in metro cars. This said, you should be aware of some scams that are periodically perpetrated against tourists. One involves İstanbul cab drivers taking your money, substituting it with lower-denomination bills, and flashing them at you insisting that you have underpaid; to avoid this situation, tally the money you are handing the driver and call for the police immediately if an argument ensues. Far more serious is someone (usually a man) who will offer assistance with directions, only to lure you to an accomplice who may attempt to mug you.

Two of the most serious offences tourists might commit are possession of illicit drugs or antiquities; both incursions are punishable by stiff prison sentences and are not to be taken lightly. Due to civil war in Syria, it's advisable stay at least 10km (6 miles) away from the Turkish–Syrian border.

D

DRIVING

Turkey's roads are not for the faint of heart and you need to drive defensively at all times. While some major highways, including the country's growing number of toll motorways, are well designed and well maintained, many roads are poorly paved, poorly marked and lit, erratically signposted and dangerously curvy and narrow, with relatively few crash barriers on cliff roads. The Turks tend to drive fast and often recklessly. In rural areas, you are quite likely to come upon flocks of sheep and goats in the road, as well as elderly and overloaded trucks, children playing football or donkey carts. All of these pose an extra hazard at night, especially with the frequent presence of unlit vehicles. Traffic lights go straight from red to green; a flashing yellow arrow means you can turn right if the road is clear even if the main light is red.

You may drive on your national driver's licence for up to three months, but an IDP is most useful for flashing at the many control points. If bringing a car into Turkey, you will need the logbook, proof of ownership, a Green Card and carnet. Check you are comprehensively insured. An official nationality sticker must be displayed at the rear of the vehicle, and the vehicle equipped with flares, a red breakdown-warning triangle, and a full set of spares (including bulbs).

Drive on the right, pass on the left and give way to the right, even on roundabouts. Speed limits are 120km/h (70mph) on motorways, 90km/h (55mph), or 80km (50mph) for big vans or caravans on rural roads; 50km/h (30mph) or 40km/h (25mp/h) if towing something in town. Drivers and all passengers must wear seat belts, and motorcyclists must wear helmets. Blood-alcohol limits are in line with European countries – 50mg alcohol per 100ml of blood – so just two beers will put you over the limit. Traffic control points and radar speed traps are common, particularly at the entrance to towns; foreigners, especially in rental vehicles, are likely to be waved through, but make sure the rental company has provided all required documentation in the glove box.

Petrol *(benzin)* and diesel *(mazot)* are readily available around larger towns and resorts, sometimes on a 24-hr basis; however, stations can be far apart in eastern Turkey. Petrol is available three grades: super, normal and lead-free fuel *(kurşunsuz)*, the latter rarer in rural districts; so-called euro-diesel is more efficient than standard. In most of the country, you can pay for fuel by credit card.

Durmak Yasaktır No Stopping
Yol Yapimı Men Working (Road Works)
Dikkat Danger
Yavaş Slow Down
Tek Yön One-way
Giremez No Entry
Şehir Merkezi Town Centre

Some useful phrases:

Driver's licence **Ehliyet**
Petrol **Benzin**
Petrol station **Benzin istasyonu**
Oil **Motor yagi**
Tyre **Lastik**
Brakes **Frenler**
It does not work **Calismiyor.**
Fill the tank, please **Doldurum, lütfen.**
I've had a breakdown **Arabam arızalandı.**
There's been an accident **Bir kaza oldu.x**

E

ELECTRICITY

220V/50Hz; continental-style 2 round-pin plugs. UK Visitors will require an adapter; travellers from North America will also need a converter.

EMBASSIES AND CONSULATES

Foreign embassies are all in Ankara, but most major countries also have consulates in İstanbul and there are also some in larger resorts.

Consulates (in İstanbul unless otherwise stated)

Australia: Ritz Carlton residences, Asker Ocağı Cad.15, Elmadağ, tel: 0212-393 8542; **Canada:** Buyukdere Cad. 209, tel: 0212-385 9700; **New Zealand:** Inonu Cad. 48/3, Taksim, tel: 0212-244 0272; **UK:** Mesrutiyet Cad. 34, Tepebaşı, Beyoğlu, tel: 0212-334 75406400; in Antalya: Gürsu Mah. 324 Sok. 6, Konyaaltı, tel: 0242-228 2811; in Bodrum: Cafer Paşa Caddesi, İkinci Emsan Evleri 7, tel: 0252-313 0021; in Fethiye, Atatürk Caddesi, Likya

İş Merkezi, Kat 2, 202, tel: 0252- 614 6302; in İzmir: 1442 Sok. 49, Alsancak, tel: 0232-463 5151; and in Marmaris: Barbaros Cad. 11, tel: 0252-412 6486; **US:** İstinye Mahallesi, Üç Şehitler Sok. 2, İstinye, tel: 0212-335 9000.

Embassies in Ankara

Australia: Ugur Mumcu Cad. No.88, Gaziosmanpaşa, tel: 0312-459 9500 (www.turkey.embassy.gov.au); Canada: Cinnah Cad. 58, Çankaya, tel: 0312-409 2700 (www.turkey.gc.ca); **Ireland:** Ugur Mumcu Cad. 88, Gaziosmanpaşa, tel: 0312-459 1000 (www.embassyofireland.org.tr); **New Zealand:** Kizkulesi Sok. 11, Gaziosmanpaşa, tel: 0312-446 3333 (www.nzembassy.com/turkey); **UK:** Şehit Ersan Cad. 46/A, Cankaya, tel: 0312-455 3344 (www.gov.uk/government/world/organisations/british-embassy-ankara); **US**: Atatürk Bulv. 110, Kavaklıdere, tel: 0312-455 5555 (http://turkey.usembassy.gov).

EMERGENCY NUMBERS (see also Police)

0212-527 4503 Tourism police
155 Police, general
110 Urban fire department
112 Ambulance

Help! **Imdat!**
I am ill. **Hastayım.**
Call a doctor. **Doktor cagirim.**
Where is the hospital? **Nerede hastane?**

G

GAY AND LESBIAN TRAVELLERS

Although homosexual activity between consenting adults over the age of 18 is legal, Turks are generally not accepting of gay lifestyles and it is illegal to print and distribute material promoting homosexuality. Members of the same sex travel and socialise together, so gay couples should feel quite comfortable travelling together. However, sexually charged contact could result in violence. Bodrum, Alanya, Antalya and Marmaris are considered the most gay-friendly resorts, though the only place with dedicated clubs is İstanbul, where the scene is centred around Beyoğlu.

GETTING THERE (see also Airports)

By air. Most international carriers fly to İstanbul. In summer, there are many additional direct flights to the resort airports of Dalaman, Bodrum and Antalya. The national carrier, Turkish Airlines (THY, www.thy.com), provides direct services across the globe, as well as domestic services. From the UK, Thomas Cook and Thomson offer flight-only charter deals, and low-cost carriers such as easyJet (www.easyjet.com), Pegasus Air (www.flypgs.com), and Jet2 (www.jet2.com) provide flights throughout the year.

By land. Travelling from other European cities to İstanbul by train is long (about 72 hours from London), but enjoyable if you have sufficient time. Trains from Europe arrive at Sirkeci Station in Eminönü, in the heart of old Constantinople. An excellent source of information is the website www.seat61.com, which has every possible routing to Turkey, and links for ticket purchases for the various legs of the journey. Global InterRail (www.interrail.eu) and Eurail (www.eurail.com) passes are valid in Turkey, but are unlikely to save you much money.

It takes up to four days to drive to Turkey from most places in Western Europe.

By sea. The only way to sail to Turkey is from Greece. There are (often seasonal) services from the Greek islands opposite to various Turkish resort-ports; www.feribot.net and www.ferries-turkey.com are useful information and booking resources.

GUIDES AND TOURS

Wherever you go in Turkey, you will encounter guides offering their services outside museums or archaeological sites. Some are properly qualified, licensed and excellent at their job; others provide entertainment at best. If you want a guarantee, hire a guide through the tourist office. Fees are not high. Don't be put off if at the end of the tour the guide offers to take you to a relative's carpet shop – it is part of the profession.

For special-interest tours and activities, the following agencies are recommended:

IN TURKEY

Middle Earth Travel, Göreme, Cappadocia, tel: 0384-271 2559, www.middleearthtravel.com. Hiking/trekking both locally and along Lycian/St Paul trails, plus conventional sightseeing.

Crowded House Tours, Eceabat, Gallipoli, tel: 0286-8141565, www.crowdedhousegallipoli.com. Battlefield tour operator.

Alternatif Turizm, Marmaris, tel: 0252-417 2720, www.alternatifraft.com. Main local outfitter for sea-kayaking, river-rafting, canyoning, trekking along this coast.

Kirkit Voyage, Sultanahmet, İstanbul, and Avanos, Cappadocia, tel: 0212-5182282, www.kirkit.com. Mountain-biking and horse-riding in Cappadocia, plus general cultural tours.

OVERSEAS

Andante Travels (UK), tel: 01722-713800, www.andantetravels.co.uk. Up-market tours to archaeological and historical sites, led by distinguished experts.

The Imaginative Traveller (UK), tel: 0473-852 354, www.imaginative-traveller.com. Variety of escorted overland tours, many family-friendly, covering all of Turkey and visiting lesser-known spots as well as the main attractions.

Cultural Folk Tours (US), tel: 1-800-935 8875, http://culturalfolktours.com. Led by musican Bora Özkök, these 15-to-27-day tours give real insight into seldom-visited parts of Turkey.

H

HEALTH AND MEDICAL CARE

You don't need any inoculations for travel to Turkey and there are no serious health risks, although the coastal area east of Alanya does have malaria in season. The most common problems for tourists are mild stomach upsets, sunburn and/or heat stroke in high summer, and alcohol poisoning. All are easily avoided – keep washing your hands, drink bottled water, eat only freshly cooked, hygienically prepared food; wear a hat and sunblock and drink plenty of water; and keep the alcohol levels down. Also, be careful in the countryside – there are poisonous scorpions, snakes and spiders.

Make sure you have full travel insurance that will cover any medical treatment you may need. You may be asked to pay for treatment upfront, so keep all receipts. Pharmacies are well stocked, and can treat many minor ailments; emergency after-hour locations are posted in all pharmacies. Your hotel will be able to get you a doctor if necessary. The quality of medical care is generally good.

Water. Tap water is heavily chlorinated and not exactly tasty (in İstanbul it is absolutely to be avoided). Turks prefer inexpensive bottled water; still water is *şişe suyu*, sparkling water is *maden suyu*. Rural springs are labelled *içilir, içibelir* or *içme suyu* (all meaning 'drinkable') or *içilmez* ('not drinkable').

Where can I find a doctor/ dentist? **Nereden bir doktor/bir disci bulabilirim?**
Where is the nearest pharmacy? **En yakin eczane neredeğdir?**
Sunburn **Güneş yanğı**
Fever **Ateş**
Stomach ache **Mide bozulması**

L

LANGUAGE

While English is spoken widely in hotels and other tourist facilities, you may well find yourself in many places in Turkey where English is unknown. Try to have at least a few words of Turkish up your sleeve: English-speaking or not, Turks will applaud your efforts.

Among Atatürk's sweeping reforms were his attempts to 'modernise' the Turkish language. As a result, since 1929 Turkish has been written in a modified Roman alphabet. Many letters are pronounced as they are in English. Some exceptions:

c like **j** in **j**am
ç like **ch** in **ch**ip
ğ almost silent, lengthening the preceding vowel
h always pronounced
ı like the sound between b and l in 'probable'
j like **s** in plea**s**ure
ö like **ur** in f**ur**
ş like **sh** in **sh**ell
ü like **ew** in f**ew**

Some basic words and phrases:

Hello **Merhaba** MEHR-hah-bah
Good morning **Günaydın** Goon-eye-DEN
Please **Lütfen** LEWT-fen
Thank you **Teşekkür ederim** Tay-shake-kur eh-day-REEM
Bon appetit **Afiyet olsun**
Cheers! **Şerefe!**
Excuse me **Ozur dilerim** Oh-ZEWR deel-air-eem
Where is…? **Nerde…?** NEH-deer…?
I don't understand **Anlamıyorum** Ahn-LAH-muh-yohr-um

I'd like... **Istiyorum...** EES-tee-yohr-ruhm
How much is that? **Bu ne kadar?** boo neh kaddar?
Is there a toilet here? **Tuvalet var mı?**
OK **Tamam**
Yes **Evet**
No **Hayır**

Numbers:

one **bir** beer
two **iki** ee-KEE
three **üc** ooch
four **dört** doort
five **beş** besh
six **altı** ahl-TUH
seven **yedi** YED-dee
eight **sekiz** sek-KEEZ
nine **dokuz** doh-KOOZ
ten **on** ohn
hundred **yüz** yewz

Days of the week:

Monday **Pazartesi** Pahz-AHR-teh-see
Tuesday **Salı** SAHL-luh
Wednesday **Çarşamba** Char-shahm-BAH
Thursday **Perşembe** Pair-shem-BAH
Friday **Cuma** JOON-ahz
Saturday **Cumartesi** Joom-AHR-teh-see
Sunday **Pazar** Pahz-AHR

M

MAPS

Good country or regional maps can be bought in bookshops in Istanbul and other touristdestinations. Consider buying one before you leave home; the best currently available overseas is Reise Know-How's 1:700,000-scale Western Turkey Mediterranean Coast and Cyprus, which covers the entire southern and western third of the country. Locally, Sabri Aydal's 1:250,000 products for Lycia, Cappadocia and Pamphylia are available. Turkish motorway maps are available at the website of the Republic of Turkey Directorate of Highways (www.kgm.gov.tr).

MEDIA

Some foreign English-language newspapers are available from newsstands in İstanbul and in larger resorts. The two local English-language dailies are the Hürriyet Daily News (www.hurriyetdailynews.com) and the Today's Zaman (www.todayszaman.com). Good news website in English are: www.turkishweekly.net and www.aa.com.tr (of Anadolou News Agency). News in English is broadcast on CNN, BBC World and Al Jazeera; the better hotels offer a satellite package including these, as well as the private Digitürk network's English-language CNBC-e and E2 channels.

MONEY

Currency. The unit of currency is the Türk Lirası (TL, Turkish Lira); 1TL is broken into 100 kuruş, which are available in coins of 5, 10, 25 and 50 kuruş, plus 1 TL. Notes come in denominations of 5, 10, 20, 50, 100 and 200TL.

Most travellers obtain cash either through the ubiquitous ATMs, or exchange sterling, euro or US$ bills at dedicated foreign-exchange booths *(döviz burolar)*; these are open much longer hours than banks, and charge no commission, though usually offer a poorer rate. Credit/debit cards are useful for air ticket and petrol purchase; most brands are accepted. Payment in foreign currency is happily accepted for purchase of valuable souvenirs (eg carpets).

O

OPENING TIMES

In general, hours are: archaeological sites, 8.30am–6.30pm daily in summer (with many variations); government offices, 8.30am–12.30pm and 1.30–5.30pm, Mon–Fri (tourist offices are often open on weekends too during summer); museums, 8.30/9am–5.30/6pm Tue–Sun (with many variations); restaurants, noon–2.30pm or 3pm for lunch, 7 or 7.30–10pm or 10.30pm for dinner (those that have music and offer drinks will often remain open longer); shops, 9am–7pm (as late as midnight during the summer season in some resorts).

P

POLICE *(polis)*

There are many kinds of police in Turkey. Municipal polis deal with petty crime, traffic, parking and other day-to-day matters; the *Jandarma*, a better trained national force, actually a branch of the army, handle serious crime and civil unrest; *Trafik Polis* monitor town streets and highways; the *Belediye Zabitası* (market police) patrol market areas with an eye out for shoplifters and dishonest merchants; and the *Turizm Polis*, who often speak English, are on hand in busy tourist areas.

POST OFFICES

Turkish post offices (www.ptt.gov.tr) are easily recognised by their PTT signs. In the major cities and resorts, the central post office is open 8am–midnight; others are open 8.30am–12.30pm and 1.30–5.30pm. Express service is faster but much more expensive; most people use courier companies for anything precious. Post offices also offer metered counter-telephone service.

PUBLIC HOLIDAYS

Turks enjoy year-round festivals (see page 141), and observe the following nation-wide holidays:

1 January New Year's Day
23 April National Independence and Children's Day
19 May Atatürk Commemoration and Youth and Sports Day
30 August Victory Day
29 October Republic Day (anniversary of the declaration of the Turkish Republic)
10 November Anniversary of Atatürk's death

The most important Islamic holidays, which drift backward 11 days annually relative to the western calendar, are Şeker Bayramı (end of Ramazan), falling in mid-summer until 2016, and Kurban Bayramı (Festival of the Sacrifice), occurring lately in mid-autumn. Both are multi-day festivals, and the country effectively shuts down for the duration as everyone who can goes on holiday. Many restaurants close during Ramazan at midday, except in tourist resorts.

R

RELIGION

Turkey is 99 percent Muslim. In İstanbul and İzmir, you will find Jewish, Armenian, Catholic and Greek Orthodox services. Non-Muslims are welcome to visit mosques, though often not during prayers. Visitors must remove their shoes (at larger mosques, an attendant will check them; elsewhere, there's a rack inside the door on which to place them). Men and women should cover their legs and upper arms (no shorts or sleeveless T-shirts) and women should cover their heads, shoulders and knees.

T

TELEPHONE *(telefon)*

Turkey's mobile phone networks offer widespread coverage; they use the European operating system, so North Americans will need a tri-band phone. Foreign visitors should not roam on their home SIM for anything other than texting; since Turkish networks are not subject to EU roaming caps, making or receiving voice calls is expensive. Instead, purchase a local pay-as-you-go SIM card (they start from around 20TL) or, for somewhat dearer rates, an international roaming SIM card (www.gosim.co.uk). To use your mobile phone with Turkish SIM card, especially in case of stays longer than two weeks, it's necessary to register it with the Turkish authorities.

Because of the prevalence of mobile use, there are fewer public phones now. They are usually blue, and take phone cards (from post offices and newsstands) or credit cards. Instructions are available in several languages. For more quiet, go to a TT (Türk Telekom, www.turktelecom.com.tr) premises. Local calls are quite cheap. To call internationally, dial 00, then the country code. Calling Turkey from abroad, its country code is 90; omit the initial zero of the 11-digit Turkish land or mobile number. Avoid phoning from your hotel room, as surcharges are horrendous.

TIME ZONES

Turkey is 2 hours ahead of Greenwich Mean Time (GMT), which places it 2 hours ahead of London, 7 hours ahead of New York, 10 hours ahead of Los Angeles, 2 hours behind Johannesburg, 9 hours behind Sydney, and 11 hours behind Auckland. Turkey observes Daylight Savings Time as in Europe: 1 hour forward the last Sunday in March, reverting to standard time the last Sunday in October.

New York	London	**Turkey**	Sydney	Los Angeles
5am	10am	**noon**	8pm	2am

TIPPING

Tips provide many Turks working in tourism with a good share of their income. Tip bellhops 2TL or 3TL a bag, and leave about 5TL per day of your stay for a hotel chambermaid. In many small hotels and *pansiyons*, the desk staff does double duty as cleaners, room service attendants, breakfast waiters and all-around service providers, and it is nice to leave a generous tip upon departure. To tip a taxi driver, simply round up the total. Tour guides and excursion-boat operators usually also expect a tip; 20–30TL per day of friendly service is appropriate. In non-fancy restaurants where no service charge or *garsoniye* ('waiter charge') is levied, 5 to 10 percent of the bill is fine; in fancier places, mandatory service charges can approach 20 percent of the bill, but leave a bit more on top if service has been good.

TOILETS *(tuvalet)*

There are plenty of public toilets, with most cafés and restaurants, petrol stations and tourist sights having facilities. They are often kept clean by a full-time warden, who will charge users up to 1TL. Most offer a mix of Western-style and Turkish squat toilets. All have little squirter-pipes aimed your nether parts, as local custom requires cleansing with running water. Carry a bit of toilet paper with you to blot yourself dry, and (usually) deposit this in a basket next to the basin, not in it. The gents' toilet is designated by *baylar*, the ladies' by *bayanlar*.

TOURIST INFORMATION

The official Turkish tourism websites are www.goturkey.com, www.tourismturkey.org and www.gototurkey.co.uk. Turkish Tourist Offices abroad:

UK: 3rd Floor, Craven House 121 Kingsway, London WC2B 6PA, tel: 020-7839 7802

US: 825 3rd Avenue Floor 5, New York, NY 10022, tel: 212-687 2194; 5055 Wilshire Blvd. Suite 850, Los Angeles, CA, 90036, tel: 323-937 8066

Tourist offices in Turkey:

Ankara: Gazi Mustafa Kemal Bulvarı 121, 06570 Maltepe, tel: 0312-231 5572

İstanbul: At Meydanı, Sultanahmet, tel: 0212-518 1802/518 8754

İzmir: 1344 Sokak 2, Passport, tel: 0232-444 7390

There are also variably helpful offices in Alanya, Antakya, Antalya, Avanos, Ayvalık, Bodrum, Bursa, Çanakkale, Çeşme, Edirne, Fethiye, Gaziantep, Kaş, Konya, Kuşadası, Marmaris and Selçuk.

TRANSPORT

A good public transport network makes it relatively easy to move between major cities and towns in Turkey without a car. Even some remote archaeological sites and beaches may be reached by public transport, but service can be infrequent.

Any town of any size has at least one *otogar* (bus station) that is the hub of local and long-distance transport. Long-distance buses, many of which travel by night, are often the only mode of transport available between cities and towns. Better companies, worth paying extra for, include Ulusoy, Varan (www.varan.com.tr), Metro (www.metroturizm.com.tr), Pamukkale and Kamil Koç.

Large towns and cities are served by local buses; buy tickets at kiosks before boarding, though in İstanbul most are now geared only for swiping of electronic, reloadable tickets called *akbil*. İstanbul,

Ankara and İzmir all have efficient, if often limited, metro networks. İstanbul, of course, has an extensive ferry network along the Bosphorus, and there are also useful car ferries and sea-buses across the Sea of Marmara.

Dolmuş fleets (often vans) also operate in most towns, and can serve as the main transport between smaller villages off major bus routes as well. They ply will drop off passengers upon request along the way. Stops are marked with a 'D'. In resorts, a *dolmuş* often provides fast and inexpensive transport to a beach or nearby archaeological site.

Numerous yellow taxis serve larger towns; make sure the meter is running and visible, and that the driver understands where it is you want to go (write it down to save problems). For trips to remote sites, it is worth doing a flat-rate deal for the morning or day, including waiting time, so you will have return transport.

Trains (www.tcdd.gov.tr) of interest to tourists are mostly confined to the triangle İstanbul-İzmir-Ankara; the best ones are cheaper than buses, more comfortable, and sometimes faster. The hi-speed trains run several times a day on three routes: Ankara–Istanbul Pendik Station (3h 30 min), Ankara–Konya (1h 45 min) and Eskişehir–Konya (1 h 30 min).

Domestic flights are numerous, serve an increasing number of hitherto obscure airports and can be surprisingly cheap. In addition to THY and Pegasus, Anadolu Jet (www.anadolujet.com), Atlas Jet (www. atlasjet.com), Sun Express (www.sunexpress.com) and Onurair (www.onurair.com.tr) provide internal services.

When is the next bus to...? **Bir sonraki otobüs kaçta kalkiyor...?**
A ticket to... **a bir bilet...**
What time does it leave? **Kaçta kalkiyor?**
How long does it take? **Ne kadar surebilir?**
How much does it cost? **Ne kadar?**

V

VISAS AND ENTRY REQUIREMENTS

Tourist visa requirements and costs vary substantially according to your nationality. All travellers need a passport valid for at least six months. Visas for 90 days are no longer granted on entry, it's necessary to apply via the Electronic Visa Application System (www.evisa.gov.tr) and pay with a credit or debit card. There are interactive kiosks at Turkish airports when you can get your visa in 3 minutes, but it's recommended to buy it in advance. In the case of the US and UK the fee is £20/$US30.

Turkish regulations permit visitors to bring all personal effects, including one camera, one music system (eg iPod), one personal computer and one video player. Duty-free import limits for luxury consumables include 1 litres of wine or spirits, 200 cigarettes, 10 cigars, and 200g of tobacco, 1kg coffee, 500g of tea and 1kg of chocolate. Exiting Turkey into the EU (particularly Greece), there is a duty-free limit for souvenir purchases (up to the value of €300). It is an offence to attempt to export 'antiquities', whose exact definition is vague but can include very old carpets. Reputable dealers will prepare a document for you stating that the purchased item is not an antiquity.

Currency Restrictions and VAT. There is no limit on the amount of foreign currency you can bring into Turkey, but sums above $US15,000 equivalent should be declared. Do not bring significant amounts of Turkish lira – you always get a better rate inside the country.

A variable (8 to 23 percent) value-added tax (KDV in Turkish) is added to most purchases in Turkey. Non-EU-resident foreigners can claim a VAT refund on departure providing they have dealt with retailers who furnished them with a Special VAT Refund Invoice. In practice, only the most expensive shops participate in the scheme

W

WEBSITES AND INTERNET ACCESS

www.biletix.com Booking for arts, music and sporting events, mostly in İstanbul and Ankara.
www.turkeytravelplanner.com American-orientated site with loads of practical tips and links to vetted service providers.
www.trekkinginturkey.com and www.cultureroutesinturkey.com Information on major trekking areas and marked long-distance routes, with on-line sales of guides and maps.
www.turkeycentral.com Useful portal with links to a variety of sites.
www.tulumba.com New-York-based shopping site specialising in all things Turkish, especially foodstuffs and music.
www.mymerhaba.com Aimed at long-term residents, and strongest on İstanbul, but wide-ranging and authoritative, with good events listings.
www.theguideistanbul.com The website of Istanbul magazine with listings, news about shopping, lifestyle and arts.
Turkey must be one of the most well connected societies in the world. Wi-fi zones are ubiquitous in bars and restaurants, and even surprisingly modest *pansiyons* will have a signal (usually free), in common areas if not every room; luxury hotels are more apt to charge for use.

Y

YOUTH HOSTELS

Pansiyons in Turkey are so reasonably priced that hostels per se are restricted to backpacker meccas such as İstanbul, Kuşadası, Fethiye, Çanakkale and Köyceğiz. Along the Lycian coast, interesting adaptations of these – arisen to get around a ban on 'permanent' buildings in protected areas – are the so-called 'treehouse' lodges, particularly at Olympos, near Ölüdeniz and elsewhere along the Lycian Way.

Recommended Hotels

Our selection of hotels includes only those that we believe will in some way enhance your stay. They may have great character, be well located or provide excellent value. Reservations are essential in better hotels almost anywhere in high season, and are highly recommended at other times.

The symbols below indicate the price range for a double room with bath, including breakfast, However, prices may vary with the season.

$$$$$	above £200 ($320)
$$$$	£130–200 ($210–320)
$$$	£75–130 ($130–210)
$$	£50–75 ($80–130)
$	below £50 ($80)

İSTANBUL AND SURROUNDINGS

Anemon Galata $$$$ *Büyükhendek Cad. 11, Kuledibi, Galata, tel: 0212-292 2340*, www.anemonhotels.com. One of the only special hotels in the new city, the Anemon is intimate, beautifully decorated and perfectly positioned within easy walking distance of Beyoğlu nightlife. The rooftop bar and restaurant has superb views across the Bosphorus and Golden Horn to the old city. 24 rooms and four suites.

Çirağan Palace Kempinski $$$$$ *Çirağan Cad. 32, Beşiktaş, 34349 İstanbul, tel: 0212-326 4646*, www.kempinski.com. The most luxurious hotel in İstanbul occupies the grounds of a palace built for the last of the Ottoman sultans on the Bosphorus. Only 11 opulent suites occupy the original palace; the other 295 standard rooms and 15 suites face the Bosphorus-side gardens and swimming pool from a new wing. Spa and four gourmet restaurants on-site.

Four Seasons Hotel Sultanahmet $$$$$ *Tevkifhane Sok. 1, Sultanahmet, İstanbul 34110, tel: 0212-402 3000*, www.fourseasons.com/

istanbul. One of the most elegant hotels in İstanbul is also one of the most unusual – it occupies a former prison. The 65 rooms and suites, beautifully appointed with kilims and handsome furniture and equipped with lovely baths, face the former prison yard or look out on the Sea of Marmara. Restaurant with a glass-enclosed courtyard, spa and health club.

Empress Zoë $$$ *Akbıyık Cad. 4/1, Sultanahmet, 34122 İstanbul, tel: 0212-518 4360/2504*, www.emzoe.com. The charms of the textiles-filled interior and of the American owner, Ann Nevans, make this small hotel a favourite with return visitors. All rooms, reached by a narrow spiral staircase, are comfortable, but best is the penthouse, with its large terrace and stunning views. 22 rooms and three suites, distributed over four Turkish style townhouses.

Pera Palace Hotel Jumeirah $$$$ *Meşrutiyet Cad. 52, Tepebaşi, 80050 İstanbul, tel: 0212-377 4000*, www.jumeirah.com. Istanbul's oldest hotel was built in 1892 to billet arriving Orient Express passengers, and the decor and graciousness of those days still prevail. Offers four-star standards (including spa and gym). Room 101 is a museum dedicated to Turkish leader Ataturk.

Sarı Konak $$$$ *Mimar Mehmet Ağa Cad. 42–46, Sultanahmet, İstanbul 34122, tel: 0212-638 6258*, www.istanbulhotelsarikonak.com. Ottoman-restoration hotels seem to be opening all the time in Sultanahmet, but this establishment run by two brothers remains one of the best. The 19 rooms and suites are simply but stylishly furnished, and many look over the Sea of Marmara. The finest views, though, are from the rooftop terrace, where snacks and drinks are served; breakfast is given in an old courtyard.

Sumahan on the Water $$$$ *Kuleli Cad. 51, Çengelköy, İstanbul 34684, tel: 0216-422 8000*, www.sumahan.com. A former *rakı* factory on the Asian shore of the Bosphorus magnificently converted into a small designer hotel with some of the finest views in the world, fabulously chic decor, a fitness centre, spa and hamam on site, plus one of the city's best seafood restaurants. A private boat links the hotel with the European shore. 24 rooms and suites.

Yeşil Ev $$$ *Kabasakal Cad. 5, Sultanahmet, İstanbul 34122, tel: 0212-517 6785*, www.yesilev.com.tr. Rebuilt former mansion on a quiet street near the sights of the old city. The 18 units vary in size, so ask for one of the larger ones; all are decorated with old bedsteads and other unique furnishings. Most face a leafy rear garden; the one suite has TV, other can watch the one in a lounge.

PRINCES ISLANDS

Splendid Palas $$$$ *23 Nisan Cad. 53, Büryükada 81330, tel: 0216-382 6950*, www.splendidhotel.net. For an atmospheric retreat from İstanbul, look no further than this wooden, 19th-century inn set in lovely poolside gardens on the largest island of the archipelago. Guest rooms are very large, and what they lack in modern amenities, they make up for with lovely old furnishings and plenty of Victorian-resort atmosphere. 70 rooms and four suites.

EDIRNE

Taşodalar $$$ *Hamam Sok. 3, behind Selimiye Camii, 22800 Edirne, tel: 0284-212 3529*, www.tasodalar.com. The town's quietest boutique hotel, this stone-built 15th-century structure is ideal for families and drivers with its private, secure car-park. Twelve rooms sport dark-wood floors and trim, though other decor mixes genuine antiques with kitsch; upstairs units have mosque views.

SEA OF MARMARA AND AEGEAN COAST

ASSOS (BEHRAMKALE)

Biber Evi $$$ *Behramkale square, tel: 0286-721 7410*, www.biberevi.com. Peppers (*biberler*) are the theme in this eco-friendly hotel – over 100 varieties in the garden, and pepper-portraying tiles in the 6 units. Ceilings and cabinetry are carved from salvaged Black Sea wood; the fireplace-lounge-bar is the big winter hit, though the upper terrace is the pièce de resistance. Host Lütfi is a font of local lore. Single night bookings are not accepted for ecological reasons.

BODRUM AND ENVIRONS

Karia Princess $$$$ *Myndos Cad 8, Eskiçeşme Mahallesi, Bodrum 48400, tel: 0252-316 8971,* www.kariaprincess.com. Probably the best town-centre accommodation. Although within walking distance of the busy waterfront, it feels quiet and secluded. A classy place capable of hosting weddings; its Turkish bath is one of the best you'll see along the Aegean coast. Open all year, but book well in advance.

El Vino $$$$ *Pamili Sok. Omurça Mah, Bodrum 48000, tel: 0252-313 8770,* www.elvinobodrum.com. Overlooking the Bodrum Castle, this hotel offers rooms and suites with all the modern amenities along with a delightful tropical garden. From the rooftop restaurant you can watch the sun set over the city. The breakfasts are exquisite.

BURSA

Çelik Palas $$$$$ *Çekirge Cad. 79, Bursa 16070, tel: 0224-233 3800,* www.celikpalas.com. Built in the 1930s on the express orders of Atatürk, this five-star hotel has since undergone a major refurbishment and can now claim to be the best accommodation in Bursa's baths district. Its hamam is one of the most sumptuous in Turkey; there's also a huge, dedicated conference centre. 141 rooms, including 21 suites.

ÇANAKKALE

Kervansaray $$$ *Fetvane Sok 13,* Çanakkale Merkez, *tel: 0286-217 8192,* www.canakkalekervansarayhotel.com. Justifiably popular hotel installed in a 1903-vintage judge's mansion and a rear annexe. Best of the mansion rooms with their mock Belle-Époque furnishings are nos 206 and 207, overlooking the garden with its single free-standing suite. Less distinguished are the annexe rooms, upstairs from the breakfast area serving above-average starts to the day.

ÇEŞME

Taş Otel $$$$ *Kemalpaşa Cad. 132, Alaçatı, tel: 0232-716 7772,* www.tasotel.com. This former Greek village near Çeşme must now have at least a dozen restoration inns of boutique calibre; Taş, installed in an 1890s-built mansion, was the first and still about the best. Breakfast is served on a terrace overlooking the lawn-set pool; just 9 rooms, so bookings – especially at weekends – are mandatory. Open all year.

İZMIR

Beyond $$$–$$$$ *1376 Sokak 5,* Kızılay Caddesi Alsancak, *İzmir, tel: 0232-463 0585*, www.hotelbeyond.com. One of a crop of boutique hotels opening in İzmir, this trendy place, right in the city centre near the seafront, makes slightly disconcerting use of six different colour palettes in the rooms (all in the name of Chakra therapy), but is stylish, comfortable and has plentiful amenities for business travellers, including a good restaurant. 60 rooms and suites.

KUŞADASI

Club Caravanserail $$ *Atatürk Bulv. 2, Kuşadası 09400, tel: 0256-614 4115*. An atmospheric inn lodged in a kervansaray dating from 1618. The courtyard shelters a lovely garden and 26 rooms (plus 1 suite) sport polished wood floors, fireplaces, kilims and other textiles. Can be noisy when tacky 'Turkish Nights' staged in the courtyard, but still good value. Open Mar–Nov.

Kismet $$$ *Gazi Beğendi Bulv. 1, Turkmen Mah., Kuşadası 09400, tel: 0256-618 1290*, www.kismet.com.tr. Originally built in 1966 by Princess Hümeyra Özbaş (1917–2000), a grand-daughter of the last sultan, this venerable self-contained resort set on its own peninsula is still run by her descendants. Because of the Ottoman dynastic connection, royalty and leadership of many states, and various domestic celebrities, have stopped in, but it's not hopelessly snooty; the 108 rooms and suites are airy and unpretentious, plus there's a large pool. Open all year.

PAMUKKALE

Colossae Thermal $$$ *Karahayıt, Denizli, tel: 0258-271 4156*, www.colossaehotel.com. The village on the plateau behind Pamukkale has been completely overtaken by large resort hotels, all with spas, taking advantage of the hot springs. This is one of the best, with two pools, several restaurants and a full health and fitness centre. 231 rooms, including 21 suites.

SELÇUK

Kalehan $$ *North end of main through road (Highway 550),* Atatürk Cad. *57, Selçuk 35920, tel: 0232-892 6154*, www.kalehan.com. Highest-standard hotel in Selçuk, with antique and mock-Ottoman decor wedded to 58 modern units, and a competent restaurant for sustenance after a day at the ruins. Extensive garden and pool, with views up to the castle just behind. Easy parking, but set back enough from the highway to minimize noise. Open all year.

MEDITERRANEAN COAST

ANTALYA

Mediterra Art $$ *Zafer Sok. 5, Kaleiçi, Antalya, tel: 0242-244 8624*, www.mediterraarthotel.com. Three carefully restored Ottoman houses within the walls of old Kaleiçi comprise this boutique hotel furnished with gleaming wood, exposed stone pointing and rugs. Courtyard pool, indoor and outdoor restaurants and bar. 28 rooms and suites.

Özmen Pansiyon $ *Zeytin Çıkmazı 5, Kaleiçi, tel: 0242-241 6505*, www.ozmenpension.com. Cheap and cheerful yet well-managed *pansiyon* with a great roof terrace right in the heart of the old town. Open all year; competitively priced airport transfers available. 25 rooms.

DALYAN

Dalyan Resort $$$–$$$$ *Sok. 12, Maraş Mah. 114, Dalyan 48840, tel: 0252-284 5499*, www.dalyanresort.com. Self-contained riverside complex that's the town's most comfortable digs, with four grades of tasteful, travertine-tiled units, an airy domed restaurant, rental canoes and a hamam with mud therapy offered. It's popular with package operators, and claims to be open all year.

KALKAN

Lizo Hotel $ *Milli Egemenlik Caddesi, Kalamar Yolu, Pk 110 Kalkan, tel: 0242-844 3381*, http://lizohotel.com. Small, family-run hotel at the back of the town, with restaurant, bar, garden and pool. Great views, friendly service and excellent food make this a firm favourite, in spite of the steep walk back after dinner or the beach.

KAŞ

Gardenia Otel $$$ *Hükümet Cad. 47, Küçükçakıl, Kaş 07580, tel: 0242-836 1691*, www.gardeniahotel-kas.com. The most ambitious boutique hotel in Kaş has just 11 varied rooms and suites distributed over four floors, their modern decor and marble floors juxtaposed with somewhat garish art in the common areas. Open May–Oct. The proprietors speak perfect American English. Buffet breakfast until 11am; no children under 12.

Hideway Hotel $$ Anfitiyatro Sokak, No 7, *07580 Kas, tel: 0242-836 1887*, www.hotelhideaway.com. This is the most attractive mid-range option in town, with especially airy third-floor rooms and a pricier luxe jacuzzi suite. Communal areas include a small plunge pool, a TV-lounge-cum-library, and a stunning rooftop restaurant with home-style cooking. Very outgoing, multilingual Belgian-Turkish hosts; credit cards accepted. Open all year.

PATARA (GELEMIŞ)

Patara Viewpoint $ *Top of east ridge road, Gelemiş, tel: 0242-843 5184/52570347*, www.pataraviewpoint.com. Long-established hotel in an unbeatable setting, American-style wall showers in the bathrooms, a pool-bar where breakfast is served, and a cushioned, Turkish-style night-time terrace with fireplace. Advantageous weekly rates; credit cards accepted. Open Apr–Sept.

SIDE

Beach House $ *Barbaros Caddesi, tel: 0242-753 1607*, www.beachhouse-hotel.com. Small, friendly hotel with 20 airy balconied rooms overlooking Side's eastern beach. The resort's first (1965) lodgings, it has plenty of character but is also very well run by an Australian-Turkish couple; there's an affiliated restaurant run by their son.

CAPPADOCIA AND CENTRAL ANATOLIA

ANKARA

Angora House Hotel $$ *Kalekapısı Sok. 16, Ankara 06240, tel: 0312-309 8380*, www.angorahouse.com.tr. One of the very few small boutique hotels in this business-orientated city, this charmingly restored Ottoman house within the citadel has just six unique rooms with carved-wood ceilings, quality bedding, antiques and rugs. Within walking distance of most attractions; helpful English-speaking proprietor.

GÖREME

Kelebek $$–$$$ *Yavuz Sok. 1, Aydınlı Mah., Göreme 50180, tel: 0384-271 2531*, www.kelebekhotel.com. Magnificent views, a small outdoor pool, a cute hamam and a range of impeccable rooms to suit all budgets make this spot a winner. Some of the 31 rooms are cut out of fairy chimneys or installed in old caves; others are in the original stone-built house.

GÜZELYURT (GELVERİ)

Karballa $$ *Güzelyurt 68500, tel: 0382-451 2103*, www.karballahotel.com. This beautiful, large village just east of the Ihlara Valley is much less frequented than those in Cappadocia proper. At its centre stands this 19th-century monastery, now converted to a comfortable hotel. Most of the 20 rooms occupy the vaulted monks' cells and are galleried, with a sitting area on one level and a sleeping loft above.

Good meals are served in the former refectory, and a swimming pool occupies one end of the tree-shaded gardens.

ÜÇHİSAR

Les Maisons de Cappadoce $$$–$$$$ *Belediye Meyd. 6, Üçhisar 50240; tel: 0384-219 2813*, www.cappadoce.com. These 16 carefully restored village houses, sleeping two to six, form a luxurious retreat ideal for families and small groups. They are equipped with kitchens, tastefully furnished and set in beautiful gardens; a gardener tends to your private patch of greenery and the management stocks your fridge before you arrive.

ÜRGÜP

Esbelli Evi $$$ *Dolay Sok. 8, Ürgüp 50400, tel: 0384-341 3395*, www.esbelli.com.tr. The cave-hotel that kick-started the restoration and conversion movement in Cappdocia is still among the very best, with ten enormous suites, a vaulted, Ottoman-style lounge perfect for having a drink with new friends, and an array of pretty gardens or courtyards. Owner Suha Ersoz prides himself on offering a home-from-home service to guests.

Serinn House $$$ *Esbelli Sok. 36 Ürgüp, tel: 0384-341 6076*, www.serinnhouse.com. Run with immense charm by well-travelled Eren Serpen and designed ultra-stylishly by Turkish architect Riftat Ergör, this tiny cave-hotel (with only five rooms) brings İstanbul chic to Cappadocia. The terrace views are superb, the minimalist furnishings surprisingly compatible with troglodytic contours, and the breakfasts excellent.

EASTERN TURKEY

ANTAKYA

Savon Hotel $$ *Kurtuluş Cad. 192, tel: 0326-214 6355*, www.savonhotel.com.tr. Boutiqe hotel in a former Ottoman soap and olive-oil factory dating back to 1860. The stone-built building offers an original architectural background to eclectic (for which read plush) decoration for the 40 rooms and three suites arrayed around a courtyard; a vaulted restaurant serves Turkish and Italian food, plus there's a fireplace bar.

GAZİANTEP

Anadolu Evleri $$ *Koroğlu Sok. 6,* Şekeroğlu Mah., *Nemrut Dağı, tel: 0342-220 9525,* www.anadoluevleri.com. Perhaps the most tastefully restored and converted of Gaziantep's old-house boutique hotels, with its 10 high-ceilinged rooms and three suites grouped around a courtyard with adjoining bar. Walking distance to the castle and museum.

NEMRUT DAĞI

Kervansaray Nemrut $$ *Karadut Köyü, Nemrut Dağı, tel: 0416-737 2190,* www.nemrutkervansaray.com. A proper hotel on the slopes of the mountain, 8km (5 miles) from the summit in the area's highest (1,245-metre/4084ft) village, this is the best place to spend the night if you want to see the sunrise from the mountain top. Rooms and restaurant are simple but adequate, there's a swimming pool and camping is allowed.

ŞANLIURFA

Cevahir Konak Evi $$$ Büyükyol Cad. *Selahattin Eyyubi Camii Karşısı, Vali Fuat Bey Caddesi, Urfa, tel: 0414-215 9377,* www.cevahirkonukevi.com. This courtyarded stone building has been converted into the city's top boutique hotel with exemplary taste (but also proper bathrooms with stall showers). Walking distance to all attractions; during summer there are *sira geceleri* (banquets with musical accompaniment) Wednesday, Friday and Saturday on the premises.

INDEX

Berlitz pocket guide

Turkey

Sixth Edition 2015

Written by Stephen Brewer
Updated by Maciej Zglinicki
Update Production: AM Services
Edited by Rachel Lawrence
Cartography updated by Carte
Picture Editor: Tom Smyth
Production: Rebeka Davies and Aga Bylica

Printed in China by CTPS

Photography credits: 123RF 32; akg images 19, 20; Dreamstime 58, 115; Frank Noon/Apa Publications 2MC, 3M, 4ML, 4ML, 4MR, 4TL, 4/5M, 5MC, 4/5T, 6ML, 6ML, 7MC, 7TC, 8, 11, 13, 16, 61, 63, 64, 66, 67, 69, 71, 75, 76, 78, 82, 84, 87, 89, 90, 94, 96, 97, 99, 100, 102, 103, 105, 107, 108, 109, 112, 121, 123, 124, 137, 142, 145, 146; Getty Images 6TL, 15, 26, 95; iStock 1, 2TL, 2ML, 3T, 3TC, 3M, 3M, 5TC, 24, 31, 37, 40, 56, 73, 79, 80, 85, 93, 111, 113, 114, 116, 117; Rebecca Erol/ Apa Publications 2TC, 3M, 4TL, 7MC, 18, 29, 35, 38, 39, 42, 43, 45, 47, 49, 50, 53, 54, 119, 126, 129, 130, 133, 134, 139, 143, 144; Turkish Tourism 22

Cover picture: Corbis

Contact us

At Berlitz we strive to keep our guides as accurate and up to date as possible, but if you find anything that has changed, or if you have any suggestions on ways to improve this guide, then we would be delighted to hear from you.

Berlitz Publishing, PO Box 7910,
London SE1 1WE, England.
email: berlitz@apaguide.co.uk
www.insightguides.com/berlitz

never have been changed. It was the best
which ever represented England in my time
To refresh your memory - here it is -
Maclaren - Ranji - Fry - Tyldesley -
Lilley - Hirst - Rhodes - Lockwood -
Braund - Jackson + Hayward -
Best of fortune to you Bill. may you
reach your Century

Yours ever
Jessop

THE CROUCHER

Other cricket books by Gerald Brodribb

The English Game
Cricket in Fiction
All Round the Wicket
Next Man In
A Book of Cricket Verse (anthology)
A Yankee Looks at Cricket
Hit for Six
Felix on the Bat
Maurice Tate
The Art of Nicholas Felix

Photograph by R. W. Thomas, 41, Cheapside, London, E.C.

Copyright. Hudson & Kearns

Gilbert L. Jessop

GERALD BRODRIBB

THE CROUCHER

A BIOGRAPHY OF GILBERT JESSOP

No man has ever driven a cricket ball so hard, so high, and so often in so many different directions. No man has ever made cricket so dramatic an entertainment.

C.B. FRY

CONSTABLE
LONDON

Published in Great Britain 1985
by Constable and Company Limited
10 Orange Street London WC2H 7EG
First published 1974 by London Magazine Editions

Printed in Great Britain by
St Edmundsbury Press
Bury St Edmunds, Suffolk

British Library CIP data

Brodribb, Gerald
The croucher: a biography of Gilbert Jessop
1. Cricket players—England—Biography
I. Title
796.35'8'0924 GV915.J4
ISBN 0 09 466360 2

To Jessica
and Mike

Contents

Foreword

IT was most pleasing to find that the publication of *The Croucher* in 1974 produced a great number of letters from that diminishing number of spectators who were fortunate enough to see Jessop in action: several had witnessed his historic innings at the Oval in 1902, and one, the late Arthur Gilligan recalled the almost frightening ovation Jessop received on reaching his century, with straw hats rocketing into the air all round the ground.

C.B. Fry described that innings as 'the greatest innings in cricket', and in *The Cricketer* in November 1973 a statistician assessed several historic test innings on the basis of a six-fold formula, and the Jessop innings came out top of the list. Several of my correspondents recalled the overpowering silence when Jessop went out to bat. No batsman has ever aroused such expectations, and then, off the very first delivery, a swish of the bat, and the ball sailed over the ropes amid an explosion of joy. Jessop never needed to play himself in: imagine his performance in modern one-day cricket. For most of his career six runs were awarded only for a hit right out of the ground, so we shall never know how many 'sixes' Jessop hit, but there is every reason to believe that no one has ever hit the ball more frequently over the boundary line, surpassing even the feats of Wellard in the 1930s.

I was glad to be able to persuade the owners to put a plaque on Jessop's birthplace in Cheltenham, and the building is now known as Jessop House, Cambray Place. In Stevenage a road has been named after Jessop, and at the county ground at Bristol there is The Jessop Tavern. I have also recently discovered that in 1966 a Gilbert Jessop Society was founded by two members of the Faculty of Law at the University of Adelaide: they thought that cricket generally was in the doldrums, and wanted a society that could represent the real spirit of the game. Ted Dexter has recently suggested a society with a similar aim. What about a Jessop Society here in England as tribute to the most exciting batsman of all time?

It was for me a dramatic moment when I showed Dexter a pair of Jessop's home-made batting gloves which he put on with some awe, and I felt that the mantle of one great cricketer had passed down to another magnificent striker of the ball.

GERALD BRODRIBB

Prologue

MY first visit to a county match was almost my last. As I entered the Hastings ground I saw a ball soaring in the air in my direction; it passed overhead, crashed on the Town Hall, and brought down a shower of slates around me. It was the most exciting moment of my nine years' life. All about me everyone was buzzing and laughing, and an old man kept on murmuring happily, 'Just like Jessop, sonny, just like Jessop!'

From that moment onwards I was completely captivated by big cricket. When the hubbub died down and I was sane enough to look at a score-card, I discovered that it was Maurice Tate who had made this roof-wrecking blow, and when I came to know him later, I used to refer to this dramatic moment in my young life. He would grin in the usual Tate way and say, 'What's a ball for if you don't hit it' – he had that simple basic approach to the game – and he would add, 'I'd like to have seen that cove Jessop do things on this ground. There was a hitter for you.'

Every time I went to the Hastings ground and someone sent a ball soaring upwards, I would hear the old men murmur, 'Ah, you should have seen Jessop, boy!' and they would point to the distant windows across the road and say, 'Through that chapel window the ball went time and again, and into those gardens behind the pavilion', and panning the whole area with their sticks, 'and landed a ball on a horse in Queen's road, and through that window of the house on the corner there, and the old woman wouldn't give it back, she wouldn't. Aah! that was Jessop! You should have seen Jessop, boy!'

Well, if that's the way he batted I should indeed have wanted to have seen him, and I came to think of Jessop as the sort of patron saint of the Central Ground. But who was he? When did all this happen? I asked my parents and my mother said: 'I can see him now coming out to bat, a jaunty little man, full of confidence and a round face and a big bat – ready for anything, and the whole crowd came alive with him, and grinned and laughed and prodded each other and said: "Now keep your eyes skinned." It was like a huge joke, but wasn't it sad when he was out! Ask your Uncle Arthur about him.'

Now I had several uncles, two twins who played a lot of good cricket and watched more, and another a schoolmaster A. W. Roberts who had played in the holidays for Gloucestershire, Jessop's county, and under Jessop's captaincy. And so I gradually became a sort of posthumous Jessop fan. I tried to imagine what it must have been like to see him in action, and I ached with regret that I had not been born early enough to be at Hastings in 1907 when he had scored that impossible 191 runs between 2.15 and 3.45. He made at least one century almost every season at the Hastings Festival, and a festival it was, what with the flowers and marquees and the ladies (including my mother), who went chiefly for the purpose of meeting people, and the famous teas served by waitresses with black dresses and silver teapots. To be seen having tea during the festival was the thing to do; the cricket was a minor item, unless of course Jessop landed a ball in the middle of the tea tables, which he sometimes did.

I pored over cricket books and found out all I could about Gilbert Laird Jessop, and by the age of fourteen – when I wrote my first piece for *The Cricketer* – I had a fair knowledge of the facts of Jessop's great innings, but this did not tell me just how he managed to be so successful with such a peculiar style, or why there has never since been any batsmen to equal his fast-scoring performances, apart from a few tail-end sloggers, who were not real batsmen at all.

In my travels round the county grounds in search of 'big hits' there was a perpetual mention of the Jessop legend, but those who had actually seen him could do little more than shake their heads, and a happy bemused look came over them as they murmured again, 'Ah, but you should have seen Jessop! He was the one!'

In 1935 a fellow Jessop fan, C. J. Britton, who had been lucky enough to have played with Jessop, produced a little book of Jessop's scores which to a degree fulfilled the wish expressed in *The Old Crocks*, a cricket book published in 1917 in which it was stated that 'A complete volume of Jessop's great performances would make a volume of quite respectable size, and I should think it would be well worth publishing'. But this was a book of facts, and did not really create the man. It might be imagined that Jessop's own book of reminiscences *A Cricketer's Log* (1922) would tell us something about Jessop himself, but though it is full of pleasant information about the great players and doings of his day, it seldom tells us about the man himself, because, unlike some, Jessop was very reluctant to talk about his own achievements. In a letter to Nigel Haig, who once asked Jessop to say 'how he did it', Jessop writes a few lines about his great 191 at Hastings, but just when we would dearly love to hear the full story, he stops and says: 'I apologise for talking about my own past deeds – a fault I seldom indulge in.'

This reluctance is really maddening, and others realised it, for James Thorpe, the artist, who knew Jessop well, once wrote that 'The doings of the man would fill a book, and what a book!' and E. H. D. Sewell, another great Jessop fan, said much the same thing.

In the mid 1940s, when I was working in Dorset, I found that Jessop and his wife were living with their parson son, who was vicar of St George's, Fordington, Dorchester. I wrote and asked whether I might have the privilege of calling on him, and I mentioned my uncle Arthur, who had played with Jessop in the county side. I received a prompt reply saying:

> Dear Mr Brodribb,
>
> I am usually on show any time except between 2.0 and 4.30. Drop in by all means if you care to next time you are in the neighbourhood. Ask Uncle Arthur when you next see him how his old college friend Richards – the umpire – is, and give him – uncle – my kind regards. He was a pretty useful performer for the old county.
>
> Yours sincerely,
>
> GILBERT L. JESSOP

I immediately fixed up a suitable time, went over to Dorchester, rang the bell at the vicarage, and there at the door was the great man. I was so intoxicated by this meeting with the hero that I did not remember as much as I should have, but I can recall his friendliness and the bright grey-blue eyes, full of the humour which his comment about being 'on show' had suggested. He was shortish, and I know I had the feeling of meeting a rather perky robin. We talked about cricket, and when I asked him about *his* big hits he promptly told me all about one made by Warwick Armstrong, which he said was the biggest he had ever seen. (Oddly enough, C. B. Fry had made the same reference to me only a few weeks before.) It was not easy to get Jessop to talk about himself. We had tea and I met Mrs Jessop and the son, the Rev. G. L. O. Jessop. I wish I could recall more, but I was not visiting him as a reporter, and could hardly have taken out a notebook. But I remember well my joy at having met him, and as I drove home it dawned on me that the perpetual comment: 'Ah, but you should have seen Jessop!' had now been fulfilled. I had seen Jessop.

When he died in 1955 his son, knowing my interest in cricket, had honoured me by writing to ask me if there were any lines from my *Book of Cricket Verse* suitable to put on his father's grave, and I subsequently had a long letter from him when he was working in Jamaica; he had come across a copy of my book *Hit for Six* in the village library, and had read the chapter about his father. The letter contained many interesting stories connected with the innings I had written about. It is clear that the son had vivid recollection of what his father had told him, and though he was too young to have seen his father in action in first-class cricket he knew all about his performances.

My interest in Jessop never abated and recently I managed to track down the whereabouts of the Rev. G. L. O. Jessop, now returned to England, and I asked him if he would give his support to my writing the story of his father and his achievements. This help has been most readily given in the way of conversation, and the loan of a number of books of cuttings kept by Jessop himself, and his wife and sister Winnie.

These volumes have been extremely interesting. The difficulty has been to give substance to the facts which tell of his incredible performances with a frequency which becomes almost monotonous. It is not too much to say that almost any one of Jessop's great innings would be the high spot of any other batsman's career. What finally persuaded me to go ahead with the story was the mention of the name Jessop in a recent match between a 'Fathers XI' and a prep. school 1st Eleven. When one twelve-year-old jumped out and drove a ball loftily for four, one of the Fathers – and he was a young father – turned to me and said: 'Bit of a Jessop, this boy.' So the name was still living, the legend still strong, even after a hundred years. I decided then to write this as a tribute for his centenary year. We have waited a long time for a second Jessop, and I am sure that there never will be one.

G. B.

1

'Jessop's Match'

'A most extraordinary little demon.'
A FELLOW ENGLAND PLAYER

THERE it was in the show case. The bat. The bat which had sprayed the field with strokes in one of the most dramatic innings ever played in a Test match. With the game good as lost, it had struck 104 runs in 77 minutes. The wood was now darkened with time, well-seasoned with a few worm holes, a heavy bat with a faded red rubber handle. And the batsman – ever generous – had given it away to a friend – 'Chris Lewis from Jessopus' it said, written by Jessop in large black writing. And now it had found its way to Lord's. A bat made by Crawford – no five star adverts., no fancy stickers, it just said: 'Crawford's Exceller'. 'Exceller' indeed, for this bat had been 'the point of rest, the calm pivotal spot' of what Sir Neville Cardus so aptly called 'Jessop's cyclone of batsmanship'.

Seventy years ago, at the Oval, this bat carved not only the Australian bowling, but also a very special niche in the history of the game. On the opening day of the Fifth Test, Monday August 11 1902, Australia won the toss, and batted first under good conditions, though the wicket was slow after rain. Rain that had interfered with play throughout the series.

In the first match at Edgbaston England had been robbed of victory after scoring 376–9 dec., when Australia replied with an all out score of 36, being totally routed on a wet wicket by Rhodes and Hirst. They followed on and were 8–0 at the close of the second day. Rain fell again that night, and next morning it seemed that the game might have to be abandoned. The afternoon however turned out fine, and because thousands of spectators had been admitted to the ground at 4 o'clock and demanded some play, the game was continued at 5.15 under almost impossible conditions. Australia had scored 46 for 2 at the close of the day, and as Test matches at that time in England were scheduled for only three days, that was the end of the match. The England team in its batting order was: A. C. MacLaren (captain), C. B. Fry, K. S. Ranjitsinhji, F. S. Jackson, J. T. Tyldesley, A. A. Lilley, G. H. Hirst, G. L. Jessop, L. C. Braund, W. H. Lockwood, W. Rhodes, and this team is considered by some to have been the best team England ever put into the field. As the Australian team were also regarded as the best ever to tour England, the whole series aroused great interest.

In the second Test at Lord's the England team remained unchanged, but rain so much interfered with play that after 100 minutes interrupted action on the first day, no further play was possible in the match. In that time England scored 102 for 2 wickets, the two being those of Fry and Ranjitsinhji, both out for nought before England had scored a run.

In the Third Test at Sheffield Ranji and Lockwood were left out; Ranji had strained a leg the day before the match, and Fry, who was not originally chosen, kept his place. Lockwood's place was taken by Barnes, who was sent for at the very last moment by MacLaren. Though Barnes bowled very well in the first innings, later events showed that it had been a great mistake to have omitted Lockwood. The scoring was low, and Australia, 194 and 289, beat England, 145 and 195, by 143 runs. In the last innings England required 339 runs to win and they made a useful start, though the spectators were much surprised to see Jessop come in as one of the opening pair. As he himself says: 'The reason for my taking first knock is that the player first deputed for the job pleaded a certain tiredness, and I snatched the opportunity to suggest that I might take his place. Now Mr MacLaren was always a firm believer in confidence, and believing that my suggestion was not tendered from any conceited motive, acceded to my request. The experiment anyway proved successful, for I was undefeated when stumps were pulled up half an hour before the usual time owing to bad light.' In the fifty minutes possible for play England had scored 73 for the loss of Abel, the score-sheet reading:

G. L. Jessop	not out	53
Abel	c Hill, b Noble	8
Tyldesley	not out	11
	Extras	1
		73–1

So a fair chunk of the runs required had been made, and what is more, thanks to Jessop, England had gone ahead of the clock.

The next morning however Jessop added only 2 more runs before being given out l.b.w. to a ball that hit him on the chest, and the umpire later apologised to him for what he realised had been a bad decision. England collapsed and were all out by lunchtime.

The Fourth Test came three weeks later at Old Trafford, and provided one of the most dramatic finishes in all Test cricket. Ranji came back into the team, and Fry, who was still out of form, was dropped, and so also was Jessop, whose absence in the field alone much weakened the side. Another blunder was the dropping of Hirst for Tate of Sussex, who though he was having a successful season as a bowler, was in no way comparable to Hirst. England lost by three runs, and to quote Jessop himself:

'No English team can ever have been picked with less regard for its fielding capabilities than this one, in which Australia just scrambled home by the narrow margin of three runs. Just three runs – and if there was one run stolen by such cute judges of runs as Australia has always bred, there must have been in their two innings as many as twenty. Since there were in all three fieldsmen on the side, Lockwood, Tate and Abel, who had not thrown a cricket-ball fifty yards for quite a number of years, it was no great marvel that Australia contrived to help herself freely in this direction.'

When the ninth wicket fell in England's second innings eight runs were wanted for victory. Poor Tate, who had already dropped a vital catch in a position he was quite unused to, came in number eleven to join Rhodes. Rain held up his arrival at the wicket, and when after an agonised wait play was resumed, Tate hit a four, but was bowled a ball or two later, to give Australia the victory. Though Tate's name is always most unfairly remembered in connection with England's defeat, the real reason lay in England's failure to save runs in the field.

After this defeat the selectors, whose blunders had been severely criticised, made several changes for the fifth Test at the Oval. Hirst and Jessop were very properly recalled, and Hayward, the local man, replaced Ranji, who was out of touch. The Australians kept to the same team that had won at Sheffield and Old Trafford. Jessop tells us that his own invitation was worded 'in somewhat rummy fashion'. Here is the letter he received from Lord Hawke, chairman of the selection committee.

Tuesday, August 5th

Dear Jessop,

Selection committee will be pleased if you will play at the Oval next Monday. They however wish me to tell you that Archie MacLaren has guaranteed that you will bowl for at least half to three-quarters of an hour at a stretch, and they sincerely hope that this is correct as it materially affects the bowling strength of the side. Richardson has given me a very nasty right thumb and I can't play this week.

Kindly reply to 107 Jermyn St.

Yours sincerely,

Hawke

Jessop promptly informed the selectors that if this stipulation really mattered, they had better choose someone else, since his fast bowling days were virtually over. They informed him that the condition was not important, but it makes the mind reel to think what might have been lost to history if they had insisted, and allowed Jessop to withdraw. In his book *A Cricketer's Log* Jessop states his pleasure at thus being enabled to take part in what proved to be such a truly wonderful game, though being the modest man he was, he tells us very little of the vital part he played in it.

I have mentioned that on the opening day Australia won the toss and batted first. At the start there was a crowd of about 12,000 which later doubled – 'A more orderly assemblage it would be difficult to imagine.' It did not rain, but the wind was cold – 'it was an autumnal rather than an August afternoon' – a remark that really might have applied to the whole season. Australia lost the first five wickets for only 126 runs, but the tail wagged and by the close of play Australia had reached a total of 324 all out. H. Trumble, who was to bowl unchanged in both innings, was top scorer with 64*. George Hirst's bowling of 5–77 makes one wonder how he also ever got left out of the previous Test. Lockwood and Rhodes had opened the bowling, as though today the England attack was to open with Snow at one end, and a much slower version of Underwood at the other. Braund (leg-breaks) and F. S. Jackson (Maurice Tate type) gave further support, and Jessop did bowl – six economical overs for 11 runs, so the selectors' odd stipulation was satisfied. England bowled their 124 overs in the six hours of play, so the spectators were not robbed of playing time.

With one side batting the whole of the first day in a three-day match England had to do something remarkable to have any chance of winning the game, and this was not to save the 'rubber', for that was already lost, and certainly not to win or hold the 'Ashes', for at that time no one bothered much about what had began as a rather feeble newspaper joke. England went in on the Tuesday simply to try to win a cricket match. Conditions were made difficult for them because heavy rain had fallen in the early morning, which made a great difference to run-getting, and after only a few overs, play was suspended for 40 minutes owing to bad light. None of the batsmen really got going. A. C. MacLaren found the wicket so awkward that he took 50 minutes over 10 runs, and Hayward stayed in 20 minutes without scoring a run. Trumble, bowling medium pace vicious off-breaks, and Saunders, a left-handed 'trundler' with an action which Jessop says he always suspected, bowled on and on, and when the sixth wicket went down at 83 it looked as if England would have no chance of saving the follow-on. The sun was at last beginning to break through, and if England were forced to follow on, any possibility of saving the match was virtually nil. After lunch Braund defended doggedly for 22 until he was out at 137–7, England being still 187 behind. But Hirst once again played his part and made a forceful 43 runs in only 45 minutes. Lockwood immediately had a go at the bowling, and was soon missed in the deep by Clem Hill whose 'sinful' catch had done much to win the fourth Test for Australia. So England survived, and eventually reached a score of 183. At the moment that the follow-on was saved Jessop felt 'as thankful as if the match had been already won'. Hugh Trumble had bowled unchanged for 31 overs and had taken 8 wickets for 65 runs. Among his victims was Jessop, bowled for 13 (scored in 8 minutes). Trumble was one of the great Australian bowlers, a sort of faster and even taller Lance Gibbs. He knew Jessop well and used to delight in teasing him when batting, for Trumble would call out 'Come on, two, it's only Jessop!', though knowing what Jessop's fielding was like, he really had no intention of trying for a run.

At 3.45 the Australians went in again with an encouraging lead of 141 runs, and victory might well have seemed to them to be a certainty, especially when in the very first over Duff was missed at mid-off by – of all people – George Hirst. He tried to take the ball too close to his face, and let it drop, to his obvious chagrin. The unlucky bowler was Rhodes, who had opened with Lockwood. With the score at 6, however, Victor Trumper played a ball from Lockwood to the offside and started to run; Duff, seeing that the ball went to Jessop, refused the call, and sent him back. Trumper turned but slipped in the middle of the pitch, and Jessop whipped the ball back to Lilley who removed the bails with Trumper still sitting on the ground. Perhaps this was lucky for England, but it was Jessop's reputation that had led to Duff's refusal, and it was just the kind of run out that MacLaren always hoped for when Jessop was about, for the Australians tended to underestimate his ability both as batsman and fielder. Jessop in his book merely states that 'Trumper was run out attempting a risky run' with no mention of himself.

This dismissal of Trumper was a critical moment in the game, and MacLaren later wrote that he regarded it as the chief cause of England's totally unexpected victory. Jessop was the Constantine, Bland or Clive Lloyd of his day, and even if he had never scored a run his place among the great cricketers would have been assured.

Trumper's dismissal was a shock that shook the Australians, and in spite of their big lead they were unable to force the pace, and runs were hard to get. Lockwood, Rhodes, and Braund bowled so well that at the close of play Australia had lost 8 second innings wickets for only 114 runs. Clem Hill (34) was out to a wonderful catch in the slips by MacLaren, and Tyldesley made a spectacular catch in the deep to get rid of Saunders.

The crowds who at lunch had felt that the match might well be finished that same day, left the ground feeling satisfied that England had fought themselves back into the game, though the odds were still much against them, for Australia were 255 runs on with two wickets still left. Even if the wicket dried out well the next day, it would still be far from easy. If any more rain fell, there would be no hope at all, for Trumble and Saunders would merely repeat their success of the morning.

In 1902 there were no detailed weather forecasts to pin your hopes and fears to. At supper time the sky was cloudless and the spirits of those who felt England were doomed began to rise slightly. Australia 255 for 8 – say, 270 to win. There might be just a chance still. MacLaren, Palairet, Tyldesley, Hayward, Jackson, Braund, Hirst, Lockwood, Lilley and Rhodes – someone might come off, and then course Jessop might make a dashing 50 or so. There *might* be a chance, if the weather held. Surely the rain could not go on wrecking England's chances yet again.

But as darkness fell, the rain blew up again from the west. Jessop was dining at the Great Central Hotel with some of his team mates, and felt that only chloroform could have dammed the sound of the falling torrents, but when the rain did ease up he tried to cheer every one up by offering to take a 10–1 bet against anyone reaching a score of 50 next day, and he took the joke further with a 20–1 offer against anyone reaching the impossible three figures. The sum at stake would scarcely have paid for a 'pot of paint', but the others took this money-for-nothing offer and felt better. Jessop, who regarded betting at cricket as anathema, says he made this absurd offer simply for the purpose of cheering everyone up, especially himself.

Wednesday, August 13, broke fine, but the ground was wet from the rain of the previous evening, and heavy dew prevented any hope of quick drying. Australia's last two wickets added seven more runs, and this meant that England needed 263 runs to win. It was clear that the pitch was totally unfavourable to batting – the sort of conditions when a score of under three figures seemed quite likely. England went in at 11.35, and after twenty minutes such a score looked almost a certainty. MacLaren, Tyldesley and Palairet were all out for only ten runs; all clean bowled by Saunders, who was making the ball flip across with his flicky wrist. The ball which beat Palairet went on to hit Kelly the wicket-keeper between the eyes and put him out of action for a few minutes. But Jackson looked confident enough when he joined Hayward, who did not, and Hayward was lucky to survive a chance at short-leg off Trumble's bowling. The score was raised to 28, when a shower fell and stopped play for 35 minutes. The weather, it seemed, was quite determined that England should make no recovery, and in the first over after resuming play Hayward was caught at the wicket; another success to Saunders, and the score now 31 for four.

Two hundred and sixty-three now seemed a ridiculous target, though Jackson was batting on in his usual cool way when Braund joined him, and they added another 17 runs before Braund was rather unluckily caught at the wicket off Trumble. The ball went high up through Kelly's gloves, but he managed to grasp it to his body as it fell. So half the side were gone for 48. The batsmen had been defeated by the sheer excellence of the bowlers, who were making the most of a brute of a wicket, and Jackson alone seemed to cope with its problems. 'He seemed to have an uncanny prescience as to which ball to play at and which to leave alone,' says Jessop who now came in to join him. I am told that as he came through the pavilion Archie MacLaren said to him, 'I bet you don't make a century!' To which Jessop's prompt reply was: 'Done'. This may perhaps have had some reference to the bet of the night before, and MacLaren was simply reminding him, but it is the odd overheard remark which any spectator would remember for ever.

As he made his way to the wicket every spectator was on his toes with expectation, longing to see the usual fireworks, but at the same time hoping he would be careful, and not throw his wicket away. Though Jessop watched the ball as closely as any of the greatest run getters, some of his strokes were a calculated risk, and the slightest error in timing could turn a glorious drive into a reckless-looking mishit. If the spectators imagined that the critical position of the game would cause Jessop to play carefully, even play himself in, they were mistaken. He took a single off the first ball and scored off the next five. Seven runs then came off the deadly Saunders in an over, and then Trumble was driven high to the pavilion awning. And the next ball went to the rails. The spectators were torn between a wish to have more and more such hits, and a feeling that this simply could not last. As it happened, Jessop was in fact being more careful than usual. He was determined not to lash out across the line of Trumble's off-breaks, for he remembered that too often he had been got out by the cunning Australian off a 'cowshot' – a new term closely associated with Jessop.

So Jessop turned his attention to Saunders instead, and drove him for four, but with his score at 22 he dashed down the wicket, and missed the ball. It kept low and Kelly missed it too. Quite undaunted by this escape, Jessop hit the next ball for four over the head of Armstrong at coverpoint, and two runs later he lashed out again and nearly got caught by Trumper at long-off. The hit was a skimmer, and swerved away from Trumper as he came in full tilt at it. Few fielders would have even got near it, but because Trumper got a hand to it, it is deemed to be a chance. Jessop watched with a dreadful sinking sensation but he survived, and at lunch the score was 87 for 5 wickets, Jackson not out 39, and Jessop not out 29, his runs being scored out of the 39 put on with Jackson, who had continued to bat superbly. What he thought of Jessop's tactics we do not know, but it makes no odds. Jackson played his way, and Jessop played like Jessop.

As the players made their way into the pavilion for lunch, the spectators thought about some refreshment and did some calculations. What *was* the position now? – 263 less 87 made 176 runs to win. Five good men had gone, but Jackson was still there. 'There is no batsman in the world whose nerve is so surely to be relied on', was a contemporary comment. But what of Jessop? Even though he so often made the impossible seem possible, he did not look like surviving with such reckless attack on such a difficult wicket. This was after all, a match against the might of Australia, and not a carefree county match. Still there was just an outside chance, and even the most pessimistic began to acknowledge it. The pavilion bell rang, and people hustled back to their seats.

There was, however, one place which remained empty when play began again. A bank clerk had dashed across from the City in his lunch-hour and saw the start of the Jackson–Jessop stand. It was P. G. Wodehouse, and he tells how formidable Trumble's bowling seemed, virtually unplayable. But the batsmen and Wodehouse stayed until the interval, and then poor Wodehouse had to hurry back to the bank, without even having a sandwich.

But the other luckier spectators now numbering 18,000 settled down to face the critical session. 'All over by tea,' said Australian supporters, and some New South Wales Lancers over for the Coronation made it very clear what they felt: their comments about Jessop were distinctly unflattering.

So the sun came out, and so did Jessop, with his big cap covering those bright grey-blue eyes, a sturdy, shortish, deep-chested man with long arms, and a jaunty and determined look.

It was soon clear that the wicket after lunch was firmer and easier, though the outfield was still very sodden, and the bowlers could turn the ball. Jessop started off with a late cut for four, then came four byes, and the 100 was up after only 80 minutes, very fast going considering the terrible start to the innings. Jessop seemed less hectic than before lunch, and was still determined not to be tempted by Trumble. On the other hand Jackson, who had looked so steady before lunch, now seemed less certain, and might have been caught in the slips. Kelly touched a snick, which went towards Trumble's left hand, but he could not hold it. Jessop went on hitting – to quote H. S. Altham, 'He "found" the ball at once and went ahead at a firm pace' – and with a clever stroke off Trumble sent the ball away through the slips to the distant corner of the Vauxhall end. Amid a storm of cheering, five scampered runs were taken, though Jackson seemed not too pleased at such speed. Another single and Jessop had reached his 50 out of 70 in only 43 minutes. So he had won his bet of the night before, and gained the first half of what he called 'his pot of paint'. Amid the applause came the murmured comment: 'If only he had been at Manchester.'

Though still watchful of Trumble, Jessop decided to attack Saunders. To quote C. B. Fry: 'Jessop then let himself loose like a catapult at the bowling, and shattered it to smithereens.' He immediately pulled Saunders for four and then later cut him for another boundary. Jackson, who had played so dominantly in the morning, was now struggling; he was beaten by a beautiful ball from Trumble, and then badly missed in the slips by Armstrong. Saunders had lost his length completely, and Jessop punished him for 17 runs in an over. He hit the first ball to square leg for four, going down on one knee to do so, put the second round to leg for four, the third ball – a full toss – was hit to the boundary at square-leg, and the fourth – a half-volley – was dealt with in the same way; off the fifth ball Jessop took a single to the off.

At long last, with the score at 145, the first bowling change was made and Saunders was taken off. His analysis, which at one time was 4 wickets for 9 runs, was now 4 for 75. In his place Warwick Armstrong was put on, bowling his awkward leg-breaks from the Vauxhall end. He put five men to leg on the edge of the ring, but Jessop stepped back and cut him for four to the open off-side, and then hit him through the leg-side cordon for four. One spectator recalls the panic among the Australian fielders as they dithered about from place to place trying vainly to stop Jessop's hits. As Jessop said later: 'This happened to be one of those lucky days when I could do nothing wrong.'

At 157, however, the Australians manged to remove Jackson who returned the ball to one of Trumble's capacious hands, the biggest hands ever seen in Test cricket. He had made 49 and had most unselfishly played second fiddle to Jessop when he saw that Jessop was in such form. Jackson himself recalls this innings: 'I was 31 when we adjourned for lunch, and Jessopus was going like a steam engine, hitting Trumble and the others all over the place. I was dying to have a go at the bowling, but I had to strangle my natural game while old Jessopus got the runs. Hughie, an artist of a bowler, if there ever was one, kept pitching them shorter and shorter, and I kept pushing them straight back. He finally trapped me – I pushed one back straight and rather low and that long lean hand shot out and just grabbed it. I think he caught and bowled me a dozen times.'

While Jessop was 'going like a steam engine' some of the spectators were beginning to feel the strain. I am told how one of them just could not bear to look. He sat with his hands over his face, murmuring 'I can't bear to look any more; and then as the next roar broke out, he would clutch his neighbour, and ask desperately: 'Is he out?' but it was just another boundary.

The Jackson–Jessop stand had taken the score from 48 for 5 to 157 for 6 in only 67 minutes. George Hirst, who had already batted and bowled so well, now came in to join Jessop, and he promptly survived a confident lbw appeal which brought Jessop acute anxiety. 'It seemed hours', he said, 'before the umpire gave his decision in favour of the batsman.' E. M. Dowson writing to Jessop twenty years later says that he was certain Hirst would be given out, as from where he was sitting in the top of the pavilion, it seemed to be the plumbest of plumb lbws. Jessop immediately launched an attack on Trumble but was still determined not to hit him to leg across the line. He straight drove him twice high into the pavilion galleries, H. K. Foster catching one of these hits as he sat at the top of the pavilion.

This last stroke, for which Jessop had only four runs, and not six, as the law was then, brought his score to 96, and with a cut for four off Armstrong he reached his century after batting only 75 minutes. This still remains easily the fastest hundred ever made in Anglo-Australian Test cricket. His second fifty had come almost unnoticed, so fast was the scoreboard flipping over. The bowling had been massacred. To quote an eye-witness: 'Hats were thrown in the air, handkerchiefs and mufflers – these were a necessity at cricket matches in 1902 – were waved, cheery voices became hoarse, and weak-chested yellers broke into coughs.' Did Jessop remember his bet? possibly not, but the applause must have broken his concentration, and after one more boundary hit which was not far off Hopkins's reach at square leg, he made the same sweep again, somewhat halfheartedly, and cocked the ball up to Noble behind square-leg:

G. L. Jessop   c Noble, b Armstrong   104

Wisden states: 'All things considered a more astonishing display has never been seen', and C. B. Fry adds: 'I should say that Jessop's 104 must rank as the greatest innings by a pure hitter ever played.' The superlatives of contemporary accounts become almost oppressive. Jessop had made these runs out of 139 in 77 minutes, his hits being a five, 17 fours, 2 threes, 4 twos, and 17 singles. One of the papers with miraculous foresight managed to keep a detailed record of the innings as Jessop played it ball by ball, and this is how it reads:

1 2 4 1 1 . . 4 4 1 . 4 . . . . 1 4 1 . 1 1 1 . 4 1 . . .
1 . 3 . 1 . 3 5 1   4 . . 4 4 4 4 1 . . . . 1 . . . . .
1 2 . . . . . . 4 . . 4 1 . 4 2 . 2 4 4 . 4 . ct.

which shows that excluding the ball from which he was out Jessop received 79 balls, of which he scored off 41, and also had 38 off which he did not score. The burst of scoring after he had passed his 50, and the speed with which he scored his last 29 runs are clearly evident.

Jessop says that the greatest satisfaction he had from this innings was his overcoming of the temptation to hit Trumble to leg with his usual sweeping pull. 'I had neither a three nor a boundary against that bowler on the leg side. I had kept to that resolve throughout, even carrying it to excess, for against Trumble when I received one or two balls on the leg stump simply "asking for it", I smothered my greed and contented myself with a single.' In this 'restrained' innings he had made a score of 104 in 77 minutes, on a bad wicket, with the game in a highly critical state, and under all the pressure of a Test match. Not that that made much difference to Jessop; the great occasion meant little to him, except a hope to do specially well for his side – 'nerve strain when actively engaged never particularly troubled me'.

Apart from the sheer joy of success and the feeling that England now had some hope of winning, Jessop must have felt satisfied that he had justified his selection and shown the redoubtable Australians that their bowling could be routed. With some facts to support it, they always had a belief that they could dismiss him cheaply – but not this time. It is good to read this comment on their acknowledgment of this great innings:

'Whatever the Australians may have thought of him – it is no secret that their opinion of him was far from flattering – they will realise what he is capable of on his great days. To fully appreciate all he did in the way of pulling and cutting straight balls off the wicket, one needed to be in line with the stumps. He had an overwhelming reception as he went back to the pavilion, the Australians joining most heartily in the applause.'

But seven wickets were down for 187, and the vanishing of Jessop's broad back also meant the vanishing of England's hopes: 76 to win and only three wickets left, but the spectators were in a state of euphoria after Jessop's innings, and as Hirst and Lockwood put up the 200, another tumultuous burst of cheering broke out. Hats flew off again, and what does it matter if a few end of season panamas and boaters get damaged? For the crowd had swelled to 22,000 when news of the lunch score suddenly suggested that there might after all be a chance of victory. Calculations became easier. Now it was 63 to win, 62 to tie. At last, after several excited appeals, Lockwood was out lbw to Trumble bowling round the wicket – 214 for 8. Lilley got a couple as soon as he came in, but at 219 he very nearly played on to Saunders, who had come back now that Jessop had gone. Four runs later Lilley hit a ball back to Trumble who just got one of his huge hands to it, but could not hold it. The fielders were almost frantic in their efforts to save runs. Noble and Darling in particular produced some miraculous saves, but now the Australians were paying for all the missed chances that had been given to them.

Hirst continued with great stolidity and calm, and among his many firm strokes was a square cut for four off Saunders, which sent the score to 230. Thirty-three runs to win. The excitement was becoming unbearable. 'So tense was the situation that the chronicling of the game became a difficult task', wrote one report. Lilley now decided to force the pace, and amid cries of 'Play up England!' drove Trumble for four; but trying to repeat the stroke he lifted the ball a little off the ground, and Darling at deep mid-off most gratefully hung on to the chance. 248 for 9. One more man to come in; it was Wilfred Rhodes, who in the previous Test at Manchester had also been concerned in a last-wicket stand, and had been left 'not out' when his partner had failed. No doubt it was some of those who had seen the sad end at Manchester that joined the troops of spectators who were now leaving the ground, unable to stand the strain. The eyes of the rest were on Wilfred Rhodes. To quote the famous words of H. S. Altham, the situation was 'Fifteen to win and two Yorkshiremen to do it'.

Jessop preparing to face his first ball.

Hitting Trumble to the pavilion.

As Rhodes came out Hirst went over to him and said a few words. Legend has it that these words were 'We'll get 'em in singles, Wilfred.' They have never actually denied this, but when A. A. Thomson some fifty years later asked Hirst whether he had really said this, Hirst's reasonable reply was that you don't remember what was said at such times. All that can be proved is that there were nine singles among the fifteen winning runs.

Rhodes had to face the last ball of Trumble's over, and he stopped it quietly. Hirst took a single off Noble's first ball, and this brought him his fifty after only 65 minutes' superb batting. More cheers, but with a touch of hysteria in them. One report says: 'Some laughed, some could not sit still, others dug their nails into their hands, while one old man was seen folding up his gloves quite methodically and making a parcel of them in his score-card – quite beside himself.'

The next ball Rhodes got an edge to, and it luckily went through the slips for four. Ten to win, nine to tie. Later in the same over Rhodes gave Australia a chance to win the game when he put a ball up in the slips dangerously near to Armstrong, who got a hand to it, lost his balance, and dropped it.

Jessop himself recalls these agonising moments: 'Every ball that was bowled produced an extraordinary sensation just as if someone was pouring cold water down my spine. I have never experienced such a feeling before, nor have I since. Twice Rhodes was almost out, Amstrong nearly getting him in the slips, and Trumble not quite reaching a return low down.' C. B. Fry also says: 'In all sorts of circumstances I have shared in all sorts of excitements. But never in one like this.'

In the following over Hirst took a single to the on off Trumble, and Rhodes had to face the remaining five balls, but one of these, as Jessop says, nearly came back as a catch to Trumble. But Hirst was not trying to 'farm' the bowling, because in the next over he again took a single off the first ball, and left Rhodes to play out the rest. Hirst added to the tension by his deliberate preparation to receive each ball. He would carefully rearrange his large pads, first one leg, then the other. He never lost his self-possession. There was no sense of hurry, not the least sign of doubt about the ultimate result, no feeling of anxiety, for after every run his right hand was held up like a semaphore telling Rhodes to stay in his ground, and take no unnecessary risk.

Trumble's next over, his thirty-seventh in succession from the start of the innings, produced a single to Hirst, a single to the off to Rhodes, another single turned into a two by an excited overthrow. The throw-in hit Hirst on the shoulder and bounced away, at which Hirst laughed, Rhodes smiled, and the Australians were not amused. So Hirst still had the bowling and took another single off the last ball of the over. Three runs to win, the sun gone in, and flecks of rain beginning to fall. Noble bowling to Hirst, who played the first five as coolly as ever, each ball with the full face of the bat, and then a sharp single off Noble's last ball, which gave Hirst the bowling again. Trumble continued and amid loud cheers Hirst pushed the ball away for another single. England could not now lose; a tie at least. Pandemonium. A parson rushed howling on to the pitch, quite demented. Rhodes played the next three balls carefully, but before the fifth ball Trumble went over to the sawdust heap, rubbed the ball in it, paused a moment, and bowled. Rhodes came forward to it, looking like an opening batsman rather than a number eleven, and he pushed the ball firmly past mid-on and ran. He himself says: 'I just ran and went on running. George was at the other end, and the crowd caught him'; and he added thoughtfully, 'If George Hirst hadn't saved the follow-on neither Jessop nor anybody else could have saved the match'. In fact, it should not have been saved at all, because as Rhodes says, 'I might have been out twice. Off my glove, the ball went down. It might just as easily have gone up.'

But such is cricket, and England had won. I suppose some fielder chased the ball and returned it, possibly not, because as the players made a headlong dash for the pavilion, the army of spectators invaded the pitch. (Beldam took a photo of them.) Hirst, coming from the farther Vauxhall end, was caught up and carried in the last few yards, and then the crowd stood and yelled and yelled and yelled. One or two burst into tears, perfect strangers shook hands with each other, even the women threw their hats into the air, some burst into song, and the Australian supporters joined in the cheering and did not begrudge England their victory. To quote a report: 'It was truly a most memorable occasion, and the throng gave vent to their pent-up feelings.'

Even the usually restrained gentlemen of the press let themselves go. For three days they had been subjected to remarks, often in bad taste, from the Australian spectators, whose reserved enclosure was in front of the press box. When the end came the pressmen let go their pent-up feelings. Even such a stickler for correct demeanour as Charles Stewart Caine, the editor of *Wisden*, stood up in his seat and waved his hat, and some of the lesser ones 'cooeed' back at the Australian spectators who had been gloating over England's apparent defeat.

Jessop says how much he envied the crowd their privilege of letting off their suppressed excitement by shouting for the players. They went on calling and each appearance set alight a new blaze of enthusiasm. It is doubtful whether Hirst ever appeared, since Trumble stated that as soon as the game was over, Hirst changed into his clothes, and was off to Yorkshire, so the crowd may have called in vain: 'We want Hirst, We want Hirst!'

And rightly so, for Hirst's achievement was truly heroic. Scores of 43 and 58*, and analyses of 5–77 and 2–7, and everything done just when it was needed. There were calls for Rhodes who, for from the time he came in, had had to face twenty balls while Hirst had faced only seventeen. There were calls for everyone, but it was Jessop most of all who set the crowd alight. They understood what Trumble meant when he said later: 'The only man living who could beat us, beat us.' Gilbert Jessop.

The spectators lingered on, until at long last the rain, which had started a few minutes before the end of the game, came down in earnest and sent them all home – bedraggled, dazed, but incredibly happy.

So England beat the Australians, and for the first time in the series, also beat the rain.

There is no doubt that Wednesday, August 13, 1902, must count as one of the greatest days in the history of cricket. Some time ago *The Evening Standard* invited readers to name the sporting event at which they would most like to

England XI *v.* Australia, Edgbaston, 1902.

have been present, and the Oval Test match of 1902 was a clear winner. It had been the scene of a battle between two magnificent teams, and the victory to England came at the very moment when a series of misfortunes, and mistakes by the selectors had given the pessimists a chance to talk of the decadence of English cricket. Victory could not have come at a more opportune moment to put the balance right, and it added an extra fillip to the Coronation gaieties. This match provided every element of the game: an ebb and flow of fortunes enough to create an almost unbearable tension for the spectators, some vicious interference by the weather, several critical missed chances, devilish bowling countered by courageous batting. The victory could not have come without Jackson's skill, Lockwood's determined attack, Hirst's cool competence, and to be honest, some lapses in the field by the Australians. Every player on the field added something to the play, but because they were the winners we tend to remember the Englishmen, and of them we most remember Gilbert Jessop. It was Jessop's innings that makes the match remembered as 'Jessop's Match'. It would have been spectacular at any time, but coming at the moment it did it can be regarded as miraculous. No novelist devising a thrilling finish would have dared to let his hero score a Test century at such a pace at such a moment in such a match.

The finish of England *v.* Australia at the Oval, August 13th, 1902. England won by one wicket. The players are being chased by the crowd.

G. L. Jessop pulling Saunders in his innings of 104 for England. The fielders are looking in the direction of square-leg. August 13th, 1902.

Letters of congratulation poured in from all over the world, and it may be of interest to quote a few of them to show the feeling this innings had created among followers in all walks of cricket. First, one from Francis Ford, one of the greatest of all left-handed batsmen. He writes from Dornoch in Scotland:

My dear Jessopus,

With the thought of the Test match still haunting me at sundry moments I write to express my delight at your wonderful 'blocking' on that occasion. Oh that I had only been there! I only wonder how on earth you did it, poking about like that too and snicking away. In this somewhat distant corner of Scotland our men were all half-cracked with delight when they got the news, me too. Golf seems to me a singularly feeble sort of game for the moment by comparison.

Buck up,

Yours ever,

Francis G. J. Ford

Now here is one from the famous umpire 'Bob' Thoms, a great character whom we meet later. His letter is written in beautiful copper-plate hand.

> W. L. Jessop, Esq.
> Sir,
>
> Bravo! Bravissimo! very much Bravissimo! Having watched you from your youthful days and witnessed you bang up the centuries with a simplicity like unto catching Tittlebats, no man was more gratified than a certain 'R.T.' to hear and know that you were again on the knock, and that at the right time too in the last great test match of England *v* Australia.
>
> With the hope that you may be found in 'Health and happiness' 'punching the leather' in your original and inimitable style, are the best wishes of
>
> Yours sincerely,
> Bob Thoms

Among the many tributes to Jessop's match-winning innings was this poetical effusion from Harry Dutton, who tells of the story in the manner and metre which Lord Macaulay used in relating the prowess of Horatius in playing an equally good innings for the Romans against the men of Tuscany. It runs like this:

When England's greatest batsmen fell
  Like chaff before the wind,
And the grand old Mother Country
  No trace of luck could find.

When the glorious pride of Somerset
  And Surrey's hero great –
The best that Lancashire could send,
  Were wiped from off the slate:

Who was it went with fearless mien,
  To guard his country's name.
To stem disaster's rushing tide,
  And save his side the game?

Who was it, once again I ask,
  That thrashed the Kangaroo –
Why, the cyclone, Mighty Jessop,
  Old Glo'ster's skipper true.

The man whom carping critics said
  Unworthy was to stand
Midst the pomp and pride of England
  To 'fend the Motherland.

Set sternly was his visage,
  Flashed fire his glorious eye
With heart of oak and nerves of steel
  He went to do or die!

For barely half a century
  Had five good wickets gone
And wanted were two hundred more
  Before the fight was won!

He recked not that with cunning rare
  Buoyed up by triumphs great,
The finest trundler in the world
  May lure him to his fate!

He only knew the Motherland
  Hoped for great things of him,
And so for tricky Trumble's best
  He went with nerve and vim!

To every corner of the green
  He drove with mighty power,
And turned despair to hopefulness
  In one brief fleeting hour.

And when at last his task was o'er,
  When closed his wondrous 'go'
Old England had a splendid chance
  To vanquish her great foe.

How bravely did bold Jackson strive
  And Hirst fight in the fray,
And Rhodes, grand Yorkshire's bonny pride
  Till glory crowned the day.

Oh! Jessop, fierce and slashing bat,
  The deed that thou hast done
Makes Chelt'nham point with pride to thee
  Her best and greatest son.

Surrey County Cricket Club.

KENNINGTON OVAL, AUGUST 11, 12 & 13, 1902

ENGLAND v. AUSTRALIA.

AUSTRALIA.	First Innings		Second Innings	
1 Mr. V. Trumper	b Hirst	42	run out	2
2 Mr. R. A. Duff	c Lilley, b Hirst	23	b Lockwood	6
3 Mr. C. Hill	b Hirst	11	c MacLaren, b Hirst	34
4 Mr. J. Darling	c Lilley, b Hirst	3	c MacLaren, b Lockwood	15
5 Mr. M. A. Noble	c & b Jackson	52	b Braund	13
6 Mr. S. E. Gregory	b Hirst	23	b Braund	9
7 Mr. W. W. Armstrong	b Jackson	17	b Lockwood	21
8 Mr. A. Hopkins	c MacLaren b Lockwood	40	c Lilley, b Lockwood	3
9 Mr. H. Trumble	not out	64	not out	7
10 Mr. J. Kelly	c Rhodes, b Braund	39	l-b-w, b Lockwood	0
11 Mr. J. V. Saunders	l-b-w, b Braund	0	c Tyldesley, b Rhodes	2
	B 5, l-b 3, w , n-b 2	10	B 7, l-b 2, w , n-b ,	9
	Total	324	Total	121

1st innings	1 for 47	2-63	3-69	4-82	5-126	6-174	7-175	8-256	9-324
2nd innings	1 for 6	2-9	3-31	4-71	5-75	6-91	7-99	8-114	9-115

ENGLAND.	First Innings.		Second Innings.	
1 Mr. A. C. MacLaren	c Armstrong, b Trumble	10	b Saunders	2
2 Mr. L. C. H. Palairet	b Trumble	20	b Saunders	6
3 Tyldesley	b Trumble	33	b Saunders	0
4 Hayward	b Trumble	0	c Kelly, b Saunders	7
5 Hon. F. S. Jackson	c Armstrong, b Saunders	2	c & b Trumble	49
6 Braund	c Hill, b Trumble	22	c Kelly b Trumble	2
7 Mr. G. L. Jessop	b Trumble	13	c Noble, b Armstrong	104
8 Hirst	c & b Trumble	43	not out	58
9 Lockwood	c Noble, b Saunders	25	l-b-w, Trumble	2
10 Lilley	c Trumper, b Trumble	0	c Darling, b Trumble	16
11 Rhodes	not out	0	not out	6
	B 13, l-b 2, w , n-b	15	B 5 l-b 6, w , n-b	11
	Total	183	Total (9 wkts)	263

1st innings	1 for 31	2-36	3-62	4-67	5-67	6-83	7-137	8-179	9-183
2nd innings	1 for 5	2-5	3-10	4-31	5-48	6-157	7-187	8-214	9-248

BOWLING ANALYSIS.

AUSTRALIA.—First Innings.

	Overs.	Maidens.	Runs.	Wickets.
Lockwood	24	2	85	1
Rhodes	28	9	46	0
Hirst	29	5	77	5
Braund	16.5	5	29	2
Jackson	20	4	66	2
Jessop	6	2	11	0

Lockwood and Rhodes each bowled one no-ball.

Second Innings.

	Overs.	Maidens.	Runs.	Wickets.
Rhodes	22	7	38	1
Lockwood	20	6	45	5
Jackson	4	3	7	0
Hirst	5	1	7	1
Braund	9	1	15	2

ENGLAND.—First Innings.

	Overs.	Maidens.	Runs.	Wickets.
Trumble	31	13	65	8
Saunders	23	7	79	2
Noble	7	3	24	0

Second Innings.

	Overs.	Maidens.	Runs.	Wickets.
Trumble	33.5	4	108	4
Saunders	24	3	105	4
Armstrong	4	0	28	1
Noble	5	0	11	0

Umpires—C. E. Richardson & A. A. White. **Stumps drawn 6.30 p.m.**

RESULT. ENGLAND WON BY ONE WICKET.

MERRITT & HATCHER, Ltd., "Cricket" Office, 168, Upper Thames Street, E.C.

And now one from a complete stranger who cannot resist saying 'thank you' to Jessop.

Dear Sir,

I trust you will allow me the liberty of writing you a few words of thanks and congratulations for your score in today's match. Doubtless you have received numerous letters from unknown correspondents; like myself all desirous of personally thanking you and congratulating you upon your great and timely effort on behalf of English cricket. Oh! if you had been at Manchester!

Yours truly,

T. S. Sidney

The Times had a leading article on the great match, and gave special attention to Jessop's innings; which made up for the previous occasion in 1896 when in a similar leader he had been censured for bowling bumpers in the Varsity match. Enough poems were written about the innings to make a book (though not a very good one), and Albert Craig, the Surrey cricket poet, would seem to have re-headed a poem he published on the first day of the match, and 'respectfully dedicated it to G. L. Jessop Esq.' in honour of his great innings.

Jessop's fellow-players were ready to talk about the innings, and when visiting Bristol a few days after the match Wilfred Rhodes answered a query about Jessop's innings with the few words: 'You know the Oval. Well, he hit 'em on yon canvas', meaning the awning over the seats in front of the pavilion. These few words told the whole story of Rhodes' wonder and admiration.

Jack Hobbs once wrote that though he was not at the Oval that day Jessop's innings was so often talked about that he felt he knew pretty well every stroke in it. And people still do talk about it.

Jessop and Jessop alone could have played it. It was not a flash-in-the-pan innings, or even a lucky table-turner by some tail-end slogger. Jessop was a legend in his lifetime, the only batsman whose name had produced an adjective to describe a certain brand of batting that is virtually unique. It may have been P. F. Warner who first referred to a batsman playing a 'Jessopian' innings. No other batsman's name appears in the book called '*The Language of Cricket*' and the only other name-use I can think of is when George Headley was referred to as 'The Black Bradman', because of his machine-like scoring. But that is not quite the same thing. Even now, some sixty years after his last game in first-class cricket, the name of Jessop is still used to describe a daring hitter of a cricket ball – though present-day batsmen do not often provide much chance for it to be used. You can try to compare one great run-getter with another, but no one can be compared with Jessop in the matter of fast-scoring. One simple fact may be enough to prove this.

Up to recent times it was customary for a side in a first-class match to score at an average pace of a run a minute, and scoring at under this pace was regarded as 'slow'. The present average in County matches is now 52 an hour. This means that an individual batsman would on the average score at half this rate. I once made a survey of the scoring rates of great batsmen based upon as much evidence as possible and covering a large proportion of their scores of over 50. Here is a selection of some of them: A. Shrewsbury 28 runs an hour; Sutcliffe, Jardine, Headley, Woodfull and Washbrook all 34 runs an hour; W. G. Grace and Hutton 36; Hayward, Mead and Hassett 37; C. B. Fry and F. S. Jackson 40; Clem Hill, Leyland, Ponsford, Hendren, Hobbs, and Hammond 43; Ames 45; J. T. Tyldesley, Bradman, Compton, MacLaren, and Hirst 47; McCabe and Donnelly 49; Valentine, E. R. T. Holmes, and K. S. Ranjitsinhji 50; George Cox, K. S. Duleepsinhji, Bartlett, and C. G. Macartney 52; R. E. Foster, Trumper and Frank Woolley 55; Maurice Tate, P. G. H. Fender and Chapman just over 60. Jessop, at 79, is out on his own. This on the evidence of all his 180 scores of 50 or more.

This means that in theory – and very much in theory – Jessop alone could score faster than the combined efforts of Grace and Hobbs. Jessop played for twenty-one seasons of first-class cricket (1894–1914) in which time he scored 26,698 runs. He made fifty-three centuries (five of them scores of over 200), and at the time of his retirement only thirteen other batsmen had scored a greater number of centuries. At the same date C. B. Fry, with five occasions, was the only batsman to surpass Jessop's record of four times scoring two hundreds in a match. Jessop's batting average in a career of 855 innings was 32·63, and he reached a score of 50 or more in every one in five of these innings – a high proportion. In one season he made over 2,000 runs as well as taking over 100 wickets, and he had another season in which he did the Double.

I give these figures to dispel any idea that Jessop was a marvellous 'slogger' who happened to have occasional purple patches of productive run-getting. If he had been merely a hitter his Test Match career would not have lasted so long as from 1899 to 1912 – a Test career longer than most, though sometimes he was left out of the England team. The England selection committee constantly argued the matter of whether to play Jessop or not. A. C. MacLaren, a frequent captain of England, always wanted to have Jessop in his side in the belief that not only could he turn any game topsy-turvy in under an hour, but he might well throw out a couple of Australians who always seemed ready to take a chance in running to him. F. S. Jackson had a high opinion of Jessop, but felt that his inclusion would be too much of a gamble.

C. B. Fry writes: 'In retrospect it looks absurd ever to have left Gilbert Jessop out of an England eleven, but not so absurd when one reviews the names of other England batsmen.' No wonder the selectors found Jessop a problem. P. F. Warner states firmly that to leave Jessop out was 'surely a mistake. His very presence was an asset in that it paralysed the initiative of the opposing captain. Jessop had only to be an hour at the wicket, or in a low-scoring game for half an hour, to alter entirely the aspect of any game. He could dominate or obliterate the time factor of any game. His contemporaries thought his name not quite good enough, and with a suggestion of the mighty and the classic, nicknamed hims JESSOPUS.'

I daresay that the enormous popularity he held among players and spectators might sometimes have tended to make the selectors fight shy of him, as though determined to show their independence of popular opinion. Like others, of course he failed sometimes, and his innings did not always go on long enough, but runs scored quickly often have an increase in value, because they open up the game, especially in three-day Test Matches.

Perhaps the most revealing facts about Jessop's capacity to 'dominate the time factor' are that only once in his career did he bat for more than three hours (this in a 'slow' innings of 240 which lasted for 200 minutes!), and that only ten times in his career of 855 innings did he bat longer than TWO hours. Even so he produced innings of 286, 240, 234, 233, 206. No wonder the word that Jessop was batting pulled the crowd into the ground; you could not afford to miss a precious moment. It is no surprise to learn that by the time he retired he had scored the two fastest hundreds yet known, and the two fastest double centuries – a record he still holds. On eighteen occasions he reached his fifty in 25 or less minutes, and in fifteen of his hundreds he reached 100 not out within an hour – a feat which has been achieved only about forty-five times in all in the history of first-class cricket. His average time for reaching a score of 100 was 72 minutes.

These facts may help to show what a unique cricketer he was; but I consider that the opinion of H. S. Altham in his *A History of Cricket* does even more to establish his greatness as a batsman. Below the heading to Chapter XXI 'The Golden age of Batting', he adds three names: 'RANJI, FRY, JESSOP.'

2

Early Days

'Well, we've found something this time.'
W. G. GRACE ON JESSOP'S DÉBUT

'TO the man who has made good, whether it be in the battle of life or the less important realm of sport, not the least interesting period of his career is that of his early struggles.'

So runs the opening sentence of Gilbert Jessop's own book of reminiscences *A Cricketer's Log* (1922) which tells us so much about his contemporaries and so little generally about himself. He does not even give his birthday.

It was on May 19, 1874, that Dr Henry Edward Jessop, surgeon, of 30 Cambray, Cheltenham, became the father of his eleventh child, who was named Gilbert Laird. 'My arrival in the world thus completed a full Jessop eleven, and three years afterwards we were provided with a substitute in the shape of my brother Osman.' I doubt if Jessop's brother and sisters would have thought of themselves as part of a cricket team, since there was no great tradition of cricket in the family. The nearest link with the game was through Mrs. Jessop, née Susannah Radford Hughes, who was distantly connected with Thomas Hughes, the author of *Tom Brown's Schooldays*, and himself a useful cricketer. But there were other sporting abilities in Jessop's father, who was an excellent shot and billiard player. He was also 'a capital hand with the gloves', and for all his size he was extremely quick on his feet, an asset inherited by Gilbert. He also possessed a natural flick of the wrist as young Gilbert's misdemeanours soon led him to discover. Dr G. A. Cardew, of Cheltenham, wrote the following description of the well-known doctor:

'Dr Henry Jessop requires the pen of an artist, but I will try to describe him as I remember him. He was a huge man of about 17 or 18 stone. He wore a broad-brimmed short topper hat, a moderate stick-up collar, with a very flashy tie, an ordinary morning coat, very large check plaid trousers, and huge boots with very broad welts, and shining black with Nubian blacking.

'Apparently he was not particular about fees, but always came home from his country rounds full of good things. He got most of his meals at patients' houses. He took me one day to Birdlip to see the landlord of the Royal George Hotel. My fee was a very good dinner at the George, with some very good old home brewed ale. Another time he took me to visit Bishop's Cleeve, first to see a case of hip disease, and then an old woman who had heart disease and dropsy. He told the daughter who kept the inn that he wanted two good fat geese for Michaelmas day which was in the following week. I accordingly received one of them, a very fine one too, and very heavy.

'To see Jessop walk down the High Street (he lived in Cambray) was a wonderful sight, as he required more than half the pavement, and he came along like a huge elephant. People cleared out of his way sharply, as he certainly would have gone over them, if they hadn't moved out of his way. He was a shrewd practical man, and the people trusted him implicitly. He told me he did not approve of my putting up fractures in a starch or plaster case, for then he would not be able to pay a visit once or twice a day, as it would be unnecessary, and he would lose a lot of fees.'

I have recently been over the house at 30 Cambray and wonder how the large family managed to fit in or exercise themselves, for the garden at the back is smaller than a squash court, and apart from the children, there were also the bulldogs which Dr Jessop bred, and each dog was allotted to the care of a particular child. One has visions of all the Jessop children, including little Osman (No. 12), known as Toddy, trailing over the countryside with their bulldogs on the many family excursions to the hills and caves of Cheltenham led by their monstrous father. Gilbert must always have been full of high spirits, and fortunately this energy from his earliest days was mainly directed towards cricket, for, as he tells us, his love of the game went right back to his toddling stage:

'My cricketing days commenced from the time when I could first toddle, and my hands were not yet big enough to grasp securely the large soft ball which in the confines of the nursery was a necessary expedient. Not for me were the various other distractions of the youthful mind, such as mechanical toys or houses built of cards, though I will not go so far as to suggest that, when the life of the ball was spent – which happened with painful frequency through the harsh treatment meted out – other amusements failed to interest me. A ball was to me what I imagine a doll is to every tiny tot of the opposite sex. I cannot remember precisely at what age a ball was first put into my hands; anyway, it could not have been at too tender an age, for my joy was mingled with tears before I had thoroughly sampled the missile.

'It was, I remember, a highly decorative article in various shades of blue and red – highly decorated, that is, before I got busy. Afterwards – if at this distance of time one may take as a criterion the vast consternation produced in the ample bosom of my nurse – I must have succeeded in obliterating all traces of the architectural beauties of a German Schloss on the one side and the green water of a sluggish stream on the other. Though Sarah had a heavy hand, I don't think I minded that half as much as the dreadful concoction of hot mustard and water which made me so terribly sick. I don't think my nurse could have been a great cricketer, for whenever appealed to – which was often – she always decided against the batsman who struck the ball with the wrong side of the bat. There was no difficulty in determining which was the correct side, for our first bat was a brush, and the marks of the bristles made themselves seen on the ball. As I had then arrived at the smacking stage – that stage in one's youthful days when one's assailant is really out to hurt – a life observation of the humanitarian instincts of all "nannies" convinces me that I must have been bordering on my fourth year.'

'When the time came to discard tunics for breeks I cannot in truth say that the pursuit of cricket was encouraged by my parents. For one thing the accommodation for the game was so severely limited. The house in which I was born in Cheltenham, 30 Cambray – why it did not rejoice in the name of street or road was always a puzzle to me – abutted on to the street, and the only outdoor exercising ground was a small garden of about eight square yards, in the centre of which was a rockery. It was not an ideal spot in which to pitch wickets, but it was a pitch upon which I spent many happy hours, none the less for it being forbidden ground. . . .

'My earliest recollection of the great game is a confused medley of broken glass and the offering up of victims to the sacrifice. It was with us an unwritten law that each in turn should bear the brunt of displeasure, and as there were five in all to participate, there was no little competition for the selection of Friday as one's day of crime. Two lickings in the same week was no joke. Space was too restricted in the apology for a garden to allow of any undue optimism as to immunity from accidents in any one day. On the leg side of the wicket lay safety; on the off the surgery windows. Small wonder, therefore, if a pronounced penchant for the "pull" should have affected my batting throughout my days.'

It might be added that Jessop's capacity for breaking windows was one that lasted throughout his career. There was fortunately one safer 'ground' which Jessop and his fellows could play on, a passageway which can still be seen. I am glad to say that plans have been made to put a plaque upon 30 Cambray to commemorate Jessop's centenary year, and the scene of his earliest cricket, about which he writes:

'To us cricket had no season. Any old time and any old place was good enough. Some of our most exciting matches were played after darkness had set in, played in an underground passage with a candle behind the wicket at one end, another behind the bowler, and one in the middle of the pitch. I'm not sure that this was not the most difficult wicket upon which I ever played, for the batsman stood on a kind of platform of indifferently laid bricks, the step up to which being some three or four yards in front of the 'block-hole', made it a matter of extreme difficulty to determine whether the ball would pitch short of the step or on the platform itself. Until it did pitch you never saw the ball at all, and consequently the bowler directed his entire attention to the serving up of straight full pitches. Sometimes the ball as urged by my sister Winnie failed to find its intended alignment, and, as soft ball became discarded for hard, adjournments of one's innings were of very common occurrence. Not until my age ran into double figures did I handle a bat with a real splice in it or finger a leather cricket ball.'

'Sister Winnie' remained a lifelong follower of her brother's exploits, and I have found the scrapbooks which she kept about him very interesting. There is one photograph of a school group of some thirty small boys, dressed in the most constricting clothing, and some wearing mortar boards and others curious flat hats. At the end of one of the rows is a healthy-looking boy with a round face. It is master Gilbert, and it is not too much to suggest that the ridiculous hat is worn at a characteristically jaunty angle. I imagine that this is a group of a school which he went to before he became a member of Cheltenham Grammar School, where he went at the age of eleven. His father was a governor of the school, and I do not think that Gilbert had to pass any high-powered selection tests to enter the school. He had no anxieties over any 'eleven-plus' exam. to inhibit his daring pulls to leg.

He was lucky to go to a school where the Headmaster, Mr John Style, was a keen cricketer who took an active part in the welfare of the school games, and what is more, realised the importance of training on the younger boys – 'he devoted no small interest in the exploits of the youngsters', says Jessop. No doubt it was he who observed that there was one small boy who had an enormous capacity to run and throw and catch, and who looked like the born games-player he was.

In the issue of the *Cheltenham Free Press* for June 8, 1886, there is a report of a match between the Grammar School and the Modern School. The game was drawn when the Modern school made 117 and their opponents replied with 38 for 6; last among the names of those who 'did not bat' is G. Jessop, who had had his twelfth birthday only a fortnight before. This must be the very first time that Jessop's name appeared in print in a cricket report. There

Gilbert Jessop at school (top left) as captain of Gloucestershire (top right) and (right) on his wedding day.

Jessop bowling, smoking, and, in his capacity as Secretary to a golf club, writing.

Beccles College XI, 1895. Jessop aged 21, is seated on the right.

Cambridge 1899, Jessop as captain in his fourth year.

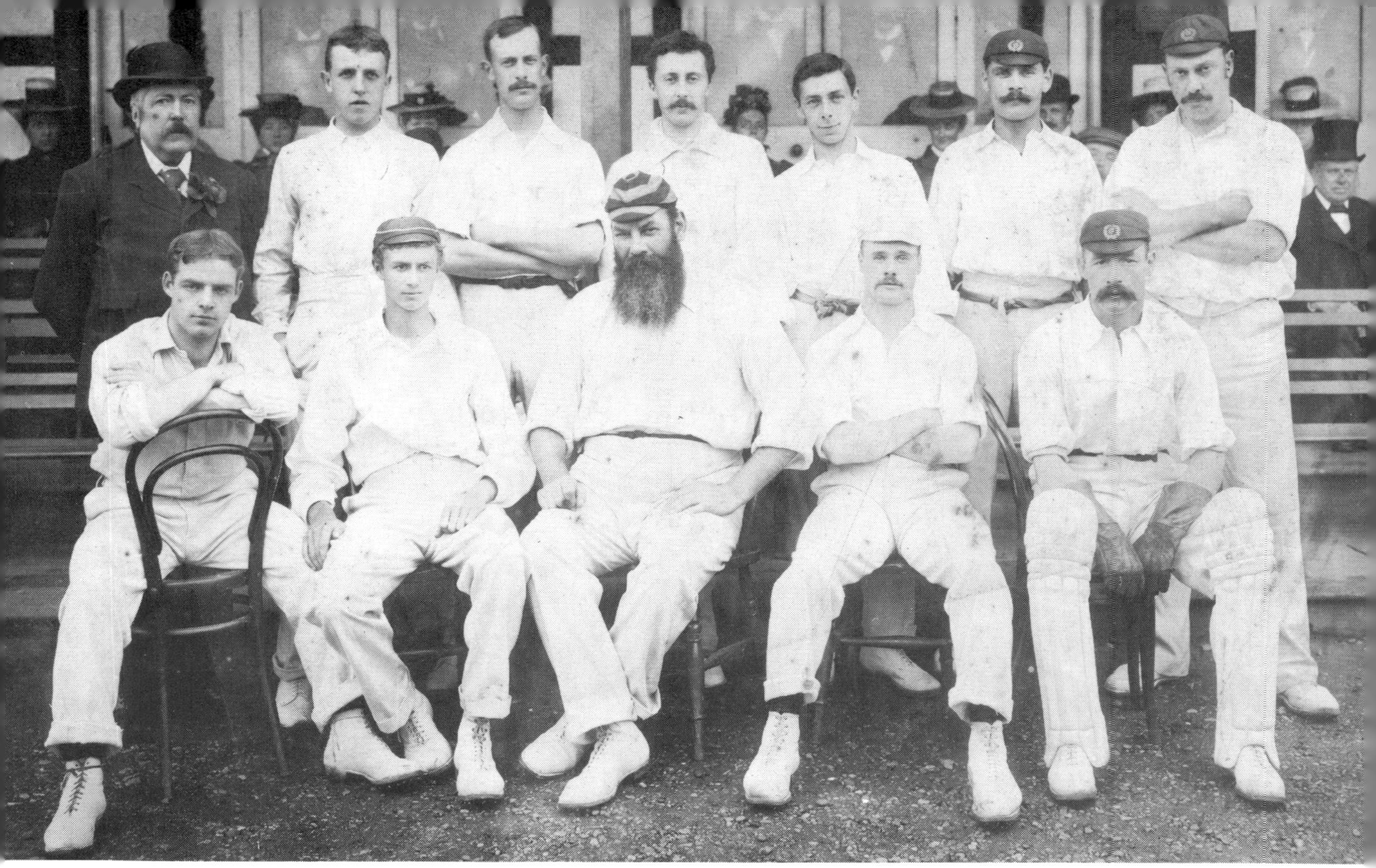

Gloucestershire 1896. Jessop is on Grace's left.

Gloucestershire 1901. Jessop as captain in one of their better seasons.

is also one other match reported in which he went in ninth and scored 3. 1886 must be the season mentioned in his book in which he says he won his 2nd XI colours and was played chiefly for his fielding at long-stop, of which he says: 'The position of a long-stop, especially on a ground inclined to be 'furrowy', is no picnic. . . . In those days the wicket-keeper did not possess the super gauntlets of today. Consequently anything in the nature of an extra fast ball which he could comfortably avoid he did not scruple to let go, so naturally the long-stop was pretty fully engaged.' Most of the school eleven were grown boys and the captain named Gustav Schneider in his last term before going to Cambridge could fairly be classed as a fast bowler, to whom 'pace meant more than direction', so little Jessop had plenty to do.

In 1887, though still aged only thirteen, Jessop seems to have taken over Schneider's role as chief bowler. There are six match reports in the local papers, and in these matches Jessop took 32 wickets, including 8 against St George's on June 4; one of these wickets was a stumping, an unusual way for Jessop to get a wicket at any time. He also moved up in the batting order, and in the match against the Modern school was top scorer with 15 out of a total of 43. This time it was Jessop himself who was stumped.

This season he won his 1st XI colours as a thirteen-year-old, and so joined that select band, including Colin Cowdrey, of those who have represented their school at such an early age.

I would dearly like to know what happened in the following year of 1888, but there are only two school matches reported in the local papers; he did not play in either of them for some reason. For the season of 1889 there are no reports at all.

In March 1890 Dr Henry Jessop died suddenly at the age of 53, and it seems that owing to lack of funds Gilbert had to leave school immediately. The Grammar School has no details as to when exactly he left, and the only reference to him is in a form list of Christmas Term 1887 when he came out thirteenth in a class of seventeen. There is only one match report in any school magazine, and that concerns the season of 1889 when he played that year for the Old Boys against the school, which is puzzling. He went in third and scored 10 in a total of 99, and then took three wickets when the school was dismissed for a mere 26. If in fact he had already left school (which seems unlikely) it is sad to think that this Old Boy was then aged only 15, and in normal circumstances might have remained at school for several more seasons. From a cricketing point of view it was perhaps a good thing that he did leave early, and thus have a chance to widen his experience. The only other evidence we have of his link with the school was that in September 1890 he played for G.S.L.V.C. ('which I read as 'Grammar School Long Vacation Club') in a

G. L. Jessop's father.

match against Swindon Hall. He made top score and took six wickets. His old friend Schneider, now at Cambridge, also played in the match.

We must be thankful for these odd glimpses into Jessop's early cricketing days, though they are disappointing as they tell us only part of the story. Such match reports in local papers are bound to be haphazard, and depend much on chance and space for any given week. The matches of the leading clubs are often ignored, while those of scratch teams are given in full – teams such as 'Cheltenham Barbers', 'Gloucester Early Closing', 'Unemployed', and there is a game of 'Cueists *v.* Markers'.

Stories of Jessop's keenness as a boy cricketer still survive in Cheltenham: how when aged twelve he once broke a man's wrist with one of his fast balls, how he used to roll out a wicket and practice with his friends in the early morning before going to school, and how when he was on his own he used to spend hours throwing a tennis ball up against the blank wall of a pub which had a field alongside it. He would practise pick-ups off the returning ball, and then fling it back again at the wall. Bradman did much the same thing as a boy when he had no one to play with.

Cheltenham Grammar School has honoured its famous old boy by naming a House after him, and Jessop's son presented the school with a large rose bowl as a cricket cup. It is inscribed: 'London Press Golfing Society. Presented by Robert Donald, Editor of the Daily Chronicle. Won by G. L. Jessop, West Middlesex Golfing Society, Sept. 28, 1908.' The meeting was at Oxhey where Ted Ray was pro. It was a day of wind and rain, and Jessop's score of 80 (48 out and 32 home) was a good one which Ted Ray said he would have been proud to achieve on such a day. This cup can be seen in the Headmaster's study, where there is also a photograph of the composer Gustav Holst, who was an exact contemporary of Jessop's, and possibly a friend of his. Is it too much to imagine the creator of 'The Planets' rolling out the wicket before breakfast?

Dr Jessop's death at such a comparatively early age must have completely disrupted the life of the family, for though the elder ones were no doubt by this time out in the world, there were several including Gilbert who had to be provided for. For financial reasons the widow could not stay on at 30 Cambray, and she moved to Somerset Cottage which is attached to Somerset House in Knapp Road. (It is now the Headquarters of the R.S.P.C.A.) This was a property owned by the family firm of solicitors, which dates back to 1792, and the sixth generation still carry on the business at 14 Royal Crescent – a wonderful spell of continuity. Mrs Jessop lived at Somerset Cottage until her death in 1908, and this was Gilbert's home base until he went to live in London. Mrs Jessop had been a nurse and married her husband when he was still a medical student, and several of the daughters became nurses. One of them, Ada, married a Dr Wilson and he took over his late father-in-law's practice, and three other sisters went to India. Kathleen became matron of Madras Hospital, Gertrude worked for the Port of Bombay authority, but she was in Madras in August 1914, and Lord Willingdon, the Governor, appointed her as matron of the hospital ship *Madras*, for which she later won a decoration; Emily, an expert in midwifery, was in charge of a Maharajah's harem. The eldest son, Walter, went to America, and became the first dentist to practise at Phoenix, Arizona. In 1892 he built a wooden house beside the mud road, and on his death his daughter Ruth lived there until 1962 when the site was sold and had a skyscraper erected upon it. It is not likely that Gilbert saw a great deal of some of his far-flung brothers and sisters, except for his younger brother Osman, and his sister Winifred, who followed his career with great devotion, as we know from the scrapbooks she kept.

We do not know what happened to Gilbert's education on the death of his father. He must have been sad to leave school so soon, though no doubt many of his friends were local boys, and he soon organised them into playing cricket with him. For some time they had played their games on a ground near the Beaufort Inn and not very far from the centre of the town. This is what he says of these days in *A Cricketer's Log:*

'After the term was over I practically lived on the ground, which we shared with a club, now defunct, called the Beaufort. Together with three or four kindred spirits, ten o'clock in the morning saw the nets hoisted into position, to remain there until the hour of six marked the arrival of the first batch of members of the Beaufort Club. The packing away of our nets did not mean for me that cricket was over for the day – far from it – for I scouted out, with now and then, when a shortage of bowlers occurred, an occasional bowl in the nets, until failing light compelled a stoppage. The easy accessibility of cricket in the holidays served as almost another season, and later I was given a chance as a batter. Strangely enough I can remember no other performances with any distinctiveness save those of the first two matches, both of which were against a team called St George's Hall. In the first which took place on our own ground, I took seven wickets for eight runs, and went a trifle better in the return game by taking eight at a cost of but five runs.

'Luck favoured me in my first efforts as a bowler, as afterwards it invariably did on first appearances. My use in the team did not end at bowling, for in crude fashion I frequently put together a useful score. Better practice came to me in the holidays when at Churchdown – a village lying midway between Cheltenham and Gloucester – strong local sides of both towns were met as well as rival villages. It was a very rare occasion upon which I did not bowl unchanged throughout both innings. Village cricket flourished around Gloucester in those days, and matches could be obtained for the asking. Two and often three games in a week were of regular occurrence, so that before I had arrived at the mature age of fifteen my match experience was already considerable. And what made such experience all the more valuable was the fact that in quite two-thirds of the matches the opponents were adults. Such practice was far more useful than hours spent at the nets.'

There are no records of the Beaufort Club, but the *Cheltenham Free Press* for August 23, 1890, records a match in which Beaufort C.C. played C. Rodgers's XI and Jessop made 2 runs and took 3 wickets for Beaufort. There are, however, a few historic sheets from scorebooks of the Churchdown Club which Jessop says 'was my first club in which I played in grown-up company. I was then 14 and always put on to bowl first.' One score sheet is dated 29.6.89 and shows that Jessop scored 30* of a match-winning score of 52 for 2 against Thurdington, and another dated June 7, 1890, shows Churchdown scoring 249 (G. Jessop top scorer with 75), followed by the dismissal of the unfortunate Churcham for only 7 runs. At one time their score was 8 wickets for 2 runs, and young Jessop's analysis reads: 5–2–0–5. Another undated sheet gives Jessop an analysis of 8–15 (7 clean bowled), followed up by a score of 68 out of a total of 114, and the scorer has written underneath 'good old Churchdown.'

In another game Gilbert's uncle Fred prevented his nephew from sweeping the board by taking four wickets himself to Gilbert's five. I wonder if the other village players ever resented the success of one so young or merely rejoiced in it. There is one tale of about this time of how he was brought into a match at the last moment as a substitute, and when it came to batting he was put in last and told not to get out and give the other batsman every chance of scoring. Gilbert played his usual game and hit up some quick runs, and it was the other batsman who was eventually dismissed, leaving Gilbert not out. The captain later was annoyed with the boy for disobeying orders and hitting out, but Jessop's reply was: 'You told me not to get out, and I didn't!'

But the time came when Gilbert had to 'pull his own weight' and earn his living, and plans were made to turn him overnight from schoolboy into schoolmaster. In those days many schools had what were virtually apprentice teachers, young, sometimes very young men, who worked more as ushers than teachers, and no doubt helped with supervision and such games as there were. The latter might well suit Gilbert and possibly make up for a lack of purely academic interests. In September 1890 a post of this kind was found for him at Alvechurch Grammar School in Worcestershire, where at the age of sixteen and a half he was appointed Senior Resident Assistant Master. It later amused him to think that at the moment when he was acting as schoolmaster his contemporaries such as C. B. Fry and 'Plum' Warner were establishing themselves as young bloods in the cricket world of their public schools. Jessop has few recollections of his time at Alvechurch except for the bitter fact that he received no salary, being given board and residence as the sole remuneration for his services. A local resident, however, many years later recalled how when young 'Mr' Jessop was batting on the Alvechurch ground it was the custom to post four boys on the other side of the field hedgerows, with two more on the road to watch where the balls went. Even as a sixteen-year-old his reputation as a hitter was being established. To quote Jessop:

'The sparsity of the staff forbade my participation in any other cricket save school matches, but I did manage to scrape in a couple of matches for the village club, and in both enjoyed considerable success. Still, though in all I did not experience more than half a dozen matches, the practice wickets were quite the best I had hitherto met with, and throughout the term from seven to eight each evening I was to be found at the nets. As a consequence, when term was over and I returned to Cheltenham for the holidays, there was a distinct improvement in my batting' – but nothing about any improvement in his Latin or his Greek, which later proved such a trouble to him.

Soon after his return for the holidays Jessop had an unexpected game for the East Gloucestershire Club against the Cotswold Hunt. His cousin Hylton, though a valuable member of the Club, wanted in this match to represent the Hunt, but if he was to do so he would have to provide a substitute. He told his young cousin that there would be an excellent lunch provided, so Gilbert agreed to play. His début for East Gloucestershire was highly successful. He took six wickets (including that of Hylton for only 4), and then scored 88 – the highest score of his career – mostly off his cousin's 'donkey-drop' leg-breaks. Throughout these holidays he averaged about four games a week in and around Cheltenham; there was plenty of cricket to be had, as the attractions of golf had not yet arrived. To quote Jessop: 'Cheltenham was full of menfolk of uncertain age who loved the game with a fervour which they spared no pains to inculcate into the minds of the young bloods.'

He recalls how in one and the same week he played under the leadership of a Prince, a Baron, a gardener, and a coachman, and as a skipper the coachman, Mr Adams of Swindon Hall, was easily the best. He was built on the lines of 'W. G.', and was a fast underhand bowler of the real old-fashioned sort. Jessop says that he never saw one of these bumping sneaks *driven* to the boundary. Mr Adams also had some of 'W. G.'s ability to spot a promising player, and he prophesied that it would not be many years before that young Mr Jessop would be playing for the county.

Jessop's keenness for cricket as a boy made him accept any chance of a game whatever the distance, but he almost always had to make his way to the game on foot. There were no motor buses to take him there and as he says: 'it would not have made much difference if there had been, because coin of the realm was almost unobtainable from the head of the house in those days'. Poor Mrs Jessop, she must have found things very difficult, but it must have been a help that Gilbert was at least housed for so many weeks in the year in his new 'job'. There was still Osman to be looked after; under the influence of his brother he also became a cricketer, a leading player with the Cheltenham Cricket Club, and later played a few games for the county, thus overcoming the unsuitable initials of 'O. W. T.' which were scarcely encouraging for a batsman.

In 1891 Jessop took a new teaching post at a school at South Woodford in Essex, and the only memorable feature of this job was that C. D. Buxton, captain of Essex, then a minor county, gave certain hints to Jessop that if he became qualified by residence, he would be given a trial for the county eleven. This was the result of an innings in which Jessop made the first century of his career, of which we happen to have a personal account, for *The Windsor Magazine* once had an article on 'My First Century' and Jessop was one of those asked to contribute. He wrote:

'My first appearance as a centurion in any match was in Essex, for South Woodford *v.* Woodford United in 1892, when I scored 112. I can remember that it was a distinctly lucky innings, remarkable chiefly for the number of opportunities I presented to the wicket-keeper. I stood a foot and a half outside my crease during most of the innings, and eventually fell a victim to my rashness, by being stumped through the ball rebounding from the wicket-keeper's pads. This habit of mine, by the way, of standing outside the crease greatly displeased the journalistic critics when I first played county cricket.'

I wonder if it was in this match that James Thorpe, the artist, first met Jessop. They were good friends in later days, and originally met at S. Woodford when Jessop with his fast bumpers 'instilled much terror into us very timid opponents', most likely in a school match.

Though Jessop's first century was not an innings he could feel very proud of, it was a milestone in his career, and he writes: 'No matter in what class of cricket, this is a great event in a cricketer's life. He may have on more than one occasion escaped the distinction by a few runs, but though the margin which divides him from his goal may have been infinitesimal, he will derive more personal satisfaction from a century than from any two ninety-odd innings.' But the matter of qualification of Essex went no further, since Jessop

'A drawing by James Thorpe.'

left the job at South Woodford without much regret. 'The prospects of advancement were indeed small, and the cricket in the area was of less good class than that around Cheltenham.' It is quite clear that Jessop was not in the teaching profession as a matter of choice, and even if he had been he would have had no prospects without qualifications or a degree. Perhaps it was at this stage that his wish to go to a university was established, but this was out of the question until his mother had more of the family off her hands. Had he been in the same situation nowadays he might well have considered playing cricket professionally, but I do not suppose that in the 1890s the idea even crossed his mind.

Meantime, what he wanted was a congenial teaching job which would enable him to play cricket, and good cricket, for it is clear that by now he was ambitious to do everything to improve his game with the immediate target of a chance to play for his home county. He had no one to push his claims, nothing except his own ability and determination. The summer of 1893 found him working much nearer home with a job at Burford Grammar School. As was customary at the time the school teams used to include several masters, thereby raising the standard of the boys and enabling good fixtures to be arranged. Apart from the school fixtures Jessop had the chance to play cricket for Witney Town Club, whose excellent standard of play was largely due to three brothers named Smith: the son of one of them, William junior, later appeared with much success for the London County team, and he came out fourth in the first-class averages for 1901. The son of another became a famous footballer who played for Reading, and eventually became captain of England. The standard of play was just suited to Jessop's ambitions. In his first year for the Witney Town Club they won the Oxford County Club competition, and it may surprise some to hear of such Cup competitions so long ago. There was, it seems, great rivalry and Jessop long remembers the night when they brought the cup back from Oxford to a triumphant welcome at Witney station.

Jessop was living at Burford not merely so that he could play for Witney Town, but to carry out a teaching job at Burford Grammar School. It was obviously a cricket-loving school, and in the school magazine *The Burfordian* for 1893 there is much cricket news and some of the earliest printed references to Jessop's skill. The 'School Notes', possibly written by the Headmaster, observe that:

'Mr G. L. Jessop, whom we welcome among us, has already made himself famous for a long distance round by his prowess in the cricket field. He is head and shoulders above any cricketers in the neighbourhood, and it is needless to say that he has been our mainstay. He is a brilliant hitter, and a really fast bowler, and besides this he thoroughly understands the game – a faculty which does not always accompany the first two.' It is not surprising to learn that the 'boys have been most keen about the game and the practices have been most thoroughly enjoyed'.

There are several legends surviving from the days when Jessop was working at Burford. One tells that a local club reluctantly told him that he could no longer play for them because he lost so many balls when batting; they were sorry about it, but they simply could not afford to have to buy so many balls. Another story tells how when an Oxford College team came to play one village, they won the toss and batted first; the last five members of the side thought that they would not be wanted for some time, so went off to the pub for a quick one. When they came back to the ground, they discovered that their side was now in the field. The first five batsmen had been skittled out by Jessop's bowling in two or three overs; as the other batsmen were absent, the innings was all over. Jessop's bowling on rough wickets must have been deadly, but he says that such wickets were good for his batting as they taught him the value of nippiness of foot and the need for watching the ball really closely, though it also led to a tendency to use a cross bat too frequently.

Among Jessop's mementoes is a silver bat shield presented by *Sporting Sketches* to record his score of 133 not out for Burford School *v.* Stow on the Wold on July 14, 1894, and there is also a letter from someone who was a boy at the school who heard later that Jessop had asked his father (a local farmer) not to reveal how young he was for the sake of his standing at the school.

In September 1894 when playing for Witney v. Victoria Club, Oxford he took 18 wickets for 32 runs.

Already at nineteen Jessop had been showing the qualities of a complete cricketer. At the end of the 1893 season he was invited to play for the Oxfordshire Colts against the county eleven, but he declined to do so as he hoped one day to get a trial for his own county. When the holidays came he was back at Cheltenham 'itching to play in any old game that might come along', and soon came the big chance that Jessop needed to further his cricketing ambitions. The opportunity to make his name came about in an odd way. Every August a trial match at Bristol was arranged between a side composed of University and Public School cricketers against the Rest of the County. The day before the match E. M. Grace sent the secretary of Cheltenham C.C. a wire which said: 'Ask Jessop to play.' Cousin Hylton was by that time a well-known club player, and the invitation was delivered to him. He was unable to accept, so Gilbert took the invitation instead. As he himself says: 'This invitation, though it did come in such a second-hand fashion, gave me more pleasure than did the invitation to appear in my first county match.' He certainly deserved this piece of luck – 'a pure fluke' he called it. Unlike the present-day cricketer of promise, Jessop had had no cricket coach, headmaster, or parent to push him, no representative school cricket in which he could advertise his ability, no one to drop a word to the right authorities. He was virtually 'self-learned', and he later stated that had he suffered the usual cricket instruction he would not have played as he did. Bradman was another who in his early cricketing years had to rely on his own resources and unfaltering determination.

On August 20, 1893, Jessop set foot on the Bristol ground for the first time; he knew all too well what a chance this was to make his name known, but he did not allow the importance of the game to upset him. He scored 53, took 4 wickets for 39, and above all fielded magnificently. C. L. Townsend, who was playing for the Public Schools XI and was already a seasoned county player, though still only seventeen, recalls in a letter written in 1945 how

Jessop ran out W. G. Grace's son: 'Jessop was bowling to him when Bertie hit a ball hard back and, as he thought, wide of Jessop, and he started to run when all of a sudden we saw the first glimpse of what this marvellous fielder could do; before he had run a few yards, Jessop had picked up the ball, and thrown down the wicket, all in one movement.' Townsend was walking round the ground with 'the old man' when this happened, and Grace seized him by the arm, and said 'Did you see that, Charlie?' This brilliant piece of fielding brought from Grace a suggestion that Jessop should play for the county as soon as he was able to next summer. 'W. G.' always had faith in Jessop's ability, and in spite of many early failures and the moanings of the critics who considered Jessop's methods outrageous, he stuck by him and just said: 'You will see!' W. G. had a great capacity for spotting promising players, and though he was always very kind to them and made them feel at home, his presence caused Jessop to state that even when he was an established county player, he always felt like a schoolboy when in the company of W. G.

The 1893 trial match was a great success, and as well as Jessop, six other players who took part later made appearances for the county. As the autumn came and the days of cricket were past, Jessop returned to his work at Burford with the comforting thought that it would be only a matter of months before he would be getting a letter inviting him to play for the county. His foot was on the first rung of a ladder which could lead him to the top.

The invitation to play for the county duly arrived, and on July 30, 1894, Jessop, now twenty, made his début for Gloucestershire. This was the culmination of all his previous efforts, right back to his toddling days of the coloured woolly ball and the broken surgery windows. The match was against Lancashire at Old Trafford. He says that without a doubt the most nervous moment of his career was when he first crossed the threshold of the dressing-room in the Old Trafford pavilion. But 'W. G.' certainly made him welcome, and to Jessop's delight Gloucestershire lost the toss and had to field first. The hard day's work of having to bowl 29 overs at a fast pace helped him to get used to the new surroundings of county cricket. It also made him realise what a long day in the field can feel like. As he had toiled away with the reward of only one wicket for 70 runs he reckoned that his prospects for future games with the county were not promising, but W. G. evidently thought otherwise, and as they went in said: 'Well bowled, young 'un, well bowled!' 'This was quite sufficient for me, and I went to bed happy that night. Naturally I looked for the next morning's papers with rather more than ordinary interest. Turning to the account of the match, I read: "If Mr Jessop's batting is no better than his bowling and fielding, he is scarcely likely to become an acquisition to the western shire" ' – a first-night critique which like many has been utterly confounded. Was not Hobbs strongly criticised for his fielding after his first season, and did not Maurice Tate announce that young Bradman was not likely to score many runs when he came to England?

When Gloucestershire went in to bat they were all out for 99, having found Mold's bowling too much for them. He was very fast, but after a few seasons of great success, he was at last no-balled for throwing, and his career came to an end. Jessop was to go in at number six, and in the last over before lunch the third and fourth wickets fell to consecutive balls, Francis run out and E. M. Grace yorked by Mold first ball. Then lunch was taken. Jessop says that it was the least enjoyed luncheon within his cricket experience, and the walk to the wicket afterwards to face the Lancashire Terror was not altogether a period of unalloyed joy. Fortunately Mold's first ball after lunch was a half-volley, and to Jessop a half-volley was always one whatever the circumstances. He drove it for four, and hit another similar boundary in the same over. Has any other batsman in the first over of his début made his intentions so clear? He continued to hit out and took his score to 29 before Mold bowled him. He was second top-scorer, and in the second innings he made 19 in another low total. W. G. stated that he had batted pluckily, smiled with satisfaction at his daring, and announced most prophetically, 'Well, we've found something this time!'

Though Gloucestershire lost the match badly, *The Western Daily Press* said that 'Jessop, the new man, may be congratulated upon the spirit and determination exhibited at a critical point in both innings'. So his début was a success. W. G. booked him for the next three matches, and though he did not do much, the invitation was extended to cover the rest of the season. In the very last match against Somerset, at Taunton, he produced his first 'Jessopian' innings. Going in with the score at 42 for 7, he knocked up 61 out of 73 in only 50 minutes, including a last wicket stand of 55 with Fred Roberts, who scored only one run. There was no doubt that the county had found a new and valuable asset. They were a very weak side and had come out bottom of the nine first-class counties then taking part in the championship (which was to be extended to fourteen counties in the following season). For what it was worth, Jessop had come out third in the batting, and second in the bowling, and *Wisden* commented that: 'Mr Jessop did uncommonly well for a first season and with increased experience should do well in the future. He certainly displayed considerable natural aptitude for the game, but in view of so many disappointments there is no inducement to indulge in any great hopes.'

In other words, the critics could not really believe that anyone could attack like Jessop and get away with it. In later times Jessop looked back with amusement on how the critics of his early days, who unanimously condemned him when he happened to fail, later changed their tune: 'My running out to Mold was condemned in those days as "rustic cricket" by a good few of those who nowadays talk of the same method as "forcing tactics".' Throughout his career Jessop never forgot the sound advice of Bill Smith of the Witney Town Club who urged him to stick to his own style and remember that a loose ball was a loose ball whether it came along on a county ground or a village green.

In these early days Jessop frequently failed to make many runs – he was primarily a fast bowler – and it is interesting to hear what C. L. Townsend, who played with him between 1894 and 1901, has to say about the young Jessop:

'When he first played he was what I would call a mere slogger, and used to dash wildly down the wicket and miss the ball, and we were all rather sceptical about his ever making a bat. It was in the last match of 1894, at Taunton, that we first had a real glimpse of what he could do. He made 61 not out in a very short time, and instead of missing the ball, hit it in all directions. He continued to be a slogger for several years but gradually cultivated his batting, and from 1899 onwards he was the finished article. I do not mean that before 1899 he did not play many extraordinary and marvellous innings, but there was always an element of chance about them; from then on I always looked upon his batting as a great art. He played every shot as he wanted to and knew exactly where he was going to hit the ball. Unless he was going to hit it out of the ground, he hit it along the ground or hit it sufficiently high to clear mid-off and no one could bowl to him a ball he could not score off.'

Once the season was over Jessop may have had hopes of going to a university, but he had to wait another year before funds made this possible. For some reason he did not stay on at Burford College, but next year took a job at Beccles College in Suffolk, a school run by Mr A. K. Hockey (known as 'Nibs'). As he was not likely to get much good cricket in what was a minor county, it is puzzling to know why he went there. His status as a county cricketer must have offered him some choice of jobs. There is no magazine to tell us anything of the part he played in the general life of the school. All we know is that in 1895 he played a number of times for Beccles College and that his figures read:

Batting	13	5	1058	219*	132·25
Bowling	168·2	64	244	100	2·44

These extraordinary figures are rather depressing because Jessop was clearly in a different class from his opponents, and he must have dominated the play to such an extent that it may have been unpleasant for the rest of the players.

Mr Hockey, the Headmaster, himself hands down the story of the great hits Jessop made during that season: 'The cricket field bordered on the railway station, and Jessop would run out of his crease and take the fast bowling before it pitched, and hit the ball over the railway sidings and station buildings, over the forecourt, and over some maltings beyond'.

There is also the inevitable legend of how one of his hits landed the ball into a coal truck passing by, and carried it on to London. We have a group photo of Beccles College Cricket team in 1895 which seems to have more grown-ups than boys in it. Jessop looks very smart in his flannels and blazer and is wearing a bow-tie. One of the boys is labelled 'Hockey', who may be a son of the Headmaster. One son of Mr Hockey later himself became Headmaster of a Prep school in Sussex, and when Jessop's son once played a game there Hockey told him how Jessop used to get people to *throw* the ball at him in the nets as no one could bowl fast enough. Beccles College had a good reputation, and Chateaubriand, the French writer was once a master there.

If Jessop's batting was devastating, his bowling was even more so. As he himself says: 'Some of the games savoured of shooting a sitting rabbit.' On May 29 against St Aubyn's School, Lowestoft, he produced analyses of 7–3 and 8–1; in the second innings he took 6 wickets in 7 balls, and he did the hat-trick three times during the match, which was a record until it was equalled by a boy in Australia some sixty years later.

On the following day Jessop was at Lord's because he had been given special permission by Mr Hockey to play for Gloucestershire against Middlesex. He was lucky to have the experience of playing in this match because on that day, May 30, W. G. Grace played an innings of 169 which enabled him to reach 1,000 runs before the end of the month of May. This remarkable feat followed several seasons in which his powers had seemed to be on the wane; here in 1895, at the advanced age of forty-seven, W. G. was back at his best. Jessop had not seen him make many runs before but 'naturally this brilliant innings of 169 captured my youthful imagination'. The Headmaster of Beccles College had originally agreed rather reluctantly to grant leave to Jessop for this one match, but W. G. now made a tactful request that Jessop should be allowed to stay away until the end of the Whitsun holiday. To his and Jessop's own surprise, the request was granted, and probably it was the fame of W. G. at this particular moment that did the trick. At any rate Jessop had the pleasure of playing in three consecutive county matches in the middle of term.

W. G. Grace realised that the Headmaster had made a generous concession in allowing Jessop time off in term time and we have a letter which he wrote to the Headmaster. It reads:

15 Victoria Square
Clifton, Bristol.
June 8, 1895

My dear Sir,

I write to thank you for your great kindness in letting Jessop off for the Surrey match. He played up well and bowled better than I ever saw him, he is a good cricketer. I shall not ask you to let him off again much as I should like to have him until the end of the season when we go north and his holidays have commenced. Again thanking you

I am,
Yours truly,
W. G. Grace

This third match was against Surrey at the Oval, and W. G. gave Jessop an exceedingly long spell of bowling in Surrey's total of 405; he bowled an hour and a half before lunch, and then afterwards three hours unchanged to end up with an analysis of 6 wickets for 124 runs in 61 five-ball overs.

When looking back later on his early days Jessop, for all his admiration for W. G., said that he was 'never a quick-change artist' in the matter of changing his bowlers, and he deplored the fact that he had been asked to bowl fast for such long spells, and believed that this action by W. G. had done much to undermine his health. For all Jessop's appearance of strength, he had in fact a poor constitution.

But whatever harm it may have done Jessop to bowl so long against Surrey he agreed that the effort may have been worth it, because as he says 'I learnt something in that match', and he goes on to state: 'In those early days I knew next to nothing about batsmanship. Whatever success I did gain in making runs I owed entirely to a good eye and a total disregard to where the ball went, so long as it did not go into a fieldsman's hands or my wicket. Batting had not for me the same interest as bowling and fielding. But the ease and grace with which Tom Hayward made his runs – he obtained one of his many centuries on this occasion – made me realise, what hours at the nets might have failed to do, that there were other methods of making runs than by sheer slogging. I cannot truthfully claim that the idea was immediately put into action, but the necessity of allowing the bat occasionally to assume a less horizontal position simmered more frequently in my mind. And from that time I began to concentrate on straighter driving. Among other faults I possessed there was one, which though producing a few fleeting moments of joy, brought to me innumerable failures. And that was the habit of endeavouring to anticipate the bowler's intention. Running up the pitch to meet slow bowling after the ball has left the bowler's hand has something to recommend it, but to leave one's crease before the ball is on its way is to ask for trouble. To pursue the same tactics against fast, or even medium-pace bowling, is, in nine cases out of ten, to label oneself the bowler's friend. For that year and the next at least, those in charge of the attack had small reason to complain of any stand-offishness in my disposition. It was not until my second year at Cambridge that I was able almost to cure myself of this suicidal propensity. Even then, in later years, especially when opposed to bowlers the immaculate character of whose length invited confidence, did the old fault occasionally crop up.'

These very enlightening comments on the nature of batting show how a determined player can discipline himself. Jessop at the start of his career realised his limitations as a batsman, admitted in fact his comparative lack of interest in batting, but then decided to take himself in hand. Even the greatest natural ability has to be organised to produce success, and only a willingness to learn from experience can lead to that. Jessop was ready to learn.

After his ten days mid-term holiday with Gloucestershire Jessop returned to Beccles and continued to slaughter the opposition, especially on June 27 when he scored 219 not out against the Royal Artillery, Yarmouth. Also playing in the college team without any qualification to do so was a Mr William Robson who happened to be spending his honeymoon on a wherry on the nearby River Waveney. One day he found the school playing cricket, got talking with the young man taking the game, and being a keen cricketer, asked if he might join in. As we read in a letter written to him by Jessop many years afterwards, he scored 34 and partnered Jessop during that innings of 219.

W. H. Robson is said to have introduced Jessop to the Stock Exchange; they became firm friends and Jessop often used to stay with the family at Barnet, near the village of Arkley, for which he used sometimes to play.

Jessop's remarkable performances during that short spell at Beccles made a great impact, and to this day his name is remembered, for a correspondent tells me that he recently heard his brother-in-law who lives there address his small son with the words: 'You great Jessop!' When asked about this, the brother-in-law said he had no idea who Jessop was: he was merely using a local expression he had heard. By July 22 Jessop had left Beccles for good, and was back in the county side. In 1895 Gloucestershire rose dramatically from being bottom in the table to fourth position, thanks mainly to Grace's wonderful recovery of form, and to young Charles Townsend's incredible bowling in July and August after the Clifton school term was over. In the month of August he played in eight matches and took 94 wickets, which still remains the record number of wickets ever taken by a bowler in a month's cricket. Another asset to the county was Jessop's advance as an all-rounder, and he gave Townsend fine support, for in one weeks' play at Bristol against Warwickshire and Sussex they together obtained no less than 38 wickets. Townsend took 22 wickets for 216 runs, and Jessop 16 wickets for 125 runs. Jessop's fiery bowling took a lot out of him, but his determination enabled him to keep going for long spells.

Though his scores were not high, he played several remarkable innings. His 63 out of 65 (in which he reached 51 in 18 minutes) was his highest, and it was the first time the Yorkshire bowlers suffered from his attack. It was of this innings that George Hirst later wrote: 'They were not all good strokes, but we did not mind that much. We learnt to respect him later on when he had repeated the dose a few times. He was one of the few great cricketers who could murder the correct theory of the game and get away with it. His wonderful eye and feet made him so confident that he could cut, pull, or at times drive the same length ball. I know, because he has done it to me.'

George Hirst, who always spoke so generously of Jessop, suffered the experience of being hit right out the ground by him at Cheltenham, Harrogate and Sheffield.

In another innings Jessop showed the value of attacking play when against Sussex at Bristol in a rain-spoilt match he made 53 in half an hour out of a total of 159 when runs were urgently needed. C. B. Fry recalled this innings of 53, for it was the first time he had seen Jessop. He wrote: 'He took part in the match with his usual electric impudence. He walked in to bat with a big cap on his small head, peak well over his nimble eyes, at a fast pace and with no fears. He set himself into his crouching pose at the wicket and projected himself first ball into a mountainous drive which fell out of harm's way in time; and I thanked my stars (if any) that I was not underneath the falling ball. He made, if I remember right, some 40 runs. It was an amazing exhibition. He fled out to drive like an amateur thunderbolt projected by Jove after too much nectar. He also flung his bat at the ball like a ballistic flail. He also delivered sundry square cuts of terrific vigour.'

In the second innings of this same match Jessop played an equally important innings of 1 not out, and seldom has so small an innings justified such a full story. The situation was that after much interruption by rain, and concentrated action on the third afternoon, the last Sussex wicket had fallen at a total which brought their combined scores equal to Gloucester's score of 159. They thus wanted one run to win, but the clock stood at 5.48, stumps were to be drawn at 6.0, so only 12 minutes were left. But with ten minutes between the innings this left Gloucester 2 minutes to make the run. Sussex assumed the game was over, but W. G. quite rightly insisted on having the chance to bat. Sussex reluctantly took the field, except for Ranji who had already changed and left. W. G. offered to act as substitute fielder for him, and selected as his two batsmen Jessop and J. J. Ferris. Jessop was to face the bowling, and Ferris wore no pads, because under cricket law of the time, if Jessop had got out the game would have been finished. Now the over would be completed. Ferris' job was simply to run like a hare if a chance arose from a hit by Jessop. Jessop was not one to be daunted by nerves, but this was an odd situation, and he might have felt disturbed by the crowding field. As he says himself, 'the getting of that one run was not quite the easy job it seems on paper, especially when the loss of a wicket meant a drawn game instead of a victory.' Fred Tate was the bowler and the first two balls beat Jessop completely, but just missed the stumps in the way Tate's great son so often did. The third ball, however, Jessop managed to push gently in the direction of W. G. fielding substitute at point, and thanks to Ferris's scamper the run was made. Jessop was applauded off the field not only for his two valuable innings, but also for his part in taking 7 wickets for 54 runs, including those of Fry and Ranji. Some years later a reporter writing in the *Daily Mail* recalled this match and invited readers to send in their ideas as to what tactics they would have used to prevent the batsman from scoring. I can imagine W. G.'s satisfaction at winning this match. He was not one to allow another side to rob him of a possible victory. It is interesting that he should have chosen Jessop – a player of little experience – to cope with this situation.

At the end of the season Jessop received an invitation to play at Scarborough. It was always a great honour to appear in the Festival matches, and it was only thirteen months since Jessop's arrival in first-class cricket. No wonder he wrote: 'To me this season of 1895 was a sheer delight. I do not honestly think that in respect of personal enjoyment any subsequent year exceeded it. Perhaps this was only natural, as I had begun to find my feet.'

There is a photograph of Jessop taken at the Oval in 1895. He is wearing a Gloucestershire cap, and sporting a moustache, and he has that unmistakable twinkle in his eye which suggests that he was finding life good.

In the issue of August 22, 1895, *Cricket* honoured him with one of that magazine's special biographical pieces, where it was stated that he had some intentions of going up to a university, though it was not yet known which one.

3

The Cambridge Years 1896–1899

'Despite the frequent interruptions by such matters as Lectures, I enjoyed my cricketing days at Cambridge.'

G. L. J.

FOR some reason Jessop did not enter Cambridge in the usual Michaelmas Term of 1895, but was not enrolled as a member of Christ's College until the following summer term. Perhaps he was working for his entrance exams through the winter. He was very nearly twenty-two – much older than most students – and within a few days of coming into residence he was playing in the Freshers match on April 30. Great things were expected of him at Cambridge after his experience as a county player, and, as usual on first appearances, he did not disappoint. He scored 102 in an hour, took seven wickets, and was the only Freshman to win a Blue that year. It is interesting to see that on the match sheet, no school is named for him. He appears as 'G. L. Jessop (Private and Christ's)': he had decided not to claim connection with Cheltenham Grammar School, which he had left when only fifteen. His ending of formal education at such an early age must have left enormous gaps in his knowledge, and it must have been very difficult for him to adjust himself to the academic work required by the university.

His chief reason for going to Cambridge was to become ordained for the Church, and this meant a considerable knowledge of the Classics. As he says: 'The season of 1896 was to me one of vast interest. It marked my first acquaintance with Plato and Fenners. Prior to my entry at Christ's College the name of Fenners had to me a more familiar ring than had that of the famous Greek author.' He did not even know the Greek alphabet, and he had to learn by heart translated portions of the Apology of Plato, with the result that he once failed an exam. by adding several more lines in English than the original Greek warranted, 'a mistake that might happen to anyone accustomed to learn Greek by heart'. It must have been a severe struggle to have to buckle down to such unpalatable work, especially when there were so many other distractions. He writes: 'One's first year at the Varsity is usually a trying time. There is so much to do and very little time to do it. Free from the restraint of school with its regularity of hours, the Fresher is rather apt to disregard the old adage of "Early to bed and early to rise, make a man healthy, wealthy and wise". Late hours never yet improved one's average.'

So no midnight oil was spent over the study of Plato, and Jessop always observed the dictum of W. G. Grace who believed that cricketing eyes needed as much rest as possible. When on tour W. G. invariably retired to bed at 10.30, and expected it of others. 'Being a blind worshipper of the Old Man, anything he did was good enough for me, and I followed his example throughout my career.' Fortunately Jessop found the dons at Christ's an 'extremely sporting lot', though they made it clear that if one was to stay at the university the entrance exam called 'Little Go' must be coped with, and Jessop began to realise that 'though they did parlously interfere with other pursuits, lectures must be attended'. As there was virtually non-stop cricket throughout the summer term, including his playing in a couple of county matches, he must have found life very full and pleasant, and as a cricket celebrity must have had a very social life.

After his success in the Freshers match he took a little time to find his form, but after a rousing innings victory over Yorkshire in which he took nine wickets, Jessop was awarded his Blue in his fourth match. But to those who had expected that he would be the best all-rounder since Sammy Woods had gone up, he was something of a disappointment. One reason for his loss of form in bowling on the hard grounds of Fenners was the condition of the nails of his left foot. When playing centre-forward for Gloucester against Warmley in a Western League game the previous March 'some thirteen stone of humanity had descended upon my toes with no fairy-like tread'. In spite of this lasting discomfort, Jessop's bowling achieved some measure of distinction because of its fieriness and his readiness to bump the ball. This tendency to bowl bumpers produced in Cambridge *Granta* circles a limerick which went:

> There was a young Fresher called Jessop
> Who was pitching 'em less up and less up,
> 'Til one of the pros
> Got a blow on the nose
> And said: 'In a helmet I'll dress up.'

or with a variant line, 'And a man with a mop cleared the mess up' – a forecast perhaps of the strange helmet worn by Patsy Hendren in the mid 1930s after he had been hit on the head. Though Jessop often bowled this fast bumping stuff from round the wicket, C. L. Townsend dispels any idea that the purpose was to intimidate the batsman. Writing in 1934 he says, 'I never saw Jessop bowl at a man in his life. Such a thing was not done in my day, thank goodness.' Jessop himself totally disapproved of the ugly body-line form of attack prevalent in the 1930s, and in a letter written to Nigel Haig in 1949 he says: 'I used to bowl about as short as anybody in my time occasionally, but my field – a long-leg, a short-leg, and a mid-on – did at any rate not prohibit the batsman from offensive strokes, nor confine him to the sole purpose of protecting himself from injury.'

The Jessop bouncers were much in evidence in his first Varsity match of 1896. He made a duck in Cambridge's score of 318, but then, under the orders of his captain, Frank Mitchell, he attacked so savagely with bumpers from round the wicket that he not only broke a stump, but damaged several of the batsmen, especially Leveson-Gower, and knocked out his own wicket-keeper. Despite the mutterings of the crowd, 'the demon bowler, as perky as ever, went on for a time with stubborn determination'. Later in the innings came one of the most unpleasant scenes ever witnessed at Lord's. In those days the follow-on was compulsory, so in order not to have Oxford batting again, the Cambridge captain arranged the deliberate bowling of two no-balls to the boundary so as to increase the Oxford score beyond the follow-on figure. This would seem now to be a reasonable way of coping with a law which later became sensibly changed, but the crowd thought it smacked of sharp practice, and to quote Jessop, 'The demonstration which followed these legitimate tactics was such as I hope never to see repeated on any English ground. The hostile ovation which we received on our return to the Pavilion was as disgraceful as it was unwarrantable. And in this atmosphere of contention we had perforce to take our second innings. Small wonder if we failed – as we eventually did.'

Some of the M.C.C. members were very hostile, and they stood and yelled abuse at the Cambridge side as they came off the field. One old man stood in the gangway so that they could not pass, and was so angry that he could not speak. As he tried to find words he just made clucking noises. Hemingway, one of the Cambridge side who also played for Gloucester, said to him: 'I'll have that one for breakfast, sir, when you've laid it.'

Next day *The Times* in a leading article deplored the actions which caused 'the University match, a contest of the most friendly and stainless character' to degenerate into such competitiveness, and Jessop's bowling came in for special censure.

'We are very far from charging the Cambridge fast bowler with a desire to destroy human life. He would not, for example, wish to harm his own excellent wicket-keeper! Yet several of his bumped-down deliveries were of almost unexampled shortness. . . . This may be, and doubtless is, the result of a rather demoniacal style, and the bowler may be recommended to modify his manner.' There cannot be many bowlers who have earned such an editorial mention in a leader in *The Times*. Jessop's 'demon' deliveries recall a story which he himself told in later days about how a ball from a whirlwind fast bowler once hit a batsman in the mouth, breaking off two of his front teeth. When the batsman came out again in the second innings, he called out to the bowler: 'Are you going to try to get the rest of my teeth this time?' To which the bowler shouted back: 'No, it's only your stumps I'm after now.'

Sir Pelham Warner refers to Jessop as being in his young days a very fast bowler, capable of bowling such a ball which once bowled F. A. Iredale, the Australian, at Cheltenham in 1899. 'It sent the off peg flying through the air a distance of nine paces, Board, the wicket-keeper, discreetly giving it a wide berth.' For some reason Jessop used to bowl quite often from round the wicket, an altogether frightening prospect for the batsman, especially on a lively pitch. One writer recalls how in 1897 on a broken wicket at Gloucester a certain Warwickshire batsman was much battered by Jessop and used to yelp every time he thought the ball was going to rise and hit him, but he stuck it out gallantly and stayed in a long time. If anyone had bowled short to Jessop, he would have welcomed it. All the greatest of fast bowlers suffered from his bat; Richardson, Mold, Kortright, Kotze and Jones were all hit hard and high by him.

Soon after the 1896 Varsity match Jessop joined the county team, and this was to be the pattern of his cricket for the next few seasons. Although he spent four summer terms at Cambridge, Jessop was in fact in residence for only seven terms in all. This was partly because owing to ill health he spent the winter of 1897 away in Cornwall. He might also have spent a term or two away doing special work for his 'Little Go' exam, though any prospects of getting a degree were doubtful from the start. Whatever his wishes and convictions, a degree was essential for one who wished to be ordained, and he must before long have been forced to give up hope of entering the Church. There is a good story told by his aunt in connection with this. Just after his university days he wrote to tell her he was coming to Cheltenham, and while there he was going to 'try out some colts', i.e. have a look at some promising young cricketers. She knew her cricket terms for she was greatly interested in the game and her nephew's exploits. She read out his letter to a friend who was staying with her, a friend whose cricket education was deficient, for she remarked rather censoriously: 'I'm exceedingly sorry to hear that Gilbert has given up the idea of going into the Church, and now I am still more sorry to hear that he is going in for horse-dealing.'

We have little information about his Cambridge days other than cricketing reminiscences, 'despite the frequent interruptions necessitated by such matters as lectures and chapels – both early and late – I thoroughly enjoyed my cricketing days at Cambridge.' It was the shortage of his chapel attendances which caused him to be 'gated', that is to say, not allowed out after 9 p.m., on the week of the Inter-Varsity billiards match. He pleaded with his tutor that his appearance in the match would be good for the esprit de corps of the college, but the tutor was adamant, and 'quite chilled' Jessop with the suggestion that his period of 'gating' would give him a helpful opportunity of doing some work for his forthcoming exams.

His scrapbooks have several items concerning his last year at Cambridge. There are some beautifully produced menu cards, including one from the Marguerites, a college club with which Jessop was connected. Another concerns a dinner given at Christ's College by the C.U.C.C. to the visiting Australian cricket team on June 9, 1899. That afternoon Jessop had bowled very successfully against the Australians, and now had to propose their health with the Provost of Kings'. This is a copy of the menu.

Consommé à la Sevigné
Salad d'homard
Attereaux à la Moderne
Quartier d'Agneau
Poulets Printaniers
Jambon de York
Asperges froides à la huile
Plombière Glacée à la Andalouse
Croutes à la Bordelaise
Dessert

After a good battle on the first innings in which both sides scored 436, the day after this dinner the University collapsed for only 122, and lost the game by ten wickets.

There is another decorated menu with its coloured ribbons for a party given by Jessop at 3 St Andrews Street on 'Mercredi, 15 Juin, 1898'. There are also several beribboned Commem. Ball Engagement Cards, two of them on consecutive days in June 1899. One is partly filled in with certain names; a Miss Duncan appears four times, while other unnamed ladies appear as 'Pinkie', 'Cerise', 'Smiler' and 'Diamond Cross'. One can almost hear now the strains of 'Herr Gottlieb's Band' coming down across the years; eighteen of the twenty-six dances were waltzes and there were three polkas, three lancers, one barn dance, and the final galop 'John Peel', in which one can imagine Jessop displaying his agility.

It is interesting to see that within twenty-four hours of these two consecutive balls Jessop was making his first appearance for England against Australia at Lord's, his selection being the result of his fine fast bowling against the visitors when they came to play the University. Jessop, bowling very fast, took six of the first eight Australian wickets.

At that early stage of the season there was a dearth of fast bowlers: Lockwood and Kortright were suffering from strains, and Richardson and W. M. Bradley were not yet in form. One of the umpires, Sherwin, said to Jessop during the innings: 'This bowling will get you into the Test team', and he wagered Jessop a new hat that he would be on the list when the team was announced. Jessop, surprised at this prophecy, took on the bet – 'the first and last time I made such a wager' – and was as he says 'later pleased to lose the wager.' So Sherwin got a new hat and Jessop within a fortnight was making his début for England as the only fast bowler in the side, which some critics found rather a doubtful selection.

Jessop recalls as the two most outstanding events of his time at Cambridge the 'hullaballo' over Women's Degrees, which he refers to as the occasion of a 'very lively rag', and the conferring of a degree on Lord Kitchener, who stayed at the Master's Lodge at Christ's College. At a reception during his visit Jessop was introduced to the guest of the evening by the tutor's wife, who referred to him as the 'President' of the Cambridge University Cricket Club instead of the 'Captain', which amused him.

A University captain must have a busy time, not least with correspondence. One letter he received was from an old Blue, Canon McCormick, who suggested that his son, who was up at the time, should be given a trial against the Australians, who were supposed to be uncertain on soft wickets against slow left-hand bowling, such as the son produced. We do not know what Jessop's reply was, but the father's request – which he begged to be kept secret – was not granted, and the son never in fact played for the University at any time.

Jessop had not originally intended to be at the University in 1899. At the end of his third year he was considering his future, and was intending at the end of the 1898 summer to go out to Rhodesia as tutor to the son of the Governor, and this might have been the end of his cricket in England. But at a meeting of the Blues after the Varsity match, it was unexpectedly suggested to Jessop that he stay on for another year, and become captain, even though he had not held any previous office. The temptation to have another season was great, the possibility of a job in Rhodesia was forgotten, and Jessop accepted the University captaincy for 1899.

But this is jumping ahead of events. In 1897 (a season which he called his 'red-letter year') he had fully recovered from his damaged toes of the previous year, and his policy of trying to play straighter, and not commit himself too early to the stroke, was beginning to produce results. There was also the satisfactory defeat of Plato which enabled him to pass 'Little Go', and an equally satisfactory defeat of Oxford. It was also the season in which he first achieved the honour of playing for the Gentlemen against the Players at Lord's. It was in fact the year in which Jessop 'arrived' as a great cricketer. His first hundred was a score of 140 for the University against the Philadelphians on June 14. The innings lasted only 105 minutes and included two remarkable hits off H. P. Baily, the chief slow bowler. In his first over, Jessop hit him into the road by the entrance gate, an enormous hit, whereupon Baily asked to be transferred to the other end where the boundary was longer. This was done, and to the vast amusement of his fellows, Baily's first ball from that end was hit clean over the distant wall into the grounds of a girl's school. Any hit right out of Fenners is extremely rare. As well as these two hits Jessop also made five or six drives which landed near the pavilion in the garden of Walter Watts, the groundsman. Someone commented to him on this succession of hits, but all Watts said was: 'If he does it many more times, he'll spoil my asparagus.' Another of Jessop's great hits on the Fenners ground was a square-cut right into the score-box. Jessop's first hundred came in what was his eightieth innings in first-class cricket, and was only his tenth score of fifty or more: those who felt that his batting had been 'disappointing' had some reasons for it, though Jessop himself said that in his early days he was not really interested in batting, and may have been less disappointed than his admirers.

It was in this season that Jessop had an interesting encounter with C. I. Thornton who is still generally acknowledged to have been the biggest hitter of all time. Comparisons between Thornton and Jessop were already being made – foolishly, because they were not really the same type. W. J. Ford, writing about hitters in 1899, says of Jessop: 'We have one of the good old sort left and were he a bigger man with a longer reach, even C. I. Thornton might at last find an equal.' When Cambridge played C. I. Thornton's XI in 1896 Jessop twice dismissed Thornton for 10 (bowled) and 16 (stumped). This must have been galling for Thornton who had been determined to show his young rival a thing or two. In the following year Thornton, now aged 47, went in tenth in the same fixture and had to face Jessop bowling fast round the wicket. 'Buns' never wore pads – just shin guards under his socks – and Jessop hit him hard on the shins, so that for most of his short stay Thornton was hopping on one leg and rubbing the other, uttering very uncomplimentary things. Though Jessop did not get him out, he made only 1 and 1, and that was a sad end to his career, for he never played again in first-class cricket.

In July of 1897 Jessop really excelled himself, 'my lucky month', he called it. He began by helping Cambridge to a good win in the Varsity match by splendid bowling and a dramatic innings of 42. The first ball he received was crashed up against the pavilion wall and rebounded far back on to the field. He went on in this manner, until after receiving only 15 balls he was caught at cover for 42, made out of 51 in only 17 minutes. His score was made up of 9 fours, 2 twos, and 2 singles. As often, the runs were badly needed. A week later he made his first appearance for the Gentlemen at Lord's, and scored a game-swinging fantastic 67 in 35 minutes, 'hitting away with a vigour he has never surpassed'. He had come in to join Francis Ford, himself a great hitter, at a critical moment and together these two put on 88 runs, of which Jessop made 67, and while this stand was on an unnecessary comment was made that Jessop made Ford look like a stone-waller.

To quote one report: 'A good parallel would be to compare the methods of the hour and minute hands of a watch.' In fact Ford was holding the side together with his scores of 50* and 79*, and subduing his natural inclinations for the sake of others. He knew it was the right moment to let this young player have his head. Here is a full report of what was Jessop's first great performance at Lord's:

'On resuming at a quarter to three Jessop went in with Ford and treated the spectators to a remarkable display. He opened with a rather faulty stroke for 2 over point's head, and he then drove Richardson to the on for 5, while a ball from Hearne he hit over the ring in front of the members' dining-room. Then in one over from Richardson 12 runs were obtained, Jessop making 11 of them. The daring young hitter first made a fine drive to the on for 4, and then jumping in several yards to the fast bowler, he got a rather lucky two, the ball dropping short of the longfield. Richardson evidently thought that Jessop would jump in again, for he dropped the next ball short, but the batsman drew himself up and hit it to the square leg boundary. In the next over from Hearne Jessop got a 4 to square leg, but with his score at 27, he gave a difficult chance wide on the off-side to Hirst, who after running some distance, and getting both of his hands to the ball, failed to make the catch. Two more 4s through the slips off Richardson went to the credit of Jessop, who had by this time made 40 while Ford was adding 5 to his score. The latter at length drove Richardson finely for 4, and also got 4 for a snick to leg off Hearne. Jessop drove Richardson for 4, and treated Hearne in a similar manner, the ball hitting the Pavilion. The rapidity of the scoring may be gathered from the fact that Jessop completed his 50 out of 65 in twenty-three minutes, and the 200 went up at the same time.

'Hayward and Attewell then took up the bowling, but Jessop went on merrily, getting Hayward to leg for 4, and in the following over from the same bowler scoring 10 runs by a 4 through the slips, 2 to the on, and 4 for a straight drive. The last was a magnificent hit, the ball dropping among the seats on the top of the Pavilion. There was a round of hearty cheering when Jessop passed Grace's score, but directly afterwards he got under a ball from Attewell, and was caught by Hayward at mid-off, the fieldsman being evidently relieved when he had made the catch. The seventh wicket fell at 224, no fewer than 88 runs having been put on in 35 minutes, of this number Jessop having made the large proportion of 67 by hitting of the most fearless description. He made some faulty hits, but that was only to be expected with the batsman taking so many liberties with the game. It was an astonishing display.'

In the end the Gentlemen fell short of victory by 78 runs, when Ford ran out of partners.

The very next day at Bristol Jessop scored 101 for Gloucestershire – his first hundred for the county – and once again it was the Philadelphians who provided him with this chance. Lest it be imagined that these overseas visitors were weak opposition, one needs to remember that among the bowlers on both occasions were J. B. King – one of the all-time great bowlers – and P. H. Clark, one of the best bowlers of the day. Three days later Jessop scored 126 out of 176 in only 95 minutes against Warwickshire at Edgbaston, an innings of which Sydney Santall has vivid recollections of W. G. Grace standing up in the verandah of the pavilion, clapping hands and shouting: 'Well hit, Gilbert!' Warwickshire had led on the first innings by 70 runs, and promptly got rid of five of the Gloucestershire second innings batsmen for 93. Then came Jessop, 'who brought about a complete change', and in the end Gloucestershire lost only by two slender wickets. Jessop made one hit off Santall to the top of the pavilion roof and made several other hits over the ring.

The next match was against Lancashire at Liverpool. When Gloucestershire were forced to follow on, they were all out in their second innings for 186, and Jessop was top scorer with 49 made in 25 minutes off the bowling of Mold, Cuttell and Briggs. He hit at least four balls over the ropes. On the following day (July 29) they moved to Harrogate to face the daunting attack of Yorkshire – champions in 1896 – which consisted of Hirst, Wainwright, F. S. Jackson, C. E. M. Wilson, Brown, and Milligan, a bowler of pace. Gloucestershire won the toss, and lost three for 72, which brought in Jessop for 20 minutes' batting before lunch. As usual he wasted no time, and when the interval came he had scored 43 out of 54 in those 20 minutes. In the next eight overs Jessop added 58 out of 64 to reach 101 out of 118 in only forty minutes. His score reads:

1 4 1 4 3 6 1 3 1 1 4 4 4 1 1 4 4 4 1 4 1 1 6 4 4 1 4 6 4 4 6 4.

Jackson finally bowled him with a vicious break-back. Thirty-three of these runs came in two consecutive overs bowled by Milligan (18) and Hirst (15).

In fact these 33 runs came off eight consecutive balls, for the last four balls of Milligan's over went 6 4 4 1, and the first four balls of Hirst's next over went for 4 6 4 4. Jessop is credited with four sixes which must have sent the ball right out of the ground, and he himself believes that at least twelve hits pitched over the boundary line. I looked in his unpublished reminiscences to see what he might have to say, but all he tells us is that he 'enjoyed forty minutes experience of the relay of six bowlers that were brought into action'. Not a word about the fact that these forty minutes produced such a score. But he did admit on another occasion that he liked playing at Harrogate because 'it was so small'.

In his earlier days Jessop often seemed just as interested in height as in distance, and many of the hits at Harrogate went a long way up. A. A. Thomson, who was living at Harrogate in 1897, but did not see the innings as he was only aged three at the time, heard all about it at an early age and almost persuaded himself that he had witnessed every stroke. The legends about it are still strong in Harrogate, including the story of one lofty hit that landed on the roof of a cab waiting outside the ground, and so startled the horse that it galloped away on the road to Leeds.

Another hit was even more remarkable, and Jessop describes it in detail in an article about Big Hits, without saying that he himself was responsible for it. He writes: 'Certainly the most extraordinary hit in my experience was one which cleared the ropes at Harrogate, the direction being over the slips' heads. It was made with the bat held almost at the same angle as one would hold a racquet and was off a bumping fast bowler. It was quite a genuine hit, not a mishit.'

The hit was in fact made off Milligan, who had some real pace, and the ball landed in the pavilion. One match report says rather critically of this hit that it was 'somewhat unorthodox'. The reports of this remarkable innings are rather unsatisfactory. I suppose things were happening too quickly for them to be reported properly, but Lord Hawke who was captaining Yorkshire in the match remembers it well, and says that when Jessop 'was in the vein he would have scored even if forty-four men were in the field. He never had theories, but he has been heard to say that the best bowling was the easiest to hit'. Lord Hawke recalls the grin of glee on W. G.'s face as he said: 'Eh, what, he gave you some, didn't he?' Jessop's success must have been very gratifying to W. G. This particular innings, to quote Lord Hawke, 'baffles description'; it was stranger than fiction, and it was the fastest hundred ever scored in a first-class match. Its time of forty minutes has been surpassed only once since then, by P. G. H. Fender, who in 1920 reached his century against Northants in 35 minutes in rather different circumstances, since Surrey had already scored over 450 runs when he went in. The third fastest hundred on record, scored in 42 minutes, also belongs to Jessop.

One last point about the famous innings at Harrogate. A note in *Wisden* states: 'Although he scored at such a tremendous pace, Jessop gave no chance.' It is almost a relief from such miracles of batting to find that in the second innings Jessop was caught without scoring, but to counterbalance that he bowled seventy-one overs and took nine Yorkshire wickets.

By the end of the season Jessop's name was on everyone's lips. All he needed now to set the seal on his success was an England cap, and if there had been Test matches in 1897 he might well have gained one. It is no surprise to find that when the next *Wisden* came out G. L. Jessop was among those selected as the 'Five cricketers of the Year'. Figures show that this honour is as difficult to achieve as being selected to play for England, since you can appear only once, and it is not confined to English cricketers. The photograph shows Jessop wearing an 'Etceteras' cap, and sporting a moustache not seen in later photos of him. The biography says: 'We have never produced a batsman of quite the same stamp. We have had harder hitters, but perhaps never one who could in twenty minutes or so entirely change the fortunes of the game.' It went on to recall the way in which he had flogged the best professional bowling in England in the Gentlemen *v.* Players match already mentioned, and how the great Tom Richardson had suffered a second time at the Oval when Jessop had treated him 'as if he had been a medium-pace bowler', when knocking off the runs in difficult conditions to give Gloucestershire her first victory over Surrey at the Oval since 1885. *Wisden* stated further that 'He is a keen judge of his own capabilities, and we have heard him say that bowling that keeps at all low is apt to get him out very soon. Taking such liberties as he does and trying to score continually off good length balls, this can readily be understood.' Another honour of a quite different type was when *The National Review* published several cricket articles by Jessop. The first one in the autumn of 1897 was about run-getting, but the honour of publication was slightly tarnished by the apparent need for a footnote which read: 'We trust that there are few readers of *The National Review* who are not aware that the feature of the past season was Mr Jessop's brilliant hitting.' I believe that this article was Jessop's first appearance in print, and the forerunner of a great many articles which proved Jessop to be an excellent sporting journalist.

It is not easy to appreciate now the extreme impact Jessop made on the cricket world in a matter of those few days in July 1897. His spectacular début for the Gentlemen, his first hundred for Gloucestershire, followed by his first county match hundred, and then that quite unbelievable innings against Yorkshire. All that happened in the course of a fortnight, and though his next eleven innings produced as many as seven single-figure scores (including five ducks) this very bad spell failed to cloud the previous glory. Something new had arrived such as the game had seldom seen before. If we want to know just how Jessop managed to transform himself from the wild slogger of his early days we can read about it, because in one of his rare moments of self-revelation Jessop has told us. In an article in *The Cricketer* in 1921 he explains about his change of stance and of grip and of his whole attitude to batting. It is one of the most interesting pieces ever written about the art of batsmanship, and here it is in full:

'In the brave old days of padless legs and tasteful top-hats the engravings of that period invariably show the attitude of a batsman at the wicket as being severely perpendicular, what in these days, when most golfers have been cricketers, and every cricketer is a golfer – more or less – would be termed a proper upright stance. Now, although at no time in my career could I boast of a classical attitude, yet at the commencement my stance closely resembled the upright. It was not until my fourth season in first-class cricket that I adopted a more horizontal position at the wicket, and the alteration was not conceived without purpose. At this time I had developed a partiality for straying up the pitch to meet the bowling. As this necessitated extreme quickness of foot, I found that I could get off the mark quicker by this crouching attitude than I could in one more upright. Practising starts for 'sprints' first gave me this idea, and though from the point of elegance the crouch has very little to recommend itself, yet something may be said for it on the point of utility.

'Anyway, it served me well, and though I may have envied at times the studied grace of Mr Lionel Palairet, and the sinuous ease of "Ranji", still, I have had small reason to regret taking up a stance which a writer once graphically described as a position whereby the aroma of the pitch could be sampled to the best advantage. The same reason – namely, running out to meet the bowling – was also responsible for my changing the grip of the bat. Formerly, I used the stereotyped grip, with the right-hand half-way down the handle. I discarded that for one which gave me greater control, especially when, as so frequently happened, one had to change one's stroke in the last fraction of a second. I placed the left hand where the right formerly was, and shifted the right down to the blade. When a batsmen chases up the pitch – be he never so quick – his intention, unless the bowler is singularly obtuse, is 'spotted', and therefore a change of length is only to be expected. The intelligent bowler pitches the ball further up in the hope of a yorker; the other kind sees his remedy in a shorter length.

'To use one's feet with only one definite object in view, namely, to hit the ball, irrespective of where it pitches, narrows a batsmen's chance of a long stay at the wicket considerably. It took a season or two to convince me of the fallacy that any kind of ball could be driven in any direction with impunity. In those early days I was too apt to forget that there were other ways of dealing with a short ball than by attempting to drive it. A fine innings of Sir Timothy O'Brien at Clifton opened my eyes to the possibilities which square cutting off the short ball offered as a means of dealing with the ball which eventually failed to turn into a drivable one. Now, if I went out with the intention of driving, and had suddenly to change tactics, this meant for me a change not only mental, but physical, because in cutting I used to always slide my hands further down the handle. When one "goes over the top" to fast bowling, one is not left much time for quiet contemplation, and it therefore seemed good to me to find one grip which would suit all purposes. I haven't the slightest doubt that the shortened grip does result, as golfers say, in loss of distance, but it more than makes up for this by reason of the greater control one has over the bat.

'As so many of my runs were obtained off the ball of what is commonly termed good length, naturally the ball was more frequently in the air than one has a right to expect from the employment of more polished and studiously orthodox methods. This being so, it was obvious that a nice regard for placing must be practised. With the old grip, though naturally not weak wristed, I frequently found that in hitting "balloons" my left wrist "flopped" a little, and consequently the ball went very wide indeed of the intended direction. I don't for one moment intend to convey to my readers the impression that with the alteration of the grip came so immaculate a control of the bat that – to vary the legend of Alfred Shaw and the "tanner" – I could plant the ball on a five-shilling piece at the distance of ninety yards, but I do claim that given the proper ball, it gave me a sufficiency of control to enable me to fetch the boundary on many more occasions in the area of ground between long-on and long-off. A shortened grip of any weapon must make for greater accuracy. Take a billiard cue, a tennis racquet, or even a brassey, and you will find that this is so. And it is guinea to a gooseberry that in hanging a picture to the wall, with one hand on the nail, the other will not be gripping the hammer at the extreme end.'

In four years Jessop had come from obscurity to fame, and with Grace now aged nearly fifty he had become the chief crowd-drawer in England. No wonder his admirers were so ecstatic. Even half an hour of Jessop made the day and he did not often disappoint. You could tell as he came in if he was really in the mood. Sydney Santall who bowled to him many times says that if he emerged from the pavilion flexing his neck slightly to one side, and occasionally giving a tug to the back of his trousers, it was a sign that the opponents were in for trouble. His personality came across to every spectator. Everything he did was vital, and A. A. Thomson recalls that merely to see Jessop cross over from cover position between the overs was 'a heart-lifting experience'.

Although Jessop drew the crowd in a way few other cricketers have ever achieved, he was not one who ever played to the gallery or relied upon the plaudits of the crowd to bring out his best. Like Victor Trumper, the crowd

Jessop in action, in each case playing a particularly characteristic shot.

'The Croucher' awaits delivery

'The Croucher' plays forward.

Four Beldam action shots of Jessop fielding. Whenever possible he tried to pick up at full stretch.

made no difference to his manner of play; he did not for example allow big hitting to go to his head as it did to Albert Trott's. He was, however, perfectly aware of the great pleasure a hitter can provide, and he made some very astute comments of the whole matter:

'The man who hits always possesses one consoling thought in success or failure, that with him goes the sympathy of the great majority of spectators. Most of them maintain firmly that "it is better to have hit and missed than never to have hit at all".

'A few old-fashioned theorists still shake their heads sadly, and endeavour to look disgusted when the ball crashes into the pavilion clock or disappears into the neighbouring gardens, but I suppose I cannot be wrong in saying that even those in their hearts are not especially saddened by the sight, while for the more ordinary sportsman, the men who have just come to see some fun, and the younger people of both sexes, the spectacle causes unqualified enthusiasm.

'Playing to the gallery in all sports is one of the most offensive forms of diseased vanity, and to hit simply to extort applause would indeed be a lamentable method of seeking cheap popularity. But it cannot be denied that there is some satisfaction in feeling that you are giving pleasure to the vast throng surrounding the field of play, that they are glad to see you appear, rejoice when an incompetent fielder gives you another life, are saddened when you retire to well-deserved obscurity. And even if the fates prove unfavourable, and your first ball, designed to disappear beyond the boundary, screws stupidly into the arms of extra-cover, and you retire dejectedly into the pavilion for an ignominous "blob", it is some slight satisfaction to feel that there is scarcely one who is not sorry for your departure. "He did his best to make things live", they amiably remark, and even cheer your retiring figure, in a kind-hearted attempt to inform you of their appreciation of your effort. . . .

'But remember that the object of each player is to do the best for his side regardless of the crowd; that we who are hitters hit because we are most use doing this, and those who play a stone-wall game do so because they are most use doing that, and that all have equal right to participate in the finest sport, whether they cause interest to the spectators or whether they cause indifference.'

This is the fullest statement ever made by a great hitter on his approach to the crowd. What would we not now give to be able to see Jessop again in action and to hear the background of the crowd noise which was always created by his presence? It is a lasting sadness that the style and performance of so unique a batsman have never been recorded on film. There is a brief snippet of news-reel film which shows W. G. Grace batting very jerkily in the nets in 1898, and some film of the Australian team of 1905 which gives us a glimpse of Trumper, but nothing so far as I know of Jessop. Even action photographs of the early twentieth-century players are rare, though we must be very grateful for the efforts of George Beldam for his photographs of great players published in 1905–6, with commentary by C. B. Fry. The twelve photos of Jessop batting have come out especially well. Fry comments that the position Jessop took up in his stance is 'very extraordinary for a big hitter', and quite misleading. The crouching attitude suggests the intention of extreme care. He always used a long-handled bat, and this meant a wide gap between the hands. The grip with the knuckles of left hand pointing down the wicket made it look as if driving would be impossible, and while waiting for the bowler he would constantly 'clasp and unclasp his hands as though fingering for a tighter grip'.

'As the ball left the bowler's hands he would make a sudden stoop with his shoulders and head almost down to a level with the top of the stumps, as though endeavouring to get the eyes as much below the ball as possible.' All this ultra-careful sighting suggested a gentle tap along the ground to the bowler and almost a sigh of relief at very survival, but what in fact happened was quite different. The crouching cat pounced, 'then he launched himself yards down the pitch with quick short steps and literally flung his bat at the ball, with the result that it went vastly hard and high somewhere between extra cover and long leg. Or else after a preliminary chassée he chivied back to his crease and threw his bat at the ball in a rasping square cut. His hitting was prodigious, but he was not a slogger. He watched the ball as carefully as did Arthur Shrewsbury. His tactics were first of all to run the bowler down to induce him to bowl short, and then apply his square-cut. He was double-jointed all over, and though his drives looked like far-flung sweeps at the ball, he really got his power from a highly developed wring of the wrists at the moment of impact.' Thus wrote C. B. Fry, and one is readily reminded of the description of the greatest batsman of the 1770s – William Beldham ('Silver Billy') of the Hambledon Club. This is what the Rev. John Mitford wrote about him in 1833:

'Beldham was a close-set, active man, about five feet eight inches. Never was such a player! so safe, so brilliant, so quick, so circumspect; so able in counsel, so active in the field; in deliberation so judicious, in execution so tremendous. It mattered not to him who bowled, or how he bowled, fast or slow, high or low, straight or bias; away flew the ball from his bat, like an eagle on the wing. It was a study for Phidias to see Beldham rise to strike; the grandeur of the attitude the settled composure of the look, the piercing lightning of the eye, the rapid glance of the bat, were electrical. Men's hearts throbbed within them, their cheeks turned pale and red. Michaelangelo should have painted him. Beldham was great in every hit, but his peculiar glory was the CUT. Here he stood with no man beside him, the laurel was all his own; it was like the cut of a racket. His wrist seemed to turn on springs of the finest steel. He took the ball, as Burke did in the House of Commons, between wind and water; not a moment too soon or late.'

The direction of Jessop's hits was often unexpected, and fielders said that they sometimes never saw the ball at all, but just heard it go past. A favourite stroke was one in which a ball pitching well outside the off-stump was hit to square-leg, unorthodox, but played with 'a beautiful correctness', and, as Fry points out, almost identical with a pull-stroke Grace developed rather late in his career. This stroke of Jessop was the one which made popular the term 'cow-shot' though it did not actually originate with him. F. B. Wilson in his *Sporting Pie* writes that it first appeared in 1904, and when he first used it in a report of a match at Cambridge his editor thought it must have been a Post Office error as he had never heard the term before. Wilson enquired of Jessop (then writing in the *Daily Mail*) about it and he said he had heard of 'the donkey-waggle' but not the cow-shot. Wilson regrets that he was not the inventor of it, whom he believed to be Gerald Winter of Cambridge. In earlier days E. M. Grace had defied the conventions by daring to pull off balls to the leg which was considered almost unsporting, and this term 'cow-shot' is still mostly used in a disparaging sense by bowlers who hate to see what they regard as a good ball dispatched in such a rude manner. Jessop had no compunction at all about playing improper strokes, which he referred to as his 'nudges'. As many as four of the twelve photos in Beldam and Fry are concerned with this one pull shot, while Plate 7 shows an off-drive with his feet well down the wicket, and a most abandoned free follow-through. Plate 8 shows the square-cut which brought him so many runs when a bowler, terrified of being driven, tended to drop the ball short. If the ball came right Jessop would be quite prepared to cut it – even off the leg stump.

Sir F. H. E. Cunliffe, who bowled against Jessop in two Varsity matches, relates how in the 1899 match 'Jessop once ran out as if to drive Bosanquet, who saw him coming, and sent down a short one as fast as he could. In a flash Jessop was back, and cut the ball first bounce against the seats in the member's enclosure under the grand stand. It rebounded to cover-point.' As Jessop always observed, such strokes merely require a certain adjustment of the feet. Though the poor bowler may have felt aggrieved to see his straight balls so savagely cut, he may have preferred this to the horrific moment when he saw Jessop advancing upon him for a low straight drive. Once at Blackpool a newcomer to first-class cricket (a left-hand bowler) put his left hand to a drive. It struck the middle of his hand and closed it, so Jessop was out. Next day not only the palm, but the whole of the *back* of the hand was quite black with the bruise that had gone right through. In plate XI the body is beautifully square on to the stroke – no two-eyed stance here, the bat is lifted high at the start of a huge free swing, and Jessop's determined jaw makes the whole picture an embodiment of attacking cricket.

These twelve photos of Jessop in action make one wish that we had more such action pictures. The only other means of discovering just how Jessop batted is to look at the numerous word pictures written about him. Best and most vivid among these are the comments of C. B. Fry. I quote in full his summing-up of the content of the photos in the Beldam and Fry book.

'The batsman who does nearly everything a batsman ought not to do – with consummate success. The insolent unorthodoxy of his methods and the combined frequency and power of his hitting mark him as truly unique.

'He holds his bat and crouches in the recognised manner of the most arrant stone-waller, and plunges straightway into play which can only be described as the height and depth of aggressiveness.

'His remarkable power in hitting comes from several sources: precision in timing, an extraordinary freedom and quickness of arm-swing, aided and accelerated by a very full use of the wrists, and a knack of hurling every ounce of body-weight into his strokes.

'His strokes presuppose a quite uncommon amount of "eye"; most of them are entirely innocent of any margin for error.

'It is not mere strength that gives almost unexampled power to his hitting; rather it is an untrammelled freedom of swing which comes from an exceptional looseness of joint. This freedom is given full and most generous play with a flashing, sword-like rapidity. Quickness, swiftness, rapidity are the features least recognised but most operative in his batsmanship. He is rapid in the full sense of the Latin adjective "rapidus" – swift, with the swiftness that devastates. He takes huge risks, which are potential at once of great success and great disaster. But the wonder of it is that he can take the risks and yet keep the odds in his own favour as against the bowler.

'To call him a slogger betrays full-fledged ignorance. Slogging is wild hitting and blind. Jessop's hitting is mildly described as enterprising; but no hitting was ever less blind. He watches the ball with a concentration which puts many an orthodox defensive batsman to shame, and which in no small degree is the secret of his success.

'If batsmen who are or hope to be hitters would study and assimilate this concentrated watchfulness, which forgets everything but the ball as bowled, then, without "crouching", they might begin to talk of playing like Jessop.'

Many years later, in 1935, in an introduction to C. J. Britton's *G. L. Jessop*, a most useful innings-by-innings record of Jessop's career, Fry tells us how every cricket writer has been tempted to try his hand at a Jessop word-picture. Fry was always ready to express his admiration for Jessop's unique batsmanship. Likewise Jessop was always ready to express his good opinion of Fry's perfect orthodox style. Once when someone told Jessop that he ought to be an automatic choice for every England side, Jessop modestly replied that if any such player existed, it ought to be C. B. Fry, not himself. The admiration was mutual, and Fry took delight in trying to describe Jessop's manner of play. Perhaps his neatest summing up is:

'If you know what a "swipe" is – I don't quite – you can call him a swiper. And he did in any case sweep the ball with a discriminating abandon I have never seen equalled.' Twenty years later in 1955 C. B. Fry was to write a notable obituary of Jessop in the *Daily Telegraph*. Nobody could have done it better, and he stresses again the fact that Jessop was a remarkably consistent scorer of runs. He was a gambler indeed, but as Jessop himself said he gambled on a system, a careful system: 'he made a success of taking what looked like the wildest chances.'

There is a very different type of pen-portrait in Albert Knight's *The Complete Cricketer*. This lengthy book was written by an old county professional, who expressed his debt to E. V. Lucas for all his help over the work. Knight writes: 'Something of the beast of prey lurks in the crouch which signalises the swish of a perfect length ball on the middle stump to the onside boundary; the lunging force of his 'forward push' which flashes by cover point to the railings, is suggestive of the smashing of a military barricade. It were impossible for me to suggest the secret of such brilliantly fearless hitting. The exhibition of it is to me appalling rather than pleasing. It leaves the game so vague, with no fixity or unity or permanence.'

Another county professional who was able to express himself well on paper was Sydney Santall of Warwickshire. Though his language is less literary than Knight's, he also used the simile of a beast of prey:

'There was something uncanny about Jessop. All one could see of the wickets when running up to deliver the ball, was the off stump. There he stood, very unorthodox with jaw stiffened, looking at you from just under the peak of his cap. He slipped his hands up and down the handle of his bat in proportion to the pace, length and direction of the ball delivered. His biggest drives were made with his hands at the top of the handle. When he pulled the short, or even good length ball, he crouched like a beast at prey, ready to spring.'

Here now are the recollections of a spectator rather than a professional player or watcher of the game. They come from the late Canon Horsefield, of Gloucestershire:

'His arrival from the pavilion was the signal for the whole field to fan out towards the boundary – he could have scored entirely in short singles if he had so wished, there being no fielder anywhere near; but he scorned (as a rule) anything but a full blooded stroke. I doubt if he knew what it meant to "leave the ball alone"; he loved them best coming in to the off stump, but a leg ball had no quarter if it was at all within reach, and with perfect timing would go square over the umpire's head.

'The stance, the tension, the silence, and then the flash as the ball sizzled on its way over the boundary are all part of one impression of grand sportsmanship and brilliant unorthodoxy, and I often felt that even the fielding side, backing rapidly away from the wicket as Jessop advanced towards it, looked forward to the opening performance as eagerly as did the crowds whose hero he always remained.'

I have already mentioned the book of Jessop statistics compiled by C. J. Britton. Here are some of his own recollections of Jessop, for he had the good fortune to have played against him. When once fielding at point Britton noticed that Jessop's hitting strokes were made 'very, very late, so late in fact as to give the impression of jerkiness, which confirms Commander Fry's "rapidus". He was also in the habit of flashing a look in the direction of point, almost unconsciously it seemed, and I assumed, rightly or wrongly, that he desired to get the hang of point's position.' I imagine that some fielders at point would have found being sighted by Jessop as though a target rather disturbing. Britton also noticed that the great power generated by Jessop seemed to come from abnormal strength in the thighs. This power was allied to extreme agility, and with his complete double-jointedness, he would have made a superb acrobat.

These various impressions may help to give some idea of what Jessop's batting was like, but nothing can express the actual pleasure of seeing him in action. It was a unique experience, and I know of only one unsatisfied customer, who when taken to see Jessop bat complained that he could see such rustic play on any village green. He began to think again when the retort came 'But could any village batsman have perpetually made runs against first-class bowlers?'

One thing no word picture or photograph can ever provide us with is the *sound* of Jessop's batting. I can remember that when Dexter was batting you were aware of this, even before you entered the ground, the moment you heard the crack of his bat.

Thanks to his efforts in July 1897 Jessop was now fully established as a cricketer ready to win his England cap when the opportunity arose. Test matches were not so frequent in those days, and overseas tours were still sponsored by individuals, not by the M.C.C. Plans were made for a team captained by A. E. Stoddart to tour Australia in the winter of 1897–8, and if Jessop's successes had come earlier in the season, he might well have been chosen; as it was the team was selected before Jessop hit the headlines, and though efforts (especially by Ranji) were made to add his name to a list which numbered only thirteen, the expense of another player on a privately sponsored tour ruled him out.

He did, however, have the opportunity of making another tour instead, for in September 1897 Pelham Warner took a team out to America on a short tour. In his book *Cricket in Many Climes*, Warner says that Ranji, Lord Hawke, and F. S. Jackson had all invited him to join them on a tour to Philadelphia in 1897, but in the end all three had to cancel their plans, so Warner decided to take a team over himself. When he arrived in New York reporters asked him questions which showed they knew little about cricket, but they had heard of Jessop and enquired how many times he had made 300, and whether his usual drives reached 200 yards. The tour aroused great interest, and five matches had been arranged, including three three-day 'Test' matches against the Gentlemen of Philadelphia, who were recently back from a tour of England. It may surprise present-day readers to hear that there was so much good cricket in America, but it was to America that the first English team to tour overseas made a visit in 1859, and by the late 1890s there was a good deal of touring in search of Anglo-American cricket. Teams from Ireland went over to Philadelphia in 1888 and 1892, Lord Hawke took a team over in 1894, Frank Mitchell in 1895, Plum Warner went in 1897 and 1898, and Ranji took a team over in 1899. All this had done much to enable the Philadelphian team which toured England in 1897 to be granted first-class status, and in 1896 Trott's Australian Eleven had been defeated by an innings by the Gentlemen of Philadelphia. At that time the town possessed four clubs with excellent grounds, and as early as 1894 22,000 people had watched Lord Hawke's team play. Though the standard began to fall by about 1908 (the last first-class tour to England) the Philadelphians in September 1912 defeated the Australian 'Triangular Tour' Team on their way home, and a year later the Germantown Cricket Club defeated another Australian touring team, which included Collins, Bardsley, Macartney, Emery and Mailey. These were two historic victories.

Philadelphia had players of 'world' class in J. B. King, who was almost the first to understand swing bowling, and P. H. Clark, another bowler of pronounced swing, but their leading players were not always available when they were wanted, and the form of the representative team varied considerably as a result. Warner's team which Jessop joined in September 1897 was considered by him to be about the equal of a good Varsity side, and was weak in bowling.

Jessop very soon realised that sea-travel did not suit him at all; 'No emigrant can ever more poignantly have regretted the disappearance from sight of the Motherland on that occasion than I did – unless it was I, myself, on a similar occasion two years later.' He was very ill all through the voyage, and the effect on his form was that though he went out with a tremendous reputation he scored only 149 runs in eight completed innings. Three 'Test' matches had been arranged against the visitors. In the first the Philadelphians raised a team stronger than any produced in England by them that summer. They batted first and scored 242, to which in reply Warner's team were all out for only 63. The first four wickets went down for nought, and J. B. King ended up with an analysis of 9–25. They followed on and did much better, to score 372, to which Jessop provided 11 before being stumped on the leg side by Scattergood to the best piece of stumping he ever experienced. In spite of this recovery, Warner's team lost by four wickets. In the second game on the ground of Merion Cricket Club – American Lawn tennis championships are played on the courts of what is still called Merion Cricket Club – the visitors started well on an unusually hot October 1st, and this is the opening passage of a report on the day's play:

'LION HATH US WHERE THE HAIR IS SHORT

'The Beast of "Johnnie" Bull having fun with the sedate Bird of Freedom
The Second Test Match

'Talk about your sulphurous canopy with all its appropriate trimmings, well, it wasn't a marker to the weather out at Haverford yesterday. It was the 1st of October it is true, that season when the burning ray business is supposed to be slack, but Old Sol's factory has been running on half time the past season, so we supposed he wanted to make up a bit for lost time yesterday. He succeeded. . . .

'But what did the spectators care! They were in the shade, weren't they! Let the players swelter, then, let the boiling beams scorch their scurvy souls if they couldn't do better than that.

'The match stands this way. Captain Warner was lucky enough to win the toss and thereby secure the advantage of the first crack at a decidedly batsmen's wicket. This side took advantage of it, and were not dislodged until they had amassed the imposing total of 322 runs in nearly four hours batting.'

Jessop's batting for the first time on the tour was up to his best, and here is part of the report on his innings.

'With the total at 115, King relieved P. H. Clark at the score-board end, and now began the spectacular hitting of the day. The hard-hitting Jessop was at last about to come off, and come off he did in a rattling manner, which, while he made the tins rattle rapidly against us, was received with generous acknowledgement by the spectators. The hard-hitting Gloucestershire batsman off-drove King to the ropes and dispatched him to cover for one. Then he lifted E. W. Clark Jr. to the ropes at long-on. He followed this by stealing one on a forward play, and Gower cut E. W. Clark for two. Jessop, having secured a new bat, cut the Belmont bowler for a single, and Gower stole one on a tap to short leg. Jessop drove King over the ropes, and then ran out four to a hit to deep leg, and then splendidly cut King to the ropes. He was hitting in a most vicious manner. Then he off-drove King for four. The curly-headed fast bowler was being most severely punished, and it seemed as if it might be good policy to bring in Baily, who had been quite effective in the morning.'

Baily had been the bowler whom Jessop had twice hit out of Fenners, and the hitting went on until 'at 3.02 he played forward on a ball from Clark that was a little too short, and met his fate at the hands of the waiting and willing Wood. He had scored his 66 runs in 55 minutes, and among them were a dozen fours.'

Philadelphia at that time had a cricket poet, Ralph D. Paine, who recalled great feats in the manner of Craig, the Surrey rimester, who sold his broadsheet poems on the county grounds. Paine's reference to Jessop as the 'human catapult' has been long remembered, and it is interesting to note that Warner in writing to Jessop refers to him as 'my dear catapault'. Here is a passage from Paine's poem on this match. Jessop and Leveson-Gower, whom Jessop had knocked about in the Varsity match of 1896, are taking the field at the end of the lunch interval:

When on the field the players flocked
  To the cow-bell's wild alarum,
The natives faced a mighty pair
  Whose purpose was to scare 'um.

At one end stocky Jessop frowned,
  The human catapult,
Who wrecks the roofs of distant towns
  When set in his assault.
His mate was that perplexing man
  We know as 'Looshun-Gore',
It isn't spelt at all that way,
  We don't know what it's for.

But as with Cholmondeley and St John
  The alphabet is mixed,
And Yankees cannot help but ask,
  'Why don't they get it fixed?'

Now, Jessop's eye is eagle-bright,
  His courage beat full high,
And he set out to demonstrate
  That 'Demon' King was 'pie'.
The wicked swat of bat and ball
  Was like the rattling roll
Of rifles in the skirmish line
  Along some wooded knoll.
The fielders ran in futile chase,
  The bowlers bowled their best,
And humming like a swarm of bees,
  The ball flew east and west.

And gasping foeman murmured oft,
  'We now can see, forsooth,
The trouble with the boundary line
  Was diplomatic truth'.
For sixty-six did Jessop crack
  In minutes fifty-five,
And all agreed this Surrey man
  Was morbidly alive.
And boundaries, twelve, a fusillade
  Flew o'er the green enclosure
As thick as Mr Milton claims
  For leaves in Vallombrosa.

But staunchly stood a seasoned Wood,
  Of just the proper timber,
Who nailed young Jessop by a catch
  In fashion swift and limber.

And so this poet with his echoes of Thomas Hood works through the day's play until:

The play was stopped and people streamed
  Toward the ivied gate –
A brace of wickets sacrificed
  For the figures one and eight.

Jessop followed up his 66 with 26 not out in the second innings, and as he also took nine wickets he was largely responsible for his team winning the game by seven wickets. Everyone was looking forward to the third match which would decide the 'series', but for some reason the Philadelphians were unable to raise a team, and the game was most unsatisfactorily cancelled. But Jessop says that the whole tour was most enjoyable, and he gives credit to Plum Warner's captaincy. It was not surprising that in spite of 'the perils of the deep' Jessop was ready enough to return to America on a similar tour two years later. At the end of the tour Jessop stayed on a week in New York with H. H. Marriott, and when he did make the return voyage it was a disaster for him. Throughout his life Jessop suffered from a weak stomach and digestive trouble, and this weakness produced throes of *mal de mer* which made him the 'worst sea-traveller in the world'.

At one stage he lay in his cabin, having discarded all his blankets, when an ice-berg passed nearby and lowered the temperature so sharply that Jessop, taken unaware, caught a severe chill, which resulted in an attack of renal colic from which he did not recover for nearly a year. He was so ill that he could not return to Cambridge for the Michaelmas term, and his doctor sent him to the mild climate of Penzance for the whole winter in order that he might not catch another chill. He was also forced to become a vegetarian from November 1897 until the following summer. He must really have been seriously ill, and though he was well enough to return to Cambridge in the following April, he could not find his usual cricket form at all, and was playing so badly that he thought of dropping out of the team. This was most disappointing after the success of the previous year. On May 30, at Whitsun, he decided to have a few days off and go and play for the county against Sussex at Hove. He consulted W. G. Grace about his health; the Old Man was much concerned about him and prescribed a different treatment; the vegetarianism was to be abandoned, and a course of champagne drinking was recommended, 'I forget whether it was Goelet 1889 or Moet 1886 for I have not the prescription by me,' says Jessop.

This change of treatment certainly led to a general improvement in his health and in his cricket, though he seldom reached the heights of 1897. But he had some good bowling days, especially for Cambridge against Hampshire with analyses of 8–34 and 4–33; eight wickets were bowled, two caught and bowled, and one lbw, which shows a remarkable single-handed performance. Apart from this bowling he won the match with a brilliant innings. When Cambridge went in with a mere 90 runs to win, they lost five wickets for 36 and were heading for defeat, but Jessop came in to score 55 not out in 45 minutes and the game was won. Later when playing for Gloucestershire against Lancashire at Old Trafford he again took eight wickets in an innings, this time for 54 runs. But his batting was generally disappointing, though he played one little innings against Essex at Leyton which helped to win the match. The opening day of the game had been spoilt by argument and ill-feeling over two decisions in which Grace was concerned, but after being dismissed for 128, Essex, thanks to Kortright, fought back, and when the final day came Gloucester wanted 148 to win. But C. J. Kortright, 'the fastest bowler in the world, was bowling with a determination I never saw exceeded', says Jessop. W. G. was hit in the stomach in such a way that you could see the seam clearly imprinted on him. The fifth wicket fell at 129, three more wickets went down for 3 runs and the score became 132–8. Jessop had gone in fifth and says that if ever there was a match he wanted to win it was this one, but during this collapse he could not get to the batting end. When Roberts the last man came in, two runs were wanted and there were two more balls of Kortright's over still to come. The first went over the top of the stumps, the next went off the edge for a single. Jessop realised that Roberts was not fast enough between the wickets to turn this into a two, so once again he had to watch instead of facing the bowling himself. Roberts was now up against the bowling of Mead. He survived an appeal for lbw, and an appeal for a catch at the wicket. Next, he had his wicket hit without the ball disturbing the bails. Jessop, when at last his turn came, had no intention of being Kortright's eighth victim, and after playing two balls drove the third into the pavilion, and the match was won. Jessops' 14 was an innings he remembered a great deal longer than many other more productive ones.

But this season he did not hold his place in the Gentlemen's team at Lord's, and not until September did he reach a score of more than 65. In his first appearance at the Hastings Festival he saved 'The Rest of England' from utter collapse in their second innings, for on going in with the score at 50 for 5, he knocked up 76 in 40 minutes overnight, and next day took his score to 112 when the last man was out at 206. This 112 not out took him only 68 minutes, made off the bowling of Tom Richardson, Hirst, Hearne, and Briggs. Hastings became one of his happiest hunting grounds, and he was to score six more hundreds there.

But on the whole 1898 added nothing to his reputation, and no doubt the purists began to moan again about his 'unsound methods'. *Wisden* explains quite firmly that 'There is little doubt that the falling off was largely due to indifferent health', and the Hon. R. H. Lyttelton in his book *Giants of the Game* says of Jessop: 'In fact it is the faculty when in form of hitting any sort of ball that makes Jessop such a quick scorer. He does not hit the ball so far as Bonnor, Thornton, McDonnell, – or several others – but what sort of ball shall I give him next is the problem to which the unhappy bowler can find no answer. Jessop will go down to posterity as a scorer of unparalleled rapidity . . . . and if ever he recovers his full health I feel sure he will repeat the feats he did in 1897.' The indifferent health was entirely due to his voyage to America in the previous autumn.

Wisden's hopes that Jessop would regain his full health were happily fulfilled in the next season. In what was his fourth year at the University he now became captain, and in his second match on May 18 he played his greatest innings yet. Cambridge batted first, and the Yorkshire attack included Hirst, Rhodes, Jackson and Brown, jun. Wickets soon went down, and at 40–3 Jessop came in. When the innings was over at 246, Jessop was left not out for a score of 171. This astonishing innings was marred by one chance when he had scored 24. Frank Mitchell, late of Cambridge University, but now playing for Yorkshire, tells how Jessop hit a tremendous ballooner off J. T. Brown, jun., towards Lord Hawke, who was fielding at point. 'I knew Lord Hawke would not be very keen, so I said: "You had better let me catch this!" . . . I missed it.'

Jessop remembers this stroke off J. T. Brown whom he considered to be the fastest bowler he had seen from Yorkshire, and who was known to many as the 'Yorkshire Windmill' because of the manner in which he slung his arm around. He writes: 'The first glimpse I had of Brown was at Cambridge where Yorkshire owing to a deluge after the completion of both of the first innings achieved an innings victory. My keenest recollection of his bowling is of one particular ball which in attempting to hit to the "on" I had succeeded in sending "mountains high" above the head of point. In all the course of my career I never saw a ball travel so high in the air at so short a distance from where it was struck. It was a catch for any of the fieldsmen within forty yards of the wicket. However, my old Varsity skipper – Frank Mitchell – elected to attempt my exit, but whether he became giddy through the prolonged arrival of the ball or whether the mishit had imparted some abnormal twist to the ball I don't know – but I had finished my second run before the ball finally slipped through his outstretched hands. This happened with my score at twenty-four and fortune decreed that I should afterwards add another one hundred and forty-seven runs to that total.'

When Jessop did give chances to the field they often seem to be worthy of mention, and they seem to be remarkably few for such a daring hitter – or in fact for any batsman.

Point was not a comfortable place to be fielding when Jessop was batting. You might get a ballooner like the one just mentioned or a skimming cut like the hit which Jessop believed to be the hardest he ever made. When playing against Yorkshire (it might have been this match) he made a half-drive, half-cut towards J. T. Brown, sen., who was fielding at point some fifteen yards away. The ball pitched just in front of Brown. He gave a squeal and jumped high in the air with his legs apart. The ball passed between them and hit the palings of the boundary without touching the ground again. Jessop remembered this hit for a long time, and so, I suspect, did Brown.

Jessop's score of 171 was made out of 206 in 115 minutes. He reached 100 in 65, and added another 71 in 50 minutes. He hit twenty-seven fours, and no doubt several of them would have counted as six under present-day ruling. It was not until 1910 that the county Advisory Committee passed a resolution that six runs should be awarded for all hits that 'drop over and clear of the boundary line or fence'. In England up to that date six runs were usually given only for a hit which sent the ball beyond the limits of the whole ground, as opposed to the playing area.

Thus many huge hits, as for example Trott's famous hit which sent the ball bouncing on the roof of the pavilion at Lord's, were awarded only four runs. No one suffered more than Jessop did from this regulation, for the general impression gained from cricket reports is that a fair number of his boundary hits landed *over* the ropes. Since 1910 there have been only eight instances of a batsman achieving forty or more sixes in a season, the highest number being seventy-two by Arthur Wellard in 1935. I am sure Jessop would have matched a similar total if his over-the-boundary hits had counted six instead of four, and his scores would have been appreciably increased.

For several years before the change of law discussions over the matter of boundary limits had been going on, and there was at one time a proposal that boundaries should be standardised, which really meant the shortening of them on the larger grounds, such as the Oval. It is interesting to see that among the advocates of shorter boundary lines were W. G. Grace, and, not surprisingly, G. L. Jessop. In fact, no 'standard' length was introduced until 1957, when the 75 yard maximum was introduced for a few years.

Jessop's innings against Yorkshire was not very well reported, but the score book shows that only two other players with scores of 24 and 14 reached double figures to support Jessop's score of 171. To quote W. J. Ford: 'Everyone else found the Yorkshire bowling unplayable', though Rhodes' twenty overs cost 80 runs for 3 wickets. Obviously Jessop had some passive support from some partners, including Sullivan, who as opening batsman stayed 80 minutes for 3, and Taylor who scored 14 must have stayed for a time, for at one spell he scored one while Jessop scored 52. As might be expected, if you were batting with Jessop you tended to let him have the bowling – not that he was greedy, but it seemed the most sensible thing to do. I have already mentioned the way in which Jessop dominated a stand with Francis Ford in the Gentlemen *v.* Players match at Lord's in 1897. Ford was a great fast-scoring left-hander with a style rather like Frank Woolley or Graeme Pollock, and he had a casual air which caused him to be described as 'six foot two of don't care', but when he saw that Jessop was in the mood, he was ready to play second fiddle to him: as a result Jessop hammered the attack of Richardson, Hearne, Attewell and Hayward (bowling on a worn pitch) to the tune of 67 out of 88 in 35 minutes. There were very few occasions when Jessop allowed himself to be outpaced by his partner, and the rarity of it makes one of them worth mentioning. This was when an England XI played the Australians at Eastbourne in 1902. On a very difficult wicket the XI were all out for 138, though V. F. S. Crawford and Jessop put on 90 for the eighth wicket in only 40 minutes. Crawford's score was 57 and Jessop's 31. *Wisden* even thought it worth mentioning that 'the Surrey man on this occasion quite eclipsed the Gloucestershire captain in vigour'. The very surprise of this makes it a compliment.

When the invitation came to play in the second Test at Lord's on June 15, 1899, it was Jessop the fast bowler rather than Jessop the batsman who was invited. He was in fact to be the only fast bowler on the side.

It was very bad luck for him that right at the start of the Australian innings he slipped in bowling and badly strained his back. He went in and had a glass of brandy and then came out again, and by the end of the innings of 421 he had bowled thirty-seven overs. In spite of acute discomfort he took three wickets, and had three catches dropped off him, two of them from Clem Hill who made 135. After the match the doctor put him into a plaster of paris cast, and for the rest of the season he bowled at half pace. He really should not have bowled at all, but as captain of Cambridge he wanted to do all he could, and continued to bowl. It is not surprising to find that the comparatively few wickets he did succeed in taking were at much greater cost than usual.

Though Jessop's bowling in the Test match was thus much handicapped, he had already batted well in England's first innings after they had made a very poor start. The terrific pace of Ernest Jones's bowling – second only to Kortright in speed' says Jessop – was too much for them, and when Jessop came in eighth at 66 for six the situation was desperate. Another wicket should have gone down almost immediately. Jessop later described it thus: 'Shortly after my arrival at the crease I hit a ball in the direction of cover point and called Jackson for a run, to which he responded, but as the fieldsman happened to be the "nippiest" cover then in existence – Syd Gregory – it looked all "Lombard Street to a China orange" that Jackson would not gain sanctuary. I say this with all sincerity that I have never experienced such a horrible moment on the cricket field as I did when the ball left Gregory's hand with the speed of a catapult with "Jacker" yards away from his haven. And then came blessed relief – the return went wide of its mark and Jackson lived to contribute a really fine innings of 73.'

After that nightmare moment when he thought that he had run Jackson out, and another calling muddle which might have been disastrous, thc scoring advanced rapidly, and at one time 32 runs came in only 15 minutes. After concentrating on singles Jessop made a mighty pull off Noble which put the ball almost into the scoring box near the entrance gate, and immediately after lunch he hit Jones 'to the covered seats in grand style'. In spite of having lost 6 wickets for 66 England put up the 150 in even time, but at last Jessop was well caught in the deep by Trumper. How often do we hear of Jessop being brilliantly caught in the deep off a good hit. He had made 51 out of the 95 runs put on in an hour, and *Wisden* was able to state that 'Jackson and Jessop together saved their side from complete collapse', as they were destined to do again three years later. Jessop's score was the second highest in an innings of 206, but owing to his back trouble there was no possibility of his being asked to play again for England that season.

July 1899 saw the end of his Cambridge days, in which for four years he had done well enough by ordinary standards, but had never really made runs in the Varsity match. Jessop himself explains that it was not a matter of suffering from 'big match' nerves, which never troubled him, but rather an over-confidence which had led him into such mistakes that in the four matches he scored only 145 runs in eight innings. In his last match he was still having to bowl with his side strapped up, which cut down his pace, and when Cambridge went in to bat in their second innings they needed 299 runs to win with only 160 minutes left. Much depended on whether Jessop could produce something special. He knocked up 46 in 25 minutes which contained some astonishing strokes. But eventually he was caught at long off and the match was drawn.

It was goodbye to Cambridge: he was now twenty-five, he had an England cap, but no degree, and he wanted a job where it might be possible to go on playing cricket. The lack of qualification might make it difficult for him to return to teaching. However, his plans for the future were briefly interrupted by another overseas cricket tour, for Ranji was planning to take a team to America as Warner had done, and though Jessop had some misgivings about the sea voyage, he was a dear friend of Ranji's, and did not like to refuse the invitation.

Ranji selected a team which, as Jessop said, was really too powerful 'to ensure any real enjoyment of the cricket'. It could have given a good account of itself even against the powers of Australia, for it consisted of Ranji, MacLaren, A. E. Stoddart, C. L. Townsend, S. M. J. Woods, Bosanquet, G. Brann, G. L. Jessop, C. Robson, W. P. Robertson, C. B. Llewellyn, A. Priestley, and Barton as baggage man. Every member of the team was fitted out most lavishly with a complete set of clothing and equipment, right down to ties and cuff links, all in Ranji's personal Nawanagar team colours.

Jessop prefers to draw a veil over the outward voyage, except to remark that the smell of Sammy Woods's cigars at around breakfast time did nothing to help the troubles of his naturally queasy stomach. When it came to the cricket the Philadelphians were easily defeated by the powerful opposition and the uncongenial soft wickets, and they lost both 'Test' matches by an innings. A report on the first match says:

'Cricket yesterday was a good deal of a joke. The joke, if such it was, was on the Gentlemen of Philadelphia, who were clean bowled, out run, out fielded and in fact out of it altogether. They were a whole innings and 173 runs out of it at the finish.

'Even the Englishmen were disappointed, for it should be remembered that Ranjitsinhji's men are true sportsmen, and although of course they wanted to win the game, they had no wish for a walk-over.

'The final act, the scrub match, in the afternoon, was a burlesque and the burlesque was the only interesting or enjoyable play of the day.'

They had 'two hours of riotous fun', during which MacLaren at one time was playing the ball with the handle of his bat. A far more detailed account is given of the ladies and what they wore, for all Philadelphia turned out and were much saddened that the Prince stayed in his hotel nursing an attack of bronchitis. Like Jessop, Ranji was also a bad sea-traveller, and had fallen ill on the voyage. Jessop was second top scorer in an innings of 435, making 64 'with many beautiful strokes, sometimes over but more often back of point'. He had a good tour, and to quote *Wisden*, 'was after Stoddart the best all-round man on the side'.

He had a nasty experience however when visiting the Negro quarter of Philadelphia, where some friends were taking him to witness a dance called the 'couchy-couchy'. Finding the experience not very edifying Jessop expressed his opinions audibly, and was strongly advised to leave. As he turned the handle of the door to go out he 'felt a rush of wind and then came a plunk on the panel of the door just above my head and looking hastily up I saw a cut-throat razor embedded in the wood'.

Just before the second Test the party were invited by Sir Thomas Lipton to go on his yacht Shamrock II to view the struggle for the America Cup, but Jessop stayed behind and was amused to see that several of the party had found the rough sea somewhat disturbing. The second Test was a repeat of the first, another innings victory. There was much local criticism over the selection of the Philadelphian team, but though disappointed in the result, the many spectators had a chance of seeing Ranji in action. He made 68 and was later interviewed by Diana, a lady reporter whose interest in Ranji represented that of many of the Philadelphian ladies. In a column headed 'Athletic Woman' she wrote:

'The Prince is a healthy-looking fellow, much more heavily built than I supposed from his picture, is most affable, speaks English with a foreign accent, but nevertheless with a fair fluency. He is British to the backbone, and as loyal a subject to Her Majesty as was ever born. One thing is certain, to his team Ranji is captain, not Prince, and there is an immense amount of thoroughbred sportsmanship in his make-up. He seems gentle and good natured and it is hard to realise that in his veins flows the blood of a royal papa, who is credited with tumbling into the Ganges 189 slaves in honor of 189 runs made by his son at Cambridge. He thinks Philadelphia contains the most beautiful girls in the world. I bowed my acknowledgments, but could not help doubting the statement being genuine: the Prince was what we would call "easy", if a mackintoshed crowd of fair maids so appealed to his sense of the beautiful.' The rest of the team do not get much of a mention when Ranji is about.

One point of interest in this second match was that Jessop was the first to notice that Bosanquet, who bowled fast-medium, was in the habit of returning balls at the end of the over with a curious delivery that was in fact the prototype of the googly. He drew this to the attention of the captain Stoddart, who prophesied that if such a ball could ever be properly controlled it would be a match-winner. Bosanquet did not take it seriously at the time, and never bowled one in a match until 1901 when his googlies became a sensational success.

The last match of the tour was at Toronto against Canada, who were likewise defeated by an innings. Though the cricket was so one-sided, the tour was socially a great success. 'I can imagine no cricket tour in which genuine good-fellowship has been bestowed upon wanderers from home with greater lavishness', writes Jessop. The only blemish was the voyage home. Though the trip was made in the *Oceanic* on her maiden voyage from America, and the weather was splendid, neither Jessop nor Ranji set foot inside the dining-saloon or on deck. They stayed in their cabins chatting across the corridor until the rattle of the chains on the gangway, 'the music of which appeared to me to have any of the productions of Messrs. Bach or Beethoven well beaten to a frazzle'.

By the end of October Jessop's extended season was over, and the problem of a career lay urgently before him. He moved to London, and took a job on the Stock Exchange.

Luckily, it was not long before events provided him with a chance of staying in cricket. Before the season of 1899 W. G. Grace had accepted the job of manager of the new London County Club, organised by the Crystal Palace authorities, and he intended to do this as well as continuing to captain the Gloucestershire county side, which he had led for so many years. But the Gloucestershire committee did not believe that he could satisfactorily do both jobs at the same time, since he was now nearly fifty-one. Grace thought differently, but feeling ran high, and after playing four games for the county, he resigned the captaincy and played his last game for the county on May 25, 1899. This was a sad end to such a famous and wonderful career and it also left the county without a captain. C. L. Troup took over the leadership temporarily, but as he had to return to India at the end of the season, the committee had to think about a permanent successor. Jessop was the obvious answer, though there was no question of his being salaried (as when a man is both captain and secretary) for E. M. Grace was still the established secretary. But the captain would have his expenses paid for several months of the year, and the rest of the time he could pursue other occupations. Jessop accepted the offer and was thus able to enliven English cricket for another fifteen memorable years.

Gloucestershire
Cricket –
Mr. G. L. Jessop.
Ronald Sinclair 1912.

4

County Captain and England Hero 1900–1904

'He is a small man, mainly composed of grit, whipcord, and jumping powder.'
CONTEMPORARY REPORT

THE coming of the summer of 1900 put Jessop's cricket on a different footing. He was no longer the university amateur helping his county after the end of term. With his appointment as county captain he was now a whole-time cricketer, and it was part of his job to be concerned with all the business and social activities which go with captaincy. These cares are sometimes said to have a bad effect on a player's own form, but Jessop says that he did not find his duties unduly harassing. 'For one thing – and a very big thing – my relations with the committee during thirteen seasons' association were always of the friendliest. We had no President who took any considerable interest in our welfare, but we rejoiced in the possession of a Chairman of the Committee – H. W. Beloe – who more than made up for any shortcomings in this respect. There can never have been a keener supporter of County cricket than Harry Beloe, nor a Chairman endowed so bountifully with ready tact. To have missed watching the play of excitement round the countenance of Gloucestershire's worthy Chairman of the Committee on the occasion of a close finish is to have missed a study of the poignant emotion which such a small thing as a simple game of cricket can at times produce on the human frame'.

It was largely due to Jessop's efforts that Gloucestershire's results in 1900 improved considerably, and they ended up seventh in the county table, though they were never to come as high again in the subsequent years of Jessop's captaincy. Like many other counties Gloucestershire seldom had enough permanent professional strength, and the amateurs, including the valuable schoolmasters, did not join the side until the second half of the season. The earlier part was a great struggle, and Jessop tried to have as few fixtures as possible in May, even though this meant a rather heavy wind-up to the summer. The 1900 season ended on a high note with five wins in the last eight games, many of these largely due to Jessop's own superb form. To quote *Wisden*: 'The presence of Jessop alone was sufficient to make most opponents apprehensive', which is about as high a compliment as can be paid to any player. *Wisden* goes on to say: 'His record is indeed worthy of W. G. Grace himself in his best days.' He scored 2,210 runs at an average of 40 – there were only four bigger aggregates that season – and he also took over 100 wickets. He thus became only the third man ever to achieve the feat of 2,000 runs and 100 wickets in a season. W. G. Grace (in 1873 and 1876), and C. L. Townsend (in 1899) were the other two to have achieved this feat previously, so Jessop made up an all-Gloucestershire trio. This great feat has been performed by only ten other cricketers since then.

Unfortunately for the home crowd most of Jessop's successes were in away matches, but at the end of August against Surrey at Bristol, he made 54 twice to be top scorer in each innings. On the last day Surrey wanted 197 to win and had the whole afternoon before them. When Holland and V. F. S. Crawford were together they looked like making the runs. It was, incidentally, in this innings that Crawford made his historic hit off Paish which sent the ball right over the top of the pavilion for a carry of 160 yards. In the end, however, Jessop clean bowled the last four Surrey batsmen to bring his side victory by 11 runs with only five minutes to go. With 108 runs and 9 wickets he showed how he could dominate a game. In the last innings he bowled thirty overs with great energy and stamina. At times he seemed to take wickets by sheer determination. Even if the pitch was slow he could still make the ball whip off it with his loose wrist.

In the previous match he had produced an analysis of 26–10–29–8 against Essex at Cheltenham. This, his best-ever performance for the county, was assisted in an odd way. While shaving that morning he cut the index finger of his right hand and put sticking plaster on it, which helped him to hurry his off-breaks. The umpire noticed this and asked about the plaster. When told of the cut he made Jessop take off the plaster, but when he saw that there really was a cut, he let Jessop put the sticking plaster on again, and continue his bowling.

1900 was the most active bowling season in his whole career, for afterwards he tended to curtail his spells of really fast bowling. In only two other subsequent seasons, 1902 and 1905, did he reach a total of fifty wickets, and many of these wickets were taken when bowling at medium pace. In 1902, a week after his great innings at the Oval, Gloucestershire met the Australians at Cheltenham, and this time Jessop showed them he could bowl as well as bat, for he had an analysis of 7–91 in in a total of 312. Three of these victims were caught at long-on by F. H. B. Champain, which suggests that he was bowling his off-breaks. In earlier days he took a high proportion of his wickets single-handed, i.e. by bowling, or lbw, or by 'c and b', and as late as 1908, when for the seeond time he took ten wickets in a match, eight of his wickets were of this sort.

We have heard how Plum Warner referred to the great speed and hostility of Jessop's bowling in his early days. Here now is something about Jessop the bowler from C. L. Townsend, who after being a boy wonder bowler in the mid-1890s, retired at an early age. This is what Townsend wrote of Jessop many years later:

'As a bowler Jessop was never quite in the front rank, but of enormous value to any side he was on. When he was bowling fast he took a great deal out of himself, and in later years had to bowl medium pace. As a fast bowler he could be very nasty as he could make the ball bound. He was never really fast like Kortright, Richardson, Mold and others. I never saw Jessop bowl at a man in his life. These things were not done in my day, thank goodness.'

Seeing that Jessop as a bowler will tend to fade from the scene, this might be the moment to mention some of the illustrious batsmen whose wickets he captured during his career. They include Trumper (seven times), A. C. MacLaren and J. T. Tyldesley (six times), Hayward, Abel and M. A. Noble (three times each), Hirst, Clem Hill, R. A. Duff, Darling, Hobbs, A. Marshal, Mead (twice each), and Fry, Ranji, Shrewsbury, J. Gunn, Perrin, J. R. Mason, Woolley, H. W. Taylor, Nourse, S. E. Gregory (once each). Even the very best batsmen sometimes found his sheer hostility too much for them. He had the same confidence as he showed in his batting, and like Trueman and Tate seemed to expect to take a wicket every ball. But, as Townsend pointed out, this uses up a lot of nervous energy. He also used a great deal of cunning, and even in his later years was always ready to experiment, developing a most successful leg-cutter to add to his sharp off-breaks. E. H. D. Sewell referred to him as the best change bowler in England.

On June 5 at Hove Jessop scored the first of his five centuries against Sussex. Gloucestershire, batting in reply to the home county's score of 391, had lost 3 wickets for 105 when Jessop came in. At lunch he had scored 21 out of 37 in 25 minutes. Soon afterwards he hit 4 fours in an over from Killick, one through the slips, one to long-leg, one through the covers, and another straight. Later he took another four boundaries in an over from G. Brann, one cover drive going over the ropes. He reached 50 in 45 minutes. He then straight-drove Relf to the roof of the covered stand at the south end of the ground. The ball bounced out of the ground and some minutes elapsed before play could be resumed. His second fifty came in only twenty minutes, so that he reached his century in 65 minutes. His last 79 had come in forty minutes since lunch. At 114 he gave a very hard chance to Ranji at point, and 142 he was dropped at long-on by Brann. Three boundaries came in one over from Tate, and four more in his next over, one of them again reaching the roof of the south stand. In the following over Jessop lifted a ball from Ranji and Vine caught him high up on the very edge of the long-on boundary, a great catch which prevented the ball from pitching yet again over the line. Jessop was out seventh with the score at 362: he had scored 179 out of 257 in only 105 minutes, the last 158 of these coming in only 80 minutes. This was his highest score in first-class cricket, surpassing his famous 171 not out against Yorkshire in the previous year.

Ten days later Jessop scored his first hundred at Lord's. Facing a Middlesex total of 291 Gloucester's third wicket had fallen at 124, but Jessop came in and scored 109 in 67 minutes off the bowling of J. T. Hearne, Trott, Roche, and an amateur Billy Williams, who was brought into the side because he had managed to get Jessop out in a club match. He did not succeed this time and his chief memory of the match is hearing Jessop's hits literally hum pass his ear 'like a swarm of bees', an experience he long remembered. Jessop actually made his 109 out of only 120 runs in 67 minutes. He reached 51 out of 57 in 30, and 100 out of 112 in exactly an hour. The *Bristol Times and Mirror* says of the innings:

'As was the case when he made his big score of 179 at Brighton, he made a target of the permanent buildings on the ground. Twice he hit balls into the pavilion, twice into the covered stand at the opposite end of the enclosure, while he had several shots at the windows of the hotel and members dining room. In fact his powerful driving was by far the best feature of his innings.'

His innings of 109 was said to have included 21 fours. It seems from the above report that at least six of these fours would now count as sixes, which would have raised his score to at least 121.

It may well be this innings about which the short-story writer Stacy Aumonier tells a good tale. He was sitting in the Mound stand on a hot afternoon, and the cricket seemed very sleepy and senseless, when suddenly a little grey-faced elderly man came to the top of the steps, looked around, and then came and sat down beside him. 'I was alone,' says Aumonier, 'and in about as isolated a position I could find in true English fashion.' The gentleman said a polite "Good afternoon", and then asked: "Excuse me, but would you mind explaining to me the finer points of this game. I've never seen it played. I'm over from the States for the first time, and I'm only here until Saturday." He took out a watch. "I can give it just forty minutes."

'Oh shades of W. G.! Explain the finer points of cricket in forty minutes. I couldn't just say that cricket was not a game at all, but a religion, and that a match lasted three days. I wanted to scream, but he sat all attentive, and I tried to do my best, while two maiden overs were bowled. Then one of the Gloucestershire men got out; bowled off his pads.

'Gilbert Jessop came in. He crouched at the wicket. The first ball – biff! ponk! bang! it went, right into the pavilion. The second ball – bang! right against a shutter by the scoring box. And so it went on. I cannot enumerate the details of that glorious innings. I do not even remember how many runs he made. All I know is that the whole atmosphere of the afternoon was changed. The somnolent old gentlemen were cheering themselves hoarse; the cake crumbs were shaken out of the waistcoats of the clergymen; the young gentlemen playing the wag were screaming and yelling. I saw the eyes of my American glow. I heard him exclaim: "Gee! Gosh! Fine! Bully! Oh, dandy!" and so on. Directly Jessop was out he had to go, and it is a joy for ever to me to know that he went back to the United States thoroughly convinced that cricket was a far more exciting game than baseball.'

This remarkable innings enabled Gloucestershire to come within 24 runs of the Middlesex score, and when Gloucestershire eventually needed 224 to win on a doubtful wicket, they lost their third wicket at 134. In came Jessop, and though he took five minutes to open his score, he helped Townsend to knock off the necessary 90 runs in only 37 minutes. Of these runs he made 58, so in the course of the game he made 167 runs in only 104 minutes. As usual with his innings, his runs were made just at the time when they were most badly needed.

Jessop's greatest match of the season came at the end of July when playing against Yorkshire at Bradford. Yorkshire were the champions in 1900, and did not lose a match during the season, but they came near to losing this one. On the opening day they scored 409, and on the following day Gloucestershire started badly, and soon lost 5 wickets for 116, Rhodes doing most of the damage. At this point Jessop came in, and, having a little luck, reached 50 in 40 minutes. He went on to make 104 out of 153 in 70 minutes before being last man out. He hit Hirst deep into the crowd, and Rhodes clean over the football stand, for which, as was announced by the press at lunch time, six runs were awarded him. Gloucestershire were still 140 runs behind, but they again fielded superbly in Yorkshire's second innings, and managed to get them out for 187. This left Gloucestershire 327 runs to win. They soon began to lose wickets, and any hope of winning was rapidly fading. The fifth wicket fell at 105, and in came Jessop. He immediately began to attack Rhodes, hitting him high over the football stand for the biggest hit of the match. The next ball but one was dispatched in the same way, and 18 runs came off the over (. 6 . 6 2 4). He later hit Rhodes over the bottom end of the Horton Park wall for six, and in his next over hit Rhodes over the football stand for another six. Four balls later he did the same thing again to record his fifth six. He reached 50 out of 60 in 25 minutes, reaching 81 in 43 minutes by the interval. His hundred arrived after only 59 minutes' batting.

With his score at 106 he was given a life, but to celebrate this he now hit Haigh to the roof of the football stand, but not over it, so he got only four. Gloucestershire were closing the gap fast, and the excitement was rising every ball. Despite the hammering he had received from Jessop Rhodes came on again at 235, confident that he would dispose of Jessop in the end. It was a matter of which would come first, Jessop's wicket or Gloucestershire's winning run. Rhodes's over went like this:

1st ball: a cut for four.
2nd ball: A hit for six over the clock of the football stand, and into the football ground.
3rd ball: Left alone.
4th ball: A hit deep into the spectators on the off-side, one of whom caught the ball, but only 4 runs given.
5th ball: Six over the football stand.
6th ball: Another magnificent drive which was sailing over the long-off boundary when Tunnicliffe, a giant of a man, ran a long way, leapt in the air, and caught the ball one-handed.

No one else could have reached the ball, and it would have been another boundary, but Jessop was out. He had scored 139 out of 182 in 95 minutes 'quite ten of which were spent in recovering the ball'. His runs came thus:

1 1 6 6 2 4 1 4 3 2 4 4 4 4 4 2 2 3 6 1 1 6 4 6 2 2 1 4 2 2 4 1 1
1 1 1 1 2 2 1 4 4 2 4 6 4 6

His only chance was the one given when he had made 106, and this was the only time he mishit the ball.

C. L. Townsend writes: 'I shall never forget the roar of the Yorkshire crowd when Jessop was in. In looking back I think perhaps this was the most thrilling game I ever played in, for Yorkshire had not been beaten for a year or two, and Jessop was making 20 or more an over; Lord Hawke was at his wits' end. We only wanted three more overs from Jessop to win, but it was not to be.'

Once Jessop was out the end came quickly, and Yorkshire won by 40 runs. The game might have been even closer had not Harry Wrathall run wild during the luncheon interval. He chased Jack Board, the not out batsman, round and round the dressing room, and so completely upset him that he was promptly bowled by Haigh.

A very great number of Jessop's runs came off the bowling of Rhodes who, in 1900, was enjoying a great season, in which he ended up top of the averages with 261 wickets at 13·81 runs each. This was fifty more wickets than anyone else, but Jessop in this innings treated him in cavalier fashion. Rhodes's analysis over the period Jessop was in makes most interesting reading:

. 6 . 6 2 4 . 4 3 . . . . 4 . 1 4 4 W . . . . 6 1 . .
. 6 . 4 . 6 . . . . . . 4 6 . 4 6 w

This shows that Jessop scored 76 runs off twenty-seven consecutive balls received from Rhodes (including the ball which got him out). In the course of these twenty-seven balls he made seven hits which counted as six, and six of these went over the football stand. We also know that in the first innings he made a similar hit off Rhodes, so that means eight out-of-the-ground sixes off Rhodes in the match. Reports show that he also hit two over-the-boundary hits off Hirst in the first innings, and two more in the second innings, one off Haigh to the roof of the stand, and one off Rhodes which was caught by a spectator. This makes twelve certain hits in the match which would have counted as six under present law, and there were also others. Jessop once admitted to me that during the match he hit Rhodes over the boundary line 'some fifteen or sixteen times', and the *Wisden* obituary notice quotes a statement that 'he cleared the ropes more than twenty times'.

Under present-day conditions for six-hitting this quantity of sixes would have set up a world record approached now only by W. J. Stewart's seventeen sixes in the Warwickshire *v.* Lancashire match at Blackpool in 1959, and J. R. Reid's fifteen sixes in his score of 296 for Wellington *v.* Northern Districts in 1962–3. It is perpetually irritating to think that owing to the delay until 1910 in the change of regulations about sixes Jessop was robbed not only of records, but of the chance of adding to his whole aggregate of runs.

I doubt whether such a good attack, which included Rhodes, Hirst and Haigh, has ever been hit so savagely as by Jessop at Bradford. Rhodes was always ready to 'buy' his wickets, and tempt his victims to destruction: but he must have been relieved when he saw Tunnicliffe's long arm snatch the ball out of the air. Jessop's innings was a second century in a match, a feat he performed four times in first-class cricket, and twice also in minor matches for the county. The odds on anyone who took such apparent risks reaching even two fifties in the same match might seem remote enough.

At the end of the great game Charles Townsend managed to get hold of the ball, and he presented it to Jessop girdled with a silver band inscribed with the simple legend 'Yorkshire *v.* Gloucestershire, July 24, 1900, 104 and 139'. Among mementoes which decorated Jessop's rooms at Brunswick Square, W.C.1, in 1901 was a pair of meerschaum pipes in a case on the cover of which was written in gold letters the words BEND OR. These pipes had been given by the owner of the horse BEND OR to the famous jockey Fred Archer after he had won the City and Suburban race on that horse in 1881. Fred Archer, a Cheltenham man, had left these pipes in his will to Jessop's father who had been his medical adviser.

As he left the ground at Bradford and was making his way to the station with his cricket bag, Jessop met a couple of young fellows evidently returning from some local cricket. One of them sidled up to Jessop, and said: 'Ay, mister, let's roob ma bag agin yourn fur look,' and he would not be satisfied until he had 'roobed' the two bags together. 'I hope it brought him luck,' added Jessop.

Though Gloucestershire did not succeed in beating Yorkshire, they went next day to Manchester and inflicted on Lancashire their first defeat of the season. On the opening day of the match Jessop was handed a telegram on the field which read: 'Our duck eggs are the best, try a couple,' but this did not succeed in putting Jessop off, for he not only took seven wickets, but after scoring 66 in the first innings, made 47 more out of the Gloucestershire match-winning score of 166–7. Fired by Jessop, the Gloucestershire fielding was said to have been 'exceptionally brilliant'. After the game Jessop found a very portly and solemn-looking man waiting for him at the gate. 'Mr Jessop,' he said, 'you're a cricketer, and ah'm a publican. Ah've joost seen tha make roons the way ah like to see them, an' ther's allus a bottle of champagne for tha in my pub whenever tha cooms to Manchester.' Jessop always liked playing up North, where he said the crowds were so full of enthusiasm and ready to applaud good play on either side. He said that he could not imagine such an experience possible at Lord's.

In the course of his first innings of 66 Jessop made a historic hit off the bowling of Cuttell which not only put up the 300 but sent the ball right out of the ground; it was the first six hit at Old Trafford for many a year. In the following season he repeated the feat by making another huge drive for six in the course of an innings of 27. It must have been at about this time that Sir Neville Cardus had his first experience of Jessop. He wrote about it in the *Manchester Guardian* in an article published in 1935:

'Thirty years ago a small boy went to Old Trafford for the first time. The match was Lancashire against Gloucestershire. The small boy contemplated for a moment the sign outside the gates: "Enter at own risk: no money returned"; but he took courage (there was not a cloud in the sky). He found a front seat and settled down to enjoy himself, though it was a shame that Lancashire were not batting. Towards lunch the small boy left his seat to buy a bottle of ginger-beer before the crowd swarmed into the refreshment-room. He was putting his money on the counter, standing on tip-toe to reach it, when suddenly there was a terrible crash. Broken bottles and splintered glass flew about and the small boy thought the end of the world had come. (Professor Falk, a German, had arranged it for the previous December; and perhaps he had only miscalculated by a few months.) A man in the bar soothed the boy's fears: "It's all right, sonny," he said, "it's only Jessop just come in." '

Some six weeks after their ordeal at Bradford, Yorkshire were to suffer again at the hands of Jessop, this time at Scarborough, where he was playing for C. I. Thornton's XI. On the opening day he hit up 95 out of 134 in a mere 50 minutes, and drove the ball three times out of the ground. It was the first time he had ever 'come off' in a match at Scarborough, and he was once again 'c Tunnicliffe, b Rhodes'. Later in the week he was playing in the Hastings Festival on what he spoke of as his favourite ground. He was playing for The South *v.* The North and on the last day, a Saturday, he scored 123 not out in 75 minutes, reaching his hundred in 55 minutes. Once again he faced the bowling of Hirst and Rhodes, though the latter did not bowl much. Jessop has something to say about his frequent meeting with Rhodes:

'I had a good deal of experience of Wilfred's bowling in 1900, for apart from the two meetings in the County Championship, we saw something of each other in the Gentlemen *v.* Players matches at Lord's and Scarborough, as well as in two North *v.* South matches, and Yorkshire *v.* C. I. Thornton's XI. We faced each other in fourteen innings – one of which was incompleted – and on no fewer than eight occasions I fell to Wilfred's wiles. Small wonder, therefore, if the cricket reports of the Yorkshire evening papers should be so frequently headed: "Jessop again falls a victim to Rhodes." Still, I had no good reason to feel that I was one of Wilfred's "rabbits", for in the course of those fourteen innings I had managed to "pouch" some six hundred and forty-seven runs. Luck as regards the state of the pitch was on my side, for only on three occasions did the conditions favour the bowler. No matter how much Wilfred was "punched" he always came up smiling for more, and as he had supreme confidence in his fieldsmen and bowled to them with unerring accuracy, he seldom failed to reap his reward.' He added that in all their meetings Rhodes never once bowled him a full pitch.

Elsewhere Jessop makes an interesting comparison between Rhodes and Bobby Peel, whom he considered to be the most difficult of all left-hand bowlers he ever met, since his flight was so deceptive. He writes: 'Rhodes' length and spin were admirable, but his flight did not appear to me to be so puzzling as that of Bobby Peel. Of the two, Wilfred was a trifle faster through the air and off the pitch, and was on hard wickets the most consistently successful. What made him, in my mind, superior to most left-handers, was the unruffled manner in which he took punishment. No matter how severe the gruelling he was seldom guilty of the weakness of bowling short. There was nothing at any time negative about his bowling; with him it was attack all the time.'

The innings just mentioned may not have been of any great importance but it kept the Saturday crowd happy to the last moment of the game. In the previous year Jessop had made another undefeated century for The Rest against the Home Counties in a game in which a draw was inevitable. He had reached about thirty-five when, just before the tea interval, he ran down the wicket to a lob from D. L. A. Jephson, missed the ball, and for all his efforts to get back, felt that he must surely be stumped. To his surprise, however, the famous old umpire Bob Thoms murmured: 'Not out . . . not out', and as he fixed the bails carefully back he said: 'Sixpenny crowd – Saturday gate – can't disappoint 'em – near thing – near thing – but not near enough for the occasion.' So the Saturday afternoon crowd had the pleasure of seeing Jessop make a century. At that time, when first-class matches began on Mondays and Thursdays, there was always the danger of a match being over before Saturday afternoon. Jessop realised this and for many years advocated the change of day for starting matches, and thanks largely to his efforts a change was eventually made.

Early in the season Jessop had bombarded Lord's, and the Oval too had been the scene of a great onslaught on the Surrey bowlers in an innings of 87. To quote *The Times*: 'He was especially severe on Richardson, and repeatedly hit the ball over the ring.' Now, in the last match of the season of 1900, Jessop was back at Lords again and on September 13 he made a historic hit there. He was playing for The South *v.* The North in a benefit match for Philip Need, of the pavilion staff. In the first innings he made 77 in 55 minutes, and in doing so hit one ball from Millward which landed on the ornamental ironwork forming the letters M.C.C. which stand on top of the roof of the north turret of the pavilion. The wickets were pitched to the grandstand side of the square, and the hit was slightly to the off-side of straight. It is reported that if the hit had gone on the line of the roof between the towers it would easily have cleared the pavilion, and won for Jessop a deserved niche in cricket history. It was only a matter of a few inches. It certainly had a much greater potential carry than Trott's hit which landed on the roof and bounced over. In the same innings he also hit a ball to the top seats of the pavilion, and at another time hit four fours in an over from Hirst, two of which went into the pavilion. So this score of 77 included at least four hits which went into the pavilion at varying heights.

Jessop achieved a hit to the top seats of the pavilion on an earlier occasion. In scoring 47 for Cambridge University *v.* M.C.C. he 'brought the house down by one of his drives off Roche, the ball pitching on the top seats of the pavilion'. Roche, on Australian who was qualifying for Middlesex, was a bowler of some speed and routed the rest of the Cambridge batsmen to end up with an analysis of 8–66. Jessop again reached the top seats during his innings of 169 *v.* Leicester in 1901, and another occasion was during his great innings of 93 against South Africa in 1907, this hit being made off Vogler. So five times at least Jessop reached the top regions of the pavilion – a feat that has been achieved only some twenty times in the history of Lord's. Though Jessop never got six runs for any of these pavilion hits, he did win six runs for a hit during his innings of 169 for M.C.C. *v.* Leicestershire in 1901 when he hit a ball to square leg clean over the entrance gate into St John's Wood road. Batting at the pavilion end when he made 63 for M.C.C. *v.* Yorkshire in 1906, he hit a ball to leg to the roof of the grandstand. The ball was lost and a new one sent for.

Though it was not counted in the first-class averages, there is one Jessop innings of 1900 which must be mentioned. That season a team from the West Indies, led by Aucher Warner, the brother of P. F. Warner, made a tour of England and played a number of three-day games with some of the counties. The tour was regarded as a success, and when the West Indies came to England six years later their matches were granted first-class status.

On June 28, 29, 30 the West Indies met Gloucestershire at Bristol, and their bowling suffered the worst mauling of the tour. On the first day, after a very bad start, Gloucestershire scored 518 for 7 wickets. Wrathall made 123, and a score of 140 was made by C. L. Townsend, who took part in a partnership of 201 for the sixth wicket with Jessop, who scored 157 of these runs. He reached 50 in 20 minutes, 83 out of 105 in 30 minutes, 102 in 43 minutes, and then added another 55 runs in 17 minutes. Jessop went in at 2.30 and was out at 3.30 – all very tidy and consistent scoring with an amazing virtuosity of stroke play. *The Bristol Times and Mirror* report states that:

'Rarely did the ball travel twice in the same direction. Nobody enjoyed this wonderful spell of phenomenal scoring more than the coloured men in the ranks of the visitors. The bowlers who were being punished, and the fielders who were called upon to work as they had probably never worked before, were hugely delighted. One of them would lie down and literally shake with laughter after a big hit, and the next minute would be making a futile effort to save another four from being placed to the credit of the batsman. When fifty was signalled as Jessop's score, this particular player turned round, and asked one of the spectators "Has he been in ten minutes yet?" His behaviour was typical of that of his colleagues. They did not know what to do to get rid of this great batsman, so they were content to admire his effort.'

Among the suffering fielders was L. S. Constantine, father of the great Learie. No doubt he told his son about the Jessop innings, and Learie himself became one of the very few cricketers whose hitting can be truly described as 'Jessopian', both in speed and method. Jessop had a habit of attacking even the best of fast bowlers, and the inexperienced and possibly erratic West Indies bowlers were torn to shreds, among them a promising bowler called Woods. C. L. R. James in his book *Beyond a Boundary* tells the full story of an amusing episode:

'One June 28th, 1900, in a match against Gloucestershire on the Bristol cricket ground, a West Indian bowler went to his captain and asked permission to take off his boots. West Indies captain Aucher Warner asked him why: he replied that he could bowl properly only when barefooted. Woods was making the best response he knew to a truly desperate situation. Wrathall, followed by C. L. Townsend, followed by G. L. Jessop, all made centuries. Jessop hit 157 in an hour. The bowling averages make curious reading. Burton took five wickets for 68 runs in 25 overs. On the figures he was not hit. If Mignon's 33·3 overs cost 162 runs he had the satisfaction of getting five wickets, including those of the century-makers. One Hinds bowled three overs which cost 72 runs and if these figures from *Wisden* are correct I would dearly like to know exactly how that happened. The men who really got it were Ollivierre with 137 runs for 23 overs, and Woods with 141 runs for 33 overs. Ollivierre, however, was a batsman who headed the batting averages for the tour. Woods was a bowler and nothing else, so that his emotion prompting a return to nature can be understood. Aucher Warner promptly refused his request. Woods returned to the bowling crease. Jessop despatched his fast balls over the boundary, out of the ground, on to roof-tops. Woods made a last attempt. 'Mr Warner,' he pleaded, 'let me take off one – just one and I could get him – just one, sir.' 'Out of the question. You can't do that here, Woods.' Dragging his feet, Woods had to endure this martyrdom, to the end encumbered by full armour.

The story is true, though perhaps of that higher order of truth which good fiction is. To West Indians it recalls the origin of many a fine bowler of sixty years ago. He came to the nets, often without shoes. He picked up the ball and bowled. In his *Cricket in Many Climes* Pelham Warner relates that he and his fellow Englishmen practised to these boys at the nets and found some of them definitely difficult. The Warners, the Austins, the Goodmans and the

Sprostons took over the best of them, shod them and clothed them, and brought them to England. Woods was one of these. His nickname was Float, after a local delicacy, as an Englishman might be called Chips from fish-and-chips. Woods was a very fine fast bowler, and it is to be hoped that he did not take his misadventure with Jessop too hard. Most of the greatest bowlers of the day were wrung through the same mill, not once but many times.'

(Hinds in fact bowled 8 overs for the 72 runs; *Wisden* is incorrect in saying it was three overs.)

We know that in the course of this remarkable innings Jessop hit as many as twenty-nine boundary fours, and that the five fours and a three which came off one over from the unfortunate Woods was the last straw reducing the fielders to a mild form of hysterics. We shall never know how many of these boundary hits went sailing over the ropes or even out of the ground. No reporter ever had time to made a note of such hits, and the innings must have been a nightmare for the scorers.

Within a few years of his arrival Jessop's hitting began to earn comparison with that of some of the great hitters of the past. W. J. Ford, himself a great hitter, writes of Jessop in *Giants of the Game* in 1899, at which time Jessop had scored only five hundreds in his first-class career:

'First among great hitters, and easily first, stands C. I. Thornton. It is now a long time since he has played in a big match, so that the rising generation must be content to know by mere hearsay of his fearless rush down the pitch, of his tremendous swing, and his gigantic drives. G. L. Jessop is a Thornton in miniature, and were he possessed of the broad hips and tall form of C.I.T., whom he certainly resembles in style, he might well rival some of his stupendous hits, though perhaps he would hardly reach the record of 168 yards 2 feet from wicket to pitch which stands to Thornton's credit, to say nothing of little pats over the old Pavilion at Lords or the old racquet-court at the Oval, and out of most grounds on which he ever played. It may safely be stated that Thornton seldom scored 50 runs in an innings without hitting at least one ball to a distance of 140 yards to the pitch, and his off-driving, even if not high in the air, was terrific. One had only to stand on the boundary to realise the tremendous pace he got on the ball.'

Ford goes on to mention George Bonnor as a good second to Thornton, but says he was a firm-footed hitter whose lunging drives lacked the beautiful crack and whip of the wrist that made Thornton so exhilarating. Jessop, unlike Thornton, Bonnor, Fowler, Ford, Sinclair and other big hitters, was not a large man for his height was only 5 foot 7 inches. Of all the hitters whom Ford mentions none could compare with Jessop as a run getter, in fact Thornton, Bonnor, Ford himself and J. J. Lyons – the top four big hitters on Ford's list – achieved only twelve centuries between them in first-class cricket, and had a combined average of 20. Even allowing for the lower run-range of their day, their scoring seems low compared with Jessop's fifty-three centuries. It has to be remembered, too, that Jessop was not one who ever 'played for his hundred', for he never became careful in the nineties like some batsmen. He took them in his stride, and in his whole career of over 850 innings he made only nine scores in the nineties, and was never out on 98 or 99.

What exactly is meant by a 'big hit'? A carry of 80 yards will produce a six on most county grounds, and on many of them, like Hastings, a straight hit of 100 yards will see the ball right out of the ground. At Hove the north wall behind the nets is 138 yards distant from the far wicket, at Lord's a carry of 91 yards will reach the railings in front of the pavilion, and one of 125 yards would put the ball on the carriageway between the pavilion and the Royal Tennis Court if the pavilion was not there. The back edge of the cantilever stands at the Nursery end is 127 yards from the pavilion end wicket. At the

Oval it used to need a carry of 118 yards to hit the ball into the seats at the Vauxhall end. This may help to give some idea of comparative distance.

Some hits have appeared vast more because of the height they reached than the distance they carried. Albert Trott's so-called 'over-the-pavilion' hit at Lord's really bounced over since it pitched on the reverse slope of the small roof at the back of the top of the pavilion. It was a huge ballooner with a carry of about 120 yards. F. T. Mann once hit a ball which hit the back wall behind the top seats when still rising, so the potential carry of that hit was far greater. As has been seen, Jessop once made a hit to the pavilion that was really far bigger than Trott's, but few people know about it, and Trott's is the one always remembered.

We shall never know what was the biggest hit ever made in first-class cricket. Very few have been measured, because the big hit so often hits something before it lands at ground level, and even when it does land in an area where it can be measured, there has been no one to note the actual spot. Of the few measured hits in a first-class match the longest is one of 160 yards when V. F. S. Crawford hit a ball over the pavilion at Bristol in 1900. Thornton has six hits made in matches which were measured at between 152 and 132 yards. Lord Tennyson made a measured hit of 139 yards 1 foot 8 inches at Southampton in 1920, and there are a few other lesser measured hits, mostly made in the last century. All we can say from evidence of the all too few measured hits is that any hit over 125 yards can be considered exceptional. This tallies with W. J. Ford's statement made in 1900 that the real *long* hit comes into the 120 to 140 yard range. He also points out that such hits are 'generally made not off a hall-marked half-volley, but off a ball that is a few inches short of that length and has fairly left the ground', i.e. a hit made with the ball 'on the up'. Jessop himself made some observation on the matter of long hits in an article in *London Opinion* in 1913. He says:

'Unlike a football ground, there is no hard-and-fast rule laid down as to the length and breadth of the playing area of a cricket field. So that our county grounds vary in size very considerably. The Oval, for instance, is almost twice the size of the Taunton ground, and Leeds might very well hold both the Harrogate and Taunton enclosures. As a general rule one finds that wickets are not pitched on most grounds exactly in the middle. There is always a near end, which is invariably that of the pavilion. The carry from the furthest wicket into the pavilion is rarely more than a hundred yards. Given a suitable delivery a carry of one hundred and forty to a hundred and fifty, I should say, would be the utmost limit of a cricket ball. Even this seems a trifle like drawing the long bow, but I firmly believe that when the Australian, W. W. Armstrong, lifted one of B. J. T. Bosanquet's googlies out of the ground at the lower end of Trent Bridge the carry was nearer one hundred and fifty than one hundred and forty. Those who are at all familiar with that enclosure will remember the trees outside the ground which tower above the grand stand, so that they will be better able to realise the carry when I say that the ball cleared those trees without touching a branch.' Both Jessop and C. B. Fry quite independently gave this hit of Armstrong's as the biggest they had ever seen. As it was made in a Test match in 1905 off the last ball but one before stumps were drawn on the first day, it must have a special place in the history of big hits.

The record books, including *Wisden*, continue to quote a hit of 175 yards alleged to have been made by Walter Fellows when practising at Oxford in 1856, but I believe this hit to have been quite unproven. If one needs a substitute for such a doubtful record I would suggest one of 168 yards made in practice at Hove in 1876 by C. I. Thornton, since the hit was actually measured by the cricket historian, James Pycroft.

All one can do about big hits is to record all the circumstances of them as faithfully as possible. Almost every ground has its legendary hits, and since they are so well remembered they must have been remarkable. Many a spectator's most vivid recollections of cricket watching concern a big hit, for there is nothing so exciting as to see a ball soaring away into the distance. As E. V. Lucas so aptly wrote:

> 'Yet even from the pedant what a deep ecstatic sigh
> When the batsman jumps to meet one, and a sixer climbs the sky'.

Jessop was always ready to 'jump to meet one', and it is sad that we shall never know how many times he hit the ball over the boundary line in the course of his long career. For more than three-quarters of his time it was necessary to hit a ball right out of the ground in order to register six runs, and though he did that more than anyone else of his day, such out-of-the-ground hits were only a small proportion of the hits which he made which put the ball over the boundary. I think it can be estimated that he must have made at least thirty-five such hits during an average season, and if we multiply this by the number of seasons he played this would give a figure of over 700 sixes. If these had really counted as six his career aggregate would have gone up considerably. Arthur Wellard of Somerset is credited with just over 500 sixes in his career, and these sixes provided over one-quarter of his total aggregate of runs. But he scored only two centuries, and compared with Jessop cannot be considered a major run-getter.

Among these hypothetical 700 sixes made by Jessop there were many superb blows which could be reckoned in the 'Big Hit' class – the hit which carries at least 125 yards. As we have said he was not a big man, but his extraordinary powers of ball propulsion overcame any loss of the height usually assumed to be necessary for a big hitter. He seldom hit the ball gently, and when he hit the stroke was full-blooded; if the hit was middled with his heavy bat the ball was likely to reach the boundary almost before anyone was aware of it, and any elevation of the stroke would put it over the ropes. It is not surprising that every county ground in England has its legends of where Jessop once hit a ball.

Every one of these hits must have produced incalculable joy for those who saw them, and possibly too for the fielding side; there must have been many a fielder who was glad to see the ball sail right over his head instead of straight at him.

Throughout the winter of 1900 Jessop was no doubt thinking about how to improve Gloucester's prospects for the coming season, for the county suffered a sad blow by the retirement from regular first-class cricket of C. L. Townsend. Though he was only 24 he had been playing ever since he was 16 and in these few years had shown himself to be one of the greatest leg-break bowlers ever. Now his work as a solicitor took him from the game, but we shall meet him again as best man at Jessop's wedding, and I had correspondence with him about Jessop in the 1940s. Gloucester missed him sadly and an added handicap was the recurrence of a strain which had caused Jessop to bowl in a plaster jacket in 1899. Jessop's fast bowling days were now virtually over, and in 1901 he took only twenty-nine wickets at a cost of 31 runs each. On one occasion, however, he really let rip in the old style, for when Sussex went in to score 327 runs to win in the match at Hove, Jessop put himself on first and sent back Fry, Goldie, and Ranji in the first two overs. To quote *Wisden*: 'Jessop fairly won the match for his side. Bowling as fast as he had ever done in his life, he quite unnerved the Sussex batsmen.'

His batting, however, was even better than ever, and in the season he scored 2,323 runs – the highest aggregate of his career. There were as usual few county matches early in May, but Jessop played in several M.C.C. matches at Lord's, and on May 16 showed he was already in form by scoring 169 out of 244 in only 105 minutes against Leicestershire. He reached 100 in an hour and at lunch time the scoreboard read: M.C.C. 214–3 (Jessop 131). He hit one ball to the top of the pavilion, and another into St John's Wood Road which counted 6. Sir Arthur Conan Doyle was also playing for M.C.C.

After his bowling success against Sussex Jessop was again at Lord's where he played one of his rare defensive innings. When Middlesex scored 483, he felt it was his duty to stabilise Gloucestershire after a poor start. He scored 46, and to quote one report: 'It was amusing to see Jessop try to play carefully as he did at Lord's on Friday. He was obviously ill at ease. A fish out of water was nothing to his extreme distress. He crouched and he straddled, he jumped out and rushed back, his mind told him not to hit, his muscles itched to knock the face off the ball. He was obviously distracted between two conflicting desires. One was to steady himself and his side, the other to give the bowling "what for" and a bit more.' His efforts were justified in the end, because Gloucestershire managed to score 266, and then the Middlesex captain inexplicably failed to make them follow on. Middlesex batted again until they too scored 266 and then declared. They were apparently afraid of what Jessop might do if he got going. Though they could not win, Gloucestershire made a comfortable start, and once the game was safe Jessop let himself go with a great innings of 124 in only 75 minutes. He made 50 in 30 minutes, increased the pace with five fours in an over from Trott, and reached his hundred by hitting a ball to the pavilion roof. At one time he scored 52 runs in 12 minutes. One report says: 'It would be difficult to describe the scene of enthusiasm which prevailed while this delightful batting was in progress. There were signs of dismay when a big drive sent the ball in the direction of Chinnery just after Jessop scored his first fifty, and when the fielder failed to make the catch, the spectators cheered and cheered again, so delighted were they at the prospect of some further tall hitting.'

This innings brought praise from many quarters, and the magazine *The King* wrote this about him:

'The air is full of Jessop's fame. There are no heroes of the war to be bracketed with Jessop. No exploits are so miraculous as his. In the morning train, at the lunch table, in the club, the talk is that Jessop has been at it again. The crowd revels in Jessop, the reporters grow lyrical over his play. If there was never so exquisite a batsman as Ranji, or a champion of such sustained mightiness as W. G. Grace, it is certain that there was never so astounding a hitter as Jessop.'

Though on a smaller scale there is one innings in 1901 which must be mentioned. It was in the return match *v.* Sussex at Bristol. Gloucestershire had to follow on 230 runs behind, and in the second over Wrathall was out with the score at 4. In came Jessop to join R. W. Rice, and in the next twenty-eight minutes he scored *all* the next 66 runs without making a single false stroke or giving anything like a chance. He received thirty-seven balls and scored off twenty-seven of them. With the score at 70 he was bowled by one of Vine's leg breaks. Rice, who had gone in first, had not yet scored. I believe that his score of 66 is the highest completed innings which has provided one hundred per cent of the runs. Gloucestershire collapsed for a total of 166, and Jessop was once again top scorer.

In the course of this innings Jessop hit a ball to the top of the pavilion, an enormous hit, since the track that runs in front of it requires a carry of 100 yards to reach it, and the pavilion stands 10 yards back from the front edge of the track. At times Jessop was awarded 6 runs for carrying the track, which sounds like a local rule. In 1907, when scoring 240 *v.* Sussex, he hit a ball from Dwyer to the face of the pavilion and got 6 runs for it, and in the following year in scoring 106 against Nottinghamshire he hit Hallam for four sixes. The first of these hits looked like being a catch to Payton standing near the edge by the score-board, but the ball sailed over his head and landed on the roof of the pavilion, breaking the back of a chair. At first only 4 runs were signalled, but a 6 was subsequently allowed. A few overs later Hallam returned and Jessop again hit him to the top of the pavilion. In the following year, when he hit 4 sixes off the bowling of Llewellyn, he put at least one of them on the top of the pavilion, and it bounced through the hatchway, and went down the stairs.

It is difficult to say what exactly 'the top' means, but a Gloucester member, Mr Cridland, who has been watching county matches for seventy years clearly recalls a hit that landed beside the clock face. All these hits were very big carries, and though he never equalled Crawford's feat of putting a ball over the pavilion, he came near to making a similar carry when he made yet another hit off Hallam which landed the ball on the boundary wall between the pavilion and the bowling green – a carry of at least 140 yards.

Jessop also made some huge hits in the opposite direction. In 1901, scoring 77 *v.* Worcester, he hit a ball right over the football stand towards long on, but it was not given 6 runs. In the same season when making 106 *v.* Warwickshire, he hit a ball from W. G. Quaife right into the football ground at Muller's orphanage end. In the following year, in the course of his innings of 50 against Nottinghamshire he again put a ball right over the stand and was given 6 runs. It may well be this hit that Jessop considers to be the biggest he ever made, for it pitched right in the middle of the ground, a huge carry. John Gunn, who was playing in that match, confirmed this hit in a letter to me. He wrote: 'I think the biggest hit I ever saw was when Mr Gilbert Jessop hit Jimmy Iremonger out of the Bristol ground and the ball went right across the football ground as well before dropping. I think that was the biggest hit I ever saw.'

Iremonger himself quite independently told me about this hit. The stand between the cricket and football ground was open back and front and had reversible seats so that both games could be served. When this great hit was made it was clearly seen by those sitting in the stand and they quickly swivelled round to see where the ball landed. The spot was marked, and a measurement made which worked out at some 150 yards. To the offside of the direction of this hit there has since been erected a refreshment place which is named the Jessop Tavern. It is right that Jessop's name should be remembered at Bristol, where the name of W. G. Grace is also honoured in the entrance gates.

One of the few occasions on which Jessop found himself a member of a really strong batting side was in the last match of the season at Lord's. A benefit match for William Yardley's widow had been arranged with two teams led by Lord Hawke and W. G. Grace, but Yorkshire had had such a good season that the match was changed to 'Champion County against the Rest of England'. On Thursday, September 12, a fine crowd turned up and because the pitch had been covered with a layer of double canvas sheeting the pitch was excellent, though the outfield was soft owing to previous heavy rain. When the second wicket of The Rest fell at 107 C. B. Fry entered; as he had made five consecutive hundreds in his last five innings, there was great interest to see if he could make another. He scored steadily and when the third wicket fell at 201 Fry had scored 48. Jessop now joined him, and after a slow start, in which he scored only 17 in half an hour, he went for the bowling. He reached 50 in 40 minutes, and when he reached 79 he overtook Fry, who 'at that time was little more than an onlooker'. Jessop's hundred came in 70 minutes (the last 83 in only 40 minutes), but Fry seemed undismayed at being so overshadowed at such an important moment, and when he duly reached what was his sixth consecutive hundred, he was wildly acclaimed. Here is a report:

'There was a tremendous scene at the usually decorous St John's Wood enclosure. Hats were waved, and the cheering and clapping went on a long time.' A few runs later Fry was caught at cover with a score of 105. His stand with Jessop had put on 204 runs in 90 minutes, of which Fry had scored 57 and Jessop 142. 'The field had grown demoralised at the hopelessness of running out either of these fliers. Hits that in the ordinary way produce singles here counted two, and some strokes which were merely half-hits or passive touches were also profited from. There was seldom any call for a run. The pair had started as the ball left the bat.' Jessop himself comments upon this marvellous running between the wickets: 'Nothing pleased me more than the number of short runs that were bagged, and this I can say with certitude that never have I had a partner with whom the essaying of a short single or the converting of a two into three runs seemed such a small risk.'

Jessop continued to hit and at the close of play his score was 176, scored in just over two hours, out of 259. The next day a huge crowd turned out to see Jessop continue his innings and he did not disappoint them. He hit Rhodes for 28 runs in his first three overs, and reached 200 in a time of 2 hours

15 minutes. Wickets were now falling fast to the bowling of Hirst, but Jessop went on to take his score to 233 before Hirst bowled him. He had added 57 out of 59, and his 233 had been made out of 318 runs in 150 minutes. Though he gave possible chances with his score at 81 and 155, he made very few mishits. Of all his many battles with Rhodes this was one of his greatest successes, and Rhodes' analysis of 43–6–179–3 tells its own story.

Of this innings *The Daily Telegraph* stated cautiously: 'One does not like as a rule to indulge in superlatives, but there can be no doubt that in his way Jessop is the most extraordinary hitter the world of cricket has yet known.'

Most newspapers were less reluctant to use superlatives, and one London report said that during the Yorkshire innings 'Jessop fielded like an angel'. Surely no cricketer has ever had so many epithets showered upon him. Angel, Idol, Marvel, Electric Battery, Wizard, Fireworks – all these terms appear in headlines, and others too.

This was truly a fine note to end the season with, and the innings brought Jessop's aggregate to 2,323. Only five others (Fry, Ranji, Abel, Tyldesley, and Hayward) scored more runs in the season of 1901, a run getting season not surpassed until 1928. Jessop's was a wonderful performance from one who not many years before had stated that he was not very interested in batting.

A few weeks later, in October 1901, Jessop was on board ship, off on his first – and last – major tour overseas. The Melbourne Cricket Club thought the days of privately sponsored tours to Australia were now over, and that a truly representative England team should go to Australia. They therefore invited the M.C.C. to send over an official side, and the M.C.C. agreed to do so. The proposal made was that Lord Hawke and A. C. MacLaren should be joint captains, the latter acting as captain on the field in the Test Matches. But so many amateurs declined to go on the tour that the M.C.C. decided to cancel their plans for the tour. Disappointed at this, the Melbourne C.C. thereupon asked A. C. MacLaren if he would arrange to bring out a team. He asked M.C.C. for permission to do so, and it was granted, but rather reluctantly, because MacLaren was not very *persona grata* in some quarters at Lord's, one possible reason being that he was a paid amateur. MacLaren found some difficulty in producing a team, and Lord Hawke did not allow Rhodes and Hirst to accept the invitation on the grounds that their going would be detrimental to Yorkshire cricket. It was not the first time that Yorkshire had shown a parochial attitude over the Test selection of their players, and Jessop for one did not approve of their attitude. In the end MacLaren was able to select a strong batting side including Jessop, Hayward, J. T. Tyldesley, Quaife, McGahey, A. O. Jones and himself, but the bowling was thin. The last choice of bowler created a great stir. He had appeared for Warwickshire in three matches in 1895–6, played twice for Lancashire in 1899, and in the last match for 1901 Lancashire gave him a further trial against Leicestershire on the strength of his good form with the Burnley Club. A. C. MacLaren was so impressed with his bowling in this match – he took six wickets for 70 – that he instantly selected him for his team for Australia. If he had not played in that one match for Lancashire, and if MacLaren had not observed his great potential, the name of S. F. Barnes might have remained unknown for ever. Fortunately MacLaren had the chance, as sole selector, to back his judgment. No official M.C.C. selectors would have dared to select a man for a tour on so little evidence.

Jessop was only too well aware of the horrors of a sea voyage and tried to cut down his troubles by meeting the rest of the team at Marseilles. But he hardly really met them then as even the waters of the Mediterranean laid him low. All he can remember of the trip is someone in a nearby cabin who incessantly sang 'The Blind Boy', in fact it was Braund with Blythe accompanying him on his violin. After suffering appallingly for thirty days Jessop recovered sufficiently in the last few days to beat Willie Quaife, a champion player, in the finals of the R.M.S. *Omrah* ping-pong championship. This practice on board ship enabled him to win the Open Tournament at the Adelaide Exhibition the day after the ship arrived, so he must have made a good recovery.

Jessop was in fact a very talented all-round games player. He won a Blue at hockey as a goalkeeper but was unable to play in the match owing to illness. He nearly won a soccer Blue and played for the Casuals as a half-back or goalkeeper between 1900 and 1904. He appeared as a wing three-quarter for Gloucester Rugby Football Club. He might, as we have heard, have represented the University at billiards, at which he once made two breaks of over 150 in a week and won the Cambridge Cue. He could run 100 yards in 10·2 seconds and took part in many sports meetings; and when he took up golf in about 1901 he soon became a scratch player, good enough to enter for the Amateur Championship in 1914.

MacLaren's team won the first Test match, and the great interest aroused in England was increased by the erection of a 'score-board' outside the office of the *Daily Mail and Herald* in Fleet Street. Similar 'score-boards' were set up in various places in England by Messrs. Johnny Walker during the 1934 Test series. After this first success the batting, apart from MacLaren himself, persistently failed, and the next four Tests were all lost. After a drought of several years the season of 1901/2 was one of the wettest on record. The visiting team found it very difficult to adjust themselves when the occasional

Deck cricket on the voyage.

dry spell came, and as always the light took some getting used to. Jessop himself says of this: 'In the clear atmosphere of Australian skies the proper sighting of the ball would appear to be a simple matter, but I, myself, did not find it so, for on days of great heat the light appears to be moving in waves much in the same fashion as shadows race over the ground when the sun becomes momentarily clouded. On two occasions do I remember becoming unsighted through this peculiarity: the first was in shaping at a drive from Warwick Armstrong on the occasion of his first appearance against us, and the second happened in playing at a ball from Charlie McLeod which eventually hit my off stump half-way up on the full pitch.'

But though MacLaren's team had its disappointments, the fielding throughout was magnificent, and Jessop said that he had never at any time figured in a side more brilliant and safe. He himself was one of its finest performers, and the Australian cricketer L. O. S. Poidevin wrote: 'In the field Jessop commands attention. His reputation at cover point is immense. He "poaches" no end of ground because he can cover so much, pick up with certainty, and return so swiftly and unerringly. Few batsmen can attempt the stolen single without jeopardising their wicket. His pick-up and throw-in are ideal, being done with one and the same action, and all the time he never seems off his balance or in an awkward position for throwing. There is a daring and devil-may-care dash about it all that charms the crowd. He is practically without a rival in England today.'

But Jessop's batting was very disappointing, only 359 runs in eighteen innings at an average of just under 20. His top score was 87 when the side scored 769 against New South Wales in their second match with the state. These runs were scored out of a stand of 109 with W. G. Quaife, and took only 57 minutes to make. In the Second Test Jessop was top scorer in the first innings, and had second highest score in the second innings, and in the Fourth Test he was again top scorer in England's total of 99, which showed his ability to make runs when the rest were finding the pitch difficult. Perhaps his greatest success on the tour was at the beginning of Australia's first innings in the same Fourth Test. In reply to England's score of 317, Australia lost four wickets for 48 runs (H. Trumble, Trumper, C. Hill and S. E. Gregory), and Jessop took all four wickets for 23 runs in a forty-minute spell. He was bowling faster than usual, and two of the wickets were the result of exceptional slip catches by Braund and MacLaren. These two, with A. O. Jones, made up the finest trio of slip fielders ever seen. Jessop did not take any more wickets in the match, but in the final Test opened the bowling as well as the batting.

In the course of a trip to visit a sheep station Jessop met George Bonnor, the mighty hitter, who had settled in the Orange District and was managing a timber business in partnership with his brother. He was still a fine figure of a man, 46 years old, but looking a great deal younger. This was the hitter with whom Jessop had sometimes been compared. Bonnor was full of reminiscences, and said that his two great regrets were not having hit a ball over the old Lord's pavilion, and not having had a single-wicket match with C. I. Thornton, the other great legendary hitter. Both these two were really super sloggers rather than batsman of the Jessop class, and it would be fair to say that their chief aim, often achieved, in every innings was to bring off a great hit.

Jessop thoroughly enjoyed his tour in Australia. 'The warmth of Australian hospitality has to be experienced to be believed, for whatever may happen to individuals on a private visit, everyone appears to conspire in making the visit of an English team one long round of continual festivities. One drawback of such tours is that cricket is apt to interrupt the flow of such social amenities.' Jessop considered that the Australians had much to teach the English in cricket organisation, especially in their consideration for the comfort of spectators. He made a great many friends and among them were the two young sons of the Governor of South Australia, Aubrey and Lionel Tennyson, who were grandsons of the poet. Jessop gave them a signed bat, and here is a letter from Aubrey thanking him for it.

Marble Hill,
Adelaide.

Dear Mr Jessop,

Thank you so much for that bat which you gave us. It was very kind of you to have taken so much trouble over getting all the signatures on it. We shall always treasure it very much as well as the ball you gave us last time. I am very glad you won the game here. I hope Mr. MacLaren's ankle is better. I hope you will have a nice and pleasant voyage home and that it will not be too rough. I hope the Australians will get thoroughly thrashed in England.

Your loving little friend,
A. Aubrey Tennyson

Aubrey's younger brother Lionel was later to became captain of England, and it was largely due to Jessop's recommendation that he became a member of the M.C.C. team to tour South Africa in 1913–14, after his dramatic entry into first-class cricket the previous summer. This bat can still be seen at Farringford, in the museum home of the poet.

The homeward voyage was to start from Fremantle, and just before they left the team was challenged to a game of soccer by some local enthusiasts. The challenge was accepted and though there were four footballers, McGahey, Lilley, Quaife, and J. Gunn who were up to League standard, the rest were rather a scratch lot. The match was billed as the 'First International Association Football Match between England and Australia', and aroused great interest. The England cricketers salvaged some of their lost reputation by winning by three goals to one. The last goal was scored by Jessop, who having abandoned his place as goalkeeper went through on his own and scored without a single opponent touching the ball.

The following summer Jessop received a letter from the British Football Association of Western Australia, inviting him to bring out a football team in 1903 to make a tour of the states and 'show young clubs here how Association Football should be played', for the game was comparatively new in Australia. Nothing, however, came of this invitation, but it shows how Jessop had attracted the interest of Australians.

The team sailed for home at the end of March, and it was the last team ever to tour Australia on a private basis, the next tour in 1903–4 being under the auspices of the M.C.C. For weeks Jessop had been dreading the long sea voyage home and wrote that the thought of it had upset his cricket. Aubrey Tennyson's hopes that it would be a pleasant voyage were quite fulfilled, however, because the team had not been long at sea before Jessop met his future wife.

Jessop was on deck playing catch with two children with a rubber tobacco pouch, and at one moment he threw wide and the pouch hit a girl walking past. Her companion remonstrated with him for such a careless act, but the girl herself only smiled. In later days she always said that Jessop had thrown wide on purpose, but he denied it and said it was an accident. As it was extremely unlikely that Jessop would make a poor throw one can only believe that she was right in what she said. If it was in fact a bad throw, then it was the luckiest misthrow Jessop ever made.

The girl's name was Millicent Annie Osborne, daughter of Mr and Mrs Alick Osborne of Hamilton, Moss Vale, New South Wales. Not many months before, her fiancé had been killed in South Africa in the war, and she later had to nurse her mother who died after a long illness. Now she was going for a well-earned holiday to England, which she had visited previously. She was descended from the Broughton family who went out to Australia in 1788.

After this disconcerting first meeting their friendship grew rapidly, and within less than a fortnight, on April 8, 1902, Jessop proposed and was accepted. When the announcement of the engagement was made in Australia, the many admirers of this beautiful girl were much upset, and one of them came all the way to England to try to persuade her to change her mind. She had no intention of doing so, and the marriage was arranged for October 8, after the end of the cricket season.

Jessop tells a story about a friend of his – a well-known batsman – who could never make runs when his fiancée was watching him. It made him nervous to such a degree that in order to regain his batting he decided to bring the date of his wedding forward. Once safely married, and his fiancée turned into a wife, his problems disappeared.

Jessop's engagement in 1902 did not upset his form, though he did not make as many runs as in 1901, for 1902 was a very wet season. His county won only three matches, but they should have won a fourth at Old Trafford. The home team were set 353 to get after Gloucestershire had declared. Early wickets went down, but several chances were missed, and with five minutes to go and the last two men in, Hallows, who had been batting patiently for two and a half hours, scooped up the simplest of catches to Jessop at cover. He dropped it, and he said later that he never could understand how he did so.

A missed catch by Jessop was so rare that it was almost worth a headline. Plum Warner, who had a cricket memory so retentive that he could remember in detail almost every innings he had played, says that he only once saw Jessop miss a catch at extra-cover. It was at Lord's in 1903, and the moment he dropped the catch he picked up the ball, and with a lightning return shattered the wicket, almost bringing him a run out instead.

Though Jessop did nothing remarkable for the county in 1902 he was in good enough form to be selected for four of the Test matches against Australia. The only one he missed was the fateful one at Old Trafford, where England lost by three runs. As Jessop's fielding regularly saved 20 to 30 runs an innings, his presence there might well have produced victory instead of defeat. He was recalled for the Fifth Test at the Oval, when he played, as we have seen, his historic innings of 104.

Even before this innings Jessop was the greatest crowd-drawer since the days of W. G. Grace. The glamour of those vital runs put him in a class that no other cricketer has since reached. He was the best-known man in England.

It has been rightly said that W. G. Grace created modern cricket as a public spectacle, and he was the first cricketer to become a household name. People flocked to see him, and there are true tales of how the match boards would say: 'Admission threepence, if Dr W. G. Grace plays, admission sixpence', and this was not because he was an especially exciting player to watch, or a particularly amusing character, but because he was such an obvious master of his craft. As C. B. Fry remarked: 'He always reminded me of Jupiter omnipotens, supremi rector Olympi.' For a quarter of a century Grace personified Cricket, and he was never better known than in the last few years of the century, after his extraordinary comeback with 1,000 runs in the May of 1895 when he was 47. Jessop said that he was always amused at the stir made by Grace's arrival at a railway station. Everything stood still until all those present had feasted their eyes on the colossal bearded figure, or welcomed him personally. 'I never remember seeing W. G. refusing to shake hands with anyone who possessed sufficient assurance to ask it of him, and the number of them who had is to me a striking tribute to the self-confidence of the British race.'

The mantle of W. G. fell rather ill-fittingly on Jessop who provided spectators with an almost hysterical excitement. When he came in to bat the whole crowd broke out into an 'audible grin', a fever of expectation which made many spectators almost afraid to look in case something went wrong. I myself used to experience the same feeling when watching George Cox batting: you wanted him to have the bowling and yet you dreaded it in case he got out. Dr E. M. Grace, son of 'The Coroner', and nephew of W. G., has recently written to me a letter in which he says, 'Jessop gave such enjoyment to the spectators that one often felt one's heart would stop for fear he would get out.'

Here is a description of the spectators' joy at a Jessop innings. It was a Bank Holiday Monday at Bristol in 1910:

'Three Gloucestershire wickets had gone down for nine runs when Jessop joined Mills, and there was a perfect roar of cheers and applause when the Gloucestershire captain was seen on the Pavilion steps. If ever a man could pardonably feel proud that man was G. L. J. on Monday. He was the big strawberry in the basket. The crowd at times was almost hysterical. That was particularly evidenced once when he had scored a five (all run) through the slips. The spectators cheered every run with a crescendo sort of cheer, and the fifth set of cheers reminded one of the finish of a five miles cycle race at Ashley Down in the good old days. And how anxiously they followed his hits when he got into the nineties. They would never have forgiven Braund if he had bowled him when he was 99. But the Bath man did not bowl the darling of the gods. Jessop just swiped him round to the leg boundary and his total was 103. The next ball Jessop undoubtedly swiped at and O. M. Samson who was fielding out near Almondsbury – at least as near there as possible – caught him high up with one hand. A mighty hit and a fine catch. 'Jessop knew what he was doing. Did Samson?'

In 1907 Jessop made a score of 240 against Sussex at Hove. Here is something from a report from *The Brighton Herald*. After headlines which stated 'JESSOP BEATS SUSSEX AT BRISTOL', it went on to say that after Gloucestershire had lost four wickets for 68 Jessop rose to the occasion with one of 'those outbursts of volcanic hitting that have given him world-wide reputation, and while the crowd cheered itself hoarse, and the Sussex bowlers seemed helpless, he amassed a score of 240'. When he was eventually out 'the crowd wanted to carry him into the pavilion, but he outpaced them and with the friendly aid of a policeman he encountered nothing more embarrassing than a multitude of pats on the back. When he came out to field later it was noted that he took point's place instead of cover as usual, and had his hand bandaged – a sign of what his innings had cost him in blisters.'

The news that Jessop was batting would cause a frantic dash to any ground, for Jessop was the most complete 'office-emptier' the game has known. W. J. Ford in the last piece he ever wrote puts it well:

'Placard a town or send a "tape" to the clubs: "Rhodes bowling a grand length", "Braund irrestible in the slips", or the like, and how many men will hurry over lunch? But "Jessop not out forty – hitting hard" will make the luncher forego his coffee and the hansoms will rattle up to Lord's'.

I have had letters from those who in their office-boy days were told to stand by to hail cabs if any of the executive had a chance of seeing Jessop in action. When enquiries were made the manager was 'unavoidably absent' on Jessop days. One county court judge admits to being a bit sharp with long-winded lawyers who kept him away from a county match – especially if Jessop was likely to perform. A Bristol correspondent tells me that the omnibuses to Ashley Down would be suddenly crowded to capacity if the news got round that Jessop was batting. One who was once employed as a boy typist would occasionally be given a shilling to go to see Jessop bat, so long as he finished his day's stint, though it might mean working till midnight, for a wage of 9s. a week. Another tells me that when a builder was putting a house on the east side of the ground at Hove he achieved a marked speeding up of the work by telling the brickies that if they reached a certain height by the time of the forthcoming match against Gloucester they would be able to see Jessop bat. The work went on so fast that they had built their 'grandstand' by the time of the match. Jessop obliged with a dramatic innings, but one of the brickies fell off in his excitement.

On one occasion, when a certain cabman was charged with illegally parking his cab at a place from where he could see over the wall of the Bristol ground, his defence was that 'Mr. Jessop were batting', and the magistrates instantly dismissed the case.

Apart from the number of poems written personally to Jessop to congratulate him on some feat, others appeared frequently in the papers. Albert Craig, the Surrey cricket poet, naturally provided some, but there are all types from parodies to serious attempts to assess his talents. But the standard was not high, and Jessop who himself occasionally tried to write verse, must have enjoyed the compliment more than the content.

Cartoonists, too, had a ready subject. 'Rip' was a great admirer and frequently drew him with comments such as 'Half an hour of Jessop is the CHAMPAGNE of cricket . . . therefore we want more. If I were rich I would found a fund to find more Jessops. What a difference you make. . . . Do you realise it? It is a great thing to make 20,000 people joyful as you did last week at Lord's.'

There are cartoons of Jessop with a bull-dog head saving England from disaster and reminding one that his father was once a breeder of bull dogs; one with Jessop literally carrying the rest of the England team on his bat; another with Jessop opening a bottle labelled 'Champagne Cricket' and offering it as physic to an ailing bed-ridden character labelled 'Slow Cricket'.

Writing many years later Jack Hobbs said that Jessop was a greater crowd drawer even than Bradman, and he added 'I am glad I wasn't a bowler,' which is as high a compliment as Jessop ever received.

The pressure of adulation must have been a burden upon Jessop, but like Victor Trumper he did not appear to be aware of it. Don Bradman at the height of his fame was forced to move from Sydney to the quieter streets of Adelaide, because he found public attention so embarrassing. Jessop was not one who enjoyed being badgered by strangers, and possibly found all the attention given to him rather overwhelming. Sir Home Gordon, writing in 1908, says: 'The personality of the redoubtable thumper to a casual acquaintance is a little grim. He nods pleasantly, but is apt to be laconic both in speech and correspondence, while he has a considerable idea of what his own business is and minding it.'

After his Oval century Jessop met the Australians again at Cheltenham a week later, and this time he reminded them that he could bowl as well as bat, for in their innings of 212 he bowled 30 overs, and took seven wickets for 91. He finished the season with a chanceless century at Hastings, a season which all through must have been coloured by the prospect of his forthcoming wedding.

'Jessop was batting.'

On October the 8th Gilbert Jessop was married at Christ Church, Lancaster Gate, the ceremony being performed by the Rev. Canon McCormick, Rector of St James, Piccadilly, who won a Blue for cricket at Cambridge in 1854, and also a Rowing Blue, the last man to win two such Blues. There was a large attendance at the wedding and, in the Australian fashion, a wedding tea was held afterwards at 115 Queen's Gate, South Kensington. Among those present were C. L. Townsend, who had acted as Jessop's best man, W. G. Grace and his son W. G. junior, A. C. MacLaren, and many other cricketers. His sister, Winnie, acted as one of the bridesmaids. The presents were 'numerous', including a handsome cheque from the Gloucestershire Committee, and a magnificent inscribed clock from members of the County Eleven. After the reception the couple departed for a honeymoon in Devon and Cornwall. One of the guests could not resist writing a poem to celebrate the occasion. It was called 'The Match of the Season' and began:

Though Lord's and the Oval have bolted their gates,
And the stands are all silent and still
Though the season has run through the list of its dates,
And the atmosphere's dreary and chill,
Yet the match of the season in all cricket eyes
Was the one that commenced neath the October skies,
The smiter is smitten, and see! he succumbs
– Like the rest of All England – to those
Who, though they are enemies, still remain chums,
And are better for being good foes.

This poem with other notes about the wedding comes from a cuttings book presented to his wife by her husband 'Laird Gilbert Jessop' on the second anniversary of their wedding, October 8 1904. They are living in a flat at 10 Kensington Square Mansions. The book is full of personal items dating back to Jessop's Cambridge days, but also contains cricket cuttings of later years.

Jessop had lived in rooms in London ever since he came down from Cambridge in July 1899, and he remained in London until the end of 1906. During that time he had three jobs, work on the Stock Exchange where he was said to be almost as popular as he was on the cricket field, the directorship of a small tobacco firm, and sporting journalism with the *Daily Mail*, though the exact dates of these jobs are not known. They probably overlapped to some extent. The job with the tobacco firm took him off to an office in the City in a top hat and morning suit. He had a three-year contract, but after about a year the firm was 'taken over' in a merger with Wills. This was very regrettable for Jessop, for though he was paid compensation for the unexpired part of the contract – he was being paid £500 a year – he would have much preferred to have kept a regular job. It is a pity that Wills did not offer him one, for a steady job would have given him some financial security. Under present-day conditions Jessop could have played his cricket and been paid for it, but there must have been times in his twenty years of county cricket when he had financial anxiety about both the present and the future. It is possible that after his marriage to may have contemplated going out to Australia and starting up a private school. His wife had property suitable for this venture at Hamilton, Moss Vale, New South Wales, but nothing came of this idea, and in about 1904 the property was sold. It did indeed become a private school, Tudor House, which still flourishes, but Gilbert Jessop was not the founder of it.

After the regrettable loss of his job with the tobacco firm in about 1903

Jessop turned increasingly to sporting journalism as a means of income. His first cricket writings date back to the days when he was still at Cambridge and in 1903 Arthur Pearson published a book on cricket which was edited by Gilbert Jessop. In the same year he began a connection with the *Daily Mail* in which he produced regular cricket notes and comments, though he was not an actual reporter on matches. The general content of these notes will be discussed in a later chapter. Jessop was now right in the world of sporting writers. He appears at a *Daily Mail* function in honour of Sir Alfred Harmsworth, and at dinners of the *Daily Mail* Cricket Club, and of the Press Club. Jessop seems to have been reasonably well paid for his journalism, but such a source of income was necessarily irregular, and perhaps not quite what he would have chosen, especially in the early days of his marriage. But if there were any anxieties they did not seem to affect his cricket.

The opening of the 1903 season found Jessop in excellent form, but there were no Test matches in which he could enhance his reputation. In the fourth match of the county season he produced one of his greatest innings. It was played against Sussex on Whit Monday, June 1st.

There was a time when Bank Holiday would ensure from county players a special effort. Certainly the 7,000 spectators who paid at the turnstiles on that day got their money's worth. Gloucestershire won the toss, but on a good wicket put on only 30 runs in the first hour. At lunch the score was 104 for 3. Jessop had come in No. 5 at 94, and had scored 9 in 10 minutes before the interval. Two more wickets fell quickly after lunch, and with the score at 129 for 5, Board joined his captain. These two scored 320 runs for the sixth wicket in a mere 2½ hours. The game was completely transformed. While Board watched, Jessop, helped by 27 runs off two consecutive overs from Vine, reached his 50 in 32 minutes. He then hastened on towards his hundred, reaching it out of 136 in 70 minutes. In another 50 minutes Jessop doubled his score, to achieve in exactly two hours the fastest double century ever made. Meanwhile Board, who was himself usually a fast scorer, continued to act as spectator. After tea the hitting went on with an almost monotonous stream of boundaries. To quote one report: 'Jessop's runs were made in a manner different to that which is usual with him. His drives were along the carpet, while his cutting was beautifully safe and clean.' There was no particular victim among the bowlers, though George Cox had one expensive over of 22 runs, 18 runs to Jessop and 4 wides, but time and again 14 or 15 runs came off an over. George Cox recalls this innings and writes:

'With regard to Mr Jessop and his "misdeeds" my feelings were somewhat mixed during that innings of 286 at Hove. One moment I would be cross, but the next, although he put your best ball to the boundary (or over the ropes) one could not but admire that wonderful footwork combined with eye and wristwork. When once he got in there seemed no method of shifting him.

'I remember Joe Vine coming to me saying, "How can you bowl to a blighter who cuts you from outside the leg peg?" This he frequently did. By the way, Joe could bowl fast leg breaks in those days and was not far removed from being the best in the country.

'We tried of course to bowl a length, but Mr Jessop soon showed you he recognised no such thing while he was at the crease or out of it – more often out. One felt he couldn't possibly continue taking such risks in batting without sooner or later making a mistake. Unfortunately for the poor bowler it was too often later.'

After reaching his 200 'amid scenes of confusion seldom surpassed on the ground' – and one paper says he showed signs of caution as he approached it – Jessop continued on his way and sailed past his previous top score of 233. Just when it seemed that he was about to make a miraculous triple century, he was out to an exceptionally brilliant catch by Ranji. Jessop describes it: 'He was fielding at long-off to Killick's bowling just in front of the south stand when the ball came in his direction in the shape of a low skimmer. As is customary with leg-break bowling when hit on the off-side, the ball towards the end of its flight increased its curl to the right, and it seemed impossible that Ranji could arrive in time to arrest its progress. Certainly I for one never thought he could, but to my astonishment the left hand shot out – and the next moment I was on my way to the pavilion. One expected that sort of thing from Ranji in the slips in those days, but scarcely "in the country".'

So once again Jessop was out to a wonderful catch, one which C. B. Fry said was the most marvellous he ever saw. He had scored 286 out of 355 in 175 minutes. He had hit 43 fours, and no doubt some of those went over the ropes, for C. B. Fry says: 'It was absurd how he planted the ball over the ropes in directions no one else ever thought of seeking.'

Seldom can a Bank Holiday crowd have been so lavishly treated, and, apart from their plaudits, Jessop received many letters, including at least two poems on postcards from strangers, one of which reads:

Oh Jessop, how we love thy tricks
When thou art careful of thy sticks
In nine nought three
May we soon see
Another brilliant two eight six.
T. A. T.

while another card from a Lancashire supporter begged Jessop not to treat them like that. There was also a letter from a Gloucestershire supporter who lived in Glasgow, and was writing on behalf of 'your many Scotch admirers'.

The details of the innings are:

1 1 2 4 1 4 1 1 2 1 4 4 4 2 1 4 4 4 1 4
4 1 4 1 4 1 4 2 4 3 4 1 1 2 2 3 1 1 4 4
1 1 4 2 4 1 3 2 4 4 4 3 2 4 4 2 2 4
4 4 1 4 4 4 1 1 2 1 1 1 3 1 3 4 2 1 1 2 2 4
2 4 2 4 2 1 4 2 2 1 1 1 1 4 2 2 2 2 2 2 4 4
3 2 4 1 1 3 4 2 4 4 4

namely 43 fours, 8 threes, 28 twos, and only 34 singles.

Earlier in the season, while Ranji and Jessop were practising on George Beldam's private cricket pitch, Ranji had told Beldam that he knew how to get Jessopus out: all you had to do was to place all your men except for silly-point on the leg-side and invite Jessop to have a go! He would surely be caught sooner or later!

After Jessop's innings of 286 against Sussex Beldam sent a wire to him saying 'Congratulations see Ranji has not discovered your weak spot', and he could well afford to say this, because not long before, when Middlesex had played Gloucestershire at Lord's, Beldam had managed to get Jessop out twice in the match.

In the very next county match, against Lancashire at Bristol, Jessop played another long innings of a different type. He scored 168 in three hours against Barnes and Brearley, whose analyses ended at 3–125 and 3–141 respectively, thanks largely to Jessop. The reports speak of Jessop as being 'slow', but such an innings from anyone else would have been regarded as outstanding. If ever he did score at a rate of under a run a minute the papers were quick to pounce, which shows how he had completely upset normal standards where time and runs were concerned. It should not be necessary to 'excuse' his time of three hours, but it is possible to do so, as evidence suggests that throughout his innings Jessop was feeling far from well.

M.C.C. were planning to take their first official team to Australia in the winter of 1903–4, and in a letter dated June 24, 1903, F. E. Lacey, the Secretary of M.C.C., wrote to ask Jessop if he would agree to make one of the team. He writes: 'All amateur expenses will be paid and arrangements will be made for the comfort and convenience of the team. Every effort will be made to make the tour a success in every way.' There were no details in this letter about the amount of money granted for expenses. Unless an amateur had private means he found it very difficult to afford to spend at least six months away on tour with no financial return other than bare incidental expenses. For a newly married man, with a living to make, it was impossible. And for Jessop there was again the daunting prospect of a long sea voyage. He refused the invitation, and for very different reasons other amateurs also declined to go.

Lacey's letter had included the words 'Warner will captain the side'. Although Warner had led teams to America and elsewhere, he was not yet captain of his county, and several amateurs felt that the honour of leading the first official M.C.C. tour to Australia should go to someone who was more experienced. So it came about that only two amateurs agreed to go with Warner, R. E. Foster, who was financially compensated as being 'assistant manager', and B. J. T. Bosanquet, who was a Middlesex friend of Warner's. All the rest were professionals, and of the whole team of 14 half were strangers to Australia. There was no Ranji, no Fry, no MacLaren, no Jones, no Perrin, and no Jessop – all of whom had been the leading amateur batsmen of 1903. Nor was S. F. Barnes selected, but this time Lord Hawke 'permitted' Hirst and Rhodes to go. In spite of these problems over selection, Warner's team did very well. They won three of the Tests, and as many as eight out of the eleven first-class matches played. Warner fully justified himself as captain.

Although he did not take part on the tour Jessop wrote regular notes and comments on the day's play for the *Daily Mail*, and kept cuttings of these reports.

Soon after his great innings of 286 a rumour arose that Jessop would not be able to play regularly for the county in 1904, and would therefore have to relinquish the captaincy. When interviewed by the *Express* he stated that if he was not able to continue the captaincy it would be entirely on business grounds, but that he had no intention of forsaking the county. His service to the county would depend on his business. If his business was supported by Gloucestershire to a sufficient extent to enable him to continue playing cricket, he would do so; but if it were imperative that he should devote more attention to business in other parts of England, he would only be able to assist occasionally. In any case, he said, his cricket would be played for Gloucestershire and no other county.

Later in the year, however, Jessop wrote a letter to the *Western Daily Press* to say that although he had practically resigned the captaincy at the end of the season he now found that his business arrangements would allow him for the future to play as much cricket as he liked.

I am not sure exactly what his business problem was, why it depended so much upon the support of the Gloucestershire people, and what happened to make his future playing now secure. All that really matters is that he was able to go on playing and giving pleasure to people for another ten years.

Jessop began the season of 1904 in the worst possible way, bagging 'a pair of specs' in his first match. He was playing for M.C.C. against London County at Lord's when he was dismissed:

	c Robson, b Odell	0 (the second victim of Odell's hat trick)
and	c Vine, b W. G. Grace	0

It was a low-scoring game and Grace also got a duck in his first innings. In his usual notes in the *Daily Mail* Jessop wrote a special piece headed: 'A PAIR OF SPECTACLES, how it feels to bag a brace', and it must be the only time a player has discussed such a sad matter in such detail. He writes:

'To be dismissed without scoring in either innings in a match is an event which one cannot look back upon without feeling a certain amount of annoyance. A couple of blobs, even though one may, perchance, claim a wicket or two, or be the medium of saving a number of runs, leaves a sting in the memory. The difference between making 0 and 1 and 0 and 0 does not seem much, but it is just that little cipher that makes all the difference.

'To describe two innings of which the actual amount was four balls, is not a difficult task, though if it were permitted to put all one's thoughts while wending one's way from the wicket to the pavilion after the second failure, it would prove extremely interesting reading! The different ways that that last fatal delivery might have been played could not be counted on the fingers of both hands. And what an interminable distance it is before one reaches the friendly shelter of the pavilion, there to pour one's feelings into friendly and sympathetic ears.'

Some years previously in 1900 he had written a piece on 'The Art of Run-getting' in which he said that the anxiety of some men to avoid 'bagging a brace of specs' not only prevented them from playing their natural game, but was a source of great amusement to onlookers. He goes on to say: 'For myself, just as I cannot see the difference it makes whether you score a century or ninety-nine runs, so it is that I am not able to perceive the difference between 'bagging a brace' and scoring nought and one.'

He apparently felt rather different about the matter when he experienced the fate himself four years later, and in 1914 he again 'bagged a brace' when playing for Gloucestershire *v.* Lancashire at Gloucester. Though there were several occasions in his career when he was out first ball, he made comparatively few ducks, and he was a reliable starter, though he seldom bothered to play himself in.

A fortnight later the cartoonist who had made the most of Jessop's two ducks at Lord's, produced another cartoon entitled 'Revenge' with the scene of Jessop dressed like a knight in armour with his foot upon the corpses of the same two ducks. The reason for this cartoon was that Jessop had just produced one of his most amazing pieces of batting. It was against Somerset at Bristol on May 18.

Gloucestershire went in with the task of scoring 298 runs to win. They made a good start, but then came rain, and when play was resumed after fifty minutes, at ten past one, they were well behind the clock. Ten minutes later their second wicket fell with the score at 98, and in came Jessop. Len Braund was bowling his leg-breaks, and Jessop regarded him and C. L. Townsend as the two most accurate leg-breakers he ever met. Braund had been very difficult to score off, and when it came to the last over before lunch he decided to try to tempt Jessop and get him caught as he had in the first innings. There were several men away on the leg-side and, apart from a deep cover-point, the off-side was practically deserted. Down came the first ball, pitching outside the leg stump. Jessop came down the wicket and gave himself room to drive the ball past cover for four. The next ball again pitched to leg but it was more tossed up. Jessop moved back and placed it rather squarer than the previous one. Another four. Braund was far too good a bowler to be upset by such tactics, and the third ball was slower still, tossed even higher with plenty of spin. Jessop was ready for it, went down the wicket in a flash, reached it on the half-volley and swung it away clean over the track to land by the tennis courts to the right of the pavilion. Braund moved a man round and bowled a faster ball straight down the leg-side. Jessop hopped back and cut it cleanly to the back of point. Four more runs. Everyone began to grow drunk with excitement, only poor Braund looking sad. He looked first at Jessop, who asked him if he was feeling all right, and then at his captain, Sammy Woods, who was chuckling to himself, knowing there was nothing to be done about it. Braund tossed up the next ball, hoping that Jessop would overreach himself, but away it went past extra-cover, who watched it whizz by half-paralysed. The scoreboard workers began to get left behind, and spectators were starting to make rapid calculations – 4 4 6 4 4 – that came to 22, and there was still one more ball to come, the last ball before lunch. Jessop gave a slight hitch to his trousers, gripped the bat more firmly, and crouched even lower.

This time Braund dropped it short. With a mighty spring Jessop leaped after it and let fly. High over the rails it went for six, and the crowd, who had grown suddenly silent, burst into frenzied cheers and rushed on to the ground. During lunch people began to work out what had happened during those last ten minutes. In fact, Jessop had received 14 balls, 3 from Palairet, 5 from Woods, and 6 from Braund, and had dealt with them like this:

0 3 4 1 4 0 4 1 4 4 6 4 4 6

to score 45 in 10 minutes. So much for being careful before an interval.

The news quickly spread around Bristol that Jessop was at it again, and when play began the crowd had increased greatly. Robson began with a maiden over to Wrathall, and then Braund had another go at Jessop. He was not the sort of bowler to be put off by his pre-lunch punishment. This over Jessop contented himself with 2 fours and 2 twos, bringing his score to 57 in just under a quarter of an hour. After that he got less of the bowling and with his score at 61 he was caught in the slips by Braund, who thus had some revenge for having been hit for 40 runs in two consecutive overs. Jessop had scored 61 out of 73 in 24 minutes, and more important, had brought the Gloucestershire score up with the clock, enabling them to make the necessary 298 runs and so win a fine match by three wickets.

This innings was remarkable for its record-breaking: 28 runs off an over was a record (though Jessop was to equal it later). But the innings was even more remarkable for its virtuosity in placing the ball, making it impossible for a bowler to keep him quiet. If the fielders were adjusted to block his stroke he took delight in putting the ball in the very spot from where the fielder had just been moved. It was the type of batsmanship that made C. B. Fry say of him that he had become less of the unorthodox hitter and more of a Victor Trumper.

A fortnight later, when scoring 87 against Middlesex at Lord's, a fast ball from Bosanquet splintered a bone in the little finger of Jessop's left hand, and in the next match against Surrey at the Oval, when Gloucestershire collapsed on a rain-damaged wicket, there was no sign of Jessop coming in to save them. When he eventually came in tenth he played a one-handed little innings of some interest. D. L. A. Jephson describes it:

'I have seen many one-handed batsmen struggle for runs. . . . I have watched them play with the care of a Scotton, but until yesterday I have never watched a man, a one-armed man, hit, and this is what Jessop essayed. He guided the bat with the left hand, and at the striking moment removed it from the handle. He pulled Lockwood to deep-square leg for two as a start. He tricked a one to mid-off, and then amid much amused applause, hoisted Smith over Chinnery's head to the mid-on boundary for 4. A 2 off Smith, and a single, and he was out caught at third-man (Holland) for 10. In my varied experience of the game I have never seen a one-handed slogger.

'Then in the field, when Surrey were preparing to bat, he stood as usual either at cover or extra and he is about as good with one hand and a couple of boots as the majority of fieldsmen with their whole complement of dilatory digits.'

He did not play in the next match but played in the next two, apparently batting normally; after a gap of ten days he appeared for Arkley club *v.* M.C.C. on June 21. He was batting one-handed again, but in spite of this scored 61 with 13 fours, and the great Kortright was among the bowlers he had to face. He often turned out for the Arkley club, chiefly because of his friends the Mudies (of Mudies Library fame) who were concerned with this Hertfordshire club.

His finger seems to have given no more trouble after this, and in mid-July he scored the third double-century of his career with a score of 206 at Trent Bridge. He reached 100 in 70 minutes and 200 in 140 minutes. He was probably even more pleased about Gloucestershire's mammoth total of 636 than his own score, for they did not often make totals like that. Jessop said that it was his soundest knock for some time, and it may have been this innings that a correspondent tells me about. His father was sitting in the pavilion, and as Jessop went in to bat he called out 'Good luck, little Gillie'. Jessop turned and thanked him, and added: 'I'll be sending you up a catch before long, so keep awake.' Not long after, Jessop made a soaring hit which sailed into the pavilion and landed quite near to where his friend was sitting. He had kept his promise.

Jessop's 206 was yet another innings in which he gave no chance, and he has some interesting things to say about chanceless innings. Writing in 1913 he says that he cannot remember seeing more than thirty centuries which could be regarded as flawless, but he was careful to stress the difference between a *catch* which should have been caught, and a *chance* which might have been caught. He thought that many reports failed to make a proper distinction. Although he often declared that statistics were anathema to him, he himself frequently produces unusual factual observations on the game such as I have never seen elsewhere.

At the end of the season Jessop played another famous innings. We have heard how often he slaughtered the attack of even the fastest of bowlers. This time his victim was J. J. Kotze of South Africa, whom Plum Warner regarded as second only to Kortright in sheer pace. The South Africans, who were not in 1904 regarded as good enough yet to be granted Test matches with England, had had a good season and this was their last match, against the South of England at Hastings. Jessop, who did not really want to play because of his lumbago, went in fifth when three wickets had fallen for only 18 runs. Wickets continued to fall, and when the seventh wicket fell at 80 Jessop had scored 36 in 45 minutes. At 23 he asked the South African captain, Frank Mitchell, under whose captaincy he had played for Cambridge in 1896, if he could have a runner. Mitchell agreed, and Seymour of Kent came out to run for him. Jessop began to hit while George Cox, who had come in ninth, propped up the other end. By lunch he had helped Jessop to add 104 runs in the last 45 minutes, most of them to Jessop, who after reaching his 50 in 57 minutes, added his next 50 in 15 minutes while Cox made one.

The lumbago wore off, Seymour was dismissed and Jessop was soon running down the wicket to all the bowlers, especially to Kotze's fastest balls. At one time Halliwell the wicket-keeper was standing up to Kotze for the first time ever. Jessop took 17 runs off Kotze's first over, and though Kotze soon had four men on the boundary Jessop kept on finding it with daring pulls. The faster Kotze bowled the harder Jessop hit him. The score at lunch was 184 for 7, of which Jessop had made 130. No doubt during the interval Mitchell enquired after Jessop's lumbago. After lunch Cox was bowled by Kotze for 17, J. T. Hearne made 14, and H. Hesketh Prichard came in last, determined to stay while Jessop went on towards his double century. He had so often seen Jessop make runs that he regarded himself as being Jessop's mascot. But poor Hesketh Prichard's intentions were not to succeed as he was out first ball, lbw to Schwarz. When the last wicket fell at 237 Jessop was left with 159; he had made these runs out of 219 in just over two hours.

Three years later, in the Test match at Lord's, Jessop was to give Kotze another hammering. His stream of boundaries at Hastings reminds one of how a lady admirer once asked Jessop if he got very tired with all that running up and down the wicket. Jessop replied modestly that he did not get very tired as he did not in fact do a great deal of running. Among the many letters of congratulation for his innings at Hastings was a card sent from Venice which said: 'What a pity you were not allowed to complete your innings. It might have reached 2,000. J. P. M.'

So 1904 ended on a high note for him, and that winter he was able to spend some time on golf, a new attraction that gave him increasing pleasure and interest.

5

Decline and Comeback 1905–1908

'To get down to hard facts, cricket matches are won by runs and not style.'

G. L. J.

IN 1905 Jessop was playing in his twelfth season in first-class cricket, and it was the first season in which his batting was regarded 'as not what it used to be', for both his average and aggregate dropped to the lowest figure since 1898, and no fewer than nineteen of his forty-seven innings were in single figures. *Wisden* sadly remarked: 'On many occasions his batting was quite disappointing, his failures being attributed to his hitting fast-footed and not getting properly to the pitch of the ball. He certainly did not jump in with his former frequency, and it was suggested that the noticeable change in his methods had been brought about by playing golf. However that may be, it is certain that as a hitter he had lost much of his former skill, and was not the same terrible batsman to the bowlers that he had been. He was so clearly not himself as a bat that after playing in the Test match at Nottingham he was left out of the subsequent England elevens, even his brilliancy as a fieldsman failing to keep him his place. He was, of course, the most valuable member of the Gloucestershire eleven, but he was no longer the commanding personality of former years.'

These are sad words on such a hero, and his supporters must have felt bitter disappointment, for when he failed the spectators felt they had been robbed of a rare experience. The first Test match against Australia at Trent Bridge was fixed for as early as May 29, a date which Jessop among others felt was too soon in the season for such an important game. Though he had made few runs Jessop was chosen for the match, and when he went in eighth in England's first innings the score was only 119. Let him describe what happened:

'My share in the winning of the rubber that year was exactly nil for I so blotted my copybook by electing to attempt to flick my first ball to leg – an uncouth manoeuvre which resulted in a disarrangement of my leg stump . . . my first and only stroke was more reminiscent of an iron shot than any stroke known to careful students of batsmanship.' So there he was, 'b Laver . . . 0', and as he walked sadly to the pavilion, he must have thought of the last innings he had played in Test cricket – his historic 104 at the Oval in 1902.

Though Jessop's fielding in the match 'was beyond praise, he stopped everything that came within reasonable distance', Jackson, the England captain, did not call upon Jessop to bat when England batted again and scored 426–5 dec. According to Fry, 'Jackson always shook his head over Jessop; he always expected our "Croucher" to try to hit the first ball bowled to him to long leg, no matter if it were a fast straight good length ball on his middle stump.' In this innings all Jackson's fears were confirmed. This was to be Jackson's great year as captain, and his opinion was virtually law. Jessop himself tells a story of how the people of the Jackson estate in Yorkshire regarded the Honourable Francis Stanley Jackson as being on a par with the Almighty, except that Jackson was a better batsman. Jessop's one irresponsible stroke made it certain that he would not be chosen again for the series under Jackson's captaincy, and though the critics protested that 'in Jessop's case form does not count for much', and reminded the selectors of the great Test innings of 1902, Jessop was not recalled. In other recollections of the match Jessop remembered how Cotter, the Australian fast bowler, who incidentally bowled Jackson for 0, made the ball jump about in an alarming way: 'Cotter is quite the shortest pitch bowler I have ever seen. I say this not even forgetting my brief career as a fast intimidator.'

Wisden has suggested that Jessop's loss of form in 1905 might be attributed to his playing of golf, and Jessop's agrees that it was in fact due 'to the previous winter's study of the intricacies of those vexatious problems which ever beset the path of the tyro at the Royal and Ancient game'. It is interesting to note that when writing twenty years later Jessop stated that an essential point in golf – keeping one's eye on the ball – must help a batsman's defence, and correct the prevalent error of playing at the pitch of the ball. . . . 'No, cricket may interfere with one's golf, but not golf with cricket.'

I think what he meant about golf upsetting his form in 1905 referred more to loss of footwork than sighting of the ball. Jessop had first begun playing golf a few years earlier, and we have in this scrapbook pictures of him receiving instruction from the great golfer Harold Hilton, who would obviously find it difficult to provide Jessop with a classical style, for he was clearly a puncher

Mr. Gilbert Laird Jessop.

with a restricted follow-through and a scythe-like action which, as his son says, was not unlike that of Lee Trevino. A magazine called *The King* has full pictorial accounts of a golf match between Cricketers and Actors played at Northwood in November 1904 with teams led by George Edwardes and G. L. Jessop: the players included Rutland Barrington, H. Hilton, W. G. Grace, G. Beldam, B. J. T. Bosanquet, G. Brann, C. O. H. Sewell, and Mornington Cannon, the famous jockey. It was possibly on this occasion that a lady accosted Jessop, whom she thought was Mornington Cannon, and she told him that it was no wonder he was not riding winners any more as he had obviously put on too much weight. We do not know Jessop's reply.

That same winter Jessop won the Suspension Bridge Cup at a meeting of the Bristol Club at Clifton, and he was clearly on the way to becoming a very good golfer, who was willing to spend plenty of time playing. There is a contemporary cutting which deplores the quantity of amateurs who were increasingly turning to golf, to the great loss of cricket. Among the older players mentioned is F. S. Jackson, and Jessop, 'who has at Burnham and Berrow been playing something decidedly better than a scratch game. There are any number of young men who would probably have been playing cricket for their counties if golf had not proved so fascinating.' Writing ten years later Jessop says that when the Cricketer's Golfing Society was founded in 1904 – he himself was the first secretary – there were ten players who were scratch golfers, whereas in 1914 there were over fifty. He agrees that cricket has suffered from players becoming attracted to golf, and using one of his frequent Latin quotations, adds: 'Facilis descensus Averno.'

Jessop was not one to complain if he was omitted from the England side and though he wrote poems he never, unlike John Snow, wrote one about being left out of the Test team. He realised that sooner or later his form would return.

Some three weeks after his disastrous Test innings at Trent Bridge Gloucestershire were meeting Somerset at Bristol. On the first day Somerset were all out for 169, and Gloucestershire replied well, Jessop being 70 at the close of play. Spectators turned up in great numbers next day, delighted that Jessop had at last found his form. Here is an account from a Bristol paper:

'Jessop batting! What an attraction the Gloucestershire captain is! As a rule the spectators are content to let the first half-hour's play slip by before taking their seats at the County ground, but this morning there was a big crowd assembled sometime before the umpires were out. There was a certainty of seeing Jessop bat, and if the hour of starting had been 6 a.m. the crowd would I think have been there. . . . The row of seats on the green in front were very nearly filled. The charming summer gowns and brightly-hued sunshades gave welcome colour to the scene, and the flower-pot stands on the popular side were all occupied. For once in a way Jessop did not disappoint, and the spectators were able to cheer his first hundred of the season, and his first century scored against Somerset bowling.' He reached his hundred in 80 minutes, added another hundred in the next 50 minutes, and when finally bowled by Braund, jumping out to drive, he had scored 234 out of 346 in 155 minutes. He had hit forty fours, and given only two chances at 31 and 155. 'It was a great innings: he was cheered to the echo on returning to the pavilion. It was quite an ovation. It was not merely a display of hand-clapping, but cheers, real hearty cheers, and many of the spectators stood up and waved their hats. They are choosing the English team for the next Test game this evening, and this innings should make Jessop's inclusion safe.'

So wrote the *Western Daily Press*, but the Test selectors took no notice of Jessop's return to form, and this return was in fact short-lived, for that was the only hundred he made in 1905. There is, though, one other match which is worth mentioning, the one against Lancashire at Old Trafford. Jessop had made 65 in the first innings, and when Gloucestershire batted again, 147 runs behind, he decided to continue an attacking policy. Walter Brearley, a rumbustious fast bowler, who had in the previous three days been bowling England to victory on the same ground, was possibly feeling weary and did not care for Jessop's treatment of him. When Jessop came in he had already been bowling for 75 minutes, but Jessop and Board showed no mercy and took 15 runs off him in an over. It seemed that Brearley would now be rested, but to quote *The Manchester Guardian*:

'To everyone's amazement Brearley again took the ball, and then came the over of the day. The first ball Jessop hit to the rails. The following five were flung clean beyond the wicket. Three of them passed clear over Jessop's head. Two fell straight into the hands of Findlay, the wicket-keeper, and the third Jessop flung his bat up to and skied it over Garnett's head. The remaining balls reached the pitch two or three yards beyond the wicket.

'It was clear after this that the Lancashire captain, MacLaren, was determined to bowl Brearley at all costs. Off the first ball of the next over Jessop was missed at the wicket, with the second, in trying to hit, he was bowled, and then Board was caught. Between them Jessop and Board had put on 98 runs in forty minutes, and 45 runs had come off three successive overs – mostly off Brearley's bowling.' *The Western Daily Press* makes the situation rather clearer, for in fact 57 runs had come off four overs, 12 off Brearley, 18 off Cuttell, 15 off Brearley, and then 12 off Cuttell. In the next over 'Brearley seemed to lose his head and five times in one over he was no-balled. The fast bowler sent several balls over Jessop's head, and this drew a remark from the Gloucestershire captain to the umpire, though it was not clear what he had said. This remarkable cricket was not to continue as Jessop pulled a ball into his wicket for 57 runs in 40 minutes, the last 34 coming in ten.'

After Jessop was out Brearley continued to bowl, and when Gloucester were all out for 198 Lancashire had an easy win. Brearley had bowled throughout the innings, and took six wickets for 106 runs.

When Jessop was dismissed he said that he had the impression that Brearley was deliberately bowling at his head. 'After being severely punished Brearley lost his head, and in an endeavour to find a better one, sought mine by aid of fast full pitches. . . . One frequently sees a bowler lose his length, but seldom his temper.' Just before this incident Brearley had behaved oddly by grabbing a bat and hitting to the boundary a ball Jessop was rolling down the wicket between overs. Brearley was not a great batsmen, and he said that he did this 'just to see how it feels to hit a four' – an unusual experience for him. He did, however, in the following season, in the Gentlemen *v.* Players match, help Jessop to make a last wicket stand of 49. As the Gentlemen eventually won by only 45 runs this was a useful effort.

Jessop and Brearley were both men of enormous self-confidence, who knew each other well, and enjoyed their lively meetings. In 1911 Brearley once had a wager with Jessop that he would take twenty wickets in the next two matches, at Leeds and Canterbury. When Brearley took only seven at Leeds, Jessop felt safe, but at Canterbury Brearley captured twelve, and would have had his wager-winning thirteen if the last man had not been dropped off his bowling. Jessop may have felt that Brearley had a rather high opinion of himself, and he enjoyed a story of how Brearley once stopped to watch some boys play cricket and decided to give them some instruction. They did not know who he was, and did not take kindly to his action. Jessop heard how Brearley had thus been snubbed, and wrote this verse about it:

> 'D'ye mean to say you don't know me, really?
> Why, I'm the famous fast bowler, Walter Brearley,
>   Take this card, my lad,
>   And just show it your dad,
> For your ignorance deserves to cost you dearly!'

Though Jessop did not see the Australians much in the Test matches, he met them in their game with Gloucestershire at Bristol at the end of August. On the last day a tame draw seemed likely, but after an Australian declaration Gloucestershire were faced with making 136 to win. Jessop altered his batting order, as he had done in two other matches in the season, but the result was disastrous, and with 15 minutes still left for play the last man, Dennett, came in to join Jessop. These two kept up their wickets till time was called, and Gloucestershire achieved a draw. Jessop's score of 23 in a total of 64 for 9 was a match-saving innings of an unusually defensive kind, and no doubt gave him more satisfaction than most of the innings he had played in 1905.

Any hopes that the new season of 1906 would see Jessop back in his best form were soon dashed, for his performance was only fractionally better than in 1905, and his highest score for the season was only 87. As the county's success depended very much on that of their captain, they had a poor time, and by the end of July they had won only one game, and lost nine (including a defeat by Cambridge). The coming of August, however, brought a remarkable change, and five out of eight matches were won, including a one-run victory over Yorkshire at Bristol, in a match that ranks high in the annals of Gloucestershire cricket. This spell of success, belated though it was, filled the members with a more hopeful feeling at a time when the whole future of the club began to seem doubtful. As with some other counties, there were not enough regular professionals, and the amateurs, with some notable exceptions, were simply not good enough. As Jessop himself sadly pointed out: 'Not all those who play in first class matches can be regarded as first-class players', but an amateur cost the club a third of what the cost was for a professional, and there was not the money to pay for more professionals. The load of responsibility carried by Jessop as captain was enough to have broken anyone less determined and resourceful than he was. There was, however, one match in 1906 which must have been very rewarding.

The final week of the season of 1906 saw two possible contenders for the championship, Kent and Yorkshire. Kent had to meet Worcester and Hampshire; Yorkshire, Somerset and Gloucestershire. When they disposed of Gloucestershire for only 164 on August 23, Yorkshire's prospects seemed good, but though the wicket was not awkward at any time, Yorkshire found the bowling of Dennett (8–86) so difficult that they finished up five runs behind the Gloucestershire total. Gloucestershire batted more doggedly in their second innings, scoring 228 and leaving Yorkshire the task of scoring 234 to win. Kent were doing well at Worcester, so Yorkshire had to win to keep in the running. The battle was on, and the extreme respect shown to the Gloucestershire bowlers resulted in five wickets falling for only 119. This put the odds slightly on the home side, but before another wicket fell the score was taken to 185, with Ernest Smith still to be disposed of, and Haigh, Myers, Hunter and Ringrose still to follow. This was the moment that Jessop took fire, clean bowling both Smith and Haigh. Amid increasing excitement, Myers, assisted by the dogged Hunter, snatched singles until, with only 11 runs wanted, Hunter was caught by Townsend off F. B. Roberts. Last man in was Ringrose. Jessop himself continues the story of what he regarded as the most exciting county match he had ever played in: 'To such an indifferent batsman as Ringrose – Yorkshire's last hope – the situation may have borne resemblance to a Christian entering an arena of lions, but outwardly there was no evidence he was seriously perturbed. Until two runs from victory he played his part manfully on the occasions when he had to face the bowling, occasions which Myers skilfully designed should be infrequent while he himself added 9 precious runs.' But at last he could not manage to hold the bowling, and Jessop put himself on for the next over against Ringrose. *Wisden* states that after sending down one ball very wide on the leg side Jessop got Ringrose lbw on the third ball of the over. This differs from Jessop's account, which possibly recalls incidents of a previous over. He writes: 'Ringrose was huddling over his bat, and never could the stumps have been so obscured. A heart-rending appeal for lbw from the first ball. The next rose over the off-stump. The third was blocked. The fourth, intended to be a fast yorker, went away very wide of Ringrose's legs (left-handers' legs in those days invariably acted like a magnet upon me), and it would have gone for four byes had not Board made a superhuman effort to get across and stop it with the fat part of his arm, thus saving me from ignominy. The next ball got through his defence for a plumb lbw. Gloucester had won by one run.'

There is a delightful reminder of this match in the pavilion at Bristol, a set of photographs of the finish with a vast hat-throwing crowd carrying their victorious captain towards the pavilion. The Committee were so elated by this victory that they had medals made and presented them to all members of the team. Lord Hawke had been so confident of a Yorkshire victory that he had previously arranged for presents to be given to wives of the players. What happened to these?

Poor Yorkshire! This defeat cost them the championship, but in spite of his feelings of disappointment George Hirst made a point of coming up to congratulate Jessop – a generous action which pleased Jessop almost as much as the result of the match. Seven years later at Sheffield Jessop was once again to win a close victory over Yorkshire by a similar dynamic last-minute effort.

What was probably Jessop's best innings of the season was in the Gentlemen *v.* Players match at Lord's, which, with no Test matches to overshadow it, was the game of the season. Forty thousand people came to see it in the three days. In the first innings Jessop was bowled for 13 by Fielder who took all ten wickets for 90 runs. In the second innings the Gentlemen had a lead of only 240 when Walter Brearley came in last to join Jessop, who had come in at 229–6. Jessop farmed the bowling and hit superbly, and when Brearley was eventually bowled, he was left with 73, scored out of 92 in an hour's batting. Fielder was still bowling with great venom and bounce, but Jessop repeatedly dropped on his right knee and lashed him high over the square-leg boundary into the Mound Stand. Had he missed the ball he might have been hit on the head, but his courage against fast bowling was always enormous. Once again his daring hitting had turned the state of the game.

Another great day for Jessop in 1906 was the birth of his son and heir on September 6. He received a card from W. G. Grace a few days later saying: 'Cannot play at Pinner, have a match with Bell at Sutton. Must congratulate you and wish mother and son are doing well. W. G. Grace.'

One telegraph of congratulation came from a small boy, who sold his possessions to pay for it, and was too shy to sign it.

There is no doubt that golf was already occupying much of Jessop's time in the winter, and as secretary-treasurer of the Cricketers' Golfing Society, founded in March 1905, he had plenty to do. During the winter of 1906 he was probably busy with the continuation of his series of 'Open Letters to Cricketers' which appeared weekly in the *Athletic News*. The first one had appeared on April 30, 1906. It took the form of a letter of 1,200 words addressed to Lord Hawke, discussing his various abilities and interests. The letter was signed 'INCOGNITUS', and the idea was evidently a success, for the series went on right through the season. The last letter was on August 27, and there had been a previous note to say that the first three readers who sent in a card by August 22 correctly naming the identity of the writer whose letters were appearing under the name INCOGNITUS would receive a selected bat signed by the author. No doubt the name had already been guessed by some: the eighteen letters had been addressed, in this order, to Lord Hawke, A. C. MacLaren, C. B. Fry, P. F. Warner, G. L. Jessop, W. Brearley, K. S. Ranjitsinhji, Bosanquet, W. G. Grace, Tom Hayward, Tyldesley, F. S. Jackson, S. M. J. Woods, Hirst, Haigh, A. O. Jones, Knox and Lilley.

There seem to have been no repercussions at the kindly but candid remarks made in the letters, and a second series followed, now appearingly openly under the name of G. L. Jessop. These names include R. E. Foster, Perrin, V. F. S. and J. N. Crawford, Trott, Blythe, Vine, G. Gunn, Board, Braund, Hayes, and J. B. Hobbs, then only in his second season. The letters are full of interest, written with great punch, and with a good deal of quotation ('Chacon à son jeu' seems a favourite one), and there are several Jessop limericks. The letter to F. S. Jackson, who, as I've mentioned, did not always favour Jessop's inclusion in Test teams, has an interesting point about the position of amateurs who were not, like Jackson, 'born with a golden spoon in their mouths', and who found it hard to afford to play regular county cricket.

The most interesting letter of this series is naturally that written to Jessop by himself, since it gives us one of the rare moments when he is ready to reveal personal information. Here it is, quoted in full from the issue of May 28, 1906:

OPEN LETTERS TO FAMOUS CRICKETERS
By Incognitus
No. V Gilbert L. Jessop

My dear Jessopus,

Now that you are no longer numbered among the tear-away

irresponsible fast bowlers, I stand no longer in awe of you. In the days of your horribly short-pitched nose-enders I would not have dared to run the risk of your ire, but now I intend to have my say. Although I can absolve you from any intention of deliberately hurting a batsman – nothing, I am sure, was further from your thoughts – yet in the art of 'pinking' your man you were a master.

It was the unhappy faculty – due more to your bowling round the wicket than from any other reason – which led to a certain individual to drop into rhyme after this fashion:

> There was a young bowler named Jessop,
> Who was pitching 'em less up and less up;
> Till one of the pros
> Who'd a blow on the nose,
> Said, 'In a helmet of brass I'll dress up'.

Notwithstanding your being chosen as the only fast bowler in the Lord's Test Match of 1899, your lack of inches prevented you from becoming a fast bowler of the very front rank. You had your days when you carried all before you, but you were never consistent. And this throughout has been the keynote of your career as a bowler. Except for an occasional 'burst', you no longer bowl anything above medium pace, and this change dates from your serious illness in 1900. Nevertheless, the stupid-looking 'stuff' which you serve up to unsuspecting batsmen does at times meet with success.

However, it is not as a bowler that you are now known to fame, but as a fast-scoring batsman. You are often quoted as an extraordinary example of the hard-hitting type of batsman, and, indeed, as being the hardest hitter of that class. But this is somewhat of a fallacy. You do at times, I grant you, Gilbert, make some prodigious hits, but you hit no harder than Georgie Hirst on the on-side, or than even 'Reggie' Spooner on the off-side of the wicket. It is not as a big hitter that you have shown yourself to be a little superior to some of your fellow cricketers, but it is in your fast-scoring propensities.

I may be misjudging you, but you seem to me to pander too much to what has been to you on not a few occasions a somewhat unfortunate proclivity. Time after time have I seen you sacrifice your wicket to this craze when there was no earthly object in your obtaining runs quickly. Just to take on instance only of this, I will remind you – even at the risk of opening up an old score – of your only appearance in the Test Matches this year.

With the game in an unfortunate position for England, you selected to hit the first ball from Laver to square-leg, and being beaten in the pace you retired to the pavilion, there to reflect over the heinousness of your crime. I will spare your feelings as to what I said then when I saw your bails go flying. If I did not choose to repeat my remarks now – under the careful eye of the Editor – I fear they would undergo expurgation, and therefore lose their force.

What is it which makes you want to hit every ball to the boundary? It must be the natural aggressiveness of your character. Your temperament is as fiery as was your bowling, and both your batting and fielding are moulded in a like shape. You have little feeling for the person's hands to whom you return the ball from 'cover', but, 'to give the devil his due', you expect the same treatment when the ball is returned to you.

Of one thing you are in no danger of being accused, and that is slackness. Whether the interest in a match has departed or not you are always the same. I would as soon see you field as I would see you bat.

You are very socialistic in your ideas of cricket legislation, and at times you are somewhat lacking in respect towards the Board of Control. Because that Board numbers amongst its members some of the aristocracy, that does not necessarily mean, my dear Jessopus, that it is not sufficiently representative of cricket. Things might be much worse – there might have been a Squirrel or a Goyd Lorge upon the Board. Anyway the dukes or the earls have no axes to grind, which is more than could be said of some people, and is some little thing to be thankful about.

Your own efforts at legislation met with some success a few years ago, when you brought in the alteration of Law 7, which put on an extra two feet in width to the bowling crease. This undoubtedly does help the bowler, especially those of the swerving variety. You have also urged the necessity of commencing all matches on Saturdays and Wednesdays, but so far with little success. Still, I am quite sure you are on the right track. Assuredly in the South the number of Saturdays upon which the working man is certain of getting a full sixpennyworth of cricket are very limited.

Your latest hobby is the pooling of gates. But you may take it from me that neither in Yorkshire or Lancashire will your voice be listened to.

Like many another cricketer, you have been entirely self-taught.

One shudders to think what might have happened to you if you had been initiated into that beautiful 'plumb' wicket style of batting which generally meets with well-merited disaster on all slow wickets.

May I, without hurting your feelings, say that your grotesque, frog-like contortions at the wicket are not altogether elegant, and that a week's careful study of a Palairet or a Spooner might repay you without detriment to your cricket.

For such a risk-taking batsman, year in and year out, the most remarkable point of your cricket has been its consistency and your relish of Yorkshire bowling. And may the latter continue for many years to come. Americans and the Philadelphians in particular know you well, for you have made your presence felt against them in both countries. Your one trip to Australia with MacLaren did not enhance your reputation and you were practically a failure. It is quite true that you had to battle on a number of sticky wickets, the season there being a wet one. You gave as a reason for your non-success your inability to accustom yourself to the glaring light. If that was so I wonder how you would fare in South Africa, where the light is even more dazzling.

Your great triumph against the Australians in that famous Test Match at the Oval must have afforded the greatest of satisfaction – you truly got your own back on that day. Was it true that you accepted a wager of 20 to 1 against your obtaining a century? If so, either you must have a lot of money or a fair modicum of 'cheek'. It has always struck me that of the latter valuable commodity you owe much of your success as a batsman. You very rarely confess that the bowler has beaten you, for you invariably scourge yourself for having given your wicket away, and I am not sure that you are not right.

Anyway, I like your 'cheek' when you are going for the bowling, and I only wish more batsmen would go and do likewise.

I should like to have seen your face when you were saluted with cries of 'Quack, quack' from some humorous spectators after you had collected a duck's egg in the second innings of your first match in Australia. I don't think the humorists would have quite seen the humour of the situation from your point of view if you had caught them 'flagrante delicto'.

On the whole, I don't think you have much cause for complaint about the treatment meted out to you by the spectators. They seem to treat you as a joke, for no sooner do you leave the pavilion than a peculiar sort of 'audible' grin seems to buzz round the ring.

Some day they may treat you seriously, but that will not be until you develop a classic style and orthodox methods. But may that day be far distant. Anyhow, if it should be permitted to you to break your own quick-scoring record, the only harm I wish you is that it may be witnessed by

Very sincerely yours,
INCOGNITUS

This letter is both enlightening and amusing, and Jessop obviously regarded it as a wonderful chance for a leg-pull. It is clear from his remarks that he would seem sometimes to regret his impetuosity, especially that rash stroke which led to his downfall in his only Test of 1905. He is prepared to make fun of his 'grotesque, froglike contortions at the wicket', admits his keen aggressiveness (rather like Tony Greig), and is aware that his radical ideas for reform were not always popular with the establishment. These letters would be worth reprinting in book form as they tell us much about nearly all the great players of the day, the one exception being Rhodes, who has to share a letter with Blythe.

By the end of December 1906 the Jessops and their three-month-old son Gilbert had left the flat at 10 Kensington Square Mansions where they had lived since their wedding day in 1902. For the next two years they were on the move and lived for a time at Littlehampton, Hythe, and East Grinstead. Then, in January 1909, Jessop was appointed secretary to the Gloucestershire County Cricket Club, and found it necessary to move to Bristol for the sake of his new job.

The summer of 1907 saw Jessop's many admirers hoping that the lean spells of the last two seasons were now over, but May and June found him with only 387 runs from 14 innings. There were increasing fears that Jessop really had lost his old touch. Perhaps it was the golf, perhaps it was some fatal loss of confidence which his type of play needed to be successful.

Jessop's loss of form resurrected some of the purist critics who wagged their heads and said that sooner or later such unorthodox batting would be bound to crack up, and that this was clearly the writing on the wall for Jessop. Such things had been said ever since Jessop came into big cricket, and in an article in *Cricket* in 1901, that splendid writer W. A. Bettesworth recalled the early years of Jessop and how a lean spell came upon him: 'But at last it seemed that the prophecies had really come true, for bad times came upon him, and he could not get runs. He seemed to have lost his nerve entirely. Whether he had done so or not, for the time being he set himself out to play the game as it was played by all orthodox players, and although by comparison with what had gone before his performances seemed tame, he showed that he could play an ordinary game as well as most other people. The memories of his brilliant innings began to fade away, when to the surprise, not to say the delight, of everybody, he started on the old tack again, and meeting with a vast amount of success, was chosen to play for England against Australia, with the unanimous approval of all critics.'

The Test selectors of 1907 were, however, quite unperturbed that Jessop had only once reached a century since the last days of 1904, and invited him to play at Lord's in what was the first Test match in which South Africa had met England in England. Jessop's last two Test innings were his 104 *v.* Australia in 1902, and his 0 against Australia in 1905, so this was a vital match for him. Another complete failure might seem to confirm that his batting was now too unreliable to satisfy even his strongest supporters.

The meeting with South Africa aroused great interest, not only as a 'first occasion', but because of the battery of South African mystery bowlers who had been puzzling the counties. In consequence the South Africans came to Lords with a record of eight wins and three draws out of the eleven games played so far. Bosanquet's new googly bowling had been so enthusiastically taken up in South Africa that there were four bowlers who 'in their different ways represented the new development', as *Wisden* put it.

How would England batsmen cope with these new problems offered by South Africa in this meeting at Lord's? The pitch had been under water on Saturday, but had recovered for a prompt start to be made on Monday, July 1. England won the toss and stayed in nearly the whole day to score 428. After a good start by Fry and Hayward England collapsed, and at ten minutes past three had lost five men for only 158 – all to Vogler's leg-breaks and googlies. At this moment Jessop came in seventh to join Braund, and in an hour and a quarter they added 145 runs, of which Jessop scored 93 before being brilliantly caught near the screen by Faulkner off Vogler. 'It was a dazzling innings', says *Wisden*, 'quite comparable to his 104 against Australia in 1902.' Jessop had no difficulty in handling spinners of a type he had never faced before. After being nearly bowled in making a huge lunge at a ball from White, which produced a roar from the large 20,000 crowd, he attacked Vogler savagely, and once hit him high among the members sitting on top of the pavilion. He reached his fifty in 45 minutes, and then attacked Kotze, the fast bowler, who had been brought on to stem the run-getting. Three fours came in one over, two pulls and a straight drive, and after he had been batting an hour Jessop's score was 82 out of the 115 put on so far with Braund. Jessop made only one mishit, when he put an intended drive over the wicket-keeper's head, and was then out off a lofty attempt to clear the screen at the

4
3
2
1
4 3 2 1
1 2 3 4
1
2
3
4

Nursery end. Jessop had made his runs in only 76 minutes, and the score had been taken from 158 for 5 to 303 for 6, which put England in a much better position. To quote A. A. Lilley: 'The whole complex of the game changed in an almost kaleidoscopic fashion.' Jessop had done it again. He had received only sixty-three balls, of which he scored off thirty-nine by means of 14 fours, 1 three, 10 twos, and 14 singles. *The Daily Express* published a chart of these hits, believed to be the first such chart ever published. One report says that 'His was an innings that scarcely any other batsman except Victor Trumper could have played.' At this time in his career we hear less about Jessop's unorthodox methods, and comparisons with Trumper were becoming common.

Thanks to this innings and Braund's persistence, which brought him a well-deserved century, England reached 428. Had the weather not broken up, they would almost certainly have won the match. In two subsequent low-scoring Test matches Vogler was never the same power after Jessop's hammering, and though Jessop did not himself do much in these two matches (his scores were 0 and 10, and 2 and 11), he had showed that the bogy of the South African mystery spinners could be dealt with, and others followed his example.

Another report stresses the extraordinary effect Jessop had on the crowd: ' "I'd give up a day's work to see Jessop," said a man with a dented bowler hat. "That's what I call cricket! Look at him now!" We looked – to see another thunderbolt speed to the boundary. "The Electric Battery" was recharged, and how the people swayed to the music of it. Real cricket critics, these, you meet them every time and every year at the big matches. They know their players and the game and recognise all the finer points. They see that Mr Jessop's greatness consists in the fact that with so vast a repertoire of stroke, he does not apply the wrong stroke to the right ball. He seems to make up his mind the moment the ball leaves the bowler's hand. Almost in the same moment the ball is at the boundary, and Mr Jessop is in repose again, almost impertinently calm. Is cricket dying? There would never be the least fear of it if Mr Jessop were a common type.'

THE GIANT OF THE WILLOW: G. L. JESSOP.

When G. L. Jessop goes in to bat a thrill of excitement runs through the crowd, for this player is the most sensational English batsman. He is the hardest English hitter, and is always good for three runs a minute. He is usually caught on the boundary, and no part of the ground—not even the clock at Lord's, which he once smashed—is safe from his terrific play. The chart of Jessop's hits in the Test Match is based upon one published in the *Daily Express*.

This great Test innings was just what Jessop needed to get him back into his old form, and the rest of the season saw him at his best. The Saturday of the same week as the Lord's Test was a historic day, as it was the first time that two captains used declarations in order to bring about a result, after rain had seemed to make a result impossible. The two captains were Jessop and his friend Sammy Woods of Somerset. The tactics they adopted were much in keeping with their sporting approach to the game, and it was Jessop who gave the lead. He described it himself later:

'Our match against Somerset at Bristol was memorable for the fact of our putting into force the closure rule twice in one day. No play had been possible on the commencing day and only a little over an hour's batting occurred on the second, in which time we scored 59 for the loss of two wickets. The third day fortunately was fine, and forcing the game we declared our innings closed at 139 for 5 wickets. To this Somerset replied with 72, and going in again we quickly knocked up 47, losing four wickets in the process, and then once more declared, leaving Somerset 115 to get in one hour and a quarter. Had Somerset chosen to do so they could have sat tight and made a comfortable draw of it, but to be content with tame tactics was never Sam Woods' conception of how the game should be played. From the start our opponents went bald-headed for the runs, and though Sam himself partially retrieved a bad start, with thirty-five minutes still remaining six wickets had fallen and sixty-one runs yet to get. The odds were distinctly in our favour until a partnership between B. L. Bisgood and C. G. Deane altered the complexion of the game so entirely as to threaten us with defeat in our turn. However, for some reason or other which I have never yet been able to fathom, just at the moment when a continuance of resolute cricket would have been at least as likely to have produced victory as defeat, a caution crept in scarcely justified by the condition in which the game then stood. The spirit in which the game had hitherto been fought vanished completely, and with two wickets still in hand Somerset left off 13 runs behind.' So the final scores read: Gloucester 139–5 dec. and 47–4 dec., Somerset 72 and 102–8, and the spectators had enjoyed a memorable day's cricket. Such bold declaration tactics came into prominence in the 1930s, especially in the hands of another Gloucestershire captain, B. H. Lyon, and though some people have considered that such forced finishes were unfair to other counties, the public saw wonderful cricket as a result. This Jessop–Woods match was the prototype of all such games.

Jessop's cricket at this time was very eventful, and another memorable day was when he and Dennett dismissed Northants for only 12 runs in the match at Gloucester. This is still the lowest score ever made in an innings in a first-class match. Dennett took eight wickets for 9 runs, and Jessop the other

Gloucestershire v. Sussex

On GLOUCESTERSHIRE COUNTY GROUND,

July 15th, 16th, and 17th, 1907.

SUSSEX.	First Innings.		Second Innings.	
1 Vine	c Jessop, b Mills	45	c Winstone, b Dennett	112
2 Mr J. G. Scott	c Board, b Dennett	0	b Huggins	6
3 Relf (A. E.)	c Champain, b Ford	45	c Champain, b Dennett	51
4 Relf (R.)	c Robinson, b Huggins	7	st Board, b Dennett	2
5 Killick	c Board, b Mills	81	b Mills	3
6 Mr. H. L. Simms	c Winstone, b Dennett	47	c Board, b Mills	49
7 Mr. C L. A. Smith	b Winstone	38	b Mills	0
8 Leach	b Dennett	10	b Dennett	12
9 Cox	b Mills	0	b Dennett	3
10 Dwyer	b Mills	15	b Dennett	0
11 Butt	not out	5	not out	3
Scorers:	B 6, l-b 1, w , n-b	7	b 2, l-b 3, w 1, n-b 1	7
H. Vernon & W. Edwards.	Total	300	Total	248

1st Innings.—1 for 0, 2- 69, 3- 89, 4-133, 5-187, 6 270, 7-270, 8 270, 9-294.
2nd Innings.—1 for 8, 2 113, 3-135, 4-143, 5-224, 6 226, 7-230, 8-243, 9-243.

Bowling Analysis—

	First Innings.				Second Innings.			
	Overs.	Mdns.	Runs.	Wkts.	Overs.	Mdns.	Runs.	Wkts.
Dennett	33	8	107	3	37.2	8	101	6
Huggins	24	7	75	1	17	5	77	1
P. H. Ford	14	3	46	1	—	—	—	—
Mills	13.2	0	53	4	21	5	56	3
Winstone	3	1	12	1	1	0	7	0

GLOS'TER.	First Innings.		Second Innings.	
1 Langdon	l b w, b Cox	40	b Cox	0
2 Board	b Cox	24	c A. E. Relf, b Dwyer	19
3 Mr. F. M Luce	b Cox	3	b Dwyer	42
5 Winstone	b Cox	0	st Butt, b Dwyer	27
8 Mills	b Cox	6		
9 Mr. G. L. Jessop	c Simms, b Leach	240		
6 Capt. C. E. B. Champain	c Smith, b Cox	8	not out	22
4 Mr. F. G. Robinson	run out	17	c Vine, b Dwyer	21
7 Huggins	b Dwyer	33	not out	5
10 Mr. P. H. Ford	b Killick	6		
11 Dennett	not out	2		
Umpires:	B 15, l-b 9, w 2, n-b	26	b 6, l-b 2, w , n-b	8
J. E. West & A Millward.	Total	405	Total	144

1st Innings.—1 for 44, 2- 52, 3- 55, 4- 68, 5-106, 6-147, 7-185, 8-293, 9-348.
2nd Innings.—1 for 5, 2- 50, 3- 69, 4- 98, 5-131, 6- , 7- , 8- , 9- .

Bowling Analysis—

	First Innings.				Second Innings.			
	Overs.	Mdns.	Runs.	Wkts.	Overs.	Mdns.	Runs	Wkts.
Dwyer	18	2	103	1				
Cox	40	9	141	6				
Relf (A. E.)	20	8	48	0				
Vine	2	0	13	0				
Leach	8	1	31	1				
Killick	10	1	37	1				

Cox bowled 2 wides.

Luncheon Interval, 2 to 2.45 p.m. Stumps drawn at 6.30 p.m.

Next Match on this Ground—GLOUCESTERSHIRE v. MIDDLESEX, August 1, 2 & 3.

two for 3 runs. The innings lasted only 47 balls. Ten days after the 'declaration' game Jessop made his first hundred for a long time. He had scored 159* against the South Africans on Sept. 5, 1904, 234 against Sussex on June 27, 1905, and his next hundred was not until July 17, 1907, when he scored 240 against Sussex, so that in fact he had one spell of some 115 innings in which he scored only one hundred. Sussex had made 300 on the opening day, and Gloucester had lost four wickets for 68 when Jessop came in. When he left, last man out, he had scored 240 out of 337 in 3 hours and 20 minutes. It was the longest innings of his career, and though 'slow' by his fastest standards, he gave no chance at all. He hit 1 six and 35 fours, and 240 was at the time the highest score of the season. He received 191 balls and scored his runs off 99 of them. The six to the face of the pavilion was a drive off Dwyer whose fast bowling was especially to Jessop's liking. The people of Bristol had not seen such an innings for a long time. A report of it said: 'He brought off several of his characteristic old-time pulls round to leg, but the bulk of his runs was made by hard cutting and driving, while it was the subject for general comment that he kept the ball unusually low.'

In the next county match Gloucestershire were at Harrogate, and Jessop had not appeared there since his historic innings in 1897 – his 101 in 40 minutes. On the first day the scores were level enough with Yorkshire 130, Gloucester 133, of which Jessop made 12, his hand apparently now recovered from the blisters acquired against Sussex. Yorkshire then made 236, which left Gloucester 234 runs to win. Three wickets went down for only 47, a familiar situation for Jessop to have to face. Within 33 minutes he had scored 74, but he did not last much longer, being bowled by Haigh for 89 made out of 111 in 45 minutes. In the end Yorkshire won by 38 runs, but another quarter of an hour from Jessop could have meant their defeat. It was an astonishing innings against Hirst, Haigh and Rhodes on a difficult wicket. He hit one ball from Hirst clean out of the ground, and hit several others into the seats. This innings is featured in A. A. Thomson's novel *The Exquisite Burden.*

A fortnight later Jessop scored 85 in 55 minutes against Essex at Bristol, making his runs off 31 of 52 balls bowled to him. We are often given these facts about the number of balls he received in an innings, and it puzzles me how this is known, for in those days the scorers did not use the sophisticated and detailed methods now customary. Who kept these facts, I wonder? Certainly with Jessop it was always worth making a note of such things.

The people of Cheltenham were given a treat when the county met Hampshire there later in the season. On the first day Gloucestershire made 131 and Hampshire 165, conditions being not at all easy for run-making. On the second day rain had fallen so heavily that it seemed likely that play would

YORKSHIRE v. GLOUCESTERSHIRE.

Played on the County Cricket Ground, Harrogate, July 18, 19, and 20, 1907.

	Yorkshire.	1st Innings.		2nd Innings.	
7	Tunnicliffe	b Huggins	1	c Langdon b Mills	1
6	Rhodes	c Langdon b Mills	69	b Dennett	13
3	Denton	c Mills b Huggins	0	c Board b Huggins	28
4	Grimshaw	c Dennett b Mills	28	c Townsend b Huggins	15
5	Hirst	c Langdon b Mills	0	c Mills b Dennett	1
9	H. S. Kaye	lbw b Dennett	5	c Mills b Dennett	0
2	Myers	c Luce b Dennett	0	c Champain b Dennett	63
8	Bates	st Board b Dennett	19	c Hale b Dennett	71
1	Rothery	b Dennett	5	c Board b Dennett	1
10	Haigh	c Townsend b Dennett	0	not out	34
11	Hunter	not out	3	st Board b Dennet	2
		Extras		Extras	7
		Total	130	Total	236

Fall of the Wickets.

1	2	3	4	5	6	7	8	9	10	1	2	3	4	5	6	7	8	9	10
13	17	83	83	88	88	112	123	123	130	7	47	67	68	94	99	163	163	232	236

Analysis of the Bowling.

	1st Innings. Ov.	Mds.	Runs	Wkts.	Wd.	2nd Innings. Ov.	Mds.	Runs	Wkts.	Wd.
Dennett	30·5	9	77	5	.	41 3	9	99	7	.
Huggins	13	8	13	2	.	15	4	52	2	2
Mills	19	6	40	3	.	20	6	45	1	.
Hale	2	2	0	0	.	2	2	..	.	.
Jessop	..	.	..	.	.	9	1	33	.	.

Collection will be made this afternoon for **DAVID DENTON'S BENEFIT.**

	Gloucester.	1st Innings.		2nd Innings.	
1	Board	b Hirst	10	b Hirst	29
2	Langdon	b Myers	7	b Hirst	0
3	C. L. Townsend	c Haigh b Rhodes	61	b Hirst	9
4	Hale	b Myers	2	c Hunter b Hirst	7
5	G. L. Jessop	b Myers	12	b Haigh	89
6	F. M. Luce	b Haigh	12	c Tunnicliffe b Rhodes	22
7	C. E. B. Champain	b Haigh	3	b Hirst	9
8	Winstone	b Hirst	19	c and b Hirst	0
9	Huggins	b Hirst	3	not out	6
10	Mills	b Hirst	2	c Tunnicliffe b Rhodes	2
11	Dennett	not out	0	b Rhodes	10
		Extras	2	Extras	12
		Total	133	Total	195

Fall of the Wickets.

1	2	3	4	5	6	7	8	9	10	1	2	3	4	5	6	7	8	9	10
12	18	24	50	104	104	111	124	132	133	1	29	47	100	158	158	173	175	183	195

Analysis of the Bowling.

	1st Innings. Ov.	Mds.	Runs	Wkts.	Wd.	2nd Innings. Ov.	Mds.	Runs	Wkts.	Wd.
Hirst	22·2	1	51	4	.	18	1	86	6	.
Myers	7	0	37	3	.	7	0	37	0	.
Rhodes	11	5	22	1	.	11·1	3	40	3	.
Haigh	8	3	21	2	.	5	0	20	1	.

Umpires—Messrs. Moss and Barlow. Scorers—Messrs. Hoyland and Vernon.

be abandoned for the day, so most of the crowd drifted away early. At twenty-past five, however, the ground was regarded as fit for play. By 5.55 Gloucester had scored 60 for 3, with Jessop at No. 5. With the outfield sodden and the ball slippery for the bowlers, Jessop was determined to make up for lost time. By ten past 6 he had scored 53, and when stumps were drawn at 6.30 he had scored 73 out of 101 in 35 minutes. His innings, ball by ball, came like this:

1 0 0 2 4 0 1 4 4 1 4 1 2 4 3 1 4 1 4 4 0 4 4 4 4 1 1 0 0 4 3 1 0 0 1 0 1

He slowed down somewhat towards the end, but his first 61 runs had come off twenty-five balls bowled to him, and he had scored off all but four.

Next day a large crowd turned up hoping Jessop would continue his fireworks, but after reaching 92 he was caught at the wicket off H. W. Persse, who thus got his revenge for having conceded five boundaries to Jessop in one over the night before. Three of these had gone into the stand. His 92 had been made out of 147 in 65 minutes off forty-one of sixty-four balls bowled to him. Once again someone had kept these details, and though they may seem monotonous, they give a very true picture of Jessop's skill.

Though it seldom showed, the wear and tear of 'carrying' a rather weak county team must have been considerable. When Jessop succeeded even the mightiest such as Yorkshire could be defeated. When he failed there were few others who could save the situation. The less serious end of season festival matches were in theory the perfect setting for such a hitter, but as Jessop himself says: 'My conception of so-called holiday cricket had been of games in which full pitches and half-volleys were to be had for the asking, but I failed to observe any courtesy of this description being ladled out at Scarborough.' In fact Jessop's early appearances there were almost a total failure, as his first twelve innings between 1895 and 1900 produced a total of 66 runs with a top score of 13. These figures are almost unbelievable, especially when compared with those at Hastings.

Jessop's finest performance at Hastings was on September 3, 1907. He was leading a team called 'Gentlemen of the South' against 'The Players of the South', and though *Wisden* states that 'it was not worthy of its high sounding title', there was a fair sprinkling of England caps. The Gentlemen batted first and made 211, to which Jessop provided one of his rare ducks. W. J. Fairservice, the Kent cricketer, recalls how Jessop pushed his first ball to point, and then missed the second, which removed his leg stump to the obvious disappointment of the large crowd. It made Fairservice feel he had done the wrong thing to have bowled out Jessop. The Players then collapsed to the bowling of Jessop and P. R. May, a Surrey fast bowler who later in his career turned to lobs. They were all out for 119 on a rain-affected pitch, and when the Gentlemen went in again at 1 o'clock, they did not do much better. Perrin, who had made a century in the first innings, was out for a duck, and just before 1.30 the third wicket went down with the score at 25, all three wickets having been taken by Dennett, Jessop's fellow team-mate and a slow left-hander who, but for Rhodes and Blythe, would certainly have become a regular England player. When play was resumed at 2.15 Jessop came in facing a situation he was well used to, but this time also facing a 'pair'. Fairservice was again bowling to him. The first ball, however, was a full toss and Jessop drove it gratefully to the boundary. He did the same to the next ball, and to quote the bowler, 'He thereupon let his hair down and gave a display which dismayed us all.'

Seeing that Jessop looked like business Albert Relf suggested to his captain H. R. Butt that 'he could get rid of the bloke'. Butt agreed, and Jessop, who had probably heard Relf's request to be put on to bowl, promptly hit Relf for 26 runs in the over. The first ball led to a sensational hit which landed the ball on the roof of a house in Station Road, where it remained. The next five all went for four, and Relf retired amidst general hilarity.

Relf was one of the steadiest bowlers in England. He had toured Australia in 1903–4, and had a remarkable ability for swinging the ball. Because of the inswingers Jessop, for almost the only time in his career, adopted a two-eyed stance when facing Relf. Normally he stood completely sideways on, and relying on his sideways stance Jessop never wore a 'box', and seldom had any need to regret it. He just considered it unnecessary. Within 35 minutes of the resumption of play after lunch the total had risen by 108 runs, 87 of them to Jessop. Jessop reached his hundred a few minutes before three o'clock after batting only 42 minutes. He thus came very near to equalling his famous 40 minutes hundred made at Harrogate ten years before. 'A change in the bowling now seemed desirable', but not at Relf's end, and Jessop first scattered the ladies sitting near Mr du Cros's marquee, and then hit a ball into the gardens of the houses in Devonshire Road, a gigantic pull, which brought his score to 154, scored in 63 minutes.

With his score at 158 Jessop made his only mishit of the innings, for he lofted a ball in the direction of square-leg. Woolley, running a long way from mid-on, made a good try for it, but failed to hold the ball. This 'chance' seemed to slow Jessop down for he took as long as 27 minutes to take his score from 150 to 191. Just when it seemed that he would reach a double century in record time – the record being the two hours he himself took to reach 200 when scoring 286 *v.* Sussex in 1903 – he skied a ball from Woolley to deep mid-off where Butt, who was normally a wicket-keeper, made an uncomfortable catch. After much juggling he managed to hold the ball between his knees after it had slipped out of his hands. I am indebted to Frank Woolley for this information, whose chief recollection of an innings which to him and others must have seemed a fantasy is the way in which Jessop's fingers were constantly working round the handle of the bat as he came up to bowl to him.

Jessop had hit 5 sixes (all out-of-the-ground hits), 30 fours, 2 threes, 10 twos, and only 15 singles. One local paper with masterly understatement said: 'Jessop played a distinctly good innings, his driving and cutting being a feature.'

This game unfortunately had little proper coverage from the newspapers. The London dailies indulged in a few superlative headlines like 'Cricket Record. Terrific Hitting, Jessop scores 191 in 90 minutes', or 'Jessop the Sixer, Hurricane hitting by 'The Wonder at Hastings, Rough on Relf', and *The Globe* burst into yet another poem including such lines as:

> We do not yawn. Believe me, that's
> But seldom done when Jessop bats',

but the actual reports are scanty, and one local paper is far more concerned with the social activities of the match, and spends more time over the ladies of Mr du Cros's marquee than the exploits of the players.

I have tried to trace recollections of those who were lucky enough to have seen this innings. G. D. Martineau was then a boy, staying at Hastings as he often did, and he chiefly remembers the wild almost hysterical excitement of the crowd. Henry Grierson recalls how he was staying on holiday at St Leonards, and hearing that Jessop was batting dashed off on an old horse bus. As he arrived at the turnstiles a ball landed among the hansoms and cabs parked where the bus station now stands by the Town Hall. Sir Home Gordon tells how during the innings Jessop 'sent more than one ball, driven as though from a gun, into the windows of a chapel on the other side of the road outside the ground, and once hit a ball so hard with the back of his bat that a boundary was scored behind the wicket'.

One difficulty in finding eyewitnesses of any of Jessop's great innings lies in the brevity of them. This one, for example, was all over between 2.15 and 3.45. If you were not there at the moment he went in you might miss most of the fun, unlike an innings by Bradman, which was likely to last a whole day.

There are many legends of Jessop's hits at Hastings, including one which landed a ball over the entrance gate and smashed a shop window where 'Colliers' now is; another of a ball through a window of a house in Station Road, whose owner was reluctant to return it. In a letter to Nigel Haig Jessop gives us his own brief memories of this innings: 'I remember at Hastings in 1907 hitting five out of the ground and eleven over the ropes which would

came to an end at 259, Butt at mid-off holding a hard hit.

In an hour and a half the Gloucestershire captain had scored 191 out of 234, and despite the tremendous pace of his run-getting he made only one real mis-hit,

have increased my score from 191 to 213. I should have enriched my bag of centuries by more than one century if the easier reward had been in vogue at the time. I apologise for talking about my own past deeds, a fault which I rarely indulge in.'

So it might have been 16 sixes under present ruling, and a new record for the books, including the fastest double century ever. As it was, this innings was numerically faster than Alletson's famous 189 in 90 minutes against Sussex at Hove in 1911, when Alletson got six runs for all his eight hits over the ropes. September 3, 1907, should surely go down in the annals of cricket as the day of one of the great batting feats of all time. It surely deserves better than the brief report in one local paper which refers to the game as 'an otherwise insignificant match redeemed by some bright play by G. L. Jessop'.

The season of 1907 saw a wonderful come-back for Jessop at a time when many sadly thought that his light was beginning to fade. His aggregate of runs was his largest since 1901. On July 30 Jessop was invited to become a member of the M.C.C. side to tour Australia under the leadership and management of A. O. Jones; 'all travelling and hotel expenses will be paid and a sum not exceeding £70 will be allowed to each amateur for incidental expenses, not including drinks at meals on land, which will be included in hotel expenses.' Jessop may have been tempted to revisit the land which he had enjoyed so much on his trip of 1901–2, and also perhaps to see his wife's family, but the hazards of the voyage and the personal expense such a trip would involve, and the fact that his son was only a year old, all outweighed the attractions. There was much general regret at his decision. At this wandering period of Jessop's life, he was no doubt increasingly concerned about his future. He was now 33, and possibly the pleasure of playing regular county cricket may have been diminished by the constant cares of leading a weak side. Speaking about this at a United Press Cricket Club dinner Jessop said that with so few professionals Gloucestershire had no hope of finishing higher than they did. The one compensation was that whereas some counties in the running for honours were often ready to play for a draw, others like Gloucestershire, could always play for a win.

The season of 1908 for Gloucestershire was very much 'the mixture as before'. There was the usual bad start, with greatly improved form in August. The matches were increased to twenty-four, and thirty-one players in all were called upon including my own uncle A. W. Roberts, brother of F. B. Roberts, who must not be confused with Fred Roberts, the left-hand bowler of earlier days. Jessop continued his return to form. In the whole season he scored 1,885 runs at an average of 41·88, which was higher even than that in his great seasons of 1900 and 1901. He was very consistent, took some useful wickets, and as a fielder was 'just his old inimitable self'. Had there been Test matches in 1908 he would certainly have been a strong candidate.

The odds on any batsman making two hundreds in the same match are always considerable, especially for an attacking batsman, but Jessop did it four times in county matches, though oddly enough in not one of these did Gloucestershire win the game. The second of these four feats was against Somerset at Bath in 1908. In the first innings he scored 143 out of 179 in 90 minutes, with only one chance, and a six and 24 fours. In the second innings, when runs were wanted quickly to allow a declaration, he made 133 out of 175, also in 90 minutes. This time he hit 25 fours and was 'more the old Jessop with daring sweeps to leg', which resulted in two chances and a few false strokes. By an odd coincidence, in each innings he received 104 balls and in each innings he scored off 53 of them, very unimaginative.

Ten days later Jessop was to produce another great innings against Sussex at Gloucester. After the usual bad start Gloucestershire had four men out for thirty-seven, but there was still time for Jessop to reach a score of 117 by lunch. When he was out he had scored 164 out of 203 in 2 hours.

In mid-August at Cheltenham Jessop fashioned one of his minor gems in an innings of 72, scoring his runs out of 83 in only 35 minutes. For once in a while he was not having to carry the side, for Gloucestershire amassed 473 in reply to Warwickshire's 286. Jessop came in at 12.55 on the second day and was out at 1.30. Ball by ball his innings read:

2 0 1 4 4 0 0 0 1 1 0 4 2 4 6 4 2 4 0 4 1 2 4 4 4 4 2 4 4

That is to say he received only thirty balls, and scored off all but seven. His 50 came up in 25 minutes, and his last 49 runs came off three consecutive overs, 16 from Charlesworth, 15 off T. A. Hilditch, and 18 off Field, who finally had him caught at the wicket by Lilley.

It was probably in this innings that Jessop made his historic hit which landed the ball into the grounds of the hospital across Sandford Road. According to W. H. Jessop, a cousin of Jessop's, who himself played for the county, this gigantic pull was made during a stand with F. H. B. Champain. The college railings on the edge of Sandford Road are 110 yards from the square, and according to one correspondent who was at that time a patient lying in a bed on the hospital terrace, the ball landed amongst them, having carried the tents, the railing and the road. Another great pull (in the opposite direction) made on the college ground was during his innings of 63 *v.* Yorkshire in 1895, when he hit a ball over the trees near the gym into Thirlestaine Road. This was most likely the six recorded off the bowling of George Hirst. Legend also talks of a hit which landed on the clock face, but pavilion clocks are all too readily associated with big hits.

At the end of the 1908 season there was a special match played on Broadhalfpenny Down, Hambledon, the scene of so many famous matches in the 1770s. Hambledon Cricket Club was not the 'cradle' of cricket so often claimed for it, for there are other older clubs, but it was lucky enough to have a distinguished writer to record its doings and so make its players famous. This memorial match was billed as 'Hambledon *v.* An England XI' – two very good sides. The match created great interest and on the opening day a granite column to commemorate the glories of the past was unveiled, and can be seen there now. Jessop scored 19 and 48, and among others who did well was my uncle A. W. Roberts who scored 69 for the England XI. It was during this match that these two were concerned in an amusing incident. A doctor friend had motored them down to the Earl of Bessborough's house, Stansted Park, then let to the Wilders. There was a breakdown, and they arrived, very late, at 1 o'clock. When Jessop went up to his room, he was about to get into bed when he found that a vast marble statue of Venus from off the staircase had been planted in his bed. He found her too heavy to move, and as it was so late he decided to share the bed with her. When the maid came in next morning with tea and a can of hot water, she suddenly noticed the figure in the bed with him, and uttering a fearful shriek fled from the room, to Jessop's great embarrassment.

These were the days when county cricket for the amateur had much of country house gaiety about it. There was a sharp distinction between the amateurs and the professionals, who were definitely paid servants of the club, and on a different footing altogether.

During the season of 1908 E. M. Grace, 'The Coroner' and elder brother of W. G., decided that the time had come for him to resign the secretaryship of the county which he had held since its inception in 1873. His son, also a Dr. E. M. Grace, has recently told me how his father conducted the job. 'He never had any secretarial aid as they do now. Anyone in his big family who could write distinctly was roped in to help addressing envelopes, folding papers and tickets, sometimes five to one envelope, and all for the love of the game.'

The committee faced the question of Grace's successor, and after due consideration the job of county secretary was offered to Jessop, with a salary of £200 per annum. He would remain captain as well. Though this meant that Jessop would be able to stay in cricket, which may have pleased him, it merely shelved the important matter of his getting a good job for when his playing days were over. Though the remuneration was nothing like so good as the directorship of the tobacco firm had once been, Jessop decided to accept the post. One condition of his becoming secretary was that he lived somewhere near Bristol, and before long he came with his wife and two-year-old son to live at Walton House, Shirehampton. The local paper said that this would be a very good thing because 'it will certainly help him in his duties as captain. His living in London has been a serious drawback to his success as captain of the team. He has not been sufficiently in touch with those on whom he has had to rely for assistance in the field, with the result that nearly every season men have played whose qualifications did not warrant their being given a trial, while others, with stronger claims, have been overlooked.'

It was further stated 'reforms are needed in many directions (but not all at once), for Gloucestershire cricket has suffered of late by close adherence to old-fashioned methods. There is every confidence that Jessop will bring his usual enthusiasm and energy to his new duties and do something to rouse the general apathy of the members, which cannot be done as in the past by mere issuing of circulars. His best chance of success will be derived from real live effort to augment the playing forces of the county, and he knows better than most men how this can be done.'

When Jessop took over as secretary he had no more assistance given to him than had his predecessor, and he used to call upon the pros and other cricketers from Bristol to come down to Walton House at Shirehampton and lend him a hand. When the job was done they would all have a meal, and go off and play some kind of squash in a large coach house nearby, or go up to Shirehampton golf course. It was all very informal, and, apart from getting a job done, much good feeling was engendered.

But really the most important business was to find new players, and there is evidence of Jessop's efforts to get around the county and arrange trial matches. Lydney Cricket Club possesses the correspondence about a trial match there in 1910, which gives us some idea of the work of a secretary and the complications of fixing up such matches. The Lydney representative, Mr W. Jones, had a son Hugh, who played in a solitary match for the county in 1914, and later died on Armistice day, 1918. Jessop must have spent much time looking for local players who could make the big step into county cricket. Just occasionally, someone like Dipper could walk off the village green into the county side, but, alas, there were only too few like that. Jessop's doubled responsibility to the county must have been a burden at times, but his spirit on the field always remained undaunted.

6

'The English Trumper' 1909–1914

'Not good enough for England scores another century.'
NEWSPAPER PLACARD

AT the beginning of 1909 there seemed to be every prospect of Jessop continuing to make big scores. The Australians were over again, and Jessop was wanted to play in the first Test at Birmingham on May 27. In the same week he had made a fine hundred against Warwickshire, and seemed in form. The Test match was a low-scoring one, in which England made 121 and 105–0 and so easily defeated the Australians whose scores were 74 and 151. Jessop made 22 in 20 minutes in an effort to improve the situation when five wickets had gone down for only 61. The second Test was on June 14. The Australians' morale was low, but it improved when they heard that Jessop had been omitted from the side. On hearing the news Jessop himself said: 'Well, I've played in the first and I don't suppose I shall be in any more.' Public feeling at his being omitted was very strong indeed. The Editor of *Wisden* later severely censured the selectors for leaving out 'the one indispensable player', and stated that 'Never in the history of Test Matches in England has there been such blundering in the selection of the England eleven.' This repeated very critical press comment. One of the Bristol papers produced an article headed:

WHY WAS JESSOP DROPPED?
Remarkable Chorus of enquiry from the cricket critics
A popular idol

How Jessop came to be left out is a mystery. It is known that MacLaren, who was a selector and captain of the team, always said he wanted to have Jessop on his side, but Leveson-Gower was not a strong supporter of Jessop and may have voted against him. The real cause of the trouble was that Lord Hawke, the chairman of the committee, was abroad at the time for health reasons, and had no say in the matter. The other blunder the selectors made was over Brearley, who was in great form, and might well have filled the fast bowler's place. It was known later that on the morning of the match MacLaren invited Brearley to play. As he had not been on the original list it is possible to understand why Brearley refused. The reason given for his refusal was that his cricketing kit was not with him. As it was, England took the field with five changes from the match-winning team of the first Test, and they lost the match by nine wickets to an Australian team which, up to then, had been in all sorts of trouble and loss of form. This unexpected victory turned the tide, and England lost the rubber.

At this distance of time it may seem much of a storm in a teacup, but the original feeling about Jessop being left out blew up again when, in the county match beginning the day after England's defeat, Jessop produced two superb centuries against Hampshire at Bristol. In the first innings he made 161 out of 295 in 95 minutes, following this with 129 in 98 minutes in the second innings. In the first innings he hit Llewellyn for 61 off four consecutive overs (12, 14, 18, 17). The newspapers went into ecstasies over the first hundred with headlines such as:

JESSOP'S BALM
A SOOTHING SYRUP
FOR SORE TEST SELECTORS
GREAT DISPLAY,

and one match account says that as he reached his hundred 'Cheers were loud and deep, for they carried a message to the *mis*-selection committee', and a facetious post-card to Jessop written on the same day as he made his 161 says: 'After comments in the press the selection committee consider your exhibition today as a display of bad temper and worse taste.'

When Jessop followed the first hundred with a second one the outburst grew even louder with headlines such as:

JESSOP AT IT AGAIN
RUBBING IT IN
MORE SALT FOR THE SELECTORS' SORES
IS HE ANY GOOD?
and NOT GOOD ENOUGH FOR ENGLAND MAKES ANOTHER CENTURY

Certainly no rejected player has ever answered the selectors more forcibly, but I doubt if Jessop really enjoyed the whole business, and he certainly did nothing to encourage it. He disliked being in the limelight. But letters flowed in to him, including one from George Beldam which began:

> Dear Jessopus,
>
> May I send you my warmest congratulations on your double. . . . Why the devil the selection committee left you and Brearley without invitations surpasses my comprehension and I told Archie (MacLaren) so. But he can't apparently have his own way! He wanted Jayes, but Haigh was given him! If ever we asked for defeat and deserved to get it, we did in this last Test. Damme, old man, I've always said I would play you for saving runs alone without taking into consideration that no team is complete without a hitter (you know I don't look upon you as simply a hitter either! You've got as many strokes in your bag as some so-called scientific batsmen). Then there is the calculation in case of a declare when you are in the side. I've never said anything else – whatever form you are in, like A. C. M. and Jacker. I would play you every time in every test! and I'm damn glad you've scored a double in this match. . . .

After the second Test Lord Hawke returned from abroad and when the names for the next Test at Leeds on July 1 came out there were five changes, and Jessop and Brearley were on the list of players. The selectors might well have been lynched if Jessop had been omitted again. A. C. MacLaren wrote to Jessop to say how glad he was to have him back. Here is the letter:

> Dear Jessopus,
>
> Many congrats on your fine performance which I was delighted to see, for you know at any rate the value I place on your presence on the England side, and it bucks me up to think that you will be with us at Leeds. I lost the Lord's game in missing Ransford, but even so we ought to have saved it, had not our batting inexcusably broken down for no reason whatever. . . . We can and will beat them with ordinary luck. Brearley could have played but would not when I saw him before the game – his bag being at Tonbridge but he would not wire for it. The wicket was a back or forward one when Austs. batted and would not have suited him, but they would not have got so many I expect. . . .
>
> Yours vy sincerely,
>
> Archie MacLaren

So Jessop was back in the England team, and it is ironic to think that after all the fuss he was destined to take such a small part in the game. After seventy minutes play on the first day he was put out of action. Here is his own account of the sad business:

'In attempting to save a sharp single past point's right hand I returned the ball from cover, and in doing so threw the ball in sideways without turning broadside on to the wicket. One does not usually look for accidents in so peaceable an occupation as fielding, but there it was – and England had to bat ten men.

'My misadventure was not without its amusing side, for on returning to the pavilion the attendant ushered in a man who professed to understand the ins and outs of all the strange little mishaps that occur to those engaged in athletic pursuits and though the next room sheltered Doctor Archie Thompson, so well known for many years as the honorary medical attendant of Australian elevens, my case was permitted to be diagnosed by the unknown 'Professor'. As far as I remember, the reason given for my strange indisposition to preserve with any ease a perpendicular position was put down by him to a temporary misplacement of one of the knobs of my backbone.'

This unknown 'doctor' was allowed to subject Jessop to violent manipulation which produced acute pain, and certainly no instant cure: the trouble was not a 'slipped disc' but a bad rupture of some of the muscles in his back. Though in later recollections Jessop says 'The joke was that we thought he was a pukka surgeon', this experience cannot have been amusing at the time, and did him considerable harm. We shall never know who the 'bonesetter' was or why he was permitted to give Jessop 'treatment'.

Big headlines announced the disaster of Jessop's accident. 'Jessop strains himself. Can take no further part in the game', and a cartoon appeared showing a bill poster sticking a cancel notice over a Test match poster at Leeds: 'There will be no fireworks display' read the notice, for, said the bill sticker, 'Wi'aht Gilbert we can't 'ave no display, 'ah reckon.' Letters poured in to Jessop expressing great sympathy, including this one from a complete stranger:

Sir,

As one of your followers and admirers I beg on behalf of friends and myself to express sorrow that you should have received such serious injury at Leeds, together with hope for your speedy recovery. You have the lasting gratitude of lovers of the grand old game for your endeavour to rescue it from the monotony and Croquet-like style so many players (who ought to know better), indulge in: You have the sympathy of the public at large and so long as you choose to play you are assured of the reception you usually get, also of the gratitude and affection of every lover of cricket. In conclusion, I would far rather it had happened to myself.

Yours faithly,
W. H. Billingham

It was a tragedy for England, too, for they lost by only 85 runs, and had Jessop been able to bat and to field the gap might well have been closed. The injury was worse than at first supposed, but after being at Leeds for a week Jessop was able to return home to Shirehampton. 'The railway authorities provided a special saloon in which an ambulance had been placed, and the injured cricketer had every attention bestowed upon him,' says one report, and a large crowd turned up to meet his arrival at Temple Meads station. He was then transferred to his home by the horse ambulance of the Bristol City and Marine Ambulance service. Mrs Jessop travelled with him. He made steady progress, and on August 20 C. B. Fry wrote to him to say:

My dear Jessopus,

I *am* so sorry to hear you have not come along quicker. I expected when once you were up you would be all right in a trice, but of course those back muscles have heavy work even in supporting the body in an upright position and all muscles quickly weaken in disuse, so you have the case not only of a muscle sore with injury but of a muscle weakened by disuse. However you will be allright directly you begin to use the muscle a bit. It will recover very quickly.

'Doctor' C. B. Fry had spoken, and he was right, because by the end of the month Jessop was able to get to Bristol to see a match and look to his secretarial duties, though he had to go home at the interval as he was not well enough. Perhaps he discussed an incident concerning Leveson-Gower, the Test selector, who had apparently been insulted by some of the members at Bristol, thinking he was responsible for omitting Jessop from the team for the second Test. I do not know exactly what it was all about, but after Jessop's visit to the ground the committee decided to send Leveson-Gower a letter of apology.

There was much concern in the Bristol papers about Jessop's absence and the effect it was having on the team and on his efforts as secretary to improve the membership. Although everyone rallied round, the team slumped to the bottom of the table and won only one of their twenty-two county matches. If ever proof was needed as to how much Gloucestershire depended on Jessop as player and captain, it was clearly shown at this moment. *Wisden* remarked, 'It was the most disastrous season in the annals of the county'.

It was soon clear that Jessop would not be playing any more cricket until the following season, and though M.C.C. was sending a team to South Africa there was no question of Jessop being even considered for it. There must have been many gloomy Gloucestershire supporters that winter, and some may even have feared that Jessop's playing days were over.

On May 16, 1910, Jessop played his first first-class innings since his accident in the previous July. It was against Somerset at Taunton, and he was out first ball. In the second innings, however, he showed that he had not lost his hitting powers, making 74 out of 109 in only 53 minutes. His supporters heaved a sigh of relief at his recovery, and noted that his speed as a fielder was as great as ever. In the match against Kent at Canterbury he made a truly remarkable catch when he ran from mid-off to chase a skier from K. L Hutchings which went far beyond the bowler. He just managed to reach the ball and held it. It was evident that his back trouble was completely mended.

One of Jessop's best transformation efforts was on July 8 when Gloucestershire recovered from being all out for 63 to gain a great victory over Worcestershire at Stourbridge. Worcestershire replied with 115, a lead of 52. Three Gloucestershire wickets fell for 45 and then Jessop launched a great onslaught. He had not been in long before he attacked his old friend Burrows, a fast bowler who holds the record for sending a bail the longest distance in first-class cricket. Jessop wrote that 'Burrows was the pluckiest bowler who ever came from Worcester. He often used to regard me as his rabbit, and he used to send me a lettuce whenever he got me out cheaply, as he did in the first innings at Stourbridge when he bowled me for 6. Next day I had reason to present Dick Burrows with enough lettuce leaves to last him every day for the rest of the season. My salad days were over and the innings at last closed.' Jessop began quietly by taking 12 minutes over his first 7 runs, but then he smote 28 runs off an over to equal his own record made against Braund in 1904. The first ball was on-driven for four, the next two pulled for six each, the fourth ball was mishit, an enormous skier to mid-off, which went so high that almost anyone on the field could have reached it. The batsman had run two and were thinking about a third, when the ball came to earth, cannoning from Taylor's fingers to the ground. Another four came off the next ball, and to finish off Jessop hit the sixth ball for another six. Poor Burrows continued to bowl, and his next two overs gave Jessop 21 more runs, making 49 off three consecutive overs. In spite of this Burrows finished up with an analysis of 7–111. Not surprisingly Jessop reached his 50 in 25 minutes, and went on to reach his hundred in an hour out of 123. At close of play he had made 106 and the score was 178–3. Thanks to him the game had swung right round. Next day Jessop continued to hit out. He lofted another huge six on to the refreshment tent, and when finally caught had made 165 out of 205 in two hours. He had hit 6 sixes and 20 fours. At the beginning of the season the new regulation by which any ball hit over the ropes would count as six runs had at long last been adopted.

It is almost superfluous to add that Gloucestershire won the match by 94 runs. The second highest innings in the match after Jessop's was G. N. Foster's 46, and no fewer than thirty of the innings were under double figures. In his next innings a few days later Jessop produced an almost carbon-copy innings with a score of 162 out of 238 against Northamptonshire at Northampton, taking 5 minutes longer.

At the end of the season Kent, the champion county, met the Rest of England at the Oval, and Jessop was invited to captain the Rest on one of the very few occasions when he was captain in a representative match. The season of 1910 was altogether a very satisfactory one in that any fears that his career might be finished after his accident could now be put aside.

There is an interesting cutting, undated, but probably from about this time, which states that Jessop was playing very good golf at Burnham 'while resting from an excursion into politics'. This reference is supported by a letter dated May 10, 1910, from the secretary of the Liberal Federation. It invites Jessop to a become Liberal candidate at the forthcoming General Election, 'if you are still a keen politician'. It is not uncommon for well-known games players to be considered as candidates, and Jessop with his keen reforming spirit in cricketing matters might well have seemed someone who might make a good M.P. He did not, it seems, take up the offer to become a candidate, but two years later, in October 1912, he received another letter on the same lines. This time, however, the letter came from the Conservative Association who approached him because they had heard he was anxious to take up political work. Another letter followed in which the representative writes: 'I am sure you would be of great assistance to the Conservative party if you would undertake an appointment with it as you suggest.' Perhaps Jessop was hoping to get a job as a Conservative agent, but nothing seems to have come of it. The reason may be that Jessop tended to change his political opinions, with the result that at the moment when one party wanted his support he no longer wanted them. He was, however, very keen on the Suffragette movement, and became chairman of one of the committees. There is a letter dated February, 1914, from his old friend the Middlesex cricketer A. J. Webbe, who invites him to come to a meeting and say a few words. But when the Suffragettes became militant and started to burn property Jessop resigned and withdrew his support.

It was clear the M.C.C. authorities thought Jessop still worth considering for representative cricket because in a letter dated May 5, 1911, the M.C.C. Secretary, F. E. Lacey, wrote to Jessop inviting him to become a member of the Selection Sub-committee to select Probable and Possible England sides for the forthcoming Test trials. The other selectors were Lord Hawke and Plum Warner, and Jessop agreed to join them. The first trial was played at Sheffield on June 1, the teams being Mr Jessop's XI *v.* Mr Warner's XI. This turned out to be a personal triumph for Jessop, who went in when six wickets had fallen for only 65 runs and scored 122 not out in a total of 234. In the second trial at Lord's on June 29 Jessop captained England against the Rest and scored 15. A third Test trial match was cancelled.

An M.C.C. team was due to go to Australia in the winter of 1911–12. The Test Trial selection committee was not the same as the Tour selection committee and despite the evidence of his good form, the selectors had not

G. L. Jessop's Team *v.* P. F. Warner's Team.

Bramall Lane Ground, June 1, 2 and 3, 1911.

G. L. JESSOP'S TEAM.	First Innings.		Second Innings.	
1 Humphreys (*Kent*)..	c Bale b Hirst...........	4	c Bale b Buckenham...	0
2 Iremonger (*Notts*)..	c Relf b Hirst...........	28	c Relf b Buckenham...	15
3 Gunn, G. (*Notts*)...	c Hirst b Buckenham...	9	run out.....................	39
4 Seymour (*Kent*) ...	b Hitch.....................	9	b Litteljohn..............	70
5. K.L.Hutchings (*Kt*)	c Mead b Hirst	2	b Litteljohn..............	53
6 Woolley (*Kent*)......	c Relf b Buckenham...	5	b Hobbs	12
7 Booth (*Yorkshire*)..	lbw b Litteljohn.........	20	c and b Litteljohn	30
12 Hearne, J. W. (*Mx.*)	....		not out	74
8 G.L.Jessop (*Glou.*).	not out	122	b Litteljohn..............	11
9 Newman (*Hants*)...	c Relf b Hirst...........	13	b Hitch	6
10 Shipman (*Leicester*)	c Buckenham b Hobbs	18	Absent ill.	
11 Strudwick (*Surrey*).	lbw b Hobbs	0	b Hirst	74
	b 1 lb 3 nb... w...	4	b10 lb 8 nb 1 w...	19
	Total.........	234	Total.........	403

FALL OF THE WICKETS.

1	2	3	4	5	6	7	8	9	1	2	3	4	5	6	7	8	9
16	37	41	43	54	65	95	173	234	0	17	103	181	188	202	236	256	277

BOWLING ANALYSIS.	First Innings.						Second Innings.					
	O.	M.	R.	W.	N.B.	WDS.	O.	M.	R.	W.	N.B.	WDS.
Hirst	18	3	74	4	...	...	19.4	5	71	1	1	...
Buckenham	14	3	43	2	...	...	25	5	97	2	...	...
Hitch.................	8	0	44	1	...	...	18	2	74	1	...	...
Litteljohn	13	1	48	1	...	...	31	4	76	4	...	...
Hobbs	2.4	0	21	2	...	...	9	1	26	1	...	...
Relf....................	...	...	...	...	...	...	8	0	32	0	...	...
Mead	...	...	...	...	...	...	2	0	8	0	...	...

P. F. WARNER'S TEAM.	First Innings.		Second Innings.	
1 Hobbs (*Surrey*) ...	c Gunn b Woolley......	22	b Booth	32
2 Mead (*Hants*)	b Newman	24	c Woolley b Booth ...	34
3 Relf, R. (*Sussex*)...	b Woolley	79	b Woolley	6
4 Ducat (*Surrey*)......	c Humphreys b Woolley	33	c Iremonger b Woolley	3
5 Hirst (*Yorkshire*)...	c Strudwick b Newman	19	b Newman	7
6 P. F. Warner (*Mx.*)	not out	60	b Woolley	28
7 A.R.Litteljohn (*Mx*)	c and b Iremonger......	2	c Booth b Woolley ...	60
8 Alletson (*Notts*) ...	c Seymour b Iremonger	15	b Newman	8
9 Hitch (*Surrey*)......	c Woolley b Iremonger	0	not out	5
10 Buckenham (*Essex*)	c and b Booth...........	21	run out.....................	0
11 Bale (*Worcester*) ...	st Strudwick b Booth...	0	run out.....................	1
	b 2 lb... nb 2 w...	4	b 4 lb 5 nb 3 w...	12
	Total.........	279	Total.........	196

FALL OF THE WICKETS.

1	2	3	4	5	6	7	8	9	1	2	3	4	5	6	7	8	9
47	51	109	164	187	194	212	212	277	63	74	79	82	92	104	189	194	194

BOWLING ANALYSIS.	First Innings.						Second Innings.					
	O.	M.	R.	W.	N.B.	WDS.	O.	M.	R.	W.	N.B.	WDS.
Shipman	5	0	16	0	...	...	...	...	...	...	...	...
Woolley	27	5	71	3	1	...	22	8	37	4	1	...
Newman	22	2	74	2	...	...	19	8	45	2	2	...
Booth................	12.5	3	40	2	1	...	10	3	12	2	...	...
Iremonger	33	8	74	3	...	...	21.5	6	57	0	...	...
Hearne..............	...	...	...	...	...	...	4	0	33	0	...	...

Umpires, Messrs. G. P. Harrison & Carlin. Scorer, Mr. Hoyland.

G. L. JESSOP'S TEAM WON BY 162 RUNS.

put Jessop's name on the list when the team was published. This omission might have been the result of a chance remark made by C. B. Fry, who was sitting-in on the selection committee as the possible Touring team captain, though he later declined the captaincy and decided not to go at all.

On August 10 C. B. Fry scored 258 not out against Gloucestershire, for whom Jessop scored 153 and 123 not out. Fry had not seen Jessop play for two years, and thought that he had still not fully recovered from his accident. He had, therefore, not mentioned Jessop when he had early in the season written in the press of likely players to go to Australia. Fry was amazed at Jessop's form in this match and wrote instantly to Lord Harris, the chairman of the selectors, urging him to choose Jessop for Australia even at this late date. On August 19 the Secretary of M.C.C. wrote to Jessop inviting him to become a member of the team. A few days before Fry had written to Jessop to explain how it came about that he had not supported Jessop's claim before. 'I said nothing when your name came up at Committee at the start simply because I had not seen you for 2 years. I merely asked: "Well, is he the same man he was?" No one seemed to know, and someone remarked that you had not recovered from your accident. Of course I was merely there by request and was not conducting matters. But what I ought to have done was to write to you, and I much regret that I did not.' It seems incredible that the selection committee should not have observed that Jessop had made a brilliant century in the Test trial, and had clearly fully recovered from his accident.

On the day on which Lacey sent Jessop the invitation to go to Australia Fry wrote again to Jessop to say how glad he was that M.C.C. had done the right thing and asked him to go, and he added some advice about making runs in Australia. He wrote:

'If you go and if you go in for straight hitting till you've made 50 and look out for the half-volley that keeps low on the Australian wickets, you should equal or beat Trumper. You do not need to have a sheer go to get runs. Your off-driving and cutting alone should get you 60 runs an hour. I would not hit in the air much in Australia, if I were you. You don't need to with all your strokes.

'Pardon an old cock for seeming to offer advice. I am so keen on your success.'

But alas, the invitation to Jessop came too late, and for one reason or another he refused. He must have been tempted, for this was yet another chance to go to Australia, and possibly to remain there. But as usual, especially where a sea voyage was concerned, he hesitated though no doubt Mrs Jessop would have been glad to see her native land again and get away from an English winter.

Meanwhile, Jessop went off to Scarborough for the Festival. Though his early appearances there had not been a success, he did very well in later years, and this year made two great hundreds.

When Yorkshire met M.C.C. in the first match they led on the first innings by 113 runs, Jessop having scored 59 out of 274 for M.C.C. Yorkshire declared in their second innings leaving M.C.C. 339 to win with only three hours of play left. R. H. Spooner set the pace with an elegant 102, but there were only 85 minutes to go when Jessop came in and over 180 runs still needed. He tore into the bowling, and in the end M.C.C. were only 5 runs short with a score of 334–7. Jessop had made 117 out of 179 in 85 minutes, and despite the pace he made no mistake until after he had passed the hundred. Once again Rhodes had a battered analysis of 9–0–68–1.

A week later Jessop played an even more remarkable innings at Scarborough. Lord Londesborough's XI were meeting the M.C.C. team about to tour Australia – the team of which Jessop was invited to be a member – as his batting ironically reminded everyone. In the first innings he made 45, and when his team went in again the second time, with a lead of 111, they put up a score of 208–3 by close of play, Spooner 89 not out and Jessop 101 not out. The partnership ended next day when Spooner was out for 94. Jessop went on to score 136, mainly off the bowling of Barnes, Douglas, and Rhodes, but 34 of his last 35 runs came off two consecutive overs from Hitch.

The season of 1911 had been one of decisions for Jessop, as apart from the matter of going to Australia, he had been coming to the conclusion that at 37 he should make other plans for his future. He had put a lot into his secretaryship for the county, but the job was not very lucrative and his son was approaching school age. Though his own form had been excellent (he had made seven centuries in the season and his average of 42·37 was the best of his whole career), the county had won only five games against twelve defeats. Jessop had had a lean spell with the toss, once losing seven times in a row. He must at times have been depressed about the county's cricket, though, according to *Wisden* 'Jessop led a forlorn hope with fine courage'.

At the annual general meeting of the club it was to be officially announced that Jessop had resigned the secretaryship: 'It is time I devoted myself to something more serious', was what he told a reporter previously, but he had nothing to say about his future plans, though he admitted the possibility of settling in Australia. There were slight hopes, nevertheless, that he might still be playing at times for the county in 1912, especially as it was the season of the Triangular Tournament between England, Australia, and South Africa. It was later confirmed that he would be able to play for the county whenever he could, but that he would be looking for a permanent job outside cricket. Whenever he did play for the county he would continue to act as captain.

In 1912, after his wonderful season of the previous year, Jessop was nothing like so successful. In his twenty-one innings for the county he averaged only 18·9, a terrible slump, and his worst average since 1898.

On May 23, however, in one of the two Test trial matches, he once again reminded people of the loss M.C.C. had suffered by his not going to Australia. In the first trial at Lord's the M.C.C. touring team met The Rest. After M.C.C. had made 509, the Rest soon lost four wickets for 26, and when the fifth wicket went down soon after, Jessop came in at number seven. Despite an attack consisting of F. R. Foster, Barnes, Douglas, J. W. Hearne, and Hitch he scored 88 in 67 minutes, enabling the Rest to reach a score of 237. In the second innings he scored 55 in an hour before Hitch caught him one-handed off a terrific return hit. In the first innings Hitch had been bowling from the pavilion end when Jessop came in. He was bowling fast with a stiff breeze behind him. His first ball was good length on the middle stump, but Jessop pulled him round for a skimming six into the tenth row of the Mound stand. Nigel Haig writes that he was sitting nearby with his uncle Lord Harris who remarked deliberately: 'That's the best stroke I've ever seen or ever will see.' Seeing that Lord Harris was never very lavish with his praises, this was something of a tribute. It was not so much the length of the hit, but the sheer effrontery of it that called forth this comment. Plum Warner also recalls a similar stroke in the same match in which Jessop mowed an in-swinger from F. R. Foster into the depths of the Mound stand. On the strength of these two innings Jessop was invited to play against South Africa on June 10, and also on July 8, but in these two Test matches his scores were only 3, and 16 and 1. In between these two matches he had acted as twelfth man in the Test against Australia at Lords.

That was the end of his Test match career, which had covered a span of thirteen years. His total Test figures read: 26–0–569–104–21·88, and he also took ten wickets at 34·5 runs each. If ever figures were totally misleading, it is these. Many times, even in a small innings, he had changed the course and tempo of the game, and the runs he saved in the field added up to even more than he made. Had he been selected more consistently he would probably have had a better record. Even in 1912 critics were still clamouring for his automatic selection, and *Punch* was making such comments as 'If I were a selector I should always say: 'Give me Jessop, and then you can put in who you like'.

Jessop's own comments on Test Match cricket are revealing:

'Until it shall come to pass that the world be challenged to a cricket contest by the inhabitants of Mars or some other planet, matches between England and Australia will continue to be regarded as the highest class of cricket. The question has frequently been put to me as to whether matches fraught with so much importance as 'Tests' yield as much enjoyment as do matches of less consequence. On the point of excitement I think – 'more', since nothing rouses the vital activity of the body to so great an extent as do meetings between exponents chosen to represent their country in any form of sport. To me it seems a difference between excitement and amusement. You always get the former in a Test Match whatever the condition of the game – the latter you *may* get in games of another class.

'This I can say, I enjoyed every minute of Test Matches, and in none did I ever experience that their importance interfered in one whit with the true spirit of the game. They were keen – deadly keen – but none the less pleasant on this account.'

As the season went on, and it was realised that his regular career with Gloucestershire was nearly over, many tributes were paid to him. After Jessop had written to K. S. Ranjitsinhji to wish him well in his rather reluctant return to county cricket, Ranji replied:

'I feel like a lame duck rather than a cricketer. You always had many balls that I couldn't play in the old days so your recent discovery is neither new nor wonderful. It is what I would expect from the "Hitting Wonder" of the world. I put you down as the eighth wonder alongside of the Niagara Falls, the Taj Mahal, and the Colossus at Rhodes, etc. etc. I am looking forward to meeting you and Mrs Jessop and also to watching you breaking the windows at Lord's and the Oval against our brethren from across the seas.'

There were other letters, including this tribute from Plum Warner, dated October 23, 1912.

Dear Jessopus,

I see it stated in the newspapers that you have retired from first-class cricket. If that is so, well, you have had a glorious career which you should be very proud of. The greatest hitter – the greatest demoraliser of bowling the world has ever seen, and nulli secundus as an extra-cover. No batsman – not even Ranji – ever has been so difficult to set a field for as you when you were "on the cob'. Lyons, Bonnor, McDonnell, Sinclair, Thornton were great hitters, but they had not your cut, and were nothing like so reliable. You have given delight to thousands and thousands of spectators and players and many a long day must elapse before another "Human catapult that wrecks the roofs of distant towns when set in his assault" as the Phila. papers called you – appears. It has been a great pleasure to have met so mighty a man, and may the best of good luck attend you and yours always in the future.

I am,

Your sincere friend and admirer,

'Plum'

Another tribute came from the pen of Albert Knight the Leicestershire professional who had keen literary interests. He wrote:

'In many ways Mr Jessop has been the most remarkable figure in the history of cricket, phenomenal alike in the extreme rapidity of his scoring and his fearless triumphant vindication of heresy. Literally a heretic, choosing his own method and a method which success alone restrains men from terming impossible. . . . He, at least, always 'got a move on'; moved indeed as batsmen might move who scent an approaching prairie fire or hear the onset of wolves. The first time one saw him play he scored some 150 runs against us, and when he left, the side felt as tree trunks must feel after some desolating storm has stripped them.' Adulation from the masses is one thing: considered tributes from fellow players must have given Jessop great satisfaction.

In January 1913 Jessop was given a presentation for all his efforts for the county. When he succeded to the captaincy in 1900 he had undertaken the daunting job of following W. G. Grace. In his first season Jessop took the side to seventh position, and it is sad to recall that never in the next twelve years of his leadership did they reach such heights again. Over the years 1900–12 Gloucester played 269 county matches – mostly under his captaincy – and they won 67 of them, their average position being eleventh. In 1909, when he was away injured, they came out bottom.

All this suggests that it must have been a struggle for the captain to keep the standard up. There were not enough good players and the side was often very weak. But the burden of captaincy does not seem to have affected Jessop's playing form, and he himself says: 'I cannot honestly say that I found my duties unduly harassing.' He certainly had to carry the batting, and in his whole career was top scorer in every one in five of the innings in which he batted. One compensation for being a weak county – 'we were always engaged upon an uphill struggle for existence' – was that unlike some counties who were anxious over every point in the table, 'we never intentionally set out to play for a draw if there was the slightest chance of snatching a victory'. Jessop fully endorsed the famous opinion of his fellow-captain of Somerset, Sammy Woods, who once declared that draws were of no use to anyone except for bathing.

At the end of 1900, in a review of the Gloucestershire season, a local paper said of Jessop: 'He has infused into the members of his side a spirit of enthusiasm and keenness that has been irresistible and to this cause alone one can trace much of the success achieved. Jessop has great faith in himself and the players under him; he is firmly convinced that a game is never lost until it is won; and by imparting this sanguine element to his colleagues, he has encouraged them to play up in a manner that has on several occasions ensured a victory when all the chances were in favour of defeat or a draw.'

This meant that sometimes his tactics were unorthodox and at times *Wisden* censures him for dangerously altering his batting order, or putting the other side in when they thought otherwise. But it was always positive captaincy, and he never spared himself personally. In several matches which ended in close victory, he put himself on to bowl at a critical moment, risking to take the blame if he failed, and in the field he always set an example which no doubt some of the weaker members found difficult to follow. One season he left out of the side an excellent batsman because his fielding let the side down. Jessop writes: 'In a way it was rather bad luck on the batsman for he had been brought up as a wicket-keeper, but in any other position he was beyond hope.' As he was not at that time a good enough wicket-keeper to displace the regular Gloucestershire wicket-keeper he had to go. It is good to know that eight years later this player, D. C. Robinson, had improved so much as a wicket-keeper that thanks to Jessop's recommendation he kept wicket for the Gentlemen *v.* Players at Lord's and the Oval, and was selected to go on the M.C.C. 1913–14 tour to South Africa.

This shows how much store Jessop set on fielding, and woebetide the player who was not on his toes, especially to Jessop's lightning returns from cover which often went unexpectedly to the bowler's end.

In one of his weekly articles in *The London Opinion* in 1912 Jessop dealt with this problem of finding enough players good enough to appear for the county. He writes:

'Whilst there are many first-class cricketers who from business or other reasons have been prevented from appearing at all in county cricket, there is also a reverse side of the medal. Many cricketers do appear without any pretensions to first-class form. An inclusion in first-class cricket does not constitute a first-class cricketer. Amateurs – those who can be relied upon to make fairly regular appearances – are overwhelmingly outnumbered by their professional brethren. Whether it be for the good of the game or not, I do not argue, but despite veiled hints which are from time to time thrown out as regards the expensiveness of some amateurs, I can assert with some authority that the cost of an amateur as compared with that of a professional is about one-third, and in some counties even less.

'Now this being so, it is somewhat excusable for a committee of an impoverished county to venture forth freely into the realms of the unknown and fasten upon any available amateur talent.

'Consequently, a few of what the old Somerset captain, S. M. J. Woods, termed "rabbits" from time to time creep in. I have my mind's eye on one in particular who was numbered on this very "Sam's" side at Bristol. So enamoured was I at the perfection to which he had brought the art of inefficiency that I was impelled to ask for what reason he was being played. "Oh," said Sam, "he isn't much of a bat; he doesn't bowl, and he can't field, but by George, what a great golfer he is!" '

In an article which Sir Home Gordon wrote in 1909 about county captains he says that while there is always plenty of praise for Jessop the batsman there should be more for Jessop the captain.

'He has to make half the runs on the side, often he must wish he could take half the opposing wickets – but his bowling is fitful – and he not only fields like a cat, but gets alertness out of the side. Only a man of his dogged temperament could do it. He vouchsafes little praise, is laconic and attentive; watches, watches, watches – his eyes are never off the game and he puts everything he knows into the most hopeless match. As captain of the Western county he exhibits the very qualities that enrich his batting. Oddly enough, the Australians were disposed to think we over-rated his powers till he gave that astounding display at the Oval. After that, Hugh Trumble observed: "I don't ever remember any other bat making me scratch my head so much." It is the famous Yorkshire bowling off which he scores most vigorously; quite a remarkable percentage of his finest exhibitions, too, have been reserved for Metropolitan grounds.'

Another contemporary comment says that of all the county captains Jessop holds the most unenviable position because of the weakness of the Gloucestershire bowling: 'There is an amount of responsibility which no man can be fairly asked to carry, no matter how bright his optimism.' Then too there are always the pavilion critics who blame everything on the poor captain when things go wrong. Jessop tells an amusing story about 'one of these species who happened to be sitting next to my wife. After mentioning my many defects, he confided to his admiring circle of the many pleasurable matches he had enjoyed at 'Lloyds'. They may have been A.1 – but scarcely cricket.'

Jessop sums up the whole situation by saying 'Generally speaking, the captain gets more kicks than ha'pence. In times of victory he is forgotten and unsung – in times of defeat his whereabouts are soon discovered. When you have got your brickbats ready I would ask you to pause – and remember the incident of the Wild West Pianist.'

At the end of 1912 Jessop decided that whatever his future occupation might be it was better for him to be living in London, and in 1913 he rented a house at 56 Courtfield Gardens, W. Ealing.

Jessop was now free to play as little or as much cricket as he wished, and this would mean that he could indulge in plenty of club cricket if he so wished. Once he had become a regular county cricketer he did not play much club cricket, partly because he had not the time, and chiefly because he did not enjoy it much. This was not from any feeling of superiority, but because it lacked the challenge which meant so much to him. As he himself once wrote:

'When the microbe of first-class cricket has entered well into one's being, the joys of second-class cricket become perhaps less compelling. Nevertheless many a small match – though individual success has been denied me – has produced for me an enjoyment frequently absent from the sterner tussles of the county championship. Even though a county may have but small hope of gaining the premiership the eternal – one might say – infernal question of points always obtrudes itself.' When he did play in club matches he entered most fully into the game, and his reason for playing was often to oblige a friend concerned with the club. In 1903, for instance, he declined an invitation to play in the Gentlemen *v.* Players match at Lord's because he had accepted a prior invitation to play for Arkley village against Hornsey. Though he made a double-century for Arkley he was sorry he had missed the great stand between C. B. Fry and MacLaren which made the Gentlemen *v.* Players match such a memorable one. One consolation, however, was that some road sweepers who had enjoyed Jessop's innings at Arkley made a collection for him which produced the sum of one shilling and fivepence-halfpenny. 'Though beer was scarcely the price it is now, the amount subsequently consumed by my patrons dug deeply into the douceur so willingly subscribed by them.'

People who played in club cricket with Jessop said how much they enjoyed playing with him, and among these was Philip Trevor, one-time cricket correspondent of *The Daily Telegraph*, who writes:

'Although so preeminent a player and a natural leader, Jessop was never one to impose himself heavy-handedly on other members of the team, and was especially understanding and helpful with the younger members of it. He never advocated that others should attempt his methods, and he was a great admirer and respecter of the great orthodox players of the day. He let it be known that they had the ability to do things he was unable to do, and he never stressed the fact that they could not do things he could do. He would play in a minor club game with as much zest as a Test match. We all enjoyed playing with him, and better still, playing under him. Of course he had definite opinions on cricket matters, but was more ready to listen to those of others, and it was always very difficult to persuade him to talk about himself.'

As might be expected, some of his club match performances were outstanding. In 1900 he scored 213 for Arkley *v.* Hornsey and a fortnight later took 11 wickets in a 12 a side match *v.* West Herts, but here is a selection of a few subsequent gems of batting. In 1902 after a county match had finished early at Tonbridge Jessop accepted an invitation to turn out for the village of South Nutfield who were playing Holmesdale. His team scored 307–8 declared, of which he made 222*. He put on 175 in 60 minutes in a stand with a local player named Harris who made 13 while Jessop made the rest. In 1901 in a scratch match at Bristol he and Sammy Woods added 142 in 22 minutes, and in the same year when leading his own county team against Liverpool and District at Liverpool he scored 140 out of 174 in 90 minutes. In 1902 he scored 141 in 70 minutes for Gloucestershire against Uddingstone at Bothwell Castle. In 1913 he was induced to turn out for Ealing against the Wanderers and scored a superb 116 out of 147 in only 55 minutes, which delighted the large crowd. To list all his great innings in minor matches would be tedious, but it must be mentioned that apart from making two hundreds in a match in four county matches, he did this feat on two other important occasions, making 109 and 106 not out for Gloucestershire Twelve against The Next Eighteen at Cirencester in 1903, and another two centuries for Gloucestershire *v.* Somerset in a friendly match at Moreton-in-the-Marsh in May 1909. Sammy Woods considered these innings on a poor wicket as most remarkable.

Not all Jessop's appearances in club cricket were successful. On one occasion he took a team down to help some fund raising, and the local spectators who knew only of his great reputation and had not often seen him bat, rejoiced heartily when the local fast bowler got him out cheaply. As Jessop returned to the pavilion he remarked sadly that whereas most spectators were glad to see him succeed, this lot seemed delighted to see him fail. It was a new experience for him. On another occasion, when playing for the *Daily Mail* team in a country match near Sutton, Jessop went in to face the bowling of the gardener's boy who bowled him first ball with a dead shooter.

The gardener's boy yelled out a delighted 'Hurrah' as he saw how he had got rid of the great man, whose previous innings had been a 200 in a county match, and he proceeded to do a series of cartwheels all round the ground until such unseemliness was put an end to.

But Jessop did not have time to play much club cricket in 1913 as he played as many as twenty-three innings in county matches with an average of 26, rather better than in 1912. This was a bonus for the county, who had not expected him to play much in 1913. Some of his play was as dramatic as in the past. The match *v.* Yorkshire at Sheffield rivalled the great match of

1906. Once again Gloucestershire won the match – this time by two runs – and Jessop dominated the game throughout.

On a wet wicket Gloucester had scraped up only 157, of which Jessop scored 67 out of 83 in an hour after being missed first ball by Percy Holmes, who had just begun to play for Yorkshire. Jessop was so frequently out caught by some exceptional catch that it is good to hear of him being able to take advantage of this piece of good luck. Yorkshire replied with 172, in the course of which Jessop took four wickets and held two good catches. The first innings battle was of more importance than usual because the county championship conditions now offered points for a lead on the first innings. Gloucestershire then collapsed and at 49 for 5 looked like giving Yorkshire an easy win. But Jessop once again rose to the occasion and hit up 40 in 37 minutes. This time he hit his first ball for four. He was then brilliantly caught in the deep, but neither the fielder nor the crowd had heard 'no-ball' called, and Jessop trotted past the wicket towards the pavilion, pretending that he was out. He resumed battle with his old foeman Rhodes, pulling him for four first ball, and then off-driving him twice for six right across the football pitch. Rhodes was taken off, but after Jessop was finally caught, the side collapsed, leaving Yorkshire only 110 runs to win. They made a poor start and at 50 for 7 the game seemed all over in Gloucestershire's favour. After a stand of 33 Yorkshire were in the running again, with Drake, who made 45, farming the bowling well. The score was 97 for 8 when C. O. H. Sewell, who was captaining Gloucestershire, asked Jessop to go on himself and take over the proceedings. With his third ball he clean bowled Sir A. W. White, the Yorkshire captain. This left 5 runs needed with the last man, Dolphin, to come in. He had made 17 in the first innings, and was quite capable of making runs, but meanwhile every effort was made to prevent Drake keeping the bowling. Dolphin made three precious singles, and then, to Jessop's delight, lunged forward to a sharply turning off-break, and, like the previous batsman, was bowled. 'As a music lover,' wrote Jessop, 'I dare confess that the sound of the contact of that ball with Dolphin's off stump afforded me as much pleasure as any exquisite rendering of Liszt's Rhapsody ever did.'

Though disappointed, the Yorkshire spectators gave their victors generous applause. 'Exciting finishes come all too seldom, and when they do occur they amply compensate for the oft dull times,' said Jessop, and the headlines once again told how 'Jessop turns the scale'. 'The Busy Idol' had dominated the game with over a hundred runs, six wickets, and four catches.

In the course of a set of articles called 'The Game of Cricket' (1900) Jessop declared that 'Bowling, the most important part of cricket lacks proper appreciation nowadays; too much kudos is bestowed nowadays on batting performances'. Right to the end of his days Jessop was experimenting with the art of bowling, and in his last few years had developed an interesting form of leg-cutter.

'Just now when Gilbert Jessop's name has been brought so prominently before the public once more by a series of performances as good as he had ever accomplished, it is satisfactory to find that he is able to devote more time to the service of his county than was anticipated when the season opened.' So began an account of the Gloucestershire *v.* Hampshire match at Cheltenham in August 1913. Gloucestershire had batted first to score 169, Jessop contributing 54 in a mere 22 minutes. He went in when three wickets had fallen for 52, and looked in form from the start. 'The spectators were never quiet. When they did not cheer or clap their hands, they laughed, so excited had they become.' When he was at last lbw to McDonell he had received twenty-four balls and scored off seventeen of them.

The report goes on to say that there was no man in England so deserving of inclusion in the side M.C.C. were to send to South Africa in the winter, but Jessop said he knew nothing about the matter of his possible selection. In fact, he was eventually asked to go, and to captain the side, but once again he declined.

Even better than some of his performances for the county were those in several other matches, and especially in the two Gentlemen *v.* Players matches. The matter of Jessop's selection in England Test teams was often heated and controversial; it might be assumed that his selection for the Gentlemen against the Players was quite automatic ever since he made his début in 1897 with a brilliant 67. Curiously, he was to surpass that score only once in his next twenty-eight innings in Gentlemen *v.* Players matches at Lords or the Oval, making 73 not out at Lord's in 1906. Between 1897 and 1913 there were seven seasons in which he did not play in the Gentlemen *v.* Players match at Lord's – the 'senior' of the two annual fixtures, but except for 1898, when he was ill, he was invited to play every year. In spite of a general belief that Jessop played better against better bowling (e.g. the Yorkshire bowling), he did not make many runs against the attacks of the leading professional bowlers. In 1913, however, at a time when he had retired from regular county cricket and was nearing the age of forty, he produced a performance that had the brilliance of sweeter days. The Oval match, with scores of Gentlemen 139 and 424–9 declared and Players 131 and 334–8 was a remarkable one. On a soft wicket, in poor light, the Gentlemen collapsed utterly to the bowling of A. E. Relf and Buckenham who were both moving the ball in the heavy atmosphere. When Jessop came in eighth the scoreboard read 28 for six, and the seventh wicket fell ten runs later. *Wisden* records: 'An utter fiasco seemed in prospect, but Jessop giving one of the finest displays in his life knocked up 81 runs in 70 minutes out of the next 111 runs, and was last out with the total at 139. M. Falcon had helped him to put on 58 runs for the last wicket: he was one of the many young players in the side, 'Plum and myself,' to quote Jessop, 'being the only bald-headed old gentlemen.' Jessop's innings was entirely free from fault, and contained a superb on-drive from J. W. Hearne to the roof of the covered stand by the main entrance.

In their turn, under similar atmospheric conditions, the Players collapsed for an even lower score, but when the Gentlemen batted again things were easier, and in the last seventy minutes of the day Jessop scored 77. The next morning he took his score to 107 before skying a ball to cover. He had made these runs out of 163 in 115 minutes, and it was his first hundred in a Gentlemen *v.* Players match at Lord's or the Oval. The cartoonists repeated their theme of showing a bulldog with a Jessop head against a background of defeated batsmen, and the caption 'The British Bulldog: Was that a cry for help?' One report tells how when he first came in Jessop was seen sweeping loose bits of turf from the wicket, at which one wag in the crowd suggested that he was really removing the cobwebs left after J. W. H. T. Douglas had been pottering about at the wicket for the last two hours. E. H. D. Sewell in a column called 'Cricket Chirps' comments: 'Jessop was – well, just Jessop. "Play him as long as he can stand up" has always been my motto about him', and he reminds readers that both innings were played when Jessop had one jet-black loose thumb-nail as the result of a crack received in a club match at Ealing.

The second annual Gentlemen *v.* Players match was to begin at Lord's next day. Jessop had not originally been asked to play, but his success at the Oval demanded his appearance at Lord's, and A. C. Johnstone, one of the Gentlemen team, generously offered to stand down, if Jessop could be found in time. It was thought that he might be coming to watch, so messengers were sent out to look out for his arrival in case he came for the start of the match. Just before the game was due to begin Jessop turned up in his top hat; and was told he was playing in the match. Jessop continues the story:

'I had come for the purpose of enjoying the match as a spectator, for I had not received an invitation to play, when a bombshell was hurled at me in the nature of an urgent request to fill a vacancy which had occurred at the last moment. Though weaponless and without my own togs, it needed no pressure for me to enter once more into the enjoyments of another tilt with the "Professors". And it came to pass when my turn arrived I waddled to the wicket closely embraced around the beam by an immaculate pair of 'Plum's' bags, feet concealed in a spare pair of Johnnie Douglas's boots – boats, I might almost say, for there was a keel on them almost the thickness of a mizzen-mast – and jauntily covering my sparse locks was a cap upon which were embroidered three scimitars. Borrowed plumes are not always satisfactory, but I had no great reason to deplore the absence of my own accoutrements. If I did occupy a more perpendicular position at the wickets on this occasion, it was not so much on account of personal inclination as it was to the doubt of the power of resistance of the dreadfully tight borrowed bags if unduly exposed to the strain of a stooping posture. The idea of undertaking that long trek back from the wicket to the pavilion in a ragged condition under the cool, critical eye of a London crowd forbade my taking any risk, and consequently I smelt less of the pitch than usual.'

In these borrowed plumes Jessop obviously found batting more difficult than he normally did. He went in at 62 for 5, and *The Times* reporter records that: 'Mr Jessop's style of play was of the wierdest description. He has undying fame as a hard hitter, and four men are put in the deep when he is batting, but it is nearly true to say that he never attempted a big hit yesterday. He mowed the ball round to leg, patted it for a single in front of him, and placed it through the slips. Nevertheless he was always scoring.' The reporter, it seems, was quite unaware of Jessop's clothing problems, but in spite of them Jessop stayed in for 70 minutes and added 107 for the sixth wicket with S. G. Smith. When he had made 63 Jessop, putting aside anxiety about his trousers, went at last for a lusty drive, which soared at a great height to Frank Woolley, who managed to hang on to it. Jessop had once again saved his side, and again underlined his liking for the bowling of S. F. Barnes. Not many batsmen have been able to do that.

When the Players batted Jessop had probably acquired more roomy trousers for he fielded magnificently, and ran out Rhodes when he had scored 49 and thought he was going for a safe single to reach his fifty. To be able to fool a canny Yorkshireman at such a moment must have given Jessop even more satisfaction than hitting him for six. It is good to know that the M.C.C. secretary wrote the following letter to Jessop to thank him for playing at such short notice.

Dear Jessop,

At a meeting of the committee held on Monday last I was instructed to write and offer you their thanks for so kindly accepting a place in the Gentlemen's side. They fully appreciate the sportsmanlike spirit you showed in helping them to make the side as representative as possible; probably at some personal inconvenience to yourself.

Yours sincerely,

F. E. Lacey.

These two great performances brought the name of Jessop right back into the limelight, and the Selection committee for the team to go to South Africa in 1913–14 soon approached him. In a letter dated August 5, 1913, Lord Harris, the chairman, says that he was delighted to hear that Jessop might be available to go with the team and what is more to act as captain. But he pointed out that F. L. Fane had already been approached over the matter of captaincy, which he would accept, but would prefer not to. There is also a letter from Fane to Jessop saying that he personally would be glad if Jessop went as captain instead of him. On August 10 there was a further letter from Lord Harris virtually assuming that Jessop would be going 'subject to the arrangements mentioned', and discussing the composition of the side. Dated three days later there is another letter from Lord Harris to Jessop saying how sorry he was that Jessop had now decided not to go on the tour after all. Fane was to be approached again about captaining the side, but in the end he did not go either, and J. W. H. T. Douglas became captain, with only two other amateurs, including the Hon. Lionel Tennyson who had burst upon the scene in 1913. His cricket had always been supported by Jessop ever since he had met young Lionel and his brother in Australia in 1901–2.

It would be interesting to know why Jessop refused at the last moment to go to South Africa, and to turn down a chance of leading an M.C.C. touring team. A possible reason might be connected with his newspaper work, as Lord Harris had mentioned in one of his letters that some rules about connection with the Press had been laid down by the M.C.C., but there was no suggestion of any difficulties. Perhaps it was just the old bogey about sea travel that turned the scales.

The decision not to go seemed to put Jessop back in form, and a few days later, at Scarborough, he repeated his 1911 performance by scoring two hundreds at the Festival. On the opening day of the Gentlemen *v.* Players match he was suffering from a heavy cold and he suggested that H. S. Altham should take his place in the team. Altham has himself told me how the team selector Leveson-Gower replied to Jessop's suggestion with the word 'Nonsense', so Jessop wrapped himself up in sweaters and scarves, and with certainly one brandy inside him made his way to the wicket to face Hitch bowling very fast down-wind. He was completely at sea for a few overs, but he survived and then proceeded to attack Hitch in such a way that he ended up with an analysis of 8–2–60–2. He hit him hard and high and produced a score of 119 made out of 172 in 105 minutes with 2 sixes and 17 fours. It was an astonishing display under any circumstances, but three days later he was to surpass even this.

The next match was Lord Londesborough's XI *v.* Kent who were quite

TO-DAY'S CRICKET.

MATCH AT COUNTY GROUND.

GLOUCESTERSHIRE v. SOMERSET.

JESSOP AT HIS BEST.

SENSATIONAL HITTING.

28 IN ONE OVER.

SCENE ON THE GROUND.

EXCITING FINISH.

BRILLIANT VICTORY FOR GLOUCESTERSHIRE.

The concluding stage of the match between

7

TEST MATCH.

MR. JESSOP SAVES THE SITUATION.

THE "ELECTRIC BATTERY AT HIS BEST.

ENGLAND 428.

STUBBORN CENTURY BY BRAUND.

By "LINESMAN."

He took grim care by the throat and choked it. He scattered the clouds of

THE CROUCHER

AT HIS BEST TO-DAY.

Magnificent Innings in the Match.

Aspect of Game Changed.

GLOS'SHIRE AHEAD.

Details of Jessop's Wonderful Game.

BY "THE SMITER."

JESSOP'S BALM

A SOOTHING SYRUP

For Sore Test Selectors.

GREAT DISPLAY

ON THE COUNTY GROUND.

(BY OUR OWN REPORTER.)

Gloucestershire have experienced such bad weather for their home matches to date this summer that the mixed weather of yesterday led to the glass being early scanned this morning, and it was quite a relief when it was found that the weather was fair to look upon. Three full days' cricket and a win for Gloucestershire over Hants would be gladly welcomed by the County Executive.

The match with Hants last summer was played at Cheltenham, and won by nine wickets by the Southern County, who placed themselves practically safe from defeat by

Jessop making a recruiting speech in Manchester.

Jessop was a scratch golfer at a time when golf was making its first serious inroad into cricket.

Jessop, dressy as usual with bow-tie and button-hole, at Dorchester not long before his death.

overwhelmed. On the opening day Jessop went in sixth and actually scored 116 out of 138 in exactly one hour. At various times he took 11 runs off an over from Fielder, 12 off one from J. R. Mason, 14 off Blythe, and then 26 off D. W. Carr, bowling his googlies from the Trafalgar Square end. This over read: 4 . 6 6 4 6. His only mishit in the innings was when his score was 52. These two hundreds were the last two he scored in first-class cricket.

The only blot on his last glorious days at Scarborough was an unpleasant experience that must have disturbed him considerably. Jessop was walking one morning to the ground with the friend with whom he was staying. Just outside the entrance they came across a runaway cab horse and tried to stop it. In the attempt Jessop's friend was struck by a shaft and killed instantly. Jessop, though much shaken, escaped serious injury.

As though unwilling to make the final end in the field he had graced so wonderfully, Jessop decided to go on playing some first-class cricket in 1914. He played only nine matches for Gloucestershire, with a top score of 78, but he was once again chosen to appear for the Gentlemen at both Lord's and the Oval. In the first innings at Lord's he made a valuable 45 out of a total of 265, but the finest comment on him was *Wisden's* note that 'Jessop's fielding in both innings was up to his highest standard.'

Owing to the outbreak of war the end of his career came unexpectedly, and there was no Scarborough Festival where he could delight spectators a final time. On August 3 and 4 at Bristol, Gloucestershire won their only match of the season. In the first innings Jessop was top scorer with an innings of 25 in a total of 111. He was out 'st Chidgey, by White', and when Gloucestershire fielded he took 4 wickets for 34. In their second innings Gloucestershire needed 77 to win. Thanks to C. S. Barnett (father of the Test batsman) who scored 32, they scraped home by one wicket, despite 5 wickets having fallen for 22. Jessop was out again in the same way 'st Chidgey, b White' – this time for only 4. Though he did not know it as he walked off the Bristol ground on the afternoon of August 4, 1914, he had played his last innings in first-class cricket.

On the outbreak of war he decided to play no more cricket and he did not play in any of the remaining five Gloucestershire matches. Never again the almost hysterical acclamation as he came down the pavilion steps, never again the cheers and claps as boundaries flew from his bat, never again the hat-waving and back-slapping as he left the wicket after a typical innings.

Looking back on his career he may perhaps have been glad that it ended quietly and without any official 'last appearance' which might have been embarrassing to one who did not really enjoy the limelight and publicity. It was all over, but he did not know that before long cricket of any kind would be all over for him. He may have been forty, but he might well have gone on playing for some time yet. W. G. went on until he was almost sixty, and Jessop's fielding was still as good as ever.

His fewer first-class games in 1914 gave him time to play some summer golf and in that year he was playing so well that he entered for the Amateur Championship. Just before the event an aunt died in Cheltenham, so he decided to scratch from the golf so that he could attend the funeral. At that moment it merely meant that his excursions into championship golf would have to be postponed for a year. Little did he know that his golfing days, too, were numbered.

7

'Innings Declared Closed' 1915–1955

'You must have many happy memories of the fun you have had, and of the pleasure you have given to countless others.'

H. S. ALTHAM

ALTHOUGH he had reached the age of forty Jessop volunteered for service on the outbreak of War, and on December 21, 1914, he was commissioned as a captain in the 14th Manchester Regiment. At about the same time the family left London and went to live in lodgings at Garfield House, Clevedon, Somerset, where they had long stays on and off for the next ten years. In the summer of 1915 he took part in a successful recruiting campaign in company with Lt. A. C. MacLaren. Jessop played a great deal of army cricket when stationed at Lichfield in 1915. He made a number of runs – including six centuries – and we have an old score-book which contains details of some of his innings. On August 28, 1915, he scored 94 for the 14th Manchester's against the 13th Sherwood Foresters, and shortly after (the date has not been filled in) he played in a Brigade match for the Red Cross Fund, leading his own XI against a team captained by Sir Robert Peel on Sir Robert's private ground at Drayton Manor, Tamworth. Jessop went in first and made 94 out of a total of 182. He hit 7 sixes including two off the great S. F. Barnes in one over. Peel had collected six professionals for his side including Barnes, who eventually had Jessop caught and ended up with an analysis of 7–84. The great bowler had not been put on to open the bowling, and I do not suppose he enjoyed being hit about by Jessop. On an earlier occasion in 1910, when Staffordshire were granting Barnes a benefit season, Jessop had kindly offered to bring a team up to Hanley, Porthill, in order to help swell the funds for Barnes' Benefit. Jessop made a century and hit Barnes hard and high. Barnes never liked being hit, but the fiercer he bowled the harder Jessop hit him. After being twice hit for six, Barnes snarled down the wicket: 'Hey, Croucher, this is my ruddy benefit, not thine.'

Jessop recalled this game against Peel's XI at Drayton Manor in a letter written to the artist James Thorpe in the early 1940s. 'Peel got six county pros including Barnes. We got 182 and they got 158, so we beat 'em. I got 94 most of 'em off my nose, for Barnes was pretty nasty on a roughish pitch. That was my last game.'

Jessop played very well that season and one of my correspondents, Mr Arthur Shaw, then a young subaltern, remembers Jessop's kindness to him after he had nearly got Jessop out first ball. It looked to be unplayable, and Shaw's heart began to leap with pleasure, until Jessop with his quick reaction managed to chop it down. That same year Lt. Shaw was in charge of collecting up Mills hand grenades after a practice, and he noticed that those thrown by Jessop were far ahead of the others, and what is more they were made, unlike the others, without Jessop exposing himself above the parapet. Just a hand and a flicking wrist appeared, as powerful and as accurate as when on the cricket field, though Jessop was never destined to throw grenades on active service.

By the early summer of 1916 Jessop had been transferred to the Lincolnshire Regiment, and was suffering from severe lumbago. He was sent for treatment to a clinic in Bath. We have his appointment card dated 29.5.16 – 'Radiant Heat, Dousing with total immersion for 30 minutes at a temperature of 210–300 degrees'. The patient was placed in a coffin-like container, and literally 'steamed-up'. If he became too uncomfortable he could raise the lid and get out, but by some accident the catch fell, and Jessop was unable to summon assistance as the attendant had gone away. When he was eventually rescued, it was found that his heart had been seriously damaged as a result of this terrible ordeal. Those two innings of 94 played in the late summer of 1915 were indeed the last times he ever appeared on any cricket field or played cricket of any sort. Years later he was able to play a little casual golf, but his serious golfing days were also over. In a matter of a few minutes the sporting life of one of the greatest of athletes had come to an abrupt end. He was only 42, and though he was to live nearly another forty years, there were no more games.

After the accident with the steam treatment Jessop was able to go back on service with the Lincolnshire Regiment, but it was soon apparent that his heart had been damaged. He was invalided out of the Army at the end of November 1917, and was able to spend Christmas with the family at Clevedon. He was then allowed to continue his service as a civilian but wearing uniform. He was stationed at Walsall, and in May 1918 his son was sent to Shardlow

Hall, near Derby, a prep. school run by an old friend of his, B. O. Corbett. A month later, whilst playing golf at Walsall, Jessop had a very serious heart attack, and it was nearly two years before he could even walk any distance. For some time the family remained at Clevedon, and as he slowly recovered he looked for a place which was less hilly where he might even be able to play some golf again.

In 1919 they were at Aberdovey for six months, and then there were brief spells at London, Dorchester, Weymouth, Tiverton and Dawlish. It was a roving life, but fortunately Jessop's health was steadily improving, and Mrs Jessop came into a small inheritance at just the moment it was most needed. Jessop could not consider any active work yet, and at this time his only source of income was from his journalism. His experience as a recruiting officer made him a strong supporter of the London Playing Fields Association. He had seen how boys brought up in the country had much better physique generally than those brought up in towns, and he was convinced that more opportunity for games would help to improve this blot on the nation's health. He made an impassioned plea in his articles for more playing fields and stressed the point that 'The open sesame to health is open spaces. To preserve land for GAME is fashionable. Let it be even more so for GAMES in the future.'

In 1919 he wrote regular comments every Saturday throughout the cricket season in *The Daily Sketch*. When this was announced, Plum Warner made a comment on it, and made it quite clear that Jessop was not in good health and would certainly never play cricket again. 'It is scarcely likely that we shall see anyone like him again for many a long day and the cricket world mourns the loss of a genius.' There was at this time a chance that Jessop might become Secretary of Surrey C.C.C., but his health was just not good enough. For such an active man the limitations of his way of life for the rest of his years must have been a terrible burden, but he seems to have remained cheerful and always had time for his many friends.

The Gloucestershire County committee wrote to ask his advice over the re-establishment of the cricket club. 'It is good to know that your interest in County cricket is unabated and that the Gloucestershire people can turn to you for advice.' Jessop must have been very interested to learn that his old friends John Tunnicliffe and Arthur Lilley, now living in Gloucestershire, had been appointed to the committee; just the sort of 'reform' Jessop would have approved of.

Among many letters we have is one from Jack Hobbs saying: 'I cannot tell you how pleased I was to get yours of 17th inst. Believe me, I highly appreciated your kind thought of me. . . . It is with sincere regret that I note your absence and I trust that ere long your health will allow you to resume your place as England's most popular cricketer.' His very old friend and fellow-player C. L. Townsend writes from his solicitor's office at Stockton on Tees to say: 'I have just been writing in reply to Bonnor and your name crops up in my thoughts so continually that I am writing these few words to let you know I still think of the many happy days we have spent together. I am grieved to hear that you have been so seedy and sincerely trust that you will soon be on the mend and able to play cricket again.' In a previous letter written some ten years before, Townsend had thanked Jessop for sending him a wedding present subscribed by various donors whom Jessop had approached. Townsend writes: 'As one looks back on one's cricket career, it is wonderful the enormous amount of friends it has brought. From a business point of view it is worth not much, but it has made life a very pleasant thing, and the joy of being a "has been" will always remain. The "never waser" misses much.'

In his letter of 1919 Townsend mentions his three sons, one of whom, 'D.C.H.' was later to play for England. He asks after Jessop's son Gilbert, now aged thirteen and about to go to Weymouth College. 'Will he be a cricketer?' asks Townsend, and the answer was 'yes', for he became a formidable player at school and later at Christ's College, Cambridge. Though he did not play for the University he appeared for Hampshire in 1933, and after that played a great deal for Dorset. He was a strong hitter and a slow bowler.

By 1920 Jessop was recovering slowly and working on a book about his cricketing days, to be published in 1922 as *A Cricketer's Log*. He was steadily getting back into the world of cricket and in April 1920 Plum Warner wrote to ask his advice about the selection of the forthcoming team to Australia. Writing in the *Daily Telegraph* Col. Philip Trevor ends by saying: 'It is good to know that at the present time Jessop the man is very much appreciated. He has, as all lovers of cricket know, been ill for a long time. At the moment of writing he is better, and likely to get better still, and congratulations to him on his recovery have been general and sincere. Well does he deserve them, for he is a fine fellow.'

Evidence of his recovery comes in the fact that in 1921 he was able to do some active reporting of the Test matches for *The Daily Mirror*. In that same year E. V. Lucas wrote in *Punch* a wonderful little piece called 'Hero-worship':

'It was my privilege not long since to receive a letter from a famous cricketer whose active career, alas! is behind him, for illness has stolen away his strength, but he still watches the game with a jealous eye and rejoices in the triumphs of others. In spite of all the prowess of the last few years, the new names and the great scores, no one has arisen to take his place. Personally I should not be surprised if none ever did.

'Seeing in the mind's eye (as I finished reading his brief missive) a vision of little running boys with autograph-books on the grass of the Oval and Lord's, through whose masses the retiring players have to force their way – few as complaisant as they used to be – I put it into an envelope and addressed it to a small nephew at school. Not that I wanted him to be fired to join this importunate army, with its pencils and its albums and its insensitiveness to rebuffs, but I wished to behave like a decent uncle and provide him with a unique and perhaps coveted possession.

'I say "perhaps", because this cricketer has not played for so long that there was the possibility that neither my nephew nor any of his companions – it is a school for really little boys – had heard of him. Their heads might be so full of contemporary giants – the Hearnes and the Hitches, the Jupps and the Jeacockes, the Meads and the – no, not Persians, Australians – that this Emeritus Titan, the delight of our eyes a decade ago, might be history so ancient as to be negligible.

'But I was wrong.

' "The letter you sent to Gerry," his fond mother wrote, "was a most tremendous success. He thought it was his duty, poor public-spirited mite, to put it up for auction for some school fund or other, and it fetched four and tenpence. But that isn't all. Each of the eleven took a tracing of it."

'I hope Mr Jessop is a reader of *Punch*.

E. V. L.'

This tribute to Jessop must have cheered him, and, better still, that summer saw his return to the golf course. He was able to play for the first time since his illness, and though he was never again the player who could break course records as he did at Buxton during a casual round there in 1915, it must have delighted him to swing a club again.

His writings were going strong. Apart from his newspaper work he wrote a series of articles for the newly founded *Cricketer* throughout the season of 1921, and the next season's issues carried excerpts from his forthcoming *A Cricketer's Log*. Within a year or so he was fit enough to undertake a regular job and on January 1, 1924, he took up an appointment as Secretary to Edgware Golf Club. The course was an easy distance from Lord's and the work was of a kind that he could do in his own time, for it was understood that he could continue with his journalism. The family came to live at 3 Sunnydale Gardens, Mill Hill, N.W.7, and for the first time in many years they had a settled home. For twelve years they lived happily at Mill Hill, and I have had a letter from someone who remembers Mr and Mrs Jessop as quiet and charming neighbours. He was now able to play golf regularly but had to take his time owing to his heart condition. Occasionally he would fill a place in the team for a golf match, and I have met someone who several times played against him on such an occasion. He was, it seems, most pleasant to play with though he appeared rather 'frail', an adjective which seems out of keeping with the Jessop of his cricketing days not so very long ago. He still hit the ball a long way, and usually won his match. Another recollection of these days comes from a young member who, setting out in the rain, borrowed Jessop's old brown beret, which he says he still carries with him in his golf bag. Jessop had little need of it after 1929 because in that year he had to stop playing altogether. Jessop had become truly golf-minded, for there is the story of a young friend driving to the Mill Hill cricket ground to play as a candidate in an M.C.C. match. He saw Jessop walking to the ground and offered him a lift, but Jessop refused it with the words: 'No, my boy, thank you but I would rather walk.' The 'candidate' then asked him where the ground was, to which Jessop's reply was 'A couple of brassie shots down this road, and then a niblick to the right!'

There are other stories of Jessop's earlier golfing days. The late director of The Central Press, Guy L'Estrange tells how he would seem to have won a medal competition at West Middlesex golf club. He was sitting in the smoke room with a clear lead of three strokes amid congratulations and drinks, when in sailed Jessop with one of the lowest scores ever put in at West Middlesex to take the prize from him. Another recollection comes from the daughter of Samuel Ryder, the donor of the famous Ryder Cup. When she was a small girl her father introduced her to a neat smiling friend whom he said was 'Someone I am immensely proud not only to have played with but to have beaten . . . just', and he went on to say she had just had the privilege of shaking hands with the great Jessop! – 'The finest cricketer of my generation'. Mr Ryder's daughter added that her father's love of cricket transcended even his delight in golf.

Another who had many happy memories of games with Jessop was his friend James Thorpe who wrote: 'Jessop played golf in the same characteristically unorthodox and unconventional style as his cricket, with a short back-swing, a strong, full follow-through of the forearms and an assured confidence which was far removed from any suspicion of conceit. With the generous allowance of a stroke a hole (or it may have been two) I was once two up on him with three to go. 'Now', he said 'you think you've got me! Well, I'm going to beat you with three bogeys.' He gave the figures for the holes and did them. He was always keen and enjoyed to the full playing any game, however apparently unimportant, and at the same time gave much enjoyment to others. This surely is the highest merit in playing games.'

Though he was absorbed with his golf Jessop had time to arrange annual cricket matches with the Edgware Police. We have the score books for 1925–6–7, and young Gilbert features well in them, which must have pleased his father. The years went on quietly, but since his terrible experience in 1916 he did not care for being closely confined and did not like travelling about much.

His *Daily Mail* duties in 1926 took him to report a Test Trial at Bristol which he had not visited since 1914. Plum Warner persuaded him to walk with him round the ground, and he was recognised and clapped. 'Old friends were delighted to meet him. He has grown a little grey, but there is still the same old lilt in his walk, and he is as keen on the game as ever. On his birthday his son made 157 and did the hat-trick' – thus wrote someone who met him then. Jessop also went to visit Walter Hammond, lying seriously ill with blood poisoning. Hammond, receiving some infection in the West Indies, played no cricket at all in 1926 and Jessop's visit must have cheered him up considerably. Other activities of these years included being Chairman of the Cricketers' Committee of the St Dunstan's Fund for Blinded soldiers, and also acting as cricket equipment adviser to Lillywhite's of the Haymarket. He kept in touch with his friends, and there is a wonderful letter from H. K. Foster written in 1932:

> You dear old fellow, Hereford
>
> What real pleasure it was to get a line from you. Do you know the reason I have always liked you is I believe due to the fact that I played on you the only dirty trick I am conscious of on the cricket field, and you took it so damn well that you won my admiration. Now look here, I may be in town for the night before the first week in May, so I want you to put on a black tie and short coat and come and dine quietly with me at the Wyndham Club. Will you do it? we should both love it; failing that I must fix up to meet you at Lord's, but we may do that as well. Curiously enough I don't seem to have any contemporaries that I care to meet – Charles (odd), Ranji (India), Jackson (too big) and so on, though there is Reggie Spooner. I would just love to see you, and I am none too well. Overwork and worry have played the devil with me. I am glad to hear that your wife is safely through her trouble and that all is well. I often wonder what has happened to your boy. Oh Jessopus! come and dine with me and we will talk and talk and

talk. . . . I wish you would come down and spend a day or two with me. I've a dear girl of 24 that you would fall straight in love with. We are very quiet here right out of the world.

You can't think what a thrill your letter gave me. A much greater one that any letter of yours gave your wife! ! ! Do you know my boy I have not had a holiday for 6 years. What about it? but where and when and how unless you come with me and we get the M.C.C. to stand the trip. Let me know that you will come and dine and I shall be happy.

Yrs ever,
Harry Foster

In 1933 Jessop had the great pleasure of having his son play county cricket for Hampshire in a couple of matches. From his earliest days he had taken a great interest in his son's cricket, and I have been told how frequently he would go to see him when he was at Weymouth College. He was always ready to help his son's friends, and would take off his coat in the nets and feed the batsman by throwing the ball overhand to a fixed point from half way down the net. One of his most regular pieces of advice to his son, based on hard-won experience, was never to commit youself to the stroke before the ball leaves the bowler's hand.

Jessop took great interest in the cricketers of Weymouth, and one especially pleasing success he had was when he converted a rather small boy called Woodd from a moderate medium-pacer into a leg-break bowler. Soon after, the college met a team of Royal Navy cricketers from H.M.S. *Barham*, who were completely diddled by these leg-breaks. A correspondent tells me that he had seldom watched anything more comical than the tough Naval batsmen reduced to quivery jelly by the wiles of a small boy.

In 1935 the Warwickshire enthusiast, C. J. Britton, published a little book which listed all Jessop's innings in first-class cricket. George Beldam, who provided the illustrations, wrote to Jessop about Britton's book and said he was 'delighted to feel that there is at last some record of your performance in figures and other details, but, alas! NO record which could give or do any justice to the manner of execution'.

In 1936 Edgware Golf Club was sold for building land, but though Jessop had many offers of jobs as a golf secretary, his health was deteriorating again, and in October 1936 he and his wife went to live at his son's vicarage at St George's, Fordington, Dorchester. His son had previously been chaplain at Queens' College, Cambridge, but now devoted himself to looking after his parents until their deaths some twenty years later.

1947. G. L. Jessop with his son G. L. O. Jessop.

The Jessops lived very quietly, but Jessop took an interest in local affairs, and his openly-stated objection to there being Exhibition Lawn Tennis on Sundays at Dorchester brought him a letter of thanks from the Lord's Day Observance Society. On a visit to Weymouth in October 1939 he had another severe heart attack, so that on his return to Dorchester he had to take life even more quietly. From then on, until his death in 1955, the extent of his exercise was a walk down to the gate of the vicarage garden. He occasionally went out in the car, but this tended to upset him.

As soon as the Second World War broke out, the Rev. Gilbert Jessop went off on service as a chaplain in the Marines. He was to be away for some six years, but the parish was conducted by visiting clergy and his parents were allowed to continue to occupy certain rooms at the vicarage. This at one time became the headquarters of a girls' public day school, evacuated from London. One of the pupils, now Mrs Mary Watson, has sent me a picture of life at the vicarage during the golden summer of 1940:

'My first impression as a resident was of green lino, acres of blackout material screening huge staircase windows, massive furniture, and dozens of bouncing girls. Word went round that the Vicar's father who lived in the house was a famous cricketer which meant little to me (the Head did not care for cricket, although as a sop to the sporting, she later introduced stoolball). The Cricketer was rarely seen, and no wonder. Hefty girls and plain spinster teachers were not the most appealing of house guests.

'Easter came and we all tumbled back to green, suburban London. But when the holidays were over I insisted on going back to the Vicarage which was the nearest thing to the boarding-school I yearned to attend, although girls were 'encouraged' to go into billets where possible. Mother fixed it.

'But what a surprise! The Vicarage was splendidly empty. Girls had vanished to join their parents in other parts of the country, or cowed had crept back into billets in the town. Four of us remained in the charge of the deputy head and a Maths. mistress. The Vicarage was a dusty desert of sun and space, with blackouts put up at the last moment those long, light evenings.

'The Cricketer became a real, live person, occupying a study just inside the front door by day, and a big bedroom over the drawing-room by night, together with his wife who, rumour had it – and there was a lot of rumour in our circle – was an Australian. We looked at her as if she was a Hottentot, but she was a small, twinkling little woman with neat feet and ankles and pretty white curly hair. They were looked after by a cheerful young maid called Nancy who cluttered around with our Mrs Tuckerman and was white-aproned in the morning, formal in a frilled cap and apron after lunch.

'Suddenly Gilbert Jessop was talking to us. He used to take a turn in the garden in the late afternoon, being very rarely seen in the morning. The Rev. Jessop appeared once or twice in Army Uniform but seemed unimpressed by our throbbing green tunics and flashing putty-coloured stockings.

'Millicent Jessop guarded her husband like a dragon. One day I was strumming on the piano after lunch and there was a tap at the door. It was Millicent. She asked me to do something else quieter for an hour because Mr Jessop always had a rest at two o'clock. Just after three she twinkled into view again. "It's all right now if you want to . . ." and her hands made playing motions in the air. "He's finished his rest."

One day Gilbert Jessop asked us if we could play bumblepuppy. We hadn't a clue, so the next afternoon after school as we toiled up the Vicarage drive we saw he'd fixed up a pole with a ball dangling from a rope at the top, and produced two tennis racquets. He coached us in the finer points and seemed to enjoy the fun as much as we did. But if we pursued him (and we did, we had no finesse whatsoever) with cries of "Teach us cricket, oh please!" he'd hurry away nervously.

After more walks and talks in the garden – he treated us with gravity and much courtesy, always expressing interest in what we were doing, always wearing a tweed hat and with matching greenish tweeds – he laid out a game of croquet for us. This was great fun. He played and so did Millicent and she outmanoeuvred us all. It was a terrific game for a Vicarage lawn. . . .'

Though this was a far cry from the Oval Test of 1902 Jessop no doubt entered into the game with just as much enthusiasm, and he provided the girls with an experience at least one of them has never forgotten. Another recollection of about the same date has been passed to me. The local midwife, when not engaged on maternity work, used to call on others, including Jessop, and the old gentleman always used to take an interest in the babies which had arrived since her last visit. He would greet her with a twinkle in his eye and ask: 'Well, nurse, what's the score?' He was amused when one day she had no babies to report, and told him 'Rain stopped play!'

His old friend James Thorpe recalls how, when he met Jessop again in 1921, after a fairly long interval, he had been shocked to see the severe traces his illness had left on him.

Many of his letters now came from friends with recollections of the distant past. Here is his reply to a letter he had received from W. H. 'Bill' Robson, who had joined in the cricket in his days at Beccles, and who later introduced him to the Stock Exchange. Robson had written to him to congratulate him on his 70th birthday.

St Georges Vicarage,
Dorchester,
25 May/44

Dear old Bill,

I am delighted as a puppy with two tails to hear about you once again. 70 is a poor score compared with 87. It makes you out to be 38 when you were so hospitable to me at Beccles. I should hope for nothing better than to crawl down the Waveney in a wherry once more with you. In your short stay at Beccles we enjoyed one or two good matches together. I remember getting 219 not out out of 271 of which your share was 34, and then getting the other side out for 43. Then those Arkley matches – how I used to enjoy them, more especially my visits to you and your good lady & the children. How splendid to think of young Harry in the 'Cumberland' helping with the good work of flogging the Huns.

My smack at them in the last War eventually clipped my wings and I have had to go pretty slow since then on account of heart trouble. Nevertheless from 1920 until 1929 I used to get a round of golf occasionally and could still hold my own at scratch, but I had to chuck it entirely after '29. When I was at Littlehampton in 1921 I tried to get in touch with you and asked Armstrong to get you down so that we could have a game, but somehow or other it did not eventuate. What an extraordinary coincidence that the photo of the Arkley team *v.* Hornsey should be at Churchdown, for that was my *first club* in which I played in grown-up company. I was 14 then and I was always put on to bowl first, and six or seven wickets was quite an ordinary thing.

I remember so well seeing poor old Jos (he was a dear fellow) at the Oval Test. I went and sat with him and a pal of his – Dru Drury – and Jos told me that when I went in for the first few overs he hid his face behind his hands – he was so afraid I would be summarily disposed of.

Yes, that was indeed a good match, and a thousand pities that the Rubber had already been thrown away thro' the idiocy of Martin Hawke and the other selectors. The team which skittled the Aussies out for 36 in the first match at Birmingham should never have been changed. It was the best that ever represented England in my time. To refresh your memory, here it is – MacLaren – Ranji – Fry – Tyldesley – Lilley – Hirst – Rhodes – Lockwood – Braund – Jackson – & Hayward.

Best of fortune to you, Bill, and may you reach your century.

Yours ever,
Jessopus

(Jessop was being modest here: he himself was playing at Birmingham and not Hayward.)

It was in 1947 that I wrote to Jessop with a request that I should visit him. Seeing how few people he used to see at that time, I consider I was lucky to arrange a visit. Here is part of his very cordial reply to my letter:

> Dear Mr Brodribb,
>
> I am usually on view any time except between 2.00 and 4.30. Drop in by all means if you care to next time you are in the neighbourhood. ...

The old humour was still there. He might tend to amuse himself by pretending that he was not willing to talk about cricket, knowing all too well that was what his visitors wished to talk about. An *Evening Standard* reporter once called upon him and afterwards wrote: 'We sipped dry sherry as he announced he was not going to talk about cricket. He then started off about cricket, came back to it later, and ended on cricket.' Jessop told him that 'too many big matches are being played. A man gets no let up. It's like the old saying about killing the golden goose', but he still followed the Test matches on the wireless, and once wrote in a letter 'Anything about Bradman bores me, a wonderful batsman, but I don't like him as a cricketer', though he approved of the way in which Bradman had tried to score off Larwood during the bodyline tour of 1932–3, stepping back and cutting him off his stumps to the open off-side field, which was exactly what Jessop used to do himself. Nigel Haig was a lifelong fan of Jessop, and once wrote to him and asked him to explain how he was able to do what he did, and his reply was a letter which is regarded almost as an historic document:

> March 1, 1949
>
> Dear Nigel,
>
> Of course I remember you, and it is not so long ago that I saw you at Lord's. In 1921 when I used to travel round with Harry Foster I plumped for you and Lionel Tennyson after that awful 1st Test, and your analysis at Lord's compares favourably with our lame ducks of today. Your question is rather puzzling. I am not aware of unique physical gifts. I should put my success down to supreme confidence, rather more acute vision than the average fellow, and perhaps the most important adjunct of all to a batsman, timing. I can quite truthfully say that on no occasion did I ever get the 'needle'. I have seen more than one of our great batsmen show obvious signs of nerves in Tests and sometimes in county matches. I shall never forget little Bobby Abel (a charming little fellow) opening the second innings with

me at Sheffield in the 3rd Test in 1902, he could hardly speak on the way to the wickets and when he did it was to suggest an appeal for bad light. I expect 'nerves' are not uncommon today, now that 'leg-theory' or body-line bowling (according to which country you belong) has been apparently fully approved. I used to bowl about as short as anybody in my time occasionally, but my field – a long leg, a short leg, and mid-on – did at any rate not prohibit the batsman from offensive shots nor confine him to the sole purpose of protecting himself from injury. Jardine has much to answer for. All this Bradman 'guff' about Test Matches promoting good feeling between the two countries could be dissipated by one ball in Australia if one of their batsmen was seriously injured in a Test. It is an ugly form of attack which judging from the West Indies and now South Africa has come to stay. I am very interested in your remarks about present day cricket. 1936 was the last season I saw. From my armchair it seems to me that there is nowadays as much negative bowling as batting, average-hunting in view of Test match prospects. The frequency of these Test tours is doing our cricket harm. If the interval between these official Tests was lengthened it would be better both physically and mentally – especially mentally for the players. I did not think that last season's selectors were particularly clever in their picking, and the dropping of Hutton savoured to me of the action of a preparatory school captain in a moment of pique. The best selection Com. of all my experience was 'Plum', Tommy Higson, and Perrin.

Statisticians were always anathema to me. It amuses me when they compare past conditions with the present, especially as regards rate of scoring. For instance for the greater part of my career one had to hit *out* of the ground for a sixer.

I remember at Hastings in 1907 hitting five out of the ground and eleven over the ropes which would have increased my score from 191 to 213. I should have enriched my bag of centuries by more than one century if the easier reward had been in vogue at that time. I apologise for talking about my own past deeds, a fault which I rarely indulge in.

Thank you for your letter. I really enjoyed it. When you next see 'Plum' give him my love and if ever you run across Harry Altham tell him that I really will thank him for his letter of *five* years ago.

Yours sincerely,

Gilbert L. Jessop

P.S. I have fined you a 'double' (when next we meet) for spelling my name with a 'double' P.

Nigel Haig wrote back with the words: 'Peccavi! a double P, what next! after that a double at your expense would be as coals of fire – ashes in the mouth, at least I think it would. . . . There was of course an easy riposte to your hand, the placing of an H at the end of my name makes the scotch blood of my clan seethe with indignation.'

At about the same time Jessop received a letter from his old friend J. B. Champain (now a bishop) – brother of F. H. B. C. – who describes how he has just had to preach at the Stanley Jackson Memorial Service – 'a most daunting occasion'. He also had a letter from the present editor of the Cricket Society's Journal, J. D. Coldham, who was at that time doing his army service. Jessop replied to him in this way:

> Dear no. 143 etc etc etc
>
> Your name has a familiar sound reminding me of a J. Coldham who played for Norfolk and also of a comestible usually associated with Turkey and without points. . . .

The bantering approach which colours so much of Jessop's writing remained to the end. His days were spent in listening to music, a great deal of reading, and taking quiet strolls down the garden, for he seldom left the vicarage now. He continued to produce the odd article. In 1950 he wrote for *The Spectator* a piece on 'Cricket Memories' as well as a review of Plum Warner's book *Lord's*. In the following year he contributed an excellent story of W. G. Grace for the M.C.C. *Book for the Young Cricketer*. He was not forgotten, and in the summer of 1952 the West of England Home Service broadcast a thirty-five minute item called *Gilbert Jessop*, written by Harold Gardiner and produced by Alan Gibson, but it did not altogether please him, and the programme had to be postponed for several weeks while certain points were cleared up. For one thing, Jessop did not care for the original title of 'The Croucher' possibly because he may have regarded the many nicknames dubbed upon him by the Press as somewhat unseemly, and he never cared much for the adulation of the public. But of all the nicknames 'The Croucher' has stuck the longest, and as it has always been used with affection and honour I have used it for this book.

In June 1953 Jessop wrote a letter to *The Daily Telegraph* about fast bowling. He was still interested in the game and if he wanted to look back he had his many scrapbooks to look at: on his wall he had two favourite pictures, one the chart of his run-making in his great innings of 93 against South Africa in 1907, and the other a watercolour of his old bat and cricket gear called 'The end of the season', which had been painted by Charles Townsend's mother.

Mr. and Mrs. G. L. Jessop at Brecon House, Clevedon, about 1928.

In January 1953 his wife Millicent had died. They had been married for over fifty years, and though she does not appear much in the story the part she played in his life was all-important. They were a most devoted couple, and he must have missed her much during the time in which he outlived her until his own death on May 11, 1955 – just a week short of his eighty-first birthday. During the strain of his wife's last illness he had developed heart dropsy. The doctor kept this under control for more than two years, but when it grew worse, he had to take to his bed in March 1955, and he died peacefully a few weeks later.

His obituary notices were manifold, and *The Times* wrote a leader entitled 'There were giants in those days' which gave tribute to Jessop and to a great boxer Tommy Burns who died on the same day. 'They added to the gaiety of the nation by being personalities in play and they had the flair of getting themselves into the thick of suddenly dramatic events. . . . These are the men the muse of History leaves on record when she deigns to turn aside from graver things and chronicle sport.' Tributes flowed in from all quarters. The *Wisden* obituary spoke of Jessop as being 'A man of engaging manners, he was a charming companion, and like most truly great men modest to a degree.' Plum Warner said: 'He was a wonderful companion, it was a pleasure to play with him or against him. Most fittingly of all, perhaps, Jessop was celebrated in a poem by G. D. Martineau which appeared in *The Cricketer*:

OH, The Croucher has gone – and the mind goes back
To the glittering age of the blade's attack,
To a field fanning out as a man strode in
With a cap drawn down and a jutting chin;

And the bowler would pray as the crowd grew still,
For Jessop – aye, Jessop! – was on the kill . . .
That crouch at the crease was a fearsome thing,
Like a panther in pose for the flashing spring.

Till the fire-winged second of leaping strength,
When the tensile arms were a match for length,
When the drive was a spry-footed, fast-flung sweep,
And the cut was a blast over point – placed deep . . .

Oh, joy to have seen him in nineteen seven!
I trammed down to Hastings and walked into Heaven –
'Tis the Croucher – the Croucher.' The gay ring roared,
And the straw hats hurtled as the sixers soared.

He is gone; but I dream of his flailing drive
(While the in-field clusters, and all survive)
And a paean re-echoes on memory's lyre –
To the Croucher, who struck with a blade of fire!

It was not quite the last word. In 1957 Jessop's name was honoured by the placing of a plaque on the house he lived in at Mill Hill; a house at his old school, Cheltenham Grammar School, was named after him, and when Stevenage new town chose names for its roads one of them was to be called Jessop Road.

8

Jessop the Fielder

'A run saved is a run made.'

OLD CRICKET MAXIM

W. G. GRACE was a keen supporter of the old cricket maxim 'A run saved is a run made'. In the course of an innings great fielders can save some twenty or thirty runs, and so begin their own innings with a considerable credit before they have scored a single. C. B. Fry, when advocating the inclusion of Jessop in the England team to tour Australia in 1911–12, recalled how in an innings of 258 not out which he played against Gloucestershire Jessop had robbed him of some 60 runs; he had counted fifteen off-drives which Jessop stopped, but which would have beaten other fielders.

There have been a few fielders in the history of the game whose reputation has been so great that their very presence has caused batsmen to refrain from attempting a run which might normally be possible. Among this select few Jessop takes a high place, and the finest compliment paid to him as a fielder is probably that made by A. O. Jones in an article on fielding in *Cricket of Today* in 1905. He writes:

'It is an old motto 'Practice makes Perfect', but that does not hold good in cricket. Even the Master, W. G. Grace, who in my opinion was as much ahead of anyone else at cricket as John Roberts was at billiards (and that is saying a good deal), was not perfect. Perhaps the nearest thing to perfection is the fielding of G. L. Jessop. Even he misses catches. It is a treat to see him in the field stopping the hardest off-drives with ease, and returning the ball with marvellous accuracy. All cricketers should strive to attain the height of excellency he was attained, and could we only become half as good as he (and there is no reason why, with practice, we should not do so) we should hear less of the drastic alterations that are proposed in the rules of cricket, there would be fewer runs made, more matches would be finished, and the grand old game of cricket would become more popular than ever.'

The legend of Jessop's skill as a fielder still lives on, and in a recent article on fielding in *Country Life*, it is he who is described as the model cover fielder, and the drawing by Chevallier Tayler is given to show the thrilling power and accuracy of his famous under-the-shoulder throw. Other cover-points may have been as accurate – Hobbs, for example, on the Australian tour of 1911–12 actually threw out no less than 15 batsmen, and Plum Warner wrote of him: 'I have never seen a cover-point hit the wicket so often, his underhand throw being particularly deadly in this respect. In Hobbs we had a cover-point the equal of any fieldsman in that position I have ever seen. Not even G. L. Jessop at his best is his superior.'

So yet again Jessop is quoted as the touchstone of excellency. His lightning throw was the quintessence of attacking fielding, and it lived again in the displays of such as Constantine, Colin Bland, Clive Lloyd and Paul Sheahan. It is intensely exciting to the spectator and even more so to the batsman.

It has been mentioned that one of A. C. MacLaren's reasons for wanting Jessop to play in every Test match in which MacLaren was captain was the likelihood of his running out one or two of the top Australians, quite apart from the runs he saved when fielding at cover, or, as he more frequently did, at extra cover. 'From either position', to quote C. B. Fry, 'he almost always hit the wicket when he threw at it.'

There is a story about one of the very rare occasions when a throw from Jessop did not hit the wicket. He was once fielding to Jack Hobbs, who always delighted in stealing short runs. After taking an especially daring one, Hobbs said jokingly to Jessop: 'I hope you don't mind.' Jessop who did not think much of Hobbs's policy of taking continual singles instead of hitting the ball to the boundary, replied: 'I don't mind at all. I reckon it's two to one on me if you go on taking chances like that.' Hobbs said: 'No, I don't think so. I wouldn't attempt it unless I reckoned the odds were on me.' A little later, Hobbs went for another short single, but Jessop came in very fast and had Hobbs at his mercy several feet short of the crease. Luckily for him Jessop's throw just missed the wicket. So Hobbs survived and honours were even.

Jessop was always disappointed if his throw did not hit the stumps, and so too was many a bowler, who sometimes preferred to let the ball go by rather than put a hand to one of those thunderbolts.

There is a valuable comment on his skill in an article in *Wisden* for 1901 by D. L. A. Jephson. He is writing about the fielding or rather the misfielding of the county elevens of 1900. There are two counties only whose fielding he can praise, Kent and Gloucestershire, and for the latter the example of their captain is largely responsible. He writes: 'G. L. Jessop, besides having saved dozens of runs, has thrown out thirty or so batsmen. Readers of this will perhaps remark to themselves – "It is all very well, but how many runs has he lost shooting at the stumps?" Yes, very likely many have been lost, but think for a moment. What is a four or many fours on a good wicket compared to the dismissal of Ranjitsinhji, Fry, Abel or Hayward. Again, rare instances occur of a ball being thrown in well so that the wicket can be broken by the bowler or the stumper, arriving the fraction of a second too late. The batsman is in, whereas had the wicket been hit he would have walked slowly, miserably, probably discontentedly, to a seat in the pavilion.'

A fine example of Jessop's ability to snap up even the most unlikely chance is told of by A. A. Lilley who recalls how once at Hastings David Denton drove a ball very hard to Jessop at extra-cover, and followed up his stroke a few paces just in case there might be a possible run. Before he could get back to his crease, Jessop had returned the ball to Lilley behind the wicket, and Denton was out – run out, without even attempting to run. Such miraculous fielding no doubt produced in many batsmen a feeling that any ball hit in Jessop's direction could lead to trouble, and many times a batsman must have stayed safely at home when in fact a reasonable run could have been taken.

Jessop delighted in luring the batsman to his destruction, and his pace over the ground enabled him to stand deeper than normal. The batsman would take a chance but he was often doomed and surprised to find the ball breaking the wicket at what he thought was the 'safe' end, for Jessop had a habit of looking towards one end and throwing at the other. Plate X in Beldam and Fry's *Great Bowlers and Fielders* shows Jessop indulging in this subterfuge. Constantine was another who was able to trick batsmen like this, and, like Jessop, saw the fun of it.

S. M. J. Woods, in his *Reminiscences*, felt that as Jessop had said so little about himself in his own book *A Cricketer's Log* he must give a full appreciation of 'The greatest match-winner there ever was or will be. . . .' 'To start with he was the best cover-point ever seen. He saved thirty runs before ever going in to bat. I say thirty at least. Maybe it was fifty, as people were afraid to run if the ball went within fifteen yards of him.' Apart from the dangers of running to him there was always the thought that any ball hit even slightly off the ground might be snapped up and caught. In his twenty-one seasons it is calculated that he took over 450 catches, and though some of these were off his own bowling, the majority were taken in the cover area. 'He practically never misses a catch and he cramps all the runs on the off-side,' wrote P. F. Warner.

In the winter of 1901–2 A. C. MacLaren took a team to Australia, with Jessop a member of the side. The trip to Australia was Jessop's one and only major overseas tour, and after that he never went overseas again. The discomfort he suffered as a result of sea travel, even in the calmest conditions, quite outweighed the pleasures of the cricket. On the Australian tour, however, though he did not make many runs, his fielding was superb, as was the rest of the team's, and it made them very popular. After MacLaren's XI had won the first Test against Australia, *The Melbourne Evening Argus* talked of two of Jessop's catches as 'marvellous in their lightning-like rapidity', and said that 'Jessop's dash at a ball resembles nothing else but a greyhound trying to pick up a hare. Imagine, if you can, a cricketer of below the medium height, with something of the build of a wrestler, a suggestion of the rolling walk of a sailor, and you have the Gloucester captain'. I doubt if Jessop would have appreciated the reference to a sailor.

Some great fielders have shown a perpetual activity, a ceaseless energy, which persists all the time, but Jessop was not like this. Here is an impression of him from Albert Knight's *The Complete Cricketer*:

'Mr Jessop usually stands at extra-cover, and more magnificent stopping and more accurate returns than his one need not wish to see. Many fieldsmen – great and clever fieldsmen – give one the idea of a rushing mighty wind – they scintillate; you realise that some wonder-working machinery is on the move to turn out a curiously perfect product. Quite a number of fieldsmen are "busy" in this Martha-like and troubled way. Jessop, on the contrary, conveys the far-away air of immobility, but for his unresting eyes, which light up and seem to illumine the body as it wakes up for its panther-like glide. Both Jessop and John Gunn have an awkward look in the corner of the eye; there is just a soupçon of luring a batsman to his fall, a certain Mephistophelean air hangs about them, which seems to say to the needy batsman scraping for an odd run, "I am the Spirit of Denial".'

In earlier days Vernon Royle was regarded as the classic cover-point, and a story is told of Tom Emmett, the great Yorkshire character. He was primarily a bowler, but though not much of a batsman, delighted in taking daring short runs – but never to Vernon Royle. If his partner called him for a run, his reply was 'Noa! I tell thee I woan't go; it's gone to t'plaace.' 'T'plaace' always meant anywhere in the region of Vernon Royle. The presence of Jessop must have created for the batsman exactly the same dread feeling. Many an opposing captain delayed a declaration and lost a chance of winning a match through fear of how Jessop's hitting could upset all run-making calculation; even more opposing batsmen must have declined a run through fear of what might happen if he called 'yes', and Jessop were to pounce.

No cricketer has ever had so many poems written about him, and I could put together a whole book of those in which Jessop has been sung in various ways and with varying competence. Here is one which tells of the dangers of taking a run when the ball has gone near him, (and as I write I read of two England batsmen who dared to run to Clive Lloyd, paying the same penalty as many did to Jessop). It appeared in an issue of *The Athletic News*, with no authorship given:

An Unwritten Rule

Here's a cricket rule,
  Batsman, prithee, learn it
Sooth, a man's a fool
  Who'd disdain or spurn it:
'When you hit a ball
  Hard and straight to Jessop,
Do not run at all
  Or your stumps he'll mess up.'

Harmless quite he seems,
  Like a tabby blinking;
P'raps immersed in dreams –
  Of the game not thinking.
Ah, that's only guile –
  He's as keen as mustard.
Up to every wile,
  So, at least, I've just heard.

For that nonchalance
  Hides a purpose stern, boys:
He's not in a trance,
  As you'll swiftly learn, boys.
Try and steal a run –
  Then your grief you'll gulp it,
For as sure as a gun
  Down will go your 'pulpit'.

For with one sharp dash,
  Like a hawk descending,
Or a lightning flash,
  He will catch you bending.
Swoop! He's got the ball!
  Whish! It's in the wicket!
Fluke? Oh, not at all –
  That's Jessopian cricket.

Cover or mid-off –
  Seldom makes a blunder.
So my hat I doff
  To this Gloucester Wonder.
Pray be warned in time,
  Batsman young and airy;
Heed my friendly rhyme,
  And be very wary.

No writer has ever written about the whole art of fielding with such an analytical approach. Jessop was not one of those 'naturals' who have no idea how they achieve their performance. He studied the skills of fielding as closely as C. B. Fry studied the matter of batsmanship. 'Fielding – to my mind, the most important branch of the game of cricket – is also, alas! even by first-class players the most neglected. Some regard it as a necessary evil, and, therefore, to be put up with, since without it batting and bowling are not feasible. How many matches are lost, I wonder, through careless fielding? I should not like to say, lest I should be accused of exaggeration. Still, the fact remains that matches are lost, and will continue to be so as long as fielding is regarded in the light in which it is. The reason why it is held in such disrespect is not far to seek. It commences from one's school-days – namely, undue prominence given to batting and bowling. A selfish reason seems to crop up; one is able to see by the scorecard what success has resulted to one's efforts in batting or bowling; but it is not recorded how well or badly, as the case may be, one has fielded.'

When he went to America, Jessop studied baseball to see if he could learn anything from it which might be of value in cricket. 'The baseball player's long swift throwing is wonderful,' he said, 'and it is taught upon scientific lines by means of wooden spools strung like a bead on a cord. But I can see nothing superior in their catching and they can show nothing like our bare-handed slip catching with the ball coming to the fielder like greased lightning.' This last remark reminds me that Jessop and A. O. Jones sometimes used to practise short catches with a piece of soap instead of a ball.

In 1913 Jessop wrote an article in *London Opinion* called 'Throwing the cricket ball' in which he acknowledged that colonial cricket teams were superior over the English in throwing over a long distance, but were no better over short distances. The reason for this might well lie in the matter of climate. He deplored the passing of 'Throwing the cricket ball' as an athletic event, but agreed that unless it was practised properly there might be a risk of throwing the arm out. He wrote another long magazine article entitled

'The Knack of Throwing', profusely illustrated; he believed that the secret lay in being ready to pick up the ball before it was actually hit. 'The books tell us that we should pick up the ball and throw it in in one action, which is clearly an impossibility, but the ball can be so picked up that there is no pause before the action of the throw begins.' That is the reason why Jessop tended to pick up the ball with his arm fully extended.

In his book *Sporting Campaigner*, the late Brigadier M. A. Green gives a good example of the point Jessop makes about saving time by being ready to throw when the ball arrives. He says that in his first match for Gloucestershire in 1912 he was put to field in the deep, and felt frightened all the time in case something came his way. At lunchtime he hoped he had survived satisfactorily when Jessop came up to him and said: 'You are the slowest deep field we have had for ages.' Green states that he nearly wept at this remark, but Jessop went on to explain that though Green ran fast enough, he slowed up before throwing and so wasted time. Green took this to heart and later became an outstanding deep fielder.

Another unusual point Jessop discusses is the amount of ground covered by a fielder during an innings. He gives the following figures from his own experience, and they are figures I have never seen mentioned elsewhere.

'We have some critics who can never see any reason for first-class cricketers becoming weary and stale. But I'll be bound that they have not thought out the number of miles an ordinary fieldsman has to traipse even when changing at the end of each over. Taking my own personal experience, and speaking roughly, I should say that my usual position from the far wicket is anything from 30 to 40 yards when a slow bowler is sending them down, and about 20 to 25 yards when anything faster is being bowled. As the crow flies, that is about sixty yards to traverse each over. In an ordinary innings of 250 runs, some sixty-five overs would be bowled, perhaps less with some teams. Well, it's nearer three miles than two to walk at the end of that innings. With a left-hander or two to worry one, it is considerably more. No wonder so many first-class cricketers begin to sigh for the joys of less excessive exercise.'

When he comes to talk about Catching he makes a point seldom understood by most spectators or pressmen, namely the distinction between a chance and a catch. A chance is one which *might* be accepted, while a catch is one which *should* be accepted. In an article written in his last season 1914 he wrote:

'Missed catches are much in evidence. I have never seen so many as this season. It has been my hobby for some time past to keep a record of catches which have gone astray – bona fide catches, and not opportunities which are vaguely alluded to as chances. During the last five years in matches in which

I have participated, the average has never been less than four. Up to date this year I see by my note-book that this average per match is exactly doubled. I have never been in a match in which every chance was successfully taken though many in which one side has had no fault.' He goes on to say that he cannot recall more than thirty centuries which have been altogether faultless. 'If anything were required to emphasise the importance of good fielding, this fact alone should do so.'

Among the difficulties facing a fielder are the awkward backgrounds caused by towering stands or buildings. He writes: 'Unless a fielder gets a fair sight of the ball anything may happen – with the odds against him. The consistently bad fieldsman is a nuisance. The slack one is an excrescence, and as such should be removed. For the fieldsman with a spurious reputation who shirks the desperate chance for fear that a "miss" should be chalked up against his record I have no use whatever.

'As an instance of a desperate chance meeting with a just reward I shall never forget a catch made by C. O. H. Sewell at Bristol in 1898. Middlesex was the visiting team; the ball was hit low and tremendously hard in the direction of long-on by C. M. Wells. Until I saw Sewell dashing in to meet it I never realised it was a possible chance. However, by flinging himself forward full length on the ground he just managed to hold the ball, incidentally depriving his elbows for the time being of a fairish portion of skin. Nine players out of ten would have been satisfied to have fielded the ball on the long hop. That catch to me stands out as the most brilliant I ever saw.'

Another such catch made out of a bare half-chance was one made by himself, and he describes it simply to explain the mechanics of such a catch. It was made in Jessop's first Gentlemen *v.* Players match at Lord's in 1897: 'One of the favourite shots of George Hirst used to be a glorious full-blooded welt towards extra-cover, and when he properly middled it the ball was not long before it reached the boundary. On this occasion George lashed out at a ball from Mr J. R. Mason who was bowling from the pavilion end, caught it fair and square in the middle of the bat and then paused – with that momentary halt which always accompanies a lusty effort – to observe developments. If the ground had been a perfectly flat one the ball must have carried the spot on which I was standing, but, swinging up the hill a trifle, it became then a matter of calculation as to whether one would be able to leap high enough. The leap was made successfully, the ball striking the tip of the fingers, bouncing from thence straight up in the air, to be clutched eventually by the two hands. If ever a man had reason to claim the injustice of fate, of a surety it was George Hirst at that moment, for few strokes have better deserved the reward of a boundary.'

Jessop was convinced that by proper regular practice everyone could improve his fielding, but it required courage as well as application. On some days his hands were black and blue after stopping some tremendous drives. But courage alone was not enough, for a fielder had to understand the importance of good fielding, with its first principle that a run saved was the equivalent of a run made. As with so many other things, it was W. G. Grace who had taught Jessop the lesson that even against much stronger teams a successful result could sometimes be gained by holding catches and saving runs. It is no surprise to find Jessop uttering the words:

'Fielding has ever been to me the most attractive feature of cricket'.

9

Writer and Reformer

'A good deal of enjoyment is obtained from the concoction of an article.'

G. L. J.

IF it were asked: 'How did Jessop earn his living?' the reply would have to be that he did a great deal of free-lance journalism. There exist copies of or references to many of his articles, and no doubt there is much more hidden among the pages of untraced newspapers and magazines. There was far greater scope for such publication in his day than there is now.

It would seem that his span of writing ranges from 1897 to 1953, and that his opening shot as a journalist was an article in *The National Review* for October 1897 on the matter of 'Run getting'. Two years later he wrote some articles about batting for the *Cambridge Independent Press*. He was at that time captain of the University side, and the second article was published on the day he first appeared for England.

The following year *The Windsor Magazine* produced the first of his many articles on the matter of fielding. By the end of 1903 he had not only written two books on cricket, but had become a regular contributor to *The Daily Mail*, for whom he wrote weekly notes on cricket for several years. This connection may have started when he sent home a report to the paper on the arrival and reception of A. C. MacLaren's team which toured Australia in 1901–2. He was virtually on the staff, and among his reports from the years 1903–5 are a report of a Southern League soccer match, some professional golf, a wrestling match and the Inter-Varsity Athletics meeting of 1905.

At about this time a number of cricketers were writing for the papers, and *The Bystander* notes that C. B. Fry, apart from being top of the batting averages, was easily the most prolific of the new tribe of cricketing-journalists. A. C. MacLaren comes a bad second on the list, with A. O. Jones, J. T. Tyldesley, Tom Hayward, Ranjitsinhji and P. F. Warner among occasional contributors. In 1909 the great Australian hitter Alan Marshal who was playing for Surrey produced a cricket article with the own illustrations.

Albert Knight, the most literary of all cricket professionals, was also an active Christian, who would stand for a moment in silent prayer after taking his guard – an action which Walter Brearley regarded as unfair, and worthy to be reported to M.C.C.

On May 12, 1904, *Punch* produced an amusing drawing by Bernard Partridge showing two batsmen running between the wickets scribbling notes as they went. The caption was 'Most of our prominent cricketers are now engaged as expert reporters by various journals'. Jessop was clearly regarded as one of the foremost of these. Many readers enjoyed such journalism, and felt that a player's comments put them truly into the picture. There were a few, nevertheless, who regarded it as unseemly for amateurs to write about the game when they were still actively engaged in it. Among these was the Hon. F. S. Jackson, who was himself a director of a national newspaper. In his Open Letter to Jackson, Jessop refers to this matter in the following words:

'As a director of an influential newspaper you have some connection with journalism, which makes me wonder why you are unsympathetic with him who wields the willow while wielding the pen. The limited-income amateur, my dear Jacker, is just as enthusiastic on the game as he who is more fortunately placed. In order to still continue his favourite pastime, he has three courses open to him. Firstly, if he is good enough, he may induce the authorities to appoint him to an assistant secretaryship; secondly, if he has any ability whatever in the direction of putting his thoughts on paper he can accept the opportunity of doing so; and lastly, he may become a professional. It may be hard for you to believe it, but a good deal of enjoyment is obtained from the concocting of an article, or the writing of such a letter, for instance, as this.

'The public having viewed you through the spectacles of the sporting journalist for many years, like to read what one fellow-cricketer thinks of another. Some fellow-cricketers may not like it, but only they who are possessed of an over-sensitive cuticle. There is this to be said of the journalistic cricketer – his practical experience of the most delightful of games leads him to take a more charitable view of affairs than he who is "stewing" for hours in a hen coop which does duty on some grounds for a press-box.

'I am sure you will pardon this digression, my dear Jacker, for this personally is the only bone I have to pick with you in any respect whatever.'

One relevant point made by Jessop was that he enjoyed writing for its own sake, as is apparent from the gusto and verve he brought to it.

As an example of his zest, and not by any means negligible erudition, the opening passage of his Open Letter to Jonah (A. O. Jones) and his team about to tour Australia in 1907–8 comes to mind:

> My dear Jonah,
>
> 'Caelum non animum, qui trans mare currunt.' You with your knowledge of Horace will at once see the point of my greeting. But it may be that the classics of Hobbs, Hardstaff & Co may have become a trifle rusty, and accordingly I will interpret: 'They change their sky, not their spirit, who run across the sea.'

Later, in speaking of the natural bowling skill of Sydney Barnes, Jessop makes the apt comment: 'Barnes nascitur, non fit.'

Commenting on the series of Open Letters of 1906 and 1907 Sir Home Gordon wrote: 'Jessop is a capable journalist of the button-holing type who relies for effect upon personal details. These abounded in his readable open letters, which usually said very little in a decidedly interesting column. The objection which was raised to his criticism shows that a sense of humour entirely depends upon the point of view.' I have mentioned some of his limericks, including the excellent one about Brearley, and here is another about C. B. Fry, who was no-balled for throwing by the umpire Jim Phillips:

> There was a young batsman named Fry
> Who at bowling oft thought he would try
> Till an umpire named Jim,
> Who was looking at him
> Said: 'Good heavens, I call that a shy!'

Jessop's delight in limericks led him to be asked to judge a limerick competition for some paper, and at that time G. J. V. Weigall wrote of him: 'Of course Jessop is a man of letters nowadays. I believe he is one of the finest judges of limericks in England.' An article on County Captains in *The Daily Mail* in 1908 supports this by saying: 'Mr Jessop, captain of Gloucestershire, is as good a judge of a run as he is of a Limerick, and that is saying a good deal.' He certainly had a nice wit as we know from the reception given to his after-dinner speeches, and I like the reply he once made to a cabby, who seeing Jessop making his way towards the cricket ground, called out 'Keb, sir – get you there quick! to which Jessop's reply was: 'No thanks, I'm in a hurry!'

Jessop's notebooks (including a half-used exercise book of his son's) are full of odd bits of writing, such as replying to the greetings of a tiresome stranger: 'I'm sure I've met you somewhere', with the words: 'Quite possibly, I've been there often', or puns like 'It's not so good to break one's neck as it is to crick-it', He obviously enjoyed playing about with words, and we come across such scraps of verse as:

Upon the piano she lbs (pounds)
Makes most deafening sbs
And the uproar that reigns
The Policeman compleigns
Keeps him nightly awake on his rbs.

and

An impudent fellow from Hawarden (harden)
Inquired without begging his pawarden
Of the learned Colquhoun
If the man in the moquhoun
Spent his knights in a nobleman's gawarden.

On which the fire-eating Earl Cholmondeley
Replied, as he looked at him glolmondeley,
With a glance at his neighbour,
Unsheathing his seighbour,
That the question was deuced uncolmondeley.

Sometimes his verses are more Wilsonian in philosophy, such as:

When all your ships are cast ashore
And trouble's knocking at the door,
You mustn't think it's time to quit –
Just light your pipe and smoke a bit.

It is usually depressing to quote puns out of context, but two Jessopian examples are: 'No good ever came out of grousing – except in August', and when writing about the superstitions of some cricketers he says: 'One player used to keep a cat's paw as a mascot: it goes without saying that he came from FURRING parts.' When once referring to his terrible tendency to seasickness he remarked: 'I hold the belt – gold or otherwise – for the championship as the worst sea traveller of the cricket world. Despite rumours which have REACHED – horrible word – me about George Hirst being no slouch in this direction.'

It may be said that limericks, puns, and Latin tags were the stock in trade of any writer of Jessop's day, but he certainly makes the most of them. He also shows a real feeling for words, as in his reference to Bosanquet's new 'mystery' breaks as PIFFLERS, and in his open letter to himself his remark about the 'AUDIBLE GRIN' which came over the face of spectators as he emerged from the pavilion is very telling.

His *Daily Mail* connection lasted on well. In 1921 he did daily reports on the Test matches, and wrote reports and comments on the 1926 series. He became captain of the Daily Mail Cricket Club, and made many friends there. He was also a member of the United Press Cricket Club, and made speeches at its functions.

Another regular commission was a series of weekly articles for *London Opinion*, which he first contributed to in 1910, when he prophesied that Alletson would shortly produce a really memorable innings, and he did so the following year. Right up to 1914 Jessop produced articles for *London Opinion* covering not only cricket, but golf, rugger, athletics, boxing and the Boat Race. They were all very readable.

Jessop's all-round interest in games caused him to be asked to write the introduction to a book called *Outdoor Sports* (Cassell, 1912, 3s. 6d.) which was a guide to beginners in all open-air sports and pastimes. Jessop, linking games and character, ends with the sentence: 'Remember that those qualities which go to build up any success that a boy may attain at any game will not desert him in the more serious battle of life. And do not forget that although every game is hedged in with restrictions, it is better to regard the spirit of the game rather than the letter of the law.'

In 1913 Jessop did a series of cricket notes for *London Budget*, and *Pearson's Magazine* and *Pearson's Weekly*, *The Illustrated Sporting Budget*, *Sporting Pictorial*, *The Sketch*, *Golf Illustrated*, *The Sunday Observer*, and *The Globe* were among others he wrote for. His scrapbooks contain a great many articles, but there is not often information to say where or when they appeared. They cover such diverse cricket topics as: 'How to keep fit?' 'Test matches I have played in',

'Does fast scoring pay?' 'Cares of captaincy', 'Trundling and trundlers', 'The L.B.W. rule', 'The demoralisation of bowlers', 'The toss', 'How to hit', and several on fielding and wicket-keeping.

One of Jessop's early notebooks is interesting because it contains all sorts of bits and pieces written out in pencil. These range from match arrangements from his Cambridge days, and pages with the names of horses he had bet on, to odd anagrams made up for fun, such as: 'Abstemiousness: One Bass Suits me', 'Complications: sit in camp cool', 'Railway station: Train Away, I lost'; and there is a poem which runs:

If a man would drop his h's,
It would make the righteous glad,
For the place of large dimensions
That is paved with good intentions,
Wouldn't sound one half as bad.

There is another poem about the exploits of a Cambridge friend who, after wrecking a billiard table with a mis-cue, goes to London, and is involved with another sort of Miss-Q. There are also household accounts (undated) which read:

Rent	£80	
Maid	26	
Washing	20	16
Gas	8	
Coals and Firing	11	5
Housekeeping	156	
Lunch and Fares	50	
	£352	1

There are details of the original membership of the Cricketers' Golfing Society, founded on March 22, 1905, of which he was the first secretary and treasurer. This is almost the only date in the book. This notebook also contains information about the fees he received for some of his writings. For editing the cricket book published by Pearson he got £30, for one season's series of thirteen articles in *The Daily Mail* he was paid 3 guineas a time. *Pearson's Magazine* paid him the then princely sum of £25 for his article on 'The American Reporter'. *The Boy's Own Paper*, and *The Golden Penny* each gave him £3 for unspecified articles, while for an article on 'Fielding' in the 'Country Life' Book of *Cricket* he writes 'ask £20'. There are original notes and rough copies of several articles of which we have the final printed version in other books of cuttings, but, alas, we do not have such projected articles as 'Cranks in Cricket', or 'How it feels to make a Test Century', which perhaps lie somewhere in the pages of some unknown magazine.

Jessop's journalism certainly kept him busy, and must have provided a reasonably steady income. After the War, when he had recovered sufficiently from his illness he produced the Fielding Section for the 1920 edition of the Badminton Library, and wrote regular weekly columns for *The Daily Sketch* in 1919–20, and *The Daily Mirror* in 1921. The birth of *The Cricketer* in the same year gave him a chance to produce weekly reminiscenses at five guineas a time, and in the following season it carried excerpts from his forthcoming autobiography. He continued to write occasional articles for *The Cricketer* after that, the last being in 1928. The publication of his autobiography *A Cricketer's Log* in the autumn of 1922 established his reputation as a writer. The review in the *Western Daily Press* says 'The book expresses the man – the great cricketer always referred to with esteem and admiration as "The Idol". To those who have had the pleasure of his acquaintanceship, Mr Jessop is a charming companion. On the cricket field he is as it were a god unto himself; in the drawing room he is equally attractive. His book is a log of his own career, but he keeps himself always in the background, referring with almost slighting briefness to his own great performances.' *The Times* says that 'except in his opening pages Mr Jessop rarely tells us anything of himself, or his experiences outside the cricket field'. It is the opening passages about his childhood days which all the critics seemed to enjoy, and they also appreciated Jessop's hero-worship of W. G. Grace, and the anecdotes about him. The general feeling was that 'the charm of the book lies in the happy outlook of a truly happy cricketer', and that the style of his writing was as breezy as that of his own cricket. There is enough quotation of *A Cricketer's Log* in this book to show what that means, though Neville Cardus in *The Guardian* thought there was 'too much journalese and too little Jessop'. *A Cricketer's Log* had an edition of 5,000 copies and brought *Jessop* in little more than £250.

Not long after its publication Jessop was approached by a publisher to write another book to be called *Cricket with the Lid off*, and to contain stories of all the disagreements and quarrels of the last thirty years in first-class cricket. He did not, predictably, accept this offer.

By 1924 Jessop was now established in his job as part-time secretary of Edgware Golf Club. He was paid £250 a year, and while he had to be present at week-ends, he could do the rest of the work in his own time. He could go to the club in the morning, deal with his correspondence, and then catch a tram from outside the golf club that took him straight to Lord's. He also went to the Oval and saw a fair amount of cricket in the years he was at Edgware. The accessibility of the club was a great asset. In 1926 he was covering the

Australian tour for *The Daily Mail* and had to travel more widely, which did not suit him, and he had to give it up. At about this time he began a connection with *The Manchester Evening News* that went on regularly until the mid-1930s. His agents Christy and Moore managed to get many of his articles syndicated, and these might appear in some half-a-dozen widely dispersed areas. At one time he let the Army on the Rhine have his articles for the special price of 10s. a week.

In 1925 Jessop had written a book for Harrap's 'Masters of Sports' series called *Cricket and How to Play It*, and illustrated it with photographs from the Beldam and Fry book. For the fielding section he overcame his natural modesty to the extent of using a photo of himself, and it has the rather odd caption of 'Under the shoulder throw by one who shall be nameless'.

He continued to produce many casual pieces, and here is a typical piece called 'Memories of Ranji':

'Ranji was the most brilliant figure in what I believe was cricket's most brilliant period. It was during the 'nineties that cricket reached its pinnacle as a national game and as a synonym of good sportsmanship. Ranji was one of the men who helped to put it there.

'On the cricket field he was magnetic to the finger-tips – and his bat became magnetic too. From the moment he stepped out of the pavilion he drew all eyes and held them. No one who saw him bat will ever forget it. He was the first man I ever knew who wore silk shirts, and there was something almost romantic about the very flow of his sleeves and the curves of his shoulders. He drew the crowds wherever he went, and at the height of his cricket days the shops in Brighton would empty if he pased along the street. Everyone wanted to see him. Whenever I bowled against him I felt as if he were impregnable. My impression was, 'I shall never get this man out'. Yet I had once bowled him for a duck. I think that on the technical side his finest equipment was his eye. I played often with him and often against him, and it always seemed to me that his eye was infallible. It showed itself later in his excellence as a shot.

'It was the speed and judgment of his eye that enabled him to reach such perfection in his leg-glide. He was the originator of that stroke. He has had many copyists since, but no one has approached his perfection in it. I never heard him complain of a wicket, and I do not believe he ever did. It have seen him make centuries on wickets that other men would regard as impossible. He had not a special reputation as a fast scorer, but when I batted with him at a Hastings Festival he scored much faster than I did.

'I never heard him say an ill word of any player, whether on his own or on his opponents' side. That's a fine epitaph for a cricketer.

'He was a severe critic of his own game. After getting 100 he would go out and practise as hard as if he had got a duck. He was upset for a whole day once when he ran A. C. MacLaren out.

'But behind all the superb brilliance of his technique and the glamour of his personality were supreme gifts of character. He was a perfect sportsman. He was a hero to me before I ever met him on the cricket field; he remained scarcely less of a hero through all the years that followed.

'He took a lofty view of the game. He believed in the team spirit, and what cricket could do to strengthen it, not only in the man but in the Empire. It was for that reason that he encouraged it so patiently and so enthusiastically in India. It was for that reason, too, that he took such trouble to develop his young relations as cricketers.

'It is a great pleasure to know that Duleepsinhji is now not only a great asset to English cricket, but is the nearest approach in these days to the now almost legendary brilliance of his uncle.'

In 1920 Jessop had been associated with J. B. Salmond in the editing of *The Book of School Sports*, published by T. Nelson, and in 1935 this book was re-issued. By this time Jessop's health was beginning to deteriorate again, and he published little more, though in 1945 there were some articles in the *Bristol Evening Post*.

It might well be thought from this considerable body of journalism that Jessop's writings were confined entirely to sport, and mainly cricket. But from quite early on he obviously enjoyed 'creative' writing of various kinds. We have among his cuttings a very odd little piece which is undated, but which I believe to date from about the turn of the century. It is difficult to associate the cool demoraliser of bowlers with such surrealist fantasy:

Extraordinary Adventures

'I stood on the deck of the steamer, with my wife on my arm and my children round me. We were sailing along with delightfully even motion over the level waters; everyone was on deck enjoying the sunshine; some were reading, others smoking, others dozing, when suddenly all were startled by an agonized cry, those that sat down stood up, and those that stood up sat down. The man at the helm rushed madly forward and shouted 'We're nearing earth fast; throw out the sandbags', and seizing my youngest child by the arm he hurled him over the car; my wife rushed forward, snatched at his boots and then fell shrieking after him. Just then the first fire engine arrived and deluged the whole place with water; huge masses of sparks flew up and volumes of smoke curled through the ancient trees. A woman shouted for help from the top of the tower; to seize a ladder and place it against the side was the work of half an hour, and I ran lightly up the steps and caught the fainting form in my arms; just as the infuriated Zulus broke from their ambush and rushed upon us, hurling tomahawks and waving assegais. How fierce they looked in the cold white light of the morning, with their teeth gleaming, and their feathers fluttering in the breeze. How should we stem this human tide? We put our rifles to our shoulders and fired; a few fell, the rest rushed madly forward, fortunately we were roped together otherwise the fall might have proved serious; as it was I firmly planted my ice axe, and disengaging my other hand hit him with full force between the eyes. He fell, but alas, too late; the express was already tearing over the bridge at eighty miles an hour; the points were open; and they lay in front. What was to be done? I seized both oars firmly in my hands and keeping her nose well up into the wind, stuck my knees in the saddle and cleared the gate in safety; the rest of the field were far behind; the race was in my own hands, when suddenly the mainmast snapped with a loud report and sent me sprawling, while the goaded animal rose on his haunches to make one final spring. I knew my last hour was come. I closed my eyes and thought of home. Just then a hansom cab drove up: I shook the two policemen from me and jumped inside, and the crowd cheered and waved their hats as I rode home an easy winner by two pounds seven and tenpence.'

Very different in content but equally inventive was a piece from *The Athletic News* called 'Some mistaken vocations' in which well-known cricketers were placed in other occupations with recommendations by Jessop. Tom Hayward becomes a Channel Pilot, A. C. MacLaren an Arctic explorer, W. Brearley the Secretary of a Benevolent Society, George Hirst Mine Host of a first-class hotel, W. G. Grace an Egyptian Sirdar, and so on.

In 1908 Jessop wrote for *C. B. Fry's Magazine* what was claimed as his first-ever short story, a piece about golf called 'Baited Bunker'. In 1909, when he was recovering from his accident in the Test match, he wrote a cricket short story for the same magazine. One of his notebooks also contains a 1,000-word fantasy called 'On the Shelf' by a Cricket Bat who holds a long conversation with other discarded cricket equipment.

During the War years Jessop had correspondence with Gunby Hadath, the writer of school stories, over the possible publication of a boys' annual based upon the idea of *Herbert Strang's Annual* to be called 'G. L. Jessop's Annual', and the same letter also has something about a playlet of Jessop's which would have to be postponed until the war was over. We learn later that the idea of the Annual was 'not feasible for the moment', and in fact nothing came of it.

In 1919 Jessop was in touch with the publisher T. Nelson about a school story to be called '*Arthur Peck's Sacrifice*'. It is written in the manner of

P. G. Wodehouse's school stories and tells of adventures at Leckenham School, which seems to have been suggested by Jessop's native Cheltenham for it is 'a town in a hollow, chiefly residential, for service folk'. That excellent artist H. M. Brock provided the illustrations.

Four years later Jessop produced another novel for boys called *Cresley of Cressingham* (Cassell, 6s.), all about a promising cricketer who leaves school to investigate an Australian mine in which his late father had invested all his money. He finds that dirty work is going on, defeats a prizefighter with a deft upper cut, saves the life of a beautiful girl, and by a miraculous stroke of luck gets the last place in an M.C.C. team that is playing a Test match at Adelaide. There is plenty of action both on and off the cricket field, and the hero, for all his high principles 'to play the game', is not a prig. It is a pity Jessop did not write more such tales, but he did produce a few short stories, one of which 'The Alligator God' (set in Africa) appeared in a volume of stories published by Collins in 1929. There is another story set in West Africa, and we have the MSS. of several school short stories such as 'An Adventurous Term', 'The Duffer', 'Dot and Carry One', 'The Mug' (set in Leckenham College), and 'The Biter Bit'. There is correspondence about the use of some of these in certain boys' annuals, but I have not been able to trace their appearance.

Jessop always took great satisfaction that the writing appearing under his name was in fact written by him. There was one occasion, however, and one only, when his name appeared over a piece of writing which he was not entirely responsible for. In about 1904 *The Daily Mail* decided to make a feature of a great All-in Wrestling match between a Turk called Medrali and a famous German named Hackenschmidt. The bout was to take place at the Albert Hall, and the paper put aside a full column on the front page for a report of it.

For some reason Jessop was detailed to cover the great contest, and went along with a friend. Within a couple of minutes one of the contestants broke a wrist and the bout was over. Jessop was faced with the prospect of filling a full front-page column, and not much action to write about. He took his friend home, set him down with a bottle of whisky, and asked him to help out by producing something. The friend – Edgar Wallace – readily obliged, and next day 'Jessop's' account of the big fight was regarded as a great success.

In 1901 a reporter from *Cassell's Magazine* came to interview Jessop, with some trepidation, because Jessop was popularily supposed to keep a bulldog for the purpose of warning off unauthorised visitors. The bulldog, however, was not in evidence, and Jessop agreed to talk so long as the question of 'throwing' bowlers was not mentioned. When asked about the matter of drawn matches, Jessop said that he felt very strongly about them, and that county cricket would die if reforms were not soon adopted, since spectators were bored by seeing so many matches left unfinished.

Nearly every cricketer had his own ideas about what should be done, but he himself thought that three simple reforms would help significantly. These were, let every match be started at 11.0 o'clock on each day and omit the tea interval, stop the 'doctoring' of wickets, and improve the standard of fielding.

One of his earliest 'causes' was the proposal to widen the bowling crease from 6 ft 8 inches to 8 ft 8 inches, which M.C.C. accepted as an amendment in law in 1902. But the cricket reform which he most constantly urged as that of starting first-class matches on a Friday or Saturday, instead of the Monday and Thursday which was the custom. In 1905 F. E. Lacey, the M.C.C. secretary, wrote to Jessop to remind him that this matter had been mooted for several years, and suggested that he should air the proposal, and find out the pros and cons, by means of his influence as a cricket writer. As secretary of M.C.C. Lacey could not himself raise a matter he supported, but Jessop could. Jessop took up the cause with great energy in his columns in *The Daily Mail*. It was generally agreed that the counties would benefit financially from providing cricket on a Saturday afternoon. The chief objectors were certain amateurs, who felt that to have to spend a Sunday in some industrial town, when they could be at home on their estates, would be a fate worse than death. Others felt that the professionals should have a quiet Sunday at home, and that travelling might be more difficult.

Though Jessop continued to plead the cause, it was not until 1912 that the experiment of a Saturday start was given a try. It immediately proved successful. But, as Jessop states in his column in *London Opinion* of July 6, 1912, even though it was a proved success 'there is a certain shyness or selfishness (what you will) among the richer counties which has prevented the innovation being persevered with. Give the working man a chance to see guaranteed cricket on Saturday afternoon and he will not be slow to take it.' Thanks to Jessop's efforts, in 1913 Middlesex, Surrey and Essex were ready to give it a try ,and the practice was likely to have become generally adopted in 1915 if the War had not prevented it. By 1920 the Saturday start was accepted, so Jessop's efforts triumphed in the end.

Even as early as 1904 Jessop was well-enough known as a reformer for *Punch* to include his name in a burlesque symposium of imaginary new magazines run by famous men on the lines of *C. B. Fry's Magazine*. The names included Winston Churchill, G. K. Chesterton, Hugh Cecil and Jessop, whose magazine was heralded as:

JESSOP'S JOURNAL

The organ of cricket reform

Edited by Gilbert Jessop C.B.

Read the Editor's sensational article

'SHOULD ROLLERS BE RUBBER TYRED?'

On another occasion *Punch* did another burlesque on Jessop in which they attributed to him imaginary articles in *The Daily Mail*, one of which dealt with the matter of RAIN, and suggests that tenders should be obtained from Maxim, Edison, Marconi and H. G. Wells on the matter of how to stop rain from falling during a cricket match. It was also suggested that in view of the increasing amount of 'ducks' being scored, an underground tunnel from the wicket to the pavilion should be made available for all those who suffered the sad experience of being out for nought. Another need was an interval every 15 minutes to allow the many cricket-playing journalists time to jot down their impressions of play on the spot. Umpires should be made to carry notebooks and telegraph forms. *Punch* had plenty of fun over Jessop and he no doubt enjoyed it, too, since it helped to establish his place as a reformer.

Another of Jessop's ideas was that of pooling gate-money at home and away matches – an idea the richer counties had little use for, though in 1902 Jessop persuaded some of Gloucestershire's opponents to give it a try, and Warwickshire for a number of years had a gate-pooling arrangement with Gloucestershire, on the condition that Jessop himself played in both matches. He was always a favourite with Warwickshire, and when they won the championship in 1911 he was chosen as chief speaker at the celebration dinner.

In his Open Letter to himself in 1906 he admits that it is no wonder that some of his radical reforms did not meet with favour with the establishment, and he sometimes made it clear that he felt Cricket, like the Jockey Club then and now, was the last resort of the ostrich. 'It is time for a radical change if we are to bring back our deserters once more to the fold', he wrote despairingly.

This particular remark was caused by the reluctant steps taken to amend the Declaration Law. Jessop felt that restrictions on declaration only encouraged big scores, which brought with them the inevitable drawn games, both of which were the bugbears of the early 1900s, when the batsmen were having all too easy a time.

Jessop considered the the publication of averages should be cut down to once a month, as they were very misleading, and even harmful, if they influenced a batsman's play.

Many of Jessop's ideas were for the purpose of removing anomalies, such as Test matches in England being usually of only three days duration, whereas in Australia more days were allowed. Conditions should be the same in both countries, even if it meant reducing the number of matches, but playing them to a finish. Another matter discussed in 1905 was the abolition of the toss in favour of allowing the visitors always to have choice of innings. Jessop constantly urged reform in the matter of the toss and said that there was no reason why tossing in *every* match should not be done away with. In the 1901–2 tour of Australia A. C. MacLaren did suggest that, after tossing for the first Test match, the choice in the other four should be alternate, but the Australians would not agree with this. To the argument that the toss always evens out over a long period, Jessop said that his own winning of the toss was more like one in three than one in two. Another correspondent suggested that the Appeal should be abolished, and the decision left to the umpires, but Jessop pointed out that if such a practice were to be adopted in all levels of cricket, then matches on the village green would be subject more to a revolution than a reformation.

The payment of players was another matter Jessop considered. Although he realised that they could not hope to earn the same rates as those given to some footballers, he thought there should be a sliding scale, and that payment made to those on overseas tours should not be a flat rate but one proportionate to their experience. In about 1903 he was the first county captain to introduce winter pay for the professionals at a rate of 30s. a week, and he always kept in touch with certain jobs, such as those offered by coal-merchants who needed extra help in the winter months, and would be ready to take on the pros for the winter. It was the old tradition that during the cricket season talent money would be given automatically to professionals who made scores of 50 or 100, or took a certain amount of wickets, but Jessop was against this type of bonus, as it too often led to selfish play by players anxious to reach the magic figure, without regard for the state of the game. Jessop thus became the forerunner of those who supported a system by which points were allotted to each player for every match, and these points eventually decided the talent money for the season.

As might be expected, Jessop had plenty to say about the organisation of the County Championship, which he believed to be nonsensical unless every county played every other county. If that was too difficult, then fixtures might have to be reduced to two-day matches (as in 1919), which would give more opportunity for valuable Test Trials, and other regional matches, with chances for Scotland, Wales and Ireland.

As early as 1910 Hampshire suggested having a county cup contest on a knock-out basis, and Jessop strongly supported it in 1914 and 1919. It was not, however, until the Gillette Cup started that full-scale cup contest took place. County qualification was another matter discussed, and Jessop was in favour of allowing school residence to count as acceptable qualification.

The perennial lbw law controversy was as active in the early 1900s as it is now, and Jessop was all for making decisions easier for umpires, possibly by marking lines right down the wicket from stump to stump. Another suggestion to counter the high scoring was the addition of an extra stump, and in a practice match between Jessop's XI and A. G. Powell's XI at Bristol in 1909 four stumps were used instead of three.

From his earliest days of cricket journalism, right to his last years, Jessop was always ready to discuss anything which might benefit the game. But, as he pointed out in one of his weekly articles in *London Opinion* in 1912, there had in the last twenty years been very few changes in the Law, the only ones being 1. the widening of the bowling crease, 2. the right to declare at any time on the second day, and 3. the option to use a new ball after 200 runs. Swerve bowling had been much cultivated after the example of such exponents as George Hirst, J. B. King, Fred Roberts and others, and some regarded the sanction of a new ball after 200 runs as highly undesirable. 'I can well fancy', said Jessop, 'many of those who regard the swerve as a doubtful blessing' muttering to themselves 'Facilis descensus Averno'.

It was the spectators who wanted to alter things to make the game more exciting to them, and Jessop wisely addressed them in an article called 'Cricket Isn't Dull' which appeared in *Pearson's Magazine* in 1914. The content of it is well expressed in the following set of notes which I found in a scrapbook. This is how they read:

> People think cricket dull. It isn't, really.
> It might however be improved and made brighter.
> Schemes which have been tried.
> Schemes which have been suggested.
> Why some are worth trying, why others useless.
> How I would improve it.
> Still, it's a splendid game as it is.
> The trouble is that people don't understand its fine points.
> Fine points made easy:
> a How a batsman's pet stroke is blocked.
> b Why batsmen leave certain balls alone.
> c Why bowlers don't bowl at the stumps.
> d Why so many catches are dropped.
> e When pad play is necessary.

It is an admirable article, illustrated with clarifying diagrams. Jessop realised that the players' game and the game witnessed by spectators were not always in accord. His last word on the problem was expressed in his usual clear-thinking and entertaining manner:

'The game is good enough for the players anyhow, and the less tinkering done with the implements the better. Those people who regard a cricket match as a spectacle ONLY are rather apt to become a trifle disappointed when matters do not happen rapidly. Either wickets must fall or runs must come quickly. The science of the game does not appeal to them; and against the cautious batsman they harbour almost a personal resentment. And then it is we hear of suggestions likely to improve cricket – of course from the spectator's point of view. I never read of such improving hints without thinking of the little girl's gift of a Bible to her grandmother, wherein, in order to improve the occasion, she inscribed therein 'With the author's compliments'.

10

A Few Facts

'Statisticians are anathema to me.'

G. L. J.

THOUGH Jessop disliked all facts and figures, and thought that all that mattered were the runs necessary to win a match ('and matches are won by runs and not by style'), his performances were often so remarkable that even the reading of them is magic. Here are a few details of his career, (see Table opposite).

This career average of 32·63 may not sound exceptional, but in the early years he was regarded chiefly as a bowler and was not yet interested in making big scores. If it is remembered too that quickly-scored runs are always much more valuable to the side, his true worth will be understood. There cannot be many batsmen who have been top scorer of their side quite so frequently. Col. Philip Trevor of the *Daily Telegraph* made the observation: 'Mr Jessop who seemingly never tries to stay in ought in the long run to have a much worse average than one or two other of those first-class batsmen who seemingly try never to get out.'

What is also interesting in a batsman who played in a manner beyond the scope of all others is that once he became a real batsman there was no great falling-off in his powers as he grew older.

Like all batsmen he had his good and bad spells, and one of his worst was immediately after his great century in forty minutes against Yorkshire in 1897. He had hit the cricketing world like a tornado with four centuries, only to follow the last one with consecutive scores of 0, 26, 43, 0 and 13, 0, 0, 90 and 2, 4 and 0, 18 and 23, 7 and 3. Another lean spell came at the end of his great season of 1900 when in August he played twelve consecutive innings for a total of 81 runs, and a top score of only 18. In 1909 he had a bad run of nine innings for 78 runs between three magnificent centuries, and he sometimes had poor spells immediately after a great innings as though almost in reaction to it.

SEASONAL FIGURES FOR BATTING

	Matches	Innings		Runs	Top score	Average	100s	50s	Top
1894	8	13	1	162	61*	13·60	–	1	1
1895	16	28	4	525	63	21·21	–	4	6
1896	20	32	1	673	93	21·22	–	4	5
1897	26	42	1	1,219	140	29·30	4	7	6
1897–8	2	4	1	110	66	36·66	–	1	–
1898	25	41	5	873	112*	24·20	1	4	6
1899	27	46	2	1,483	171*	33·70	3	9	5
1899–1900	2	2	0	72	64	36·00	–	1	–
1900	31	58	3	2,210	179	40·18	6	19	10
1901	32	58	1	2,323	233	40·75	5	15	10
1901–2	10	18	0	359	87	19·94	–	1	3
1902	28	49	3	1,562	126	33·95	4	12	8
1903	22	36	0	1,382	286	38·38	2	8	8
1904	25	42	1	1,450	206	35·36	2	9	12
1905	28	47	2	1,197	234	26·60	1	9	6
1906	24	44	1	1,199	87	27·88	–	9	7
1907	27	48	0	1,754	240	36·54	3	11	16
1908	26	48	3	1,885	164	41·88	4	12	11
1909	12	19	0	665	161	35·00	3	4	5
1910	20	36	2	1,142	165	33·58	4	7	7
1911	26	49	4	1,907	153	42·37	7	13	10
1912	23	36	0	804	127	22·23	1	7	5
1913	19	36	1	1,244	119	35·54	3	11	12
1914	12	23	1	498	78	22·63	–	2	5
	491	855	37	26,698	286	32·63	53	180	164

N.B. The column on the right marked 'top' refers to the number of times in which he was top scorer in a complete or virtually complete innings, a proportion which works at his being top-scorer in every one in five of the innings in which he batted.

One very consistent spell came in 1900 when he made nine fifties in the course of fifteen consecutive innings, ending with the scores of 109 and 58* 82 and 62, which was the only time he made as many as four consecutive fifties, though he made two scores of over fifty in a match on nineteen occasions. In 1903 he made two consecutive scores for Gloucestershire in county matches of 286 and 168, but made a score of 6 *v.* London County sandwiched in between. In 1913, almost at the end of his career, he had a successful batting spell which reads: 59 and 68, 3 and 7, 1 and 10, 81 and 107, 63 and 1, 0 and 82, 67 and 40, 87 – as consistent a spell as he ever had at any time.

A Breakdown of his Scores

An analysis of his scores is revealing, and works out like this:

Score	0– 9	296 times
	10– 19	146
	20– 29	103
	30– 39	70
	40– 49	60
	50– 59	40
	60– 69	31
	70– 79	24
	80– 89	23
	90– 99	9
	100–124	23
	125–149	14
	150–199	11
	over 200	5
Total innings		855

Seventy of his under-10 scores were ducks (including two 'pairs') and since 34 per cent of all his scores were under 10, and 17 per cent of his scores were between 10 and 19, there was a fifty–fifty chance that if you went to see Jessop he would be out before he had scored twenty.

The only comment he ever made of any special batting superstitions was about the score 13. He wrote:

'For my part I used once to make strenuous efforts to avoid the thirteen mark until one lucky innings served to rid my mind of this bugbear. Thirteen saw my finish of the first innings of the Oval Test of 1902, and by the aid of a single which I desperately wished to turn into a two, I arrived at the same mark in the second innings. However, the spell became unstuck, and I succeeded in persuading myself that, after all, there was some merit in even "a bakers's dozen". The sharp-run single was very much more in evidence in the old days than it is now.'

The fifty mark never seemed to bother him, nor did he tend to get out on reaching it, like so many batsmen. The nineties never created any feeling of anxiety for him, and he made only nine scores in the nineties, and never a score of 98 or 99. Once he reached his hundred he tended to pile on the runs ever faster, and his 'hundred average' of 140 is better than Hobbs's of 134 and is about the same as Boycott's and Richards'.

The fifty-three centuries which came in his 855 innings works out at one in every sixteen innings, and as he pointed out he would have had several more to his name if the present Law regarding sixes had been in operation in his time.

How He Got Out

Here is an analysis of the way in which Jessop was dismissed, with a percentage given for his innings, and on the right-hand side under 'General percentage', a figure which represents a survey of some half of the 150,000 wickets which fell in first-class cricket in England between 1919 and 1950. It gives some comparison:

How out	Times	Jessop percentage	General percentage
Bowled	247	30	32
Caught	473	57	47
Lbw	21	2	13
Stumped	66	8	4
Run out	9	1	3
Hit wicket	2	–	1
	818	(completed innings)	

Here are a few notes under each heading:

Bowled It is difficult to think of 'defence' with such a player, but figures show that Jessop was in fact more difficult to bowl out than Hutton, W. G. Grace, or Ponsford. In the season of 1905 when something went wrong with his technique, he was clean bowled in 23 of his 45 completed innings – the only season in which he was bowled out more times than he was caught.

Caught Jessop's unique attacking play caused him to hit many balls into the air, but though some were genuine 'catches' he often hit the ball so hard that they were not really chances at all except for the bravest or most expert fielder. Jessop himself said that it was rare for a batsman to reach a hundred without offering a catch to the fielding side, and by a catch he meant something that actually went to hand. Writing in 1904 he said that in the first thirteen matches played by Gloucestershire no less than fifty *catches* were missed off the bowling of George Dennett, and these were actual catches that went to hands (other than Jessop's).

Time and again we read that Jessop made his score without a faulty stroke, but very occasionally he had an innings in which he enjoyed some luck, and never more so than against Warwickshire at Gloucester.

'This is a small ground around which tower lofty trees making the proper sighting of the ball – especially off a big hit – somewhat hazardous. In seven balls I received four lives. Two in succession went off long-on's fingers to the ropes. This is not being to the liking of the opposing skipper, H. W. Bainbridge, he dismissed the luckless fielder to another position, and took up the position himself. Two balls after, up went another skier, if anything a trifle more mountainous, under which the Warwickshire leader – a notoriously safe outfield – placed himself, but the ball again refused to connect, and once more slipped over the line. The fourth life came from the first ball of the next over, but despite these four lives only forty runs were recorded. How many lives would have been required to score a hundred runs on that day is beyond my calculations.'

Jessop was frequently out to spectacular catches on the boundary and at times there was some doubt about them. After scoring 57 against Sussex at Hove in 1901 'Jessop sent the ball soaring up in the air till it seemed it would go well over the heads of the spectators. Fisher ran back until he was among the people sitting round the edge of the boundary, and amid a great shout took the ball high up with one hand. The batsman appealed on the ground that the ball was over the boundary when caught, but the umpire ruled against him.' Jessop had suffered another unfortunate experience at Hove in the Bank Holiday match of 1896. He was fielding right on the edge of the ring, with the crowd all round his feet, when a lofty hit came towards him. As he struggled his way amongst spectators amid cries of 'Miss it!' someone finally succeeded in making him do so, by firing off a ginger-beer bottle at him.

Stumped No batsman has ever left his ground so far or frequently, but Jessop regarded this as a calculated risk which brought him a number of runs. His one weakness as he knew was making up his mind to come down the wicket before the bowler bowled, and a relative of his, Group-Captain Vernon Jessop, tells a delightful story of an old cricketer he met who told him how when he was once bowling to Jessop he saw Jessop coming, stopped and 'failed to release the ball'. Jessop went on coming, so the bowler walked towards him. They met in the middle of the pitch, and the bowler said: 'Eh, Gilbert, was there something you wanted to say to me, lad?'

Jessop's excursions must have made the wicket-keepers full of expectation, and there is a recollection of W. G. Grace watching the Gloucestershire *v.* Kent match at Dover in 1912. Seeing Jessop out 'st Huish, b Carr . . . 0', the Old Man rose in wrath and called shrilly across the field: 'I saw you, Freddie: I saw you take the ball in front of the wicket!'

Run Out Jessop was exceedingly quick between the wickets, and Rockley Wilson says it was hell to bat with him as he insisted on running two for any stroke into the deep, regardless. He must have been a scamperer like Evans, or Pawson, or Mike Griffith, but he was seldom run out or ran others out, so good was his calling – unlike some great batsmen. M. A. Green tells how, in one of his early matches for Gloucestershire in 1912, he was batting with Jessop, who tapped the ball to cover. The next moment Green found Jessop beside him at the non-striker's end. Thanks to a bad return Green was able to get in, and Jessop was able to reassure him with the words: 'Don't worry, I do that only when I have made a duck in the first innings.'

Jessop was not, like Hobbs, addicted to single-snatching, except when it was necessary to farm the bowling. There is one correspondent who tells me that when he was once playing in a club match Jessop came in to join him with the side wanting a hundred to win and an hour to go. As Jessop passed he humourously quoted the legendary words: 'We'll get 'em in singles!' The runs were made, but not in singles.

LBW I cannot imagine any batsman being out less frequently than Jessop who suffered only twenty-one lbw decisions in his whole first-class career. His crouching stance sometimes led to appeals when the ball hit him on the head and he was out this way at Lord's in 1904 after scoring 87.

Many a captain must have had some special scheme for getting Jessop out. We have heard how Ranji had told Beldam he had a new plan to dismiss him, the result in that case being an innings of 286. W. A. Bettesworth in an appreciation of Jessop in an issue of *Cricket* in 1901 says: 'I am still anxious to see some slow bowler try my suggested experiment of giving him a series of consecutive full pitches, with a well-placed field; there must surely be a slow bowler somewhere in the world who could bowl ball after ball so that it would pitch close to the top of the stumps.' Bettesworth's 'Spedegue Dropper' idea never seems to have been tried out.

In 1901 a brave interviewer was about to ask Jessop if he thought the captains of fielding sides opposing him would be able to devise any special means of getting him out. Jessop apparently divined what the man was thinking and made the following cryptic statement: 'There is one way, I believe, in which the captain of the opposite side could often bring my innings to an abrupt close. But you can't expect me to give the secret away. Luckily for me, none of the county captains have discovered it yet. When they do discover it, perhaps I shall retire from first-class cricket.' Jessop may have been serious in this remark, but it is quite in keeping with his sense of fun to be pulling the interviewer's leg.

I have asked several present-day cricketers how they would have curbed Jessop if he were playing today, and they have made the following observations: (*a*) The standard of fielding today is much better than it was in his time, and there are seldom any 'passengers' in the field. (*b*) The art of defensive field-placing has developed considerably, though today the Proctors and Richards can penetrate even the tightest of fields, and I daresay Jessop would have been able to do likewise. We read how when he came in to bat the fielders were placed all round the boundary, but he often found the gaps by the sheer speed of the hit, which made even the spectators fearful. (*c*) Far fewer balls are bowled in the day's play than used to be, owing to the excessively long-runs of so-called fast bowlers, the absence of spinners, and general time-wasting. Not even Jessop could score fast if balls were not bowled to him.

Jessop's 'Bêtes-noires' (and others)

Even a great batsman tends to have certain weak spots, and G. J. V, Weigall once stated that he thought the only kind of ball which bothered Jessop was one that came low off the pitch. Jessop confirmed this, and C. B. Fry once warned Jessop about meeting such balls when he went to Australia.

Jessop also says that there were certain bowlers whom he regarded as his 'bêtes-noires'. They included, among medium-pacers, M. A. Noble, the Australian, and Tom Hayward who, he said, could turn the ball smartly from the off even on the plumbest of wickets. Among left-handers he regarded Bobby Peel as the most difficult bowler he ever played against because of his deceptive flight. Another left-hander who troubled him was Blythe, who he thought was a better bowler than Rhodes, but whereas Rhodes loved a fight and big occasions, Blythe loathed it and became literally sick under the pressure of a Test match.

Rhodes had the pleasure of getting Jessop's wicket more often than any other bowler, but this was largely because of the frequency with which they met. In *all* matches in which they were in opposition there were eighty-nine innings in which Jessop batted and in which he might have faced the bowling of Rhodes, and Rhodes got him out thirty-one times. Another left-hander whom Jessop respected was Hargreave of Warwickshire 'whose balls seemed to come on further than you thought and what looked like a half-volley became a yorker'.

Next on the list of bowlers who frequently dismissed Jessop–fourteen times – was his old friend Hugh Trumble, who among other things could turn the ball sharply from the off. It will be remembered how in his great 1902 Test innings Jessop disciplined himself not to hit across the line when facing Trumble. Mr. R. L. Arrowsmith has sent me some interesting information concerning Fairservice of Kent, who thought that Jessop was sometimes vulnerable to off-spinners. In the seventeen matches in which Fairservice faced Jessop he got him out seven times, six of them in the course of ten matches in 1904–1908.

There were few fast bowlers who ever really bothered Jessop, who thought that Tom Richardson was without doubt the greatest fast bowler he ever met, and one who never deliberately tried to intimidate the batsman. For sheer pace Jessop placed Kortright top of the list of the English fast bowlers he met, the next on the list (in order of pace) being Richardson, Mold, Sammy Woods, Hitch, Lockwood, Woodcock, N. A. Knox, Brearley and W. M. Bradley.

Jessop also mentions that there were several bowlers whom he looked forward to facing. Among these were Rhodes, Bland of Sussex, and the immortal Sydney Barnes, who would not have been pleased to read such a statement.

Centuries, Stands, and Monopolies

In the course of his first-class career Jessop made fifty-three centuries in first-class cricket, and at the end of 1914 – the end of his career – only thirteen other batsmen had made more centuries than he had. His highest scores were:

286	out of	355	in	175	minutes	for Gloucestershire *v.* Sussex	Hove	1903
240	,,	337	,,	200	,,	,, Gloucestershire *v.* Sussex	Bristol	1907
234	,,	346	,,	155	,,	,, Gloucestershire *v.* Somerset	Bristol	1905
233	,,	318	,,	150	,,	,, Rest of England *v.* Yorks.	Lord's	1901
206	,,	317	,,	140	,,	,, Gloucestershire *v.* Notts.	Trent Bridge	1904
191	,,	234	,,	90	,,	,, Gents of South *v.* Players of South	Hastings	1907
179	,,	257	,,	105	,,	,, Gloucestershire *v.* Sussex	Hove	1900
171*	,,	206	,,	115	,,	,, C.U. *v.* Yorks	Cambridge	1899

He made six hundreds against the bowling of Yorkshire, and five each against Sussex and Hampshire.

He made two hundreds in a match on four occasions:

104 and 139	for Gloucestershire	*v.* Yorkshire at Bradford	1900
143 and 133*	,, ,,	*v.* Somerset at Bath	1908
161 and 129	,, ,,	*v.* Hampshire at Bristol	1909
153 and 123*	,, ,,	*v.* Hampshire at Southampton	1911

The biggest partnerships in which he took part were:

320 for 6th wkt.	Jessop 286 and J. H. Board 71	*v.* Sussex	Hove	1903
209 for 3rd wkt.	Jessop 127 and D. C. Robinson 90	*v.* Worcester	Worcester	1912
204 for 4th wkt.	Jessop 233 and C. B. Fry 105	*v.* Yorkshire	Lords	1901
195 for 2nd wkt.	Jessop 136* and R. H. Spooner 94	*v.* M.C.C.	Scarborough	1911
176 for 5th wkt.	Jessop 164 and J. H. Huggins 29	*v.* Sussex	Gloucester	1908
161 for 6th wkt.	Jessop 139 and P. H. Bell 31	*v.* Surrey	Bristol	1911

The runs made from all his scores of a hundred or more show that in these innings he made 72 per cent of all the runs made while he was batting – a very high proportion. But he had many remarkable spells in which he dominated the run-getting to an even greater extent. These include:

	66 out of 66		Gloucestershire *v.* Sussex	Bristol	1901
	63 ,, 65		,, *v.* Yorkshire	Cheltenham	1895
	75 ,, 80		,, *v.* Notts.	Trent Bridge	1908
and	78 ,, 86		,, *v.* Notts.	Trent Bridge	1908
	76 ,, 82		,, *v.* Notts.	Bristol	1901
	92 ,, 106		,, *v.* Sussex	Bristol	1903
	109 ,, 120		,, *v.* Middlesex	Lords	1900
	116 ,, 138		Lord Londesborough's XI *v.* Kent	Scarborough	1913
	126 ,, 159	(110* of 122)	Gloucestershire *v.* Worcester	Bristol	1902
	143 ,, 179		Gloucestershire *v.* Somerset	Bath	1908
	161 ,, 199	(total 295)	,, *v.* Hampshire	Bristol	1909
	164 ,, 203		,, *v.* Sussex	Gloucester	1908
	165 ,, 205	(total 261)	,, *v.* Worcester	Stourbridge	1910
	171* ,, 206	(total 246)	C.U. *v.* Yorkshire	Cambridge	1899
	179 ,, 257		Gloucestershire *v.* Sussex	Hove	1900
	191 ,, 234	(total 313)	Gents of South *v.* Players of South	Hastings	1907
	286 ,, 355		Gloucestershire *v.* Sussex	Hove	1903

Rate of Scoring

Though time is not the most satisfactory way of reckoning the scoring rate of an innings, it is usually the only way available. Jessop's fastest fifties were:

50* in 15 minutes	(61 in 24)	Gloucestershire *v.* Somerset	Bristol	1904
53* in 15 ,,	(92 in 65)	,, *v.* Hampshire	Cheltenham	1907
51* in 18 ,,	(63 in 28)	,, *v.* Yorkshire	,,	1895

In all, including the above, there were eighteen occasions when he took his score from 0 to 50 within 25 minutes, but in only four of these did he go on to reach a hundred. He was sometimes comparatively 'slow' over his first fifty runs.

His fastest hundreds were:

101 in 40 minutes	(101 in 40)	Gloucestershire *v.* Yorkshire	Harrogate	1897
100* ,, 42 ,,	(191 ,, 90)	Gents of South *v.* Players of South	Hastings	1907
100* ,, 53 ,,	(139 ,, 90)	Gloucestershire *v.* Surrey	Bristol	1911
100* ,, 55 ,,	(123* ,, 75)	South *v.* North	Hastings	1900
100* ,, 55 ,,	(126 ,, 95)	Gloucestershire *v.* Notts.	Trent Bridge	1902
100* ,, 55 ,,	(119 ,, 75)	Gloucestershire *v.* Sussex	Hastings	1907
102* ,, 55 ,,	(116 ,, 60)	Lord Londesborough's XI *v.* Kent	Scarborough	1913

He also reached his hundred within the hour on eight other occasions, which gives him fifteen such hundreds, about one-third of *all* 'hundreds in an hour' ever recorded in first-class cricket. His fastest double centuries were:

200* in 120 minutes	(286 in 175)	Gloucestershire *v.* Sussex	Hove	1903
200* ,, 130 ,,	(234 ,, 155)	,, *v.* Somerset	Bristol	1905

200* ,, 135	,,	(233 ,, 150)	Rest of England *v.* Yorkshire	Lords	1901
206 ,, 140	,,	(206 ,, 140)	Gloucestershire *v.* Notts.	Trent Bridge	1904

These times fill the first, second, fourth and seventh places in the list of fastest double centuries ever made, and had the boundary law been different in his day his score of 191 in 90 minutes at Hastings in 1907 would have beaten all of these. In that innings he reached 150 in only 63 minutes – easily the fastest 150 ever made. His average time for taking his score from 0–100 was 72 minutes.

His fifty-three centuries were scored at an average rate of 82·7 runs an hour, while his 127 scores of 50 to 99 were made at an average rate of 76·32 runs an hour. Together his 180 scores of 50 or more were scored at an average rate of 79·08 runs an hour.

Only four of his hundreds were scored at a rate of less than a run a minute, and only twenty-seven of all his over 50 scores were scored at a rate of less than a run a minute.

Only once did he bat for more than three hours, only ten times for more than two hours, and only thirty-five times in all did he bat for more than 90 minutes. No further comment is needed.

Modern scorers can no doubt tell at a glance just how many balls each batsman has received. This was not so in Jessop's time, but it seems that scorers of his day used sometimes to make a special note of the balls Jessop received, and we are lucky enough to have this information on at least twenty of his innings. Here is a list of the best of these, listed in order of merit, according to the average of runs per ball received:

61 off 19 of 24 balls	2·54	Gloucestershire *v.* Somerset	Bristol	1904
72 ,, 23 ,, 29 ,,	2·49	,, *v.* Warwick	Cheltenham	1908
54 ,, 17 ,, 22 ,,	2·45	,, *v.* Hampshire	Cheltenham	1913
116 ,, 35 ,, 57 ,,	2·03	Lord Londesborough's XI *v.* Kent	Scarborough	1913
66 ,, 25 ,, 36 ,,	1·83	Gloucestershire *v.* Somerset	Bath	1906
66 ,, 22 ,, 37 ,,	1·79	,, *v.* Sussex	Bristol	1901

also:

93 ,, 39 ,, 69 ,,	1·34	England *v.* S. Africa	Lords	1907
102 ,, 41 ,, 79 ,,	1·30	,, *v.* Australia	Oval	1902

For sheer speed of scoring there has never been any top-class batsman to approach him. The only man who can be regarded as at all comparable is the late Lord Constantine, but only in a very limited degree as a batsman, as he made only five centuries (with a top score of 130), and had a batting average of barely 25. He did however have a scoring rate of 75 runs an hour for the

30 or so fifties he made, and his unorthodox play had a true touch of Jessop. There is really no one else, though there are one or two out-and-out sloggers like Jim Smith, of Middlesex, who scored their runs even faster than Jessop on the rare occasions when they reached fifty. Smith's rate for his 16 fifties comes out at over 100 runs an hour. F. Barratt, Guy Earle, Hitch, and C. I. Thornton all have scoring rates which reach or even surpass that of Jessop, but any comparison between them and Jessop would be ridiculous.

Hitting Spells

Jessop from time to time made a bowler's life intolerable, and here is a note of some devastating overs suffered by a bowler.

28 runs (4 4 6 4 4 6) off L. Braund scoring 61 *v.* Somerset – Bristol 1904 (he took 12 more runs off Braund's next over).
28 runs (4 6 6 2 4 6) off R. D. Burrows scoring 165 *v.* Worcestershire – Stourbridge 1910.
26 runs (6 4 4 4 4 4) off A. E. Relf scoring 191 *v.* Players of South – Hastings 1907.
26 runs (4 0 6 6 4 6) off D. W. Carr in scoring 116 *v.* Kent – Scarborough 1913.

He took 22 runs off an over from J. Vine when making 164 *v.* Sussex at Gloucester in 1908, and off A. E. Lewis when making 133* *v.* Somerset in 1908. He took 20 runs off an over from W. Rhodes at Bradford in 1900, A. E. Trott at Lords in 1901, E. B. Dwyer at Hove in 1906, H. W. Persse at Cheltenham in 1907, and W. East at Northampton in 1910.

He took 34 runs off two consecutive overs bowled to him by Hitch at Scarborough in 1911, 46 runs off nineteen consecutive balls bowled to him by D. W. Carr at Scarborough in 1913, and 61 runs off four consecutive overs bowled to him by C. B. Llewellyn at Bristol in 1909.

We shall never know how many of the fours he hit would today count as sixes, but we do know that when he scored 47 *v.* the Australians at Hastings in 1899 he once hit Howell three times in three balls high over the ropes, and the 14 runs he made off this over would now count as 20.

As I write these facts and figures I can imagine the voice of Jessop calling the whole of this chapter 'a lot of nonsense', but I hope some readers will find it more interesting than he would.

The Bat

Jessop possessed exceptionally strong wrists and forearms which enabled him to use a bat heavier than usual. Most batsmen use bats which weigh between 2 lb. 2 oz. and 2 lb. 6 oz., but Jessop's bats were at least 2 lb. 10 oz. and his favourite bat weighed 3 lb. 4 oz. He scored over 4,000 runs with this bat in about 1901 until it eventually fell to bits. During the 1901–2 tour of Australia Jessop lent W. G. Quaife, a very small man, a bat that weighed 1 lb. more than his usual bat of 2 lb. 2 oz. and Quaife made good use of it. A Kent journalist, Albert Kinross, once told Jessop that he could hit just as hard as Jessop if he had a bat like his, whereupon Jessop sent him a bat inscribed

'From one slogger to another', but it weighed 3 lb. 5 oz. and Kinross could hardly lift it.

I have a letter from one who as a small boy was once allowed the privilege of oiling Jessop's bats, and Jessop showed him how to rub the oil in with the end of a broomstick handle. Jessop's bats in particular must have been looked upon with awe, so fearful was the fire-power of them. In 1906 there was an auction of bats arranged for the benefit of the Cricketers' Benevolent Fund. A bat of W. G. Grace's sold for as much as £50, one of Trumper's for £42, one of Ranji's for 13 gn. One of Jessop's fetched £8.

Jessop the Bowler and All-rounder

An early chapter has told of the nature and performance of Jessop's bowling, and it will be remembered that he won his first England cap as a bowler. Here is a record of his annual figures:

	Overs	Runs	Wickets	Average
1894	138·2	264	16	16·80
1895	460·3	873	50	17·23
1896	696·3	1,773	74	23·71
1897	983·3	2,071	116	17·99
1897–8	93	229	11	20·80
1898	682·1	1,547	69	22·42
1899	747·3	2,061	66	31·22
1899–1900	51	103	11	9·33
1900	820·1	2,185	104	21·00
1901	297·2	902	29	31·10
1901–2	129	397	12	33·08
1902	371·2	1,014	53	19·13
1903	245·2	705	20	35·25
1904	233·5	535	25	21·40
1905	519·1	1,602	64	25·03
1906	347·5	1,200	34	35·29
1907	120·5	381	17	22·41
1908	141	348	22	15·81
1909	53	119	10	11·90
1910	4	21	0	—
1911	52·2	189	8	23·62
1912	124·1	299	18	16·61
1913	230·1	650	26	25·00
1914	137·4	436	18	24·22
		19,904	873	22·79

Of these wickets 839 were taken in England, and 34 on tours overseas. His average number of balls bowled for each wicket taken works out at 49.

Here is a note of his best performances, sometimes linked with a batting success as well.

4–33 and 5–38 (and 50 and 40)	Gloucestershire *v.* Warwicks.	Bristol	1895
5–33 and 2–21 (and 53 and 1*)	,, *v.* Sussex	Bristol	1895
5–13 and 2–44	,, *v.* Lancs.	Old Trafford	1895
6–59 and 3–80	C.U. *v.* Yorkshire	Cambridge	1896
5–52 (and 44 and 66)	Gloucestershire *v.* Middlesex	Clifton	1896
5–19	C.U. *v.* Yorkshire	Cambridge	1897
6–65	C.U. *v.* O.U.	Lord's	1897
7–92	Gloucestershire *v.* Warwicks.	Gloucester	1897
4–80 and 2–62 (and 1 and 126)	,, *v.* Warwicks.	Edgbaston	1897
4–106 and 5–71 (and 101 and 0)	,, *v.* Yorkshire	Harrogate	1897
5–36	M.C.C. *v.* Yorkshire	Scarborough	1897
5–55 and 4–70 (and 66 and 26*)	Warner's XI *v.* Philadelphia	Merion	1897–8
8–34 and 4–33 (and 9 and 55*)	C.U. *v.* Hampshire	Cambridge	1898
6–45	C.U. *v.* Surrey	Cambridge	1898
8–54	Gloucestershire *v.* Lancs.	Old Trafford	1898
5–18	C.U. *v.* M.C.C.	Cambridge	1899
5–48	Gloucestershire *v.* Warwicks.	Bristol	1899
7–61	,, *v.* Yorks.	Huddersfield	1899
6–52 and 2–30 (and 64)	Ranji's XI *v.* Philadelphia	Haverford	1899–1900
8–29	Gloucestershire *v.* Essex	Cheltenham	1900
3–55 and 6–72 (and 54 and 54)	,, *v.* Surrey	Bristol	1900
8–82 (and 77 and 12)	,, *v.* Kent	Catford	1900
2–42 and 5–25 (and 66 and 47)	,, *v.* Lancs.	Old Trafford	1900
7–77 and 1–45 (and 2 and 126)	,, *v.* Worcester	Bristol	1902
8–58 and 3–40	,, *v.* Middlesex	Lord's	1902
7–91	,, *v.* Australians	Cheltenham	1902
2–46 and 6–33	,, *v.* Sussex	Bristol	1905
4–44 and 4–54 (and 74)	,, *v.* Surrey	Bristol	1905
5–26 and 5–80	,, *v.* Surrey	Bristol	1908
5–14	,, *v.* Kent	Cheltenham	1912
4–57 and 2–3 (and 67 and 40)	,, *v.* Yorkshire	Sheffield	1913
4–34 and 1–7	,, *v.* Somerset (his last match)	Bristol	1914

ENVOI

'No other personality in the world of sport can make or mar a man's pleasure as Gilbert Jessop can. His failure is accepted as a personal misfortune; his success inspires a feeling of joy that everyone shares.'

CONTEMPORARY COMMENT

Index

This is an index of all persons mentioned in the text with the exception of Gilbert Jessop himself.

ACKNOWLEDGEMENTS

I am extremely grateful to Gilbert Jessop's son, the Rev. G. L. O. Jessop, for his co-operation in every way, including the loan of family scrapbooks, letters and photos, without which this book could hardly have been possible.

My acknowledgements are also due for the use of certain passages from Gilbert Jessop's own book *A Cricketer's Log*, which I reproduce by permission of Christy and Moore; to *The Cricketer* for certain passages from articles by G. L. Jessop; to Mr G. D. Martineau for use of his poem 'The Croucher', which originally appeared in *The Cricketer*; the piece 'Hero Worship' by E. V. Lucas, and the drawing 'Spoiling Sport' by Bernard Partridge, are reproduced by permission of *Punch*; I am grateful to Mr C. L. R. James for use of a passage from *Beyond a Boundary*.

I wish to express my thanks for use of some material from the late C. J. Britton's book *Gilbert Jessop*. The Jessop scrapbooks contain cuttings from which I have quoted, but I fear that the majority of them have no information as to their source. I am sorry if I have unwittingly used pieces without permission. *Wisden* as usual has proved a valuable means of checking facts.

My thanks also go to Mr Keith Silk for his photographic help, and to the many correspondents who have most kindly sent me material of all kinds, and especially to Mr R. L. Arrowsmith, Mr J. F. Burrell, Mr M. R. Coghlan, Mr David Frith, Mr Desmond Eagar, Mr Stephen Green, Mr Cyril Hollinshead, Mrs Pringle, Mr J. W. Scott and family, Mrs Mary Watson, Dr E. M. Grace, Mr J. J. Boswell and Mr J. D. Coldham. I acknowledge with thanks the use of certain photographs taken originally by Mr G. W. Beldam.

Prints for plates 6 and 7 have been supplied by the MCC Library; plate 8 has been provided by Mrs Anne Pye, and the photograph on page 187 by the Reverend E. V. Tanner; the end papers come from a letter kindly loaned by Mr Coghlan – for all of which my thanks.

would be summarily disposed of —
es - that was indeed a good match -
nd a thousand pities that the Rubber
ad already been thrown away thro' the
idiocy of Martin Hawke & the other
Selectors. The team which skittled
the Aussies out for 36 - in the
rst match at Birmingham ...